Tip O'Neill and the
St. Louis Browns of 1887

Tip O'Neill and the St. Louis Browns of 1887

Dennis Thiessen

Foreword by Mark O'Neill

McFarland & Company, Inc., Publishers
Jefferson, North Carolina

ISBN (print) 978-1-4766-7290-8
ISBN (ebook) 978-1-4766-3667-2

LIBRARY OF CONGRESS AND BRITISH LIBRARY
CATALOGUING DATA ARE AVAILABLE

LIBRARY OF CONGRESS CONTROL NUMBER: 2019942441

© 2019 Dennis Thiessen. All rights reserved

No part of this book may be reproduced or transmitted in any form or by any means, electronic or mechanical, including photocopying or recording, or by any information storage and retrieval system, without permission in writing from the publisher.

Front cover illustration of Tip O'Neill by Jesse Loving
(Ars Longa Art Cards)

Manufactured in the United States of America

McFarland & Company, Inc., Publishers
Box 611, Jefferson, North Carolina 28640
www.mcfarlandpub.com

To my father, Samuel Thiessen, my son, Geoffrey,
and my grandsons, Ryan and Jeremy—
playing catch from one generation to the next

Table of Contents

Acknowledgments ix

Foreword by Mark O'Neill 1

Preface 5

1. October 18 to October 23, 1886: Champions of the World — 17
2. From Pitcher to Left Fielder — 24
3. Core Players: St. Louis Browns — 33
4. "Anything to Win" — 43
5. October 24, 1886, to April 15, 1887: Off-Season — 56
6. April 16 to May 24: Batting for Average — 63
7. Two Cycles — 75
8. May 25 to July 11: Injury and Struggle — 79
9. Featured Games: Batting and Fielding — 95
10. July 12 to August 10: A Slow Return to Form — 101
11. Long Hits — 110
12. August 12 to September 8: Batting for Power — 116
13. Batting Streaks — 129
14. September 9 to October 9: American Association Champions — 135
15. October 10 to October 26: St. Louis Loses to Detroit in the World Championship — 144
16. A Season of Firsts — 154

Epilogue 159

Appendix A: Resolution of Discrepancies in Game-Based Statistics 171

Appendix B: Tip O'Neill—Single-Season Batting Records and Feats in 1887 183

Appendix C: Tip O'Neill—Career Statistics 189

Chapter Notes 191

Bibliography 233

Index 237

Acknowledgments

In a project that began in 2011, I have met or corresponded with many people who have had a significant impact on the warp and woof of this book. Though they are not always cited by name, I nonetheless applaud the people who created the resources I used in this study and who led and served in the organizations I visited or contacted. I will be forever grateful for the time and effort of those who gave so much, likely more than they realized, to this publication.

In the study of James "Tip" O'Neill's extraordinary 1887 season, I examined game accounts in newspapers of the times to generate the stories that animate each of the following chapters. Digitized copies of nineteenth-century newspapers were available through a growing number of online archives (e.g., LA84 Foundation; Historical Newspapers). I also turned to online sources for statistics relevant to the performances of James O'Neill, the Browns, and the American Association. Unless otherwise specified, I relied on the statistics reported in Baseball Reference (see https://baseball-reference.com). I also found the numerous resources on or linked to the website of the Society for American Baseball Research (SABR) quite useful (e.g., Baseball Biography Project, *Baseball Research Journal* Archives).

As valuable as these online sources were, many of the 19,000 items in my James O'Neill database came from microfilm reels of nineteenth-century newspapers that I obtained through interlibrary loans organized by the Resource Sharing Department in the Robarts Library at the University of Toronto. In particular, I commend the work of the resource-sharing specialists for their capacity to locate and to secure these resources in a timely manner. They searched far and wide, contacting not only other universities and public libraries but also archives and societies (e.g., The State Historical Society of Missouri).

On occasion, rather than wait for the resources to come to me through interlibrary loan, I went to the resources. For example, I repeatedly visited the Library of Congress in Washington, D.C., to take advantage of its exhaustive repository of microfilm copies of nineteenth-century newspapers, photographs and images. Similarly, I spent time in the Stephen A. Schwarzman Building of the New York Public Library, the San Francisco Public Library, and the Free Library of Philadelphia.

Between 2011 and 2017, I worked two or more days each year in the Giamatti Research Center of the National Baseball Hall of Fame and Museum in Cooperstown, New York. Guided by Cassidy Lent, the knowledgeable, diligent, and caring Reference Librarian at the Research Center (and previously by her predecessor, Freddy Berowski), I was able to uncover numerous documents and reference materials on James O'Neill's life and career. John Horne, Coordinator of Rights and Reproductions, Photo Archives, was also instrumental in locating many of the photographs and images used in this book.

As part of my inquiry into James O'Neill's early years, I travelled to Woodstock, Ontario, Tip's hometown, to explore the information available from the Oxford County Historical Society, the County of Oxford Archives, the Woodstock Public Library, and the Woodstock Museum (Adam Pollard, Collection and Exhibit Coordinator). I also accessed valuable materials in London, Ontario, in the Archives and Research Collections Centre at Western University and in the Diocese of London (Debra Majer, Archivist).

I owe a debt of gratitude to those who provided me with photographs and images. In addition to the National Baseball Hall of Fame and Museum, the Library of Congress, the New York Public Library, and the Woodstock Museum, I thank Rucker Archives, the Metropolitan Museum of Art (New York–Art Resource), the St. Louis Cardinals Hall of Fame and Museum (Paula Homan, Manager and Curator of Hall of Fame Museum), and the Canadian Baseball Hall of Fame and Museum in St. Marys, Ontario (Scott Crawford, Director of Operations) for enabling me to enrich the visual quality of the written text with so many engaging images. I especially appreciate the generous support from Jesse Loving, the owner and artist of Ars Longa Art Cards. He created the image of James O'Neill that adorns the cover of this book.

As I immersed myself in the study of the life and career of James O'Neill, I proudly joined two interrelated baseball communities, one within the world of SABR and the other in a growing network of Canadian baseball researchers. In particular, I pay tribute to the following SABR groups: Nineteenth Century Research Committee (Peter Mancuso, Chair) and the gang who gather each year at the Frederick Ivor-Campbell 19th Century Base Ball Conference; Baseball Records Research Committee (Trent McCotter, Chair); and three SABR chapters (Hanlan Point Chapter, Toronto; Quebec Chapter, Montreal; Bob Broeg St. Louis Chapter). I also extend my heartfelt gratitude to baseball researchers in Canada, especially Bill Humber, Brian Martin, Patrick Carpentier, and those who attend the annual Canadian Baseball History Conference (Andrew North, Coordinator).

I consider myself quite fortunate to have had the opportunity to meet three of James O'Neill's relatives: Liz Farrell and Mark O'Neill in Ottawa, Ontario, and Bill O'Neill in Toronto, Ontario. Liz, Mark, and Bill are the grandchildren of D'Arcy O'Neill, Tip's youngest brother. I will always remember their affection for their famous great-uncle and their interest in the book. I am especially pleased that Mark O'Neill, the president and chief executive officer of the Canadian Museum of History, in honor of his great-uncle, agreed to write the Foreword to this book.

I am greatly indebted to the invaluable support of Alan Cantor and Lisa Juan. Each provided timely, creative, and much-needed technical expertise, which immeasurably improved the organization and design of the final manuscript.

Finally, with much love and admiration, I thank my wife, Elizabeth Campbell, who is also a professor at the University of Toronto. She is the best scholar and writer I know and the best friend I have ever had. She offered ideas about the structure of the book; helped me to sort out which stories to tell and how best to evoke an understanding of James O'Neill through various narrative devices; made editorial suggestions to improve the text; and was uncanny in her ability to deliver a laugh, a frown, or a puzzled look just at the right moment. Elizabeth was unwavering in her dedication to this project, something and someone to cherish always.

Foreword by Mark O'Neill

To a professional athlete, having an asterisk next to one of your records is like having an albatross around your neck. An asterisk generally means there is something uncertain about the achievement. It is like dragging the word "but" around behind you: "Sure, he was good, but—."

There is probably no baseball player who carries around a bigger asterisk than Canadian-born James Edward "Tip" O'Neill. Born in Springfield, Ontario, and raised in Woodstock, Ontario, O'Neill played major league baseball in the United States during the 1880s.

His achievements should be the stuff of legend. O'Neill was only the second professional player to achieve a Triple Crown: highest batting average, most home runs, and most runs batted in during a single season. He is one of only four baseball players ever to hit for the cycle twice in a season—a single, double, triple and home run in a single game. He has the all-time mark for setting the most batting records in one season with 10 records in the American Association and eight records in the majors.

And then there is the record that stands tallest in his meteoric career, namely, that Tip is the player with the highest single-season batting average of all time in Major League Baseball.

This is the statistic with the asterisk. This is the giant "but" that has always hung over a record some baseball historians consider the greatest in the sport—while others consider it little more than a carnival sideshow trick. Views on Tip O'Neill's career have always ranged from one extreme to the other. I have known about this polarity for some time because I am his great-nephew.

Even without the family connection, I would have found the story of my great-uncle fascinating. He began his baseball career as a star pitcher in southwestern Ontario. The "Woodstock Wonder" then went off to seek fame and fortune in New York City during the early 1880s. He was one of the sport's first sluggers, which made him hugely popular with fans. He also possessed movie-star good looks, repeatedly attracting attention from ladies in the stands. Stories swirled around him. On one occasion, Tip reported late for spring training because he had become engaged to a dancer in New York (although he never married). Another time, he graciously responded to a request from an admiring female fan in St. Louis, hitting the ball exactly where she requested.

James "Tip" O'Neill and the St. Louis Browns of 1887 is an impeccably researched retelling of my great-uncle's life and baseball career. It places special emphasis on the 1887 season, the year Tip O'Neill won the batting championship with an officially recognized average of .492, and his team, the St. Louis Browns (later the Cardinals), played the Detroit Wolverines for the world championship. The baseball season of 1887 has its own asterisk, for reasons you will learn in the book.

Anyone reading news reports and sports journals from 1887 would be struck by the importance of baseball to the city of St. Louis. What is largely forgotten today is how important baseball was to Canada during those same years. In the late–19th century, there was a constant migration of Canadian ball players to the pro and semi-pro leagues in the United States. In southwestern Ontario, where Tip was raised, baseball was as popular—if not more so—than lacrosse, football or even hockey.

Although he broke into the professional leagues in the United States as a pitcher, Tip was moved to the outfield during his third season. He is particularly remembered today for his prowess at bat. He was a slugger in a sport that until then had emphasized the scientific advancement of the base runner. More often than not, Tip advanced runners with a hit, while others on the team, notably Charlie Comiskey, the player-manager of the Browns, and Arlie Latham, the Browns' third baseman, relied as much on bunts to move runners from base to base.

Tip O'Neill always swung, and the fans loved him for it. In fact, two of the three theories on how he got his famous nickname are based on how hard he hit the ball. The first explanation was related to the many foul balls he would hit, while waiting patiently for a pitch that he might be able to knock out of the park. The second theory is connected to the fact that it appeared that Tip's effortless swing would do nothing more than gently "tip" the ball forward on contact. Yet more times than not, the ball shot off his bat with lightning speed as it soared deep into the outfield. The other theory is that the name was given to him as a teenager in Ontario, after a memorably bad performance during a high-school production of "Tip and Slasher."

However he got his nickname, Tip soon became the most popular player on the St. Louis Browns. Many of the sluggers of the late-19th century—Willie Keeler of the Baltimore Orioles, Buck Ewing of the New York Gothams, and others—were fan favorites. No one, however, was more popular than Tip—so much so, in fact, that "Tip" soon became the requisite nickname for any O'Neill boy in St. Louis. After a few years, it even became the requisite nickname for any O'Neill boy in the United States. The Speaker of the United States House of Representatives for many years—Thomas Phillip "Tip" O'Neill—was nicknamed after my great-uncle. So common did the moniker become that my great-uncle began to refer to himself, later in life, as the "Original" Tip O'Neill.

Despite his many records and his immense popularity as a player, he is still not represented in the plaque gallery at the Baseball Hall of Fame in Cooperstown, New York. Nor is he a household name like Comiskey—and likely never will be. As the President and Chief Executive Officer of the Canadian Museum of History, I know that history is never a fixed mark, is never static, and that it is quite common for people and events that seem important at the time to be nearly forgotten a mere few years later. Tip O'Neill's fame in the 1880s—and his nearly forgotten legacy today—is a classic example of this phenomenon.

For historians, stories like this are a reminder that, when attempting to describe a place, or an era accurately, it is important not only to study government documents and newspapers of record, but also journals and letters, receipts and photographs, personal effects and first-hand memory. In Tip's case, it is also important to imagine walking the streets of St. Louis in 1887 as the Browns rise above all.

Dennis Thiessen has done a remarkable job of doing just that. This book will appeal not only to the serious baseball historian but also to anyone with an interest in the sport or the era. It is also sure to be appreciated as a classic narrative of great achievement, cut down by the vagaries of fate and the outside pettiness that often accompanies fame.

While my great-uncle's achievements may be largely forgotten today, he has not disappeared completely. The annual award presented by the Canadian Baseball Hall of Fame to the best Canadian player is called the Tip O'Neill Award. In 1994, Tip O'Neill was also inducted into Canada's Sports Hall of Fame. The honor came exactly one century from the year he moved back to Canada after retiring from Major League Baseball. During his two decades in Montreal (1894–1915), he supported the development of baseball in the city and the province, assisting with various amateur and professional teams (e.g., Montreal Baseball Club in the Eastern League). In 1897 and 1898, he worked as an umpire in the Eastern League and, periodically, in various local leagues in or near the city. He died of a heart attack in 1915, at the age of 55.

I attended the Canada's Sports Hall of Fame induction ceremony, and it was a great honor to see my great-uncle join the ranks of people like Boom Boom Geoffrion, Tom Longboat, Nancy Greene and Rocket Richard. It was also one more reminder, for me, that history is much more than grand events or powerful people speaking from podiums. Sometimes, it is the sound of a hockey puck hitting the boards of an outdoor arena, so early in the morning that the sun has yet to rise. Or a young boy rounding the bases of a sandlot diamond in Woodstock, Ontario, after hitting the ball farther than anyone thought possible.

People make history every day. In the pages of this book you will find a piece of sport history most of us have forgotten. It is, in the end, a beautiful retelling of the story of James Edward O'Neill, the Woodstock Wonder and the world's "Original" Tip O'Neill.

Mark O'Neill, the great-nephew of Tip O'Neill, is the president and CEO of the Canadian Museum of History.

Preface

James "Tip" O'Neill, the star left fielder for the St. Louis Browns, was the champion batsman of the American Association in 1887 with a phenomenal .492 batting average. In the early days of my research, I found a 1911 source that lauded O'Neill's 1887 batting performance as "a record that has never been excelled before or since,"[1] and another one, 100 years later, that claimed it was "The Greatest Season You Don't Know About."[2] Never excelled but not known about? How could it be possible that some baseball fans do not know about one of the greatest seasons in history, indeed, one with the highest batting average ever officially recorded?

As my research progressed, I began to appreciate why many might not know much about the 1887 season, O'Neill's performance that season, or for that matter James O'Neill himself. If the number of published books on baseball is any indication, most researchers and authors seemed more interested in writing about teams, players, or events after 1900.[3] Those committed to the study of nineteenth century baseball sometimes faced formidable challenges in the conduct of research on this period. For much of the twentieth century, the records of nineteenth century baseball were either difficult to access or, if available, were frequently incomplete or inconsistent. As accessibility improved, so did the number of publications on nineteenth century baseball. However, many of the books, chapters, and articles written in the last four decades on nineteenth century baseball focus more on players and teams in the National League and not on those in the American Association. With some notable exceptions, much less has been written on the American Association or, for my purposes, on the St. Louis Browns.[4] Apart from a few short biographical chapters or sketches,[5] most of the information available on O'Neill comes from vignettes that appear in books or articles on the Browns or his teammates, or in statistical summaries of his career. In other words, we do not know much about O'Neill's incredible season because he played in the nineteenth century, because he did not play in the National League, because it can be problematic to study nineteenth century games and seasons, and because there are no in-depth accounts of his life and career. And, perhaps even more to the point, researchers and writers appeared reluctant to delve into a season and, by implication, a batting champion that were repeatedly criticized, discounted, or re-cast in the years that followed.

The 1887 season was a year of rule changes, more than in any other season in history, as rulesmakers struggled to get the offense-defense balance right, specifically between those rules that favored the pitcher and those that favored the batsman. Although many of the rule changes were widely accepted and endured for many seasons thereafter, two that gave the advantage to the batsman came under considerable attack. One of the new rules gave the batsman an additional strike, that is, he was called out after four strikes.[6] In the second and more controversial rule, the batsman was assigned a hit and a time at bat for a base on balls. While both rules lasted only the one season, the impact of these changes endured for decades, especially when it came to what stature, if any, to afford to O'Neill's .492 batting average.

I decided to study the history of ".492" from the late nineteenth century to the twenty-first century. In particular, I wanted to understand how various historians, statisticians, and commentators made sense of and represented his 1887 record. As the history of his batting average will show, the stature and indeed survival of O'Neill's .492 average became embroiled in a debate about how best to address the base-on-balls-as-a-hit scoring rule in force in 1887. Those who chose to honor the scoring rules of the day, which I dub the conventionalist position, accepted O'Neill's .492 batting average as the highest batting average in 1887, a record that was officially recognized by the American Association at the end of the 1887 season and in the 1888 *Reach's Official American Association Base Ball Guide*. Those who believed that statistics in one year should be as comparable as possible to those in other years, which I call the revisionist position, favored one rule for walks for every season, that is, a base on balls should never be counted as a time at bat or a hit.[7] In the revisionist stance, O'Neill's batting average had to be recalculated after excluding his walks from his hit count and times at bat, a process that in 1969 formally and retroactively reduced his average to .435.[8] Over the years, the debate between these two positions played out in various forums, batting his average between .492 and .435, and to points in between.

Wheeler Wikoff, the president and secretary of the American Association, announced the official averages in early November of 1887. O'Neill headed the list of 112 players with an individual batting record that was presented in four columns: "No. of Games—123 games; No. of B.H. (Base Hits)—277; No. Stolen Bases—30; and Av. B.H. to A.B. (Average of the number of Base Hits-B.H. to the number of times at bat-A.B.)—.492."[9] Although there was not an at-bat column (A.B.), since the published official averages included his number of hits and batting average, it is possible to calculate that O'Neill had 563 times at bat.[10] No other "official" statistics on O'Neill's 1887 performance were published. In the spring of 1888, *Reach's Guide,* in a two-page feature, honored "James E. O'Neill" as the "Champion Batsman of the American Association," with a one-page article that commented on his 1887 batting performance and his career and a second page that displayed a full-page portrait of O'Neill. Of his batting, the *Reach's Guide* stated:

> James E. O'Neill, a magnificent portrait of whom accompanies this sketch, stands at the head of the American Association as its champion batsman, having attained the unprecedented average of .495. He has the proud distinction of being America's Champion batsman and has won his way to the front on genuine, hard hitting, with little or no assistance of the phantom order.[11]

The reference to "little or no assistance of the phantom order"—critics of the base-on-balls rule often referred to walks as phantom hits[12]—reinforced the point that O'Neill was a hard hitter and a worthy batting champion who did not rely heavily on the rule that counted bases on balls as hits for his success. However, it also unwittingly began what became a common refrain, namely to note the rule any time O'Neill's .492 batting average was listed or mentioned.

In late April 1888, a few weeks after the release of the *Reach's Guide,* O'Neill was celebrated in St. Louis at Sportsman's Park prior to the start of a game against Cincinnati.

He received a medal as the best batsman on the Browns in 1887. Judge Scott delivered the following toast:

> Mr. O'Neill. Your magnificent batting record in the year 1887, with an average of .492 stands unexcelled, and within all human probability is unapproachable. It is the best ever made by any player, and places you at the head of your profession in that department of the game. Excellent as has been your work in the left field and elsewhere you must still be content to be crowned "king batter." This honor has not been gained by luck or accident. Your almost unerring gauge of the delivery of the ball and marvelous skill in execution has made you the terror of all pitchers. Often you have turned almost certain defeat into victory by your timely "stick" work. Remember that he who is crowned in the athletic arena must be vigilant and unceasing in effort, lest his honors be lost. Continue therefore your splendid work at the bat and should the boys at any time during the season get into a hole, just tip them a ball over the fence. Now sir, I have the honor and pleasure on behalf of the Mermod & Jaccard Jewelry Company to present to you this elegant pair of diamond sleeve buttons which you have fairly won, and you may keep and prize them as a souvenir of your success.[13]

The 1888 *Reach's Guide* was the first edition that included a photograph of the champion batsman in the American Association. In previous years, the *Guide* included a drawing or sketch of the leading batsman. The accompanying text on the opposite page of the portrait noted that O'Neill was a "natural batsman" who "wields his bat gracefully as well as effectively" (National Baseball Hall of Fame Library, Cooperstown, New York).

As various record guides or books started to appear, O'Neill's .492 batting average was increasingly presented with an accompanying note, parenthesis, or asterisk. For example, in its overview of the 1887 season, *The Sporting Life's Official Base Ball Guide 1891* stated: "The Association's leading batsman was O'Neill, of St. Louis, with .492, this high percentage being due to the fact that in this season, all bases on balls, under the rules, counted as hits."[14] This qualification of O'Neill's record became all but standard practice, and continued so in numerous sources well into the twentieth century.[15]

Not content with simply clarifying O'Neill's 1887 achievement with an asterisk, some sought to discredit any and all achievements attained in this season. Ferdinand Cole Lane, the editor of *Baseball Magazine* between 1912 and 1937, through his own writing as well as the articles he published, was especially pointed in his criticism of O'Neill's record. In his 1911 article, "Who is the Greatest Player in the History of Baseball?," Lane systematically argued that O'Neill's "phenomenal record of .492 was made under vastly more favorable conditions than those enjoyed by his rival," which here referred to Ty Cobb, whom Lane concluded was the more supreme batsman.[16] Four years later, *Baseball Magazine* published an article by John Ward, a former pitcher and shortstop in the National League,[17] entitled, "1887, the Black Sheep of Baseball Records." Ward went further in his condemnation of records established in 1887:

> One thing is true. This year was a grand display of exaggeration and misrepresentation. Its records are fictitious and should be abolished without scruple. The year 1887 has too long basked in a false glory. The year 1887 should be placed under the ban of reason. The year 1887 should be labeled in all the records books "untrustworthy." Its records as such should be abolished. Tip O'Neill holds no record in our category. Ty Cobb would have run rings around him at his own game. And the other records of that memorable year were no better than hundreds of others made by the old-timers in the days when the rules were lax and favorable.[18]

In an effort to add statistical heft to his argument, Ward estimated that O'Neill's average would have been no better than .344 if walks were not counted as hits, a batting average that paled in comparison to Ty Cobb's 1911 record of .420.

In 1922, Ernest Lanigan, author of the *Baseball Cyclopedia,* joined the chorus of critics. Although he had O'Neill at the top of a list of the leading hitters ranked in descending order according to batting average in a season, Lanigan marked O'Neill's average and those of all 1887 batsman with an asterisk, which at the end of the list was succinctly explained in the following notation: "Four strikes; bases on balls counted as hits and charged as at bats."[19] In the section preceding this list, entitled "O'Neill's Mark of .492 Not a Real Mark," Lanigan asserted:

> The highest batting average credited to a major league player—the .492 belonging to James F. O'Neill of the St. Louis Browns is really not the highest real mark, for that year batters received base hits when they got passes. Once the writer checked, as far as he could, the performance of Tip the First and found that if passes were taken away from him he would have batted in the neighborhood of .400."[20]

The following year, Lane added further weight to this growing attack on 1887 and O'Neill's batting record with his article, "One Batting Championship That Never Was Deserved." He characterized the season of 1887 as "the wildest, weirdest year in all baseball history," largely due to the "folly" of the rulesmakers who "suffered a mental lapse and let the averages go on a glorious, wholly illogical spree" by allowing "a base on balls to rank as a hit."[21] In a bold stroke to close the books on O'Neill's record once and for all, Lane unequivocally proclaimed:

> Now the plain facts of the case are these. Any record that was made in 1887 is a record in name only. It has no substance, no foundation. Baseball men have been kowtowing to the memory of J. E. "Tip" O'Neill too long. They set him on a pedestal above all other batters, a pedestal that looked very pretty, but rested on the veriest quick sand of flimsy fiction. J. E. "Tip" O'Neill did not make more hits than any other batter on record as the record books held to be the case. He did not outhit all other major league batters past or present. He is not entitled to any honors as baseball's premier hitter.[22]

The rest of the article laid out the facts in support of Lane's challenge to "the nebulous quality of O'Neill's claims to batting supremacy."[23] Based on a review of 1887 game reports completed by baseball statistician Al Munro Elias, Lane proclaimed that O'Neill's numbers were lower than previously recognized. The Elias findings showed O'Neill with 273 hits, "and not the 277 hits the record books give him."[24] Furthermore, Elias determined that O'Neill had at least 53 bases on balls and went to bat 564 times. When the 53 walks were excluded as hits and times at bat, O'Neill's batting average was .431, based on 220 hits divided by 511 times at bat.[25] Lane went on to point out that O'Neill's recalculated batting average was not as high as either Hugh Duffy's average of .438 in 1894 or Willie Keeler's average of .432 in 1897.

Interestingly, Lane did not use Elias's figures to recalculate O'Neill's batting average applying 1887 scoring rules. Had he done so, O'Neill's average would change to .484 based on 273 hits (220 hits plus 53 bases on balls) divided by 564 times at bat (511 at-bats plus 53 times at bat when he got a hit on each base on balls). I suspect that Lane would not have included this recalculation for the simple reason that to do so would have implicitly recognized the legitimacy of tabulating a batting average that scored a base on balls as a hit. He was not about to endorse the base-on-balls-as-a-hit rule and, by implication, the records of the 1887 season, especially the batting average of James O'Neill, through any statement or gesture. In effect, Lane's line of argument was consistent with the revisionist stance outlined above.[26] He wanted the same scoring rules for calculating records, in this case batting averages, to be used in every season.

In 1948, yet another article appeared in *Baseball Magazine*. Instead of setting O'Neill's record against that of Ty Cobb, as had been the case with Lane in 1911 and Ward in 1915, Cliff Bloodgood, in his article "Ted Williams vs. Tip O'Neill," demonstrated that, if walks had counted as hits between 1939 and 1947, Williams would have topped O'Neill's mark of .492 in four of his six seasons to date. As with past articles, Bloodgood readily disparaged the achievement of O'Neill in 1887: "In 1887, James F. 'Tip' O'Neill of the St. Louis club of the American Association then recognized as a major league, amassed the altitudinal batting average of .492 for the season. This mark is still carried in the record books, an eyesore to the statisticians and historians of the game, for it is a grim joke. Tip no more deserved that inflated average than a buffalo has license to fly."[27] O'Neill's record-setting batting average had clearly become a symbol for all that was wrong with the 1887 season. His historic record of .492, all but buried by Lane, seemed like it was on an endangered list by most others.

O'Neill himself had foreshadowed the confusion and criticism that might arise from records set in a season when bases on balls were counted as hits. In a 1938 article on the five batters with the highest batting averages, John Foster quoted from an interview with O'Neill some years after his 1887 performance. O'Neill reflected:

> I was never very pleased with the addition to the rule that increased the batting average with the addition of the base on balls. Of course, it made my batting percentage higher and that was most welcome, but it was not a legitimate boost to batting. I never got over the old-fashioned idea, and I guess there was a great many just like me, that whenever I got a base on balls the pitcher had just as much to do with it as the batter.
>
> I felt proud, of course, to have such a high mark in batting, but I used to tell the other players it never will be accepted as a reward for batting alone, but it would always be said that in some way or another it would be a record combining the base on balls with the base hit. That, as a matter of fact, would be making up two records in one, and there would not be a very good explanation as to why it was done. It would neither be an actual batting percentage nor could it be a good record of the number of base on balls received during the season, and the seeker of information would be compelled to go through a process of subtraction to find out what the actual batting percentage of the player might be. This would be too much work for the fan and he would resent it.[28]

However, amidst the emerging asterisks, criticisms, and on O'Neill's part, doubts about the status of his 1887 record, there were some in the first half of the twentieth century who retained their admiration for what O'Neill achieved that season and indeed in his career.

From time to time, especially among those who had played or witnessed baseball in the 1880s, O'Neill's record held a special place in their memories. For example, in 1911, William W. Aulick, a sportswriter for the *New York Times*, wrote a series entitled, "One Hundred Notables in Baseball." In the issue dedicated to O'Neill, he marveled at the fact that O'Neill could achieve such a record with one arm permanently damaged: "As it was, this .492 mark stands as far and away the best bit of workmanship achieved by any batsman whose name has come thundering down through the ages, but at that it represented only the effort of a man whose 'arm had given out.'"[29] In 1919, Charles Comiskey, O'Neill's captain and manager for nine of his ten years in the major leagues, while acknowledging the influence of the rules changes in 1887, commended O'Neill on his batting when something more than a walk was required:

> In the outfield, I had one of the greatest of all fly chasers and base runners in Curt Welch, and one of the greatest sluggers in the history of the game in Tip O'Neill. In 1887, I believe it was, he hit for an average of .492, the biggest percentage ever rung up in the major leagues, but it must be taken in consideration that in the year bases on balls counted as hits. Still when walks were not profitable Tip was there with the bat.[30]

These positive comments notwithstanding, by the middle of the twentieth century, the memory of O'Neill's batting achievements of 1887 had receded into the distant past. Other than the Bloodgood article noted above, there were few published materials of or references to the 1887 season or to O'Neill's batting championship.[31] His .492 average continued to appear in the record books invariably marked with a symbol, asterisk, or parenthesis to designate its exception-to-the-rule status and accompanied by an explanation of how the base-on-balls-as-a-hit rule made O'Neill's high percentage different from those of other batting champions. Fast forward to 1968, when the season of 1887 and O'Neill's .492 average were under scrutiny once again, this time implicated in a larger effort to develop a more comprehensive record of baseball statistics and a more systematic approach to regulate these records.

Any meaningful debate about O'Neill's .492 batting average, or indeed any informed discussion on many of the nineteenth century statistics, was marred by the incomplete and inconsistent information available. In 1967, Information Concepts Incorporated (ICI) began a project whose purpose was to build "a data bank of major league baseball's existing statistics."[32] Shortly thereafter, ICI joined with The MacMillan Company to develop a format for an encyclopedia that would, among other things, display the results of the ICI research. Major League Baseball supported the ICI research project, and the publication of *The Baseball Encyclopedia: The Complete and Official Record of Major League Baseball*.[33] By 1968, Major League Baseball formed a Special Baseball Records Committee "to establish rules governing record-keeping procedures."[34] The Committee's 17 decisions informed both the work of ICI and the content and format of the encyclopedia that was published in 1969.

One of the 17 decisions made by the Special Baseball Records Committee in 1968 had a direct bearing on the status of O'Neill's .492 batting average: "Bases on balls shall always be treated as neither a time at bat nor a hit for the batter. (In 1887 bases on balls were scored as hits and in 1876 bases on balls were scored as outs.)"[35] Based on the ICI research, *The Baseball Encyclopedia* listed O'Neill with 517 times at bat, 225 hits, 167 runs, and 50 bases on balls.[36] The ICI data also clarified the breakdown of O'Neill's 85 extra-base hits—52 doubles, 19 triples, and 14 home runs. With specific numbers for each type of hit (including 140 singles), ICI was also able to determine O'Neill's total bases and to include a calculation of .691 for his slugging average. From the ICI study, then, we had a better understanding of the hits that defined his batting average.

Following the decision of the Special Baseball Records Committee, with O'Neill's 50 walks no longer counted as hits or times at bat, his batting average was adjusted to .435.[37] The saga of his .492 batting average had officially come to an end, as did the need to add an asterisk or a parenthesis each time his .435 batting average appeared in future record books. The unmarked revision of O'Neill's batting average, however, came at a cost. The decision did not reflect the rule in force in 1887 and, by implication, neither did the normalized average of .435. While the revisionist-based decision made the scoring of walks consistent with how walks were handled in all other seasons—a perceived advantage when it came to comparing batting averages across seasons and eras—it robbed the history of the 1887 season of one of its most distinct features. This historical theft took away 57 points from the previous official average for O'Neill reported in the 1888 *Reach's Guide*. It also moved his average down a notch in its all-time ranking. O'Neill's .435 average, still impressive to be sure, was now the second-best batting average of all time, behind Hugh Duffy's 1894 record of .440.[38]

Since 1968, numerous historians have questioned the wisdom of some of the decisions made by the Special Baseball Records Committee. David Voigt, one of the most ardent critics, exclaimed: "Until the erroneous decisions of the Special Records Committee are overturned, the long history of major league baseball will be blighted by its misguided zeal to make past records fit modern standards."[39] In 2001, Jerome Holtzman, Major League Baseball's official historian, reversed the Special Baseball Records Committee's decision on bases on balls in 1887:

> Major League Baseball is pleased to announce that, beginning with this seventh edition of *Total Baseball*, all batting averages are recorded as they were at the time they were reported, and not in accordance with the decision of a 1968 Special Baseball Records Committee.... Revisionist history is admirable when new and undisputed evidence is brought forth. But this was an abomination, an absolute falsehood and twisting of the known facts for the singular purpose of regulating history to conform to previous and subsequent standards. It was a grievous corruption. If a walk was a hit in 1887 it should stand as a hit forevermore.[40]

In this announcement, James O'Neill was acknowledged as the batting champion of the 1887 American Association. His .492 average, however, was not reinstated but corrected. Based on the numbers determined by the ICI research and the scoring rules of 1887, O'Neill had 275 hits (225 hits in singles, doubles, triples, and home runs plus 50 hits by bases on balls) in 567 times at bat for an average of .485. The once-honored mark of .492 that had subsequently survived for decades, albeit impaired with asterisks, had been sent to the grave for a second time. It had first expired in 1968 by a fatal stroke of the Special Baseball Records Committee when it cut 50 hits from Tip's record and was replaced by the walk-less average of .435. Temporarily resuscitated by Holtzman's 2001 ruling, .492 perished once more, this time succumbing to an alleged arithmetic error.[41]

Despite the declaration by Holtzman, most reference books and online databases (e.g., Baseball Reference, Retrosheet) continued to list O'Neill with a .435 batting average in 1887. To date, the seventh and eighth editions of *Total Baseball* are the only major compendia that include O'Neill's "new" average of .485.[42] After three decades of revisionist rule, the various keepers of the records seemed more interested in working with seasonal statistics that are as comparable as possible and, in the case of the 1887 records and O'Neill's batting average in particular, were less concerned about representing the numbers according to the scoring conventions of the times.

At the National Baseball Hall of Fame and Museum in Cooperstown, New York, one of its displays gives some recognition to O'Neill's record in the 1887 season and to the debate that surrounds this record. On a poster entitled, "Highest Batting Average in a Season Since 1876," Hugh Duffy is featured immediately below the title, with a side-angle photograph of his head and shoulders on the right side of the poster and his batting average of ".440" placed in bold, large print in the center of the poster just to the left of the image. "HUGH DUFFY" appears in capital letters just below Duffy's photograph and ".440." Below Duffy's name, there is an 18-line statement that suggests how O'Neill can also be considered for the highest single-season batting average:

> For record books that regard the National League's first year (1876) as the start of major league play, Boston's Hugh Duffy is generally cited for holding the mark for highest single-season batting average:

.440 in 1894. But another player from baseball's early days has a legitimate claim to the title. In 1887, baseball implemented two rules which lasted just one season: a walk counted as both a base hit and at bat (today it counts for neither), and a strikeout occurred after *four* (italics in original), not three, strikes. At season's end, more than a dozen players posted batting averages above .400, with Tip O'Neill leading the way with a .485 mark. While one cannot retroactively "correct" for the advantage batters gained for the extra strike, most modern-day statisticians have accounted for the unusual walk rule. In so doing, O'Neill's mark has been retroactively dropped to .435.[43]

The Hall of Fame then in effect acknowledges the existence of both conventionalist (.485) and revisionist (.435) averages, without directly taking sides, other than through the fact that Duffy's photograph and .440 batting average appear prominently at the top of the poster.

At least one other contemporary source of baseball records lists a different batting average for O'Neill. The Elias Sports Bureau, the official statistician of Major League Baseball, in *The Elias Book of Baseball Records*, lists O'Neill's average at .442,[44] which is the highest batting average for a season. *The Elias Book of Baseball Records* has Duffy ranked second with an average of .438.[45] O'Neill's batting average had previously appeared as .442 in the tenth and final edition of *The Official Encyclopedia of Baseball*.[46]

In summary, the history of O'Neill's .492 average is a story of twists and turns, challenges and doubts, some near-fatal moments followed by revivals, only to be lost recently in translation. The storyline of his batting average is inextricably tied to the changing status of the 1887 rule that counted bases on balls as hits and times at bat. The rule has been historically mired in a debate between conventionalists who argued that the scoring rules of the day should be respected and revisionists who insisted that scoring rules should be normalized for all seasons. O'Neill's .492 performance stood as the best official batting average in history until 1969, albeit usually demarcated with an asterisk or parenthesis to clarify or qualify his achievement, and periodically challenged by those who found his record questionable if not unworthy (e.g., Lane, Ward, Lanigan, Bloodgood). After the ICI research in the late 1960s, the decisions of the Special Baseball Records Committee in 1968, and the publication of *The Baseball Encyclopedia* in 1969, O'Neill's batting average was normalized to .435, relegating him to second-best on the all-time list of best averages for a season. From 1969 until 2001, following the guidelines set in the revisionist edict issued in 1968, few sources mentioned O'Neill's .492 average. Holtzman's decree in 2001 halted the revisionist era in record-keeping. With the 1887 batting records, he called for walks to be restored as hits and for batting averages to be recalculated. O'Neill's average was corrected to .485, putting to rest, presumably once and for all, any further reference to .492, the official average announced by the president of the American Association at the end of the 1887 season. Although O'Neill's new average returned him to the top of the standings with the highest batting average for one season in history, few people subsequently cited .485. Most compendia and online databases maintained the revisionist creed and consequently continued to list O'Neill's normalized average of .435. However, given the Elias Sport Bureau's average for O'Neill at .442, which vaulted Tip into first place when batting averages of every hitter exclude walks as hits or times at bat, the matter of who is the all-time leader in a season with a normalized average is also in some dispute.

As the above discussion illustrates, much of what is known about O'Neill's batting championship in 1887 is centered on the somewhat confusing tale of how his .492 batting average was questioned, challenged, and changed over the years. Prior to the Computer

Age (1969–present) of baseball statistics,[47] there were few articles or references that provided further details about the hits that animated O'Neill's batting average and distinguished this season.[48] One of the first revelations came from an unlikely source. Given his previous efforts to denigrate O'Neill's .492 batting average, F. C. Lane, in his role as editor of *The Little Red Book of Major League Baseball* (1939–48), nevertheless, was the only record-keeper prior to 1950 who listed another mark that O'Neill set in 1887: Leading Leagues in all three departments—Doubles, triples, homers-season—James E. O'Neill, St. Louis AA, 46 doubles, 24 triples, 13 homers, 1887. Also led League in batting percentage, .492; 1887.[49] The numbers cited for doubles, triples, and home runs were different from those found in the ICI research, which, as noted above, listed Tip with 52 doubles, 19 triples, and 14 home runs. Regardless of the discrepancy in the two sets of figures, the numbers in both were high enough for O'Neill to lead the American Association in "all three departments."

Following the ICI research in 1969, other batting feats started to appear in various record books or compendia. By the 1980s, O'Neill's name appeared in various publications for hitting for the cycle twice in 1887.[50] Into the 1990s, *Total Baseball* confirmed that in 1887, O'Neill drove in 123 runs,[51] which along with his Association-leading batting average (.485) and home runs (14), eventually led to O'Neill's inclusion on the list of batsmen who won the Triple Crown.[52] These emerging revelations brought further distinctions to O'Neill's 1887 batting record, providing additional insights into a performance that was for too long overwhelmed by the swirling story surrounding his batting average.

By the turn of the twenty-first century, the computer had not only contributed to the explosion of statistical data but also made these data more accessible. Less distracted by O'Neill's so-called inflated batting average, historians and statisticians discovered or confirmed new facets of O'Neill's extraordinary season. For example, following in the footsteps of Lane, David Nemec in his 2004 book, *The Beer and Whiskey League. The Illustrated History of the American Association—Baseball's Renegade Major League*, expanded the number of offensive categories in which O'Neill led in 1887, asserting that he "became the only player ever to top a major league in hits, runs, doubles, triples, home runs, total bases, slugging average and batting average" in the same season.[53] Seven years later, Nemec added: "Once the season started, however, O'Neill rocketed to perhaps the most dominant offensive season in history."[54] It is time to probe beneath and beyond these numbers, to examine the basis of these recent claims, such as those made by Nemec, and to chronicle the various batting stories that illuminate O'Neill's "rocket-like" season.

In the following chapters, I take you back in time to James O'Neill's world in 1887, to a remarkable season of soaring achievements. I tell the story as it unfolded in 1887, fully committed to honoring the conventionalist proclamation of Holtzman in 2001: "If a walk was a hit in 1887 it should stand as a hit forever." Testing the limits of how many lives O'Neill's original batting average can have, I resurrect .492, to give it due regard as the batting average of record, officially recognized by the American Association in 1887. I also honor ".485," the average that was painstakingly calculated from ICI research, the most rigorous study ever conducted into statistics of the nineteenth century. It seems possible that O'Neill's conventionalist average could land on .492, .485, or somewhere in between. In the course of reconstructing the story of O'Neill's season of batting supremacy, I take another look at his batting average and associated batting statistics, in order to confirm or revise those numbers that currently define his 1887 performance.

The story opens in Chapter 1 at the 1886 world championship series between St.

Louis, the American Association champion, and Chicago, the National League champion. It is here that the 1886 season ended and where, I argue, the 1887 season began. In the world championship series, O'Neill led all batsmen on both teams with a batting average of .400, a bar that he sustained and indeed significantly exceeded in 1887.

Chapter 2 is the first of three chapters that describe some of the contexts that frame O'Neill's story as it unfolded in 1887. It provides a biographical sketch of O'Neill, with a brief snapshot of his early years, a comment on the origins of his nickname of "Tip," and an overview of his eight years as a pitcher, the last of which was when he joined the St. Louis Browns in 1884. The chapter describes O'Neill's transition in 1885 and 1886 to an outfielder and his emergence as one of the leading batsmen in the American Association.

Chapter 3 introduces eight players on the Browns who, along with O'Neill, formed the core of the Browns' team that, entering 1887, had won the last two championships in the American Association (1885–1886) and, in 1886, the world championship. In comparison to Chapter 2, the profiles of his teammates show how they differed from the background, qualities, and strengths that O'Neill brought to the team. Chapter 4 follows with an analysis of the Browns' style of play, an orientation to the game that combined skill and headwork with noisy coaching, incessant kicking, tricks, rough play, and an insatiable drive to win.

Chapter 5 picks up the story of O'Neill and the St. Louis Browns from the end of the 1886 world championship to the start of the 1887 season. It recounts some of O'Neill's experiences during the off-season, the tensions between the Browns' players and the owner, and the Browns' and O'Neill's struggles in a pre-season rematch against Chicago.

Chapters 6 to 14 recount the story of the 1887 regular season. Five of the nine chapters, in alternating sequence, examine one of five phases of O'Neill's regular season. Each phase covers a similar number of games and is organized around themes that characterize the play of O'Neill, especially his batting, during the phase. The following table lists the number of each phase-based chapter, the beginning and end dates of the phase, the number of games played by O'Neill in the phase, and the substantive title of the chapter, which suggests the thematic focus of O'Neill's play during this period:

Chapter	*Dates*	*Games Played*	*Title of Chapter*
6	April 16 to May 24	24	Batting for Average
8	May 25 to July 11	28	Injury and Struggle
10	July 12 to August 10	25	A Slow Return to Form
12	August 12 to September 8	24	Batting for Power
14	September 9 to October 9	23	American Association Champions

The phase-based chapters highlight such areas as O'Neill's sustained and timely hitting in three or more games in a row; his numerous multi-hit games; his ability to get on base; and his capacity to score and drive in runs. In addition, they document his forgettable games at bat, his struggles with injuries, his miscues on the base path, and his occasional lapses in the field. Weaving through O'Neill's stories, these five chapters also convey tales of O'Neill's teammates, narrative accounts of their skillful and strategic work on the field, their antics and tricks, their aggressive play, and their squawks and squabbles.

Following each the first four phase-based chapters is a chapter that examines one of O'Neill's noteworthy batting feats in the 1887 regular season, the first three of which address the following: hitting for the cycle (Chapter 7); featured games for batting, fielding or both (Chapter 9); and long hits (Chapter 11).[55] Chapter 13 explores a fourth batting feat, O'Neill's numerous hitting streaks, some which involved consecutive times at bat when he got on base; others which spanned more than 20 games in a row where he had at least one hit; and one which included a number of games in a row with one or more long hits.

The story of O'Neill's extraordinary year closes in Chapter 15 with the Browns' loss to Detroit in a 15-game series for the world championship. The chapter comments on the marked difference between the Browns' dramatic win over Chicago in 1886 and their initially hard-fought but in the end disappointing performance against Detroit in 1887. It elaborates how this contrast in the two series was especially evident in O'Neill's poor performance at the plate in the Detroit series.

Chapter 16 examines O'Neill's 1887 standing in 12 batting categories (hits, singles, doubles, triples, home runs, runs batted in, long hits, total bases, on-base percentage, slugging percentage, on-base plus slugging percentage, batting average). It describes how O'Neill led the Browns and the American Association in most batting categories and in a majority of the batting categories in the major leagues (National League and American Association), in many cases with record-setting performances. The chapter concludes with a comparison between O'Neill and eight other batsmen in the twentieth century who have had seasons when they led in ten or more batting categories.

In the Epilogue, I outline some of O'Neill's major accomplishments in the last five years of his major league career (1888–1892); describe his life in Montreal (1894–1915) and his sudden death on New Year's Eve of 1915; and review the various ways O'Neill's baseball career has been honored over the last 30 years. I conclude the book with the hope that the story of O'Neill's 1887 season reclaims and revives a legacy that is much deserved but not yet fully appreciated.

1

October 18 to October 23, 1886: Champions of the World

CRACK! The ball exploded off the bat of James "Tip" O'Neill, the left fielder of the St. Louis Browns. The collision of bat and ball pierced the air like the shot of a gun to start a race. The infielders froze as the ball whistled overhead on a line to deep left-center field. O'Neill and Abner Dalrymple, the left fielder of the Chicago White Stockings, took off together, albeit in different directions, O'Neill in a headlong pursuit to make the circuit of the bases and Dalrymple in a frantic chase to run the ball down in time to throw out O'Neill before he scored. The race turned out to be no contest. The ball somehow threaded its way through a maze of carriages in left-center field and sped onwards to the brick fence, a distance over 400 feet from home plate.[1] Just as Dalrymple picked up the ball, O'Neill touched home, with Bob Caruthers, the Browns' pitcher, scoring ahead of him. After only three batsmen in the first inning, O'Neill's home run gave the St. Louis Browns a 2–0 lead. The Browns went on to score ten more runs in this one-sided, 12–0 rout. The win tied the Series at one win apiece in a seven-game challenge match to determine the champions of the world.

At the start of the first inning, Arlie Latham, the Browns' third baseman, strolled to the plate amidst a torrent of shrieks and howls from the Chicago crowd. After his antics in the first game of the series (a 6–0 win for Chicago), the *Chicago Inter Ocean* chastised the "clown Latham" as a "hoodlum" who engaged in disgusting and "obscene talk on the ball field."[2] Resolute and calm in the face of such derision, Latham rapped his bat on the plate and readied himself for the first pitch from Jim McCormick, the Chicago pitcher. Latham repeatedly bunted the ball foul, rattling McCormick to the point that the flustered pitcher tossed six called balls, sending Latham to first with a base on balls. On a pickoff attempt by McCormick, the first umpire, Jack McQuaid, called Latham out. Charles Comiskey, the captain and first baseman of the Browns, challenged the call, but Joe Quest, the second umpire, supported McQuaid's decision. The kicking[3] intensified as "players gesticulated wildly and the crowd hooted."[4] Latham ran across the field to protest the call to John Kelly, the referee,[5] who was positioned behind second base. After five minutes of wrangling, Kelly reversed the decision, Latham returned to first base and promptly stole second. When Caruthers swung at and missed the third strike, King Kelly, the Chicago catcher, slyly dropped the ball as a ploy to get Latham to edge further off second. As Caruthers ran to first, Latham took steps towards third. Without warning, Kelly picked up the dropped ball and threw Latham out at second. The crowd guyed[6] Latham for how easily Kelly duped him into a pickoff that this time was successful. Unfazed, Latham resumed his duties as the third base coacher and continued in his relentless banter and taunts of opposing players, fans, and umpires alike. Caruthers was safe at first and two pitches later crossed home plate on O'Neill's home run.

In Chicago's first at-bat, the leadoff batter was George Gore, the center fielder, who lined a sharp single to right field. Two batters later, Cap Anson, the first baseman and captain of the White Stockings, successfully emulated the "fouling" style of Latham (repeatedly bunted the ball foul) and took his base on balls. Fred Pfeffer, the Chicago second baseman, flied out to Dave Foutz, the Browns' right fielder. Gore and Anson moved up to third and second base, respectively. Ned Williamson, the shortstop, grounded out to Bill "Yank" Robinson, the Browns' second baseman, leaving the two runners stranded. As it turned out, Gore's hit was the only one that Caruthers allowed in the eight-inning game.[7] Caruthers "twirled the ball for all that he was worth."[8] It was not until the seventh inning that another Chicago runner made it to third base. Caruthers struck out five, walked two, and delivered no wild pitches. Only five batted balls left the infield (Gore's single and four fly outs). He retired the Chicago batters in order in innings three, four, five and six. Aided by a strong fielding performance, Caruthers had the Chicago batters off-balance all afternoon.

Neither team scored any runs in the second and third innings. O'Neill, however, was involved in two incidents in the third inning. McCormick, "remembering things that were,"[9] gave O'Neill his base on balls. O'Neill ran to second as Bill Gleason, the Browns' shortstop, hit a ground ball down the third base line that the umpire called foul. As O'Neill sauntered back to first, the ball was returned to McCormick, who threw it to first in time for Anson to tag O'Neill. Anson argued that according to National League rules (which were the rules of play for all games played in Chicago), the runner must run back to first, and if he did not, he should be declared out.[10] Kelly, the referee, intervened and re-affirmed that O'Neill was safe. Moments later, Gleason hit a ground ball to Tom Burns, the third baseman, who wheeled and threw to second to get O'Neill for the first out in what Chicago hoped would be a double play. The second baseman, Pfeffer, caught the ball and touched the bag for the out just as O'Neill knocked him down and fell on top of him, thus preventing Pfeffer from throwing to first to complete the double play. Anson protested, arguing that O'Neill had deliberately obstructed the second baseman. The umpire restated that O'Neill was out at second but dismissed the charge that there was any obstruction on the play. The crowd hissed loudly at O'Neill as he ran off the field.

The Browns surged into a 7–0 lead on two runs in the fourth inning and three runs in the fifth. Sloppy play on the part of the White Stockings enabled the Browns to score two runs in the fourth inning. Foutz, the right fielder, led off with a single to left and went to second when Abner Dalrymple momentarily fumbled the ball. Albert "Doc" Bushong, the Browns' catcher, followed with a fly ball to left field that dropped in front of Dalrymple when he lost the ball in the sun. Foutz took advantage of the sun-induced misplay by the left fielder and scored the Browns' third run. Bushong moved to third on Latham's groundout to the pitcher. Caruthers hit a pop-up to Burns, the third baseman, who muffed the easy fly for the third of four errors he made in the game. Bushong came home on the error.

CRACK! On the first pitch of the fifth inning, O'Neill duplicated his earlier feat with his second home run of the game. His "corking line drive"[11] followed the path of his first home run but "did not touch the ground until it almost reached the carriage fence."[12]

Unlike the hissing in the third inning, the Chicago crowd cheered wildly as O'Neill made the circuit. The *Chicago Tribune* recounted these two home runs:

> O'Neill's two home-run hits down into the lower left-hand corner of the field away behind the carriages were the prettiest ever made on the grounds. The second one went so far that Dalrymple hadn't reached it when O'Neill crossed the plate.[13]

Bill Gleason, the next batter, hit a single and went to third base on a safe hit by Curt Welch, the Browns' center fielder. With runners on first and third, Welch initiated the first leg of a delayed double steal. He started for second slowly, then momentarily hesitated as if uncertain about whether to continue, hoping to entice the catcher to throw to second. As the catcher fired the ball to second, Gleason took off from third to score the sixth run, successfully completing the second leg of the plan.[14] Welch tallied another run on Foutz's triple to the clubhouse in right center field.

The Browns completed the scoring with five runs in the seventh inning. With one out, Welch walked and moved to second when Pfeffer, in his rush to get a double play, failed to pick up the slow-rolling ball that dribbled off Foutz's bat. Both Welch and Foutz scored on a single to left field by Yank Robinson. Dalrymple threw to catch Welch on his run for home, but the ball sailed over the head of the catcher. McCormick rushed in to cover the plate in anticipation of a relay throw from the catcher to prevent one or both runners from scoring. As Welch touched the plate, his "arm collided with that of the pitcher,"[15] a bump that the *Cincinnati Commercial Gazette* said "knocked the breath out of McCormick."[16] Some newspapers did not report the initial contact by Welch, but were instead appalled by the rough play they felt was instigated by McCormick, namely a blow to Welch's neck with a force that dislodged his cap. Angry words were exchanged, but for the many who expected to see Welch retaliate with his fists, they were surprised when Welch walked away.[17] The *St. Louis Republican* praised Welch for his "self-restraint" in the face of McCormick's "cowardly and ungentlemanly action."[18]

Amidst the tussle at home between Welch and McCormick, Robinson made it to third base. He scored on Bushong's groundout to Anson at first base. On a hit to the left side of the infield, Latham made it to second on the shortstop's throwing error and then hustled home on Caruthers' opposite-field triple, his second hit off the wall in left field (he doubled in the sixth). O'Neill drove in the 12th run of the game with a single to center field. After the eighth inning, the game was called on account of darkness.

In addition to the cheers from those fans in attendance, the St. Louis cranks[19] in Missouri celebrated the victory from afar. Telegrams of congratulations poured into President Chris Von der Ahe, the owner and president of the St. Louis nine.[20] The bettors from the day before had put even more down on a St. Louis victory in Game Two and were rewarded handsomely for their loyalty. As the innings went by, the betting was no longer on who was going to win the game but on what the chances were that Chicago would be shut out. The Chicagos were indeed "Chicagoed"[21] by their very own Browns. Having lost 6–0 in Game One, the Browns, in the 12–0 victory, had given the White Stockings a "double dose of the medicine"[22] they had received the day before. The loss was the worst drubbing of the season for Chicago and only their ninth loss at home. One St. Louis reporter turned to poetry to express his delight at the Browns' win:

> There was a windy city growing
> On the southeast side of a lake's marsh edge,
> And the greatest fakes in the dawn came groping

> Down through its paths from the day's low ledge;
> Its base ball club, full of Anson folly,
> Blowed and blustered in sickening style—
> Swore it would drown in melancholy
> The Browns, and rake St. Louis' pile.
>
> They played one game in that charming (?) city
> And piled up scores 'gainst nothing, so
> That they felt neither love, nor pity
> For the club that came out of the sunset's glow.
> Another they played while the fit was on them,
> While victory sat cross-legged on their heads,
> While the bay rums and laurel profusely bedecked them,
> And the streets were afloat in infinite reds.
>
> But Caruthers met them at Fame's bright gateway;
> O'Neill barred the path that they longed to climb,
> And a shadow fell on their footsteps straightway—
> A shade that grew dark when the umpire called "Time!"
> They wrestled with Fate, but he fain would linger
> To see them knocked down by the golden gate;
> "Twelve" "Goose-eggs!" he said, pointing one stern finger—
> That was how they were done in innings eight.
>
> Chicago was mad, and its language winding
> Colored the depths of infinite air;
> They were queered in a way that was past all finding,
> And there wasn't a doubt they were done up fair.
> "We thought they were babies," quoth Anson mildly,
> "This wasn't the easiest game we played!"
> And the gang will never cease kicking wildly
> When they think of the foolish bets they made.[23]

Led by O'Neill and Caruthers, the Browns thoroughly outplayed Chicago in Game Two. Confidence was high among the St. Louis fans and players alike. Game Three would be a different story.

In the third one-sided game in a row, the Chicagos reversed their fortunes of the previous day with a dominating 11–4 win over the Browns. John Clarkson, the Chicago pitcher, scattered nine hits, had five strikeouts, and allowed no earned runs. Brimming with confidence from his triumphant performance in Game Two, Caruthers persuaded Von der Ahe to let him pitch Game Three, despite the objections of Comiskey.[24] In contrast to his pitching gem in Game Two, Caruthers struggled out of the gate and never recovered. He threw 12 balls to start the game. He was pounded for 12 hits, four for extra bases (double, triple, two home runs). The St. Louis newspapers roundly criticized the Browns for pitching Caruthers two games in a row, as did some of the players, most notably Kid Gleason, Latham, and O'Neill. Gleason bluntly argued, "It was dead wrong to put him in," while O'Neill commented that the "pitching had been miserably managed, and this from the start disconcerted the whole team."[25]

Throughout the series in Chicago, the local newspapers were unwavering in their rant about Latham's coaching.[26] To be sure, some of the Chicago fans began to enjoy his outlandish behavior and increasingly relished the chance to jeer him when he made a mistake or when one of his exhortations backfired. For example, in Game One, when O'Neill struck out in his first two times at bat after Latham yelled to him, "Eat 'em up,

Jim!" the fans laughed and hooted at Latham for his lack of inspirational coaching.[27] Most of the Chicago newspapers, however, saw little humor in Latham's antics. For example, the *Chicago Times* exclaimed that Latham "made an antiquated idiot of himself in a vain attempt to rattle the veteran players of the Chicago team by continual loud-mouthed and useless coaching."[28] The *Chicago Tribune* begrudgingly granted that Latham's "incessant howling ... was funny for about fifteen minutes," but then felt "it grew tiresome ... [and became] the worst nuisance ever inflicted upon a Chicago audience."[29] After Game Four, the *Chicago Daily News* had had enough. It concluded: "Mr. Latham is a capital baseball player; he gains nothing but an evil reputation for himself by the tiresome exhibitions of alley wit—he certainly does not disconcert his opponents, and as certainly he does hurt base ball as a profession every time he opens his yawp."[30]

After Game Three, the teams boarded a train to travel to St. Louis for the next three games in the Series. They arrived in the morning, checked in the hotel, and were at Sportsman's Park in the afternoon to ready themselves for Game Four. The Browns won three in row in St. Louis to capture the championship of the world, four games to two. Unlike the three games in Chicago, only the Browns' 10–3 win in Game Five was one-sided. Games Four and Six were hard-fought and closely contested matches that the Browns won, 8–5 and 4–3 respectively.

In Game Four, Chicago seemed to make the same mistake for which the Browns were so vehemently criticized, namely to pitch their ace, Clarkson, in back-to-back games. It was, however, Foutz, the Browns' pitcher, who got off to a rough start as Chicago took a 3–0 lead after one inning. By the end of the fourth inning, Clarkson initially proved the skeptics wrong by holding the Browns to two unearned runs on two hits and three Chicago errors. In the third inning, O'Neill hit a triple into the crowd in right field, driving in the Browns' second run. O'Neill tried to stretch the triple into a home run but was thrown out on a relay from the right fielder to the pitcher to the catcher.[31] Chicago clung to a 3–2 lead as St. Louis went to bat in the bottom of the fifth. In a calculated move, Kelly, Clarkson, and Anson decided to walk O'Neill intentionally, once in the fifth inning and again in the sixth. The strategy failed. In both innings, the base on balls to O'Neill loaded the bases. Gleason followed with a single in the fifth inning, scoring two runs to put the Browns ahead, 4–3. Comiskey knocked in another run to extend the lead to 5–3. Chicago tied the score with two runs in the top of the sixth inning. In the bottom of the sixth, once again the Browns responded with three runs, the last two on Gleason's timely hit after Clarkson intentionally walked O'Neill. The decision to take the bat out of O'Neill's hands for a second time in as many innings allowed the Browns to regain the lead. Chicago failed to score in the top of seventh.[32] The game was called because of darkness, with the Browns victorious by a score of 8–5.

Chicago did not have a pitcher available for Game Five. Clarkson had pitched three of the first four games and needed a break. McCormick was sick and did not make the trip to St. Louis. Flynn, the White Stockings' third pitcher, had a lame arm. Albert Spalding, the owner and president of the White Stockings, wanted Mark Baldwin, a recently signed minor league pitcher, to start Game Five, but Von der Ahe refused to allow a pitcher who had not been with the team in 1886. Rather than press the point, Chicago started the shortstop, Ned Williamson, in the box. After the Browns scored two runs in the first inning, Jim Ryan, the right fielder, replaced Williamson.[33] The Browns went with Nat Hudson, their rookie pitcher, who turned in a strong performance, giving up just three hits and no earned runs. Caruthers was the best St. Louis batter on the day. He went three-for-four at the plate with a triple, had two runs batted in, and scored two runs. O'Neill had two singles in four times at bat. He was again thrown out on the base path when he tried to go from first to third on a single by Gleason. The lopsided 10–3 victory gave the Browns three wins against two losses, their first lead in the Series.

In the sixth and deciding game, St. Louis and Chicago battled ten innings before the Browns emerged victorious. Caruthers and Clarkson formed the pitching duel, Caruthers starting his third game on two days' rest and Clarkson taking the ball for his fourth game on one day's rest. By the fifth inning, Chicago had a 3–0 lead. After six innings, Clarkson had faced just 19 batters, with O'Neill being the only man to reach first with a base on balls in the first inning. With one out in the seventh inning, O'Neill ended Clarkson's no-hitter with a triple but was tagged out when he over-ran third base. Chicago still had a 3–0 lead going into the bottom of the eighth inning, when the Browns finally struck back to tie the score, 3–3. Comiskey opened the eighth with a single and Welch followed with a bunt down third that he easily beat out. Burns' unwise throw to first was wide of the base, allowing Comiskey to score the Browns' first run and Welch to hustle down to second base. Foutz flied out to center field. Welch advanced to third on a passed ball. Robinson flied out to Anson. Bushong took his base on balls. Latham stepped to the plate. He paused to shout to Bushong: "Stay there, Bush, and I'll bring you both in."[34] Two pitches later, Latham hit a triple to left field over Dalrymple's head; Bushong and Welch scored. To all those who had ridiculed Latham for his howling, brazen antics, and clown-like demeanor, he had the last laugh. When it counted, Latham made good on his audacious promise: "I'll bring you both in," he blustered, and he did.

The game remained tied

In celebration of the St. Louis Browns' undisputed championship of the world, memorabilia abounded. Team photographs were available in programs or on cigar boxes, soap tins, banners, or blankets. The above poster was one of the souvenirs produced to mark the Browns' 1886 victory over Chicago (Library of Congress, Prints and Photographs Division, Reproduction Number LC-DIG-ppmsca-18392).

until the tenth inning. Welch was first to bat. He leaned over the plate, got hit by a pitch, and was sent by the umpire to first base. The Chicago team complained that Welch had not tried to get out of the way of the pitch. The umpire reversed his decision. On the next pitch, Welch hit a single to center field. Foutz hit a sharp grounder that the shortstop could not handle. The Browns had men on first and second. Robinson laid down a sacrifice bunt; both runners moved up a base. Bushong came to bat. On the second pitch, Kelly, the Chicago catcher, motioned to Clarkson for a low outside pitch. Clarkson threw high and inside. The ball went to the backstop and Welch ran home with the winning run.[35]

The Browns were the world champions. Bedlam broke out in Sportsman's Park as fans poured onto the field. Fans ran helter-skelter, leaping in delight, shaking hands or hugging friends and strangers alike, yelling and cheering at the Browns' triumph. Some of the players threw their caps into the air; others performed somersaults. As a toast to the monumental achievement of the Browns, a few of the fans hoisted the players to their shoulders and carried them in a celebratory march around the field and eventually to their dressing rooms. Three cheers rang out repeatedly throughout the city. Fans who had gathered in downtown St. Louis outside the *Globe-Democrat* office, in pool-rooms, or at the merchants' exchange heard the news of the win seconds after it happened as officials at each of these sites received an update by telegraph or telephone and then excitedly shouted out or hastily posted the final score on boards for the anxious crowds.[36] The headline, "St. Louis Crazy,"[37] aptly captured the hysteria that gripped the city well into the night.

One day later, the Browns won the city championship with a 6–5 win over the Maroons, the St. Louis team in the National League.[38] The Browns were now the champions of St. Louis, the American Association, and the world. James "Tip" O'Neill was the champion batsman on the championship team. In the six-game series against Chicago, he led all batsman in batting average (8-for-20 or .400), total bases (18), total base average (18 for 20 or .900),[39] extra-base hits (4), triples (2), and home runs (2). Unknown at the time, O'Neill's world-class performance in the World Series was a harbinger of things to come. In 1887, O'Neill would become the champion batsman again, this time over a full season, and in support of the Browns' successful pursuit of their third consecutive championship of the American Association.

2

From Pitcher to Left Fielder

Between 1885 and 1887, Tip O'Neill was one of the core players on the St. Louis Browns. In the infield, Charlie Comiskey was at first base, Yank Robinson at second base, Arlie Latham at third base, and Bill Gleason at shortstop. The outfield consisted of O'Neill in left field, Curt Welch in center field, and, in 1886 and 1887, either Dave Foutz or Bob Caruthers in right field.[1] During these three years, Caruthers and Foutz were the dominant pitchers, with Doc Bushong doing much of the catching. Prior to O'Neill's arrival in St. Louis, he had gone through various transitions in his baseball career. The following narrative retraces O'Neill's development as a baseball player from Canada to the United States, specifically from Woodstock, Ontario, to New York to St. Louis; from amateur to professional baseball player; and from pitcher to outfielder. It was always a story of promise, but one where the promise changed and became both different and greater than O'Neill likely ever envisioned.

The baseball card below introduces O'Neill with a sketch of the player, including the following information: birth date and birth place; throwing and batting handedness (right or left); height and weight; position(s); nickname(s) (under the heading "Also Known As"); batting and fielding statistics for 1885 and 1886; and qualities or traits that best characterize his play on and sometimes off the field (under the heading "Known For").

James Edward O'Neill was born on June 15, 1860, in Springfield, Ontario, Canada.[2] He was the second oldest of eight children of James and Mary O'Neill.[3] His father was a hotelkeeper. In 1867, after living in three towns, O'Neill and his family moved to Woodstock, Ontario. After managing and living in two of the local establishments, by the early 1880s, the family settled in a hotel that bore the family name (O'Neill House).[4]

In the 1870s, the population of Woodstock grew from 4,000 to 5,000. The town was a commercial and social hub for the region. Nancy Bouchier, in her book, *For the Love of the Game. Amateur Sport in Small-Town Ontario 1838–1895,* added that Woodstock was a sports town: "From the mid–1860s on, organized team sport competition took hold of the public's imagination and emerged as a mainstay of local recreation, entertainment, and urban boosterism."[5] Baseball was the first team sport to gain some notoriety in town, with the Young Canadians as the most popular team in the 1860s.[6] Though O'Neill was only a young lad when he moved to Woodstock, he likely got swept up in the local interest in baseball.

In the mid–1870s, O'Neill attended the De La Salle Institute in Toronto, a secondary Catholic boys' school where baseball was a popular sport.[7] On his return to Woodstock,

O'Neill dedicated himself to becoming a pitcher. One winter, as "the story goes, an American hotel guest showed young Jim how to throw a curve ball, which he then practiced all winter long in an adjoining vacant dance hall."[8] By 1877, Ed O'Neil,[9] as he was initially called in the Woodstock newspapers, was a member of the Woodstock Actives, a baseball team that likely aspired to the heights reached by the Young Canadians in the previous decade. In the following year, O'Neill, as the pitcher and newly-elected field captain,[10] led the team to the amateur championship of Canada.[11]

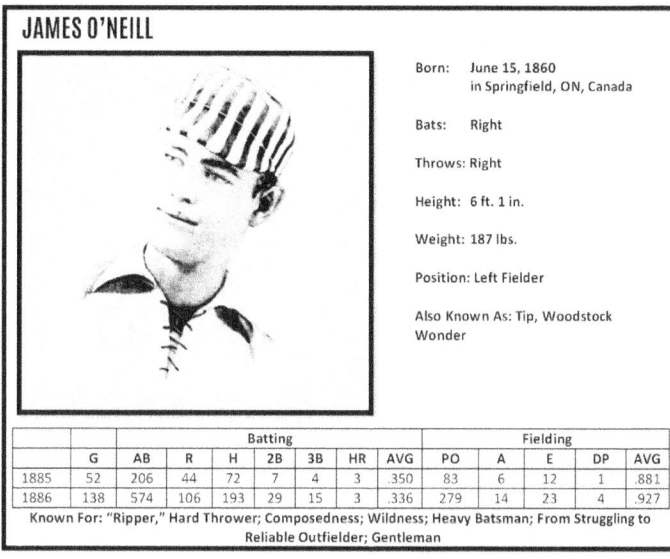

JAMES O'NEILL

Born: June 15, 1860 in Springfield, ON, Canada
Bats: Right
Throws: Right
Height: 6 ft. 1 in.
Weight: 187 lbs.
Position: Left Fielder
Also Known As: Tip, Woodstock Wonder

	Batting								Fielding				
	G	AB	R	H	2B	3B	HR	AVG	PO	A	E	DP	AVG
1885	52	206	44	72	7	4	3	.350	83	6	12	1	.881
1886	138	574	106	193	29	15	3	.336	279	14	23	4	.927

Known For: "Ripper," Hard Thrower; Composedness; Wildness; Heavy Batsman; From Struggling to Reliable Outfielder; Gentleman

The image in O'Neill's baseball card comes from a team photograph entitled: "Champions. St. Louis Browns. American Association. 1886" (The Rucker Archive).

The first time that James O'Neill was identified in the press by the nickname of "Tip" occurred in 1879 in the *Woodstock Sentinel-Review*, his hometown newspaper. It appeared in a note that refuted a rumor that "Tip" had "accepted an offer from a foreign club for his services,"[12] without any comment on why he was called Tip. The *Woodstock Sentinel-Review* continued to refer to O'Neill by his nickname in some of its game reports of the Actives in 1880–1881, and from 1882 onwards, in its occasional updates on O'Neill's baseball career as it unfolded in the United States between 1882 and 1892, again without explaining how he got his moniker.[13] Once O'Neill left Woodstock, first to New York for two years (1882–1883) and then to St. Louis in 1884, his nickname did not immediately follow him to these American destinations. There is no record of the New York newspapers using his nickname in either 1882 or 1883. Similarly, in his first two years in St. Louis (1884–1885), other than the *St. Louis Post-Dispatch's* acknowledgment that Tip was what he was "familiarly called" among his teammates,[14] most references in the St. Louis newspapers identified him by his last name. It was only after his breakout year in 1886, when he was among the top batters in the American Association and the leading batsman in the world championship, that newspapers regularly cited Tip when reporting on the play of O'Neill.

While three plausible explanations of the origin of his nickname emerged over the years, O'Neill himself never disclosed how this nickname began, nor did he confirm any of the explications offered by others. In 1891, as O'Neill neared the end of his career, Campbell, the St. Louis columnist for *Sporting Life,* asked and answered the question: "Have you heard of the story of Jim O'Neill's nickname?" Campbell explained that O'Neill's nickname emerged during a brief dramatic episode in his youth. Pulled to the stage, James starred as "Tip" in the farce "Tip and Slasher." His less-than-successful schoolboy performance drew catcalls and comments from the audience—presumably some of whom were his Woodstock teammates—who yelled "Slide!" "Judgment!" "Play

Ball!" and "You're Rotten!"[15] From that inauspicious stage debut, Campbell argued, O'Neill bore the nickname of Tip, or so goes the 1891 story in *Sporting Life*.

The other two explanations of O'Neill's nickname were based on his approach at the plate. In 1904, Chris Von der Ahe recalled: "The nickname 'Tip' was given to him because he merely seemed to 'tip' the ball when batting. He stood at the plate straight as an arrow, a giant in physique, and it seemed that he would just push out his bat and the ball would shoot like lightning."[16] The third explanation, the most frequently cited account of the origin of O'Neill's nickname, surfaced in secondary sources several years later. Illustrative of this third option, Canada's Sports Hall of Fame provides the following comment on how O'Neill got his nickname: "A powerful and consistent hitter, O'Neill knew how to wait for his pitch. He would deliberately foul off ball after ball until the pitcher gave him what he wanted, eventually earning him the nickname 'Tip.'"[17] While O'Neill may have preferred one or both of the above baseball-related explanations of his nickname to the less flattering tale spawned by his failure as a tragedian, during his playing years O'Neill never divulged to the press why he was called "Tip." Furthermore, with the exception of the farcical explanation proffered by *Sporting Life* a year before O'Neill ended his career, the newspapers that reported on his games seemed to have no interest in the origin of his nickname—he was just Tip.

From 1877 to 1884, O'Neill pursued a career in pitching, plying his trade in

In this carte-de-visite, James O'Neill (left), the pitcher of the Woodstock Actives, and Virgil Lee, his catcher, pose for a picture in their Actives uniform. The above photograph (along with a team photograph) was taken shortly after the Secretary of the Canadian Base Ball Association sent the team a streamer that read: "Actives, of Woodstock, 1887, Champions of Canada" (courtesy the Woodstock Museum NHS).

different places and at different levels. After his amateur years in Woodstock (1877–1881), O'Neill went on to the professional ranks in New York, in 1882, with the New York Metropolitans, an independent team that was also part of the League Alliance; in 1883, with the New York Gothams in the National League; and finally, in 1884, with the St. Louis Browns in the American Association.[18] As the starting pitcher for St. Louis in the opening game of the 1884 season, when the Browns beat Indianapolis, 4–2, O'Neill likely felt that he would finally get his chance to become one of the starting pitchers, a goal that, for the most part, had alluded him in New York. However, he was unable to overcome a chronic sore arm, and so by late June, O'Neill was relieved of his pitching duties. After eight years as a hurler, he now had to take his lame arm to left field and to follow a different career path, one based on becoming a renowned batsman.

It was likely difficult for O'Neill to leave the pitcher's box. Throughout his eight years as a pitcher, O'Neill had shown more than promise. In his amateur years, he had a 41–14 win-loss record (with two ties),[19] throwing two no-hitters.[20] In 1882, in his role as an alternate pitcher with the New York Metropolitans, he won 25 games and lost 10, including six wins and eight losses against National League teams and three wins and no losses against American Association teams. The *New York Clipper* published a profile of O'Neill prior to the start of the 1883 season that began: 'James E. O'Neil … is acknowledged to be one of the most promising professional pitchers of the present period.'"[21] Unfortunately, in the following two years, O'Neill struggled to make good on this assessment.

In 1883, O'Neill was less successful with the New York Gothams of the National League, registering a 5–12 win-loss record. Late in the season, he was loaned to the independent Hartford club, where he played in 19 games, 11 in which he pitched, winning seven and losing four, two of the losses to League teams (Chicago, Buffalo) and one to an Association team (New York Metropolitans).[22] In October, he threw two no-hitters in a span of 26 days, one when he was still with Hartford, beating Holyoke 11–1, and the other when he was on loan to the New York Metropolitans, beating Allentown 22–0.[23] Despite an injury-marred season in 1884, his first year with the Browns, O'Neill had a 11–4 record, with a winning percentage of .733, the highest in the American Association that year. In short, Tip showed more than promise. He could win games, between 1877 and 1884 compiling an 89–44 record, four of his wins on no-hitters. But in the end, he could not sustain this promise on a regular basis as a pitcher for a major league team. What went wrong?

O'Neill had a swift fastball and a puzzling curve. He could effectively change the pace of his pitch and had good command of the ball. He had a slow and deliberate delivery, pausing between pitches to size up the batter and to determine which pitch to throw. When ready, he exploded across the box, his arm fully extended backward and then propelled forward in a whip-like motion, releasing the sphere just as he planted his right foot at the far line of the box.[24] Regrettably, this unique pitching style did not always serve O'Neill well in his first three and a half years in professional baseball in New York and St. Louis. Even in O'Neill's first game in the box as a professional, a match between the Metropolitans and Princeton, there were problems that, unknowingly at the time, foreshadowed his eventual downfall as a pitcher.

On April 17, 1882, the Metropolitans handily beat Princeton, 18–9, in spite of O'Neill's pitching. He was moved to center field after only two innings. The *New York Clipper* bluntly assessed O'Neill's initial pitching performance:

> The new pitcher had been spoken of as "a ripper" in regard to his speed, and so proved to be, and a very damaging one, too. He was tediously slow in delivery, watched the bases in the old way without

the least regard to signals from his catcher, and though Clapp promptly returned balls to him for a quick delivery when the batsman was out of form, he never once took advantage of it. O'Neil was limited to two innings of pitching, and in this short period, he gave four men their bases on called balls, and as many bases on wild pitches, one run being given on a passed ball, he nearly using up Clapp. Pitching as he did in this game, he would require about a half-dozen new catchers a season.... What O'Neil might do were he to study the art of pitching we cannot say; but by judging his exhibition in this game, he has nothing but speed to recommend him.[25]

This quote pointed to many of the concerns that would eventually be his undoing as a pitcher.

Being a "ripper" was not always a good thing in the years that O'Neill pitched. The catcher had limited protective gear and relatively thin gloves and so could be at risk of injury with a pitcher who threw at some pace. O'Neill had a number of managers who were reluctant to take a chance on his speed.[26] His hard throwing also led to a second concern, namely his bouts of wildness, a problem that arose in a number of games throughout his professional pitching career. When O'Neill lacked control, he issued more bases on balls, threw more wild pitches, and sent his catcher diving or scrambling after his erratic pitches.[27] A third area of concern was his somewhat unorthodox delivery. He took a long time between pitches, a deliberately slow start to his delivery that, once in motion, became an exaggerated and sometimes violent thrust across the box before his release. This awkward and hurried movement may well have enabled him to rip the ball with considerable velocity, but it also contributed to his wildness.

The delivery also likely put a strain on his arm, and, consequently, was probably a factor in the fourth concern, the number of injuries he sustained. In 1882, O'Neill injured his hand in August and did not play for the rest of the season.[28] With the Gothams in 1883, he developed a sore arm and did not pitch or play in the field for most of August. In 1884, as noted above, O'Neill was bothered by pain in his arm for the first two months of the season. When he asked Von der Ahe in mid–June to relieve him of his pitching duties until his arm improved, Von der Ahe, on the advice of his own doctor, insisted that O'Neill return to the rotation two weeks later. O'Neill was not able to overcome his sore arm. For the remainder of the season, he started just three games in June, two in July, and one in August.[29] Fortunately for O'Neill, he had batted well in the games in which he pitched. He stayed in the Browns' lineup as the left fielder. With the pitcher's box behind him, O'Neill turned his attention to the batter's box, and so began his transition from a hard thrower to a heavy batsman.

O'Neill had been successful in the past in the batter's box. In his amateur days, he was one of the leading batters for the Woodstock Actives.[30] In 1882, in his less-than-memorable pitching debut with the New York Metropolitans against Princeton (described above), he led the team with five hits in five times at bat. Despite such limited playing time, O'Neill developed a reputation as an "excellent batsman."[31] In the 1884 season, at the point when O'Neill was moved into the outfield, he was leading the Browns with a .321 batting average.[32] By season's end, he finished second on the team in batting with an average of .276, with Fred Lewis, the center fielder, first at .323. O'Neill also led the team with three home runs and was second with 11 triples.

With more playing time, O'Neill got more notice in the St. Louis press. The fans liked what they saw at the plate, as did Von der Ahe and Comiskey. They also appreciated the character of their pitcher-turned-left fielder. After a raucous 1883 season marred by a series of discipline problems, Von der Ahe was relieved to sign a player who would not bring any trouble to the team. Based on a conversation with James Mutrie, the manager of the New York Metropolitans, Von der Ahe felt that the team was getting, in O'Neill, a courteous and cooperative player who was "a good man, a fine player, and a perfect gentleman."[33] Early in the 1884 season, he was described by the *St. Louis Post-Dispatch* "as one of the most reticent, reserved and modest men in the business."[34]

O'Neill, however, was not always reticent, reserved, or gentlemanly. On July 1, 1884, after the Browns beat Baltimore in St. Louis, 11–5, O'Neill left the Lindell Hotel in the early hours of the morning with Lewis, the Browns' center fielder, and three of the Baltimore players—Hardie Henderson, Gid Gardner, and Bob Emslie (who had also played in Ontario when O'Neill was with the Woodstock Actives)—to continue their imbibing at the "disreputable" Maude Abbey House.[35] "O'Neill, the great,"[36] irritated by a comment made by one of the women who worked at the House, threw a spittoon at her. In the ensuing melee, someone blew the police whistle. O'Neill and Emslie escaped before the police arrived. Gardner was questioned and then allowed to leave. Lewis and Henderson were arrested. Baltimore fined Emslie $100 and Henderson $150, and expelled Gardner.[37] Lewis was initially expelled, then reinstated but not before he swore in front of the judge that he would not drink any evil spirits for six months.[38] O'Neill was neither fined nor reprimanded.[39] His reputation as a gentleman apparently remained intact.

As the Browns readied for the 1885 season, many of the newspapers were excited about the team's chances. After O'Neill hit a home run in one of the pre-season exhibition games, the *St. Louis Sunday Sayings* declared: "Jim promises to make all the fielders hunt leather this year."[40] However, O'Neill had a slow start at the plate in the first 11 games, managing only eight hits in 40 times at bat for a .200 batting average, a record that, for the most part, went unnoticed. By the time the Browns went on a 17-game winning streak (May 5 to June 1), O'Neill had pulled out of his slump, hitting a torrid .481 (36 hits in 75 times at bat) during the run. Unfortunately, O'Neill was injured in mid–June. Prior to his injury, Tip had played in 38 games, bursting forth with 16 multi-hit games, including one five-hit game and four four-hit games. At the point when he was hurt, he led the Association in batting with a .381 average. When he returned in September, he had not fully recovered from his injury and thus struggled to regain his batting form for the remainder of the year. In a season when he appeared in only 52 of the 112 games played by the Browns, O'Neill still led the team with a batting average of .350, finishing second in the Association.[41] Curt Welch, the Browns' center fielder, was second at .271. What might have been a stellar year for O'Neill was cut short by injury. Those who wondered what O'Neill might do if he ever played a full season got their answer in 1886.

After three seasons in the major leagues (1883–1885), O'Neill had played in only 153 games. He finally completed a full season in 1886, missing one game in August due to an injured hand.[42] Based on the monthly batting records published by *Sporting Life*, for most of the season O'Neill, Foutz, and Caruthers took turns leading the Browns in batting. By late August, Foutz fell back, leaving O'Neill and Caruthers to compete for the best batting average on the Browns. O'Neill edged ahead of Caruthers at the end of August (O'Neill hit .418 in August) only to be overtaken by Caruthers at the end of the season (O'Neill hit .286 for the last month). Even though Caruthers and O'Neill had similar batting averages for the last few weeks of the season, the St. Louis newspapers repeatedly reported that O'Neill was the only batsman who had a chance of catching Guy Hecker, the Louisville pitcher and first baseman, for the batting championship. Before the American Association announced the official averages, those in St. Louis were convinced that O'Neill had the best average on the team.⁴³ Accordingly, during the last game of the season O'Neill was presented with the E. Jaccard & Co. gold medal for the best batting average on the Browns.⁴⁴

In a close race for the batting title of the American Association, Guy Hecker won the crown with an average of .341. Pete Browning, an outfielder on Louisville, finished second at .340, and Caruthers and Dave Orr, the first baseman on New York, tied for third with a .338 average. O'Neill came next at .336.⁴⁵ On the Browns, Tip led in hits (193), singles (146), triples (15), and total bases (261). His 146 singles set a new single-season record in the major leagues.⁴⁶ He had 65 multi-hit games, with one five-hit game and four four-hit games. O'Neill, the "heavy batsman," the hitter with the "giant swing," "the surest and hardest batters of the American Association," had arrived.⁴⁷

On defense, O'Neill spent most of 1884 and 1885 getting used to the demands of chasing down fly balls, scooping ground balls, and figuring out the kind of positional play that Comiskey demanded of outfielders. He had played some games in the outfield in his two years in New York, but these few times in the field did not fully prepare him for the challenges of being the everyday left fielder. O'Neill eventually adapted to his new position, but some things did not come naturally or quickly. Although initially slow to react to a ball hit into left field, he steadily improved to the point that he became a reliable fly catcher. However, he struggled with ground balls. Furthermore, with the continued soreness in his right arm in 1884, he did not make many attempts to throw out runners.⁴⁸ In subsequent years, he never recovered the full strength in his arm and, consequently, his total assists and double plays each season were invariably lower than most of the outfielders in the Association.

In 1886, O'Neill played over 170 games in left field, including regular season games, pre- and post-season games, and exhibition games. It was an exhaustive schedule that nonetheless enabled O'Neill to make significant improvements in his outfield play, so much so that 1886 was arguably the best defensive year he ever had. O'Neill's fielding average of .927 was third-best and his 279 putouts were second-best among all Association outfielders. Welch, the center fielder, led the Browns and the Association in both areas with a fielding average of .952 and 297 putouts. In the 1886 world championship, O'Neill was the only regular outfielder on either St. Louis or Chicago to have a fielding average of 1.000.

O'Neill's throwing numbers in 1886, 14 assists and four double plays, were the highest numbers he put up in his career. O'Neill ranked 14th in assists and tenth in double plays among all Association outfielders. In a 2–0 loss to Philadelphia late in the season, O'Neill had his strongest throwing game as an outfielder, certainly in 1886, and possibly the best of his eight seasons as a full-time left fielder (1885–1892). In this game, Denny Lyons, the Philadelphia third baseman, was on third when Jack O'Brien, the first baseman, came to bat:

> O'Brien sent a long fly to left center which O'Neill caught and then by a superb throw to Latham caught Lyons at third. O'Neill made another nice throw in the next inning, when McGarr, who had opened with a hit and reached second on Bushong's low throw, tried to come home on Bierbauer's hit to left, which O'Neill fielded in such good style that the runner was caught at the plate.⁴⁹

These successful throwing numbers and events notwithstanding, O'Neill was still careful not to strain his weakened arm and thus was selective about when and how often he tried to cut down runners who sought to advance a base.

The Browns in 1884 had already established a reputation for daring running. O'Neill was able to reach a good speed in situations that called for him to advance two or more bases, such as when he ran from first to third or second to home, tried to stretch a double into a triple or a triple into a home run, or chased down a long fly ball. However, he did not have explosive speed, and, consequently, was not quick off the mark to catch up to a ball hit to left field.[50] On the base path, he also was not quick out of the batter's box to beat out a ground ball or quick to get a jump on the pitcher in an attempt to steal second base. This lack of quickness did not stop O'Neill from taking the kinds of chances that some of his more daring teammates took regularly as they fielded hard-hit balls or ran the bases. From time to time, O'Neill was successful in these chances and was applauded for it.[51] In most cases, however, he exhibited neither the speed nor the savvy to make good on the risks he took.

In 1886, the first year that stolen bases were tallied, O'Neill rarely attempted to steal a base off the pitcher or to steal a base on a hit.[52] He was hampered by his lumbering takeoff. He also lacked judgment about when it was best to try for a stolen base. On close plays, O'Neill was further disadvantaged by his inability to slide.[53] As a result, O'Neill was caught stealing more often than the nine bases he stole.

Once on the base path, O'Neill had some problems determining when to go for an extra base on a hit and how to evade attempts to pick him off base. Trying for an extra base whenever the opportunity presented itself was in line with the Browns' commitment to bold base running. Although failure to gain the extra base was not usually criticized, O'Neill often seemed more reckless than daring. For example, during the 1886 season, he was thrown out trying to stretch a triple into a home run[54]; attempting to score when he hit a ground ball that was thrown wild to first and rolled into right field[55]; and bolting for home from third base on a ground ball to the shortstop.[56] He also was "caught napping"[57] after either drifting too far from the base or not hustling back to the base after each pitch or when a play was over. In these lapses of concentration, O'Neill was vulnerable to a quick throw by the pitcher or catcher.[58]

After three years with the Browns (1884–1886), O'Neill, the base runner, was still a work in progress. He embraced Comiskey's charge to take chances. Yet when he was faced with the split-second decisions that a base runner must make, sometimes he hesitated and the chance was lost, and sometimes he stormed onwards hoping to find the chance on the way, but it was not there to be found. In either case, O'Neill was not a base-running threat, except perhaps to his own team.

O'Neill had moved on. His pitching days were behind him. His future was now as one of the core Browns, as the everyday left fielder. In 1885–1886, he quickly developed into one of the leading batsmen in the American Association and was the top batsman in the Browns' victory over Chicago for the 1886 world championship. His hometown newspaper commended Tip for the "greatest batting in the series," concluding with a reflection about what might have been: "On the field he is excelled by few, and he has the satisfaction of knowing that the cultivation of the art of batting and fielding has kept him from being a member of that great and motley crowd—the broken-down pitchers."[59] Tip had also become quite popular with the St. Louis cranks (fans). After he hit a "mighty three-bagger to the right field fence," the *St. Louis Republican* exclaimed: "The dude's popularity never weakens if one is to judge by the cheering of men and the clapping of ladies' tiny little hands in yesterday's game."[60] By 1886, the cheers were not only for his batting but also for his fielding. His strong performance in the field, especially in putouts and fielding average, suggested that his uneven fielding record of 1884 and 1885 might well be behind him. As the world championship neared the end, *Sporting Life* confidently asserted: "Jim O'Neill, besides being the best batter in the country, has covered left field in a manner that was an honor to his club and a credit to himself."[61] Expectations were high for the offensive and defensive contributions O'Neill would make to the Browns in 1887. *The Sporting News* hailed Tip as the "hardest hitting batsman in the country,"[62] and two weeks later, predicted that he would "be the leading batter of the American Association this season."[63] The prediction proved prophetic, although it likely did not fully anticipate how extraordinary O'Neill's 1887 season would actually be.

Thus ends the first of three chapters on the contextual forces that most influenced what O'Neill accomplished in 1887, namely, O'Neill's life story (Chapter 2), his teammates (Chapter 3), and the Browns' style of play (Chapter 4). In this chapter, the biographical portrait reconstructs Tip's life and career prior to 1887, with a particular emphasis on how his first two years as the full-time left fielder set the stage for his 1887 run for the batting championship. Chapter 3 introduces eight of O'Neill's teammates who, during 1885 and 1886, developed together into the core players of the team. O'Neill's story in 1887 and those of his teammates were implicated in the ongoing experiences they shared on and off the field. As part of a team, O'Neill's achievements were also situated within the style of play enacted by the Browns, a topic pursued more fully in Chapter 4. These three contexts framed the narrative of Tip O'Neill, the champion batsman of 1887.

3

Core Players: St. Louis Browns

The St. Louis Browns won the American Association championship four years in a row (1885–1888). For the first three years of their championship run, the team relied on nine core players: Charles Comiskey, first baseman; William "Yank" Robinson, second baseman; Walter "Arlie" Latham, third baseman; William Gleason, shortstop; James "Tip" O'Neill, left fielder; Curtis Welch, center fielder; David Foutz, pitcher, right fielder; Robert Caruthers, pitcher, right fielder; Albert "Doc" Bushong, catcher.

The core players brought fame to St. Louis in 1885, when they finished first in the American Association and tied Chicago (National League) for the world championship. As described in Chapter 1, in 1886, this same nine led the St. Louis club to the championship of the American Association and to the championship of the world in their victory against the same Chicago club. And the core players were there again in 1887, when they won the championship of the American Association for the third time in three years and played Detroit (National League) for the world championship.

This chapter introduces each of the eight core players with a baseball card like the one used for O'Neill in Chapter 2. Following the card, each profile highlights the player's batting, base running, fielding, or pitching (in the case of Foutz and Caruthers), in some cases, with examples from his performance in 1885 and 1886. It also notes whether a player had other responsibilities (e.g., Comiskey's role as coach, captain, and manager; coaching of Latham and Gleason) or exhibited certain characteristics in the way he played the game (e.g., daring base running, aggressive tactics). Though alluded to in some of the profiles, the Browns' style of play is examined in greater detail in Chapter 4.

Charles Comiskey

In 1882, the inaugural year of the American Association, Charles Comiskey signed with the St. Louis Browns to play first base. He was made captain of the team in 1883, a position that included coaching responsibilities, usually along the third base line. By 1885, Comiskey assumed the positions of captain and manager on an ongoing basis, while continuing as the regular first baseman. This profile focuses on his record as a first baseman.

Comiskey quickly established himself as one of the premier first basemen in the game. He was one of the pioneers who changed how the position was played. Malcolm MacLean declared: "He managed to make first base what it had never been before—a

The 1885 St. Louis Browns were the first team in the city to win a major league championship. It was also the first of three years in which the nine core players introduced in Chapters Two and Three played together. In the back row, left to right, are: Albert "Doc" Bushong, Curtis Welch, Sam Barkley, David Foutz, James "Tip" O'Neill, and William Gleason. In the front row, left to right, are: William "Yank" Robinson, "Arlie" Latham, Robert Caruthers, George McGuiness, William Sullivan, and Hugh Nichols [Nicol]. Chris Von der Ahe, the owner, is in the upper left corner, and Charles Comiskey, the captain, is in the upper right corner (The Ruckers Archive).

playing position of equal possibilities with second, short, and third."[1] He played off the bag and well back of it, closer to second than other first basemen of his day, but not so far as to expose the line to an easy hit. Comiskey also expected the pitcher or second baseman to cover first if he ranged off the bag to snag a ground ball, a line drive, or a short fly ball into right field.[2]

On offense, Comiskey was more known for his daring base running, "rattling his opponents with his aggressive and reckless style. He never eased up no matter what the score, and he was among the first to use the head-first slide."[3] The Browns were defined by their fearless base running, a reputation that was first spawned by the example Comiskey set.

As a batsman, Comiskey was also a model for others on his team, demonstrating how a batter should advance runners with a hit if possible, and with a sacrifice hit or bunt, if necessary.[4] Comiskey was one of the players most responsible for the re-emergence of the bunt in the mid–1880s, effectively using it as a strategy to advance a runner or to get on base.

In many ways, Comiskey's approach to the game as a player quickly became the style of the team once he took over as manager of the Browns in 1885. It was a style that privileged "mind over mere brawn"[5] and instilled a dedication to winning by any and all tactics.

William Robinson

William "Yank" Robinson joined the Browns in 1885 as a change catcher and utility player. In his first three seasons with the Browns (1885–1887), he proved his worth as a utility player, playing every position during these years. The ambidextrous Robinson became the everyday second baseman in 1886. Robinson was known for his rough play on the base paths and, defensively, for knocking about opposing runners as they rounded second base. He was also the consummate trickster, always ready to take advantage of an opposing player's miscue or lapse in concentration.

Robinson was an adept

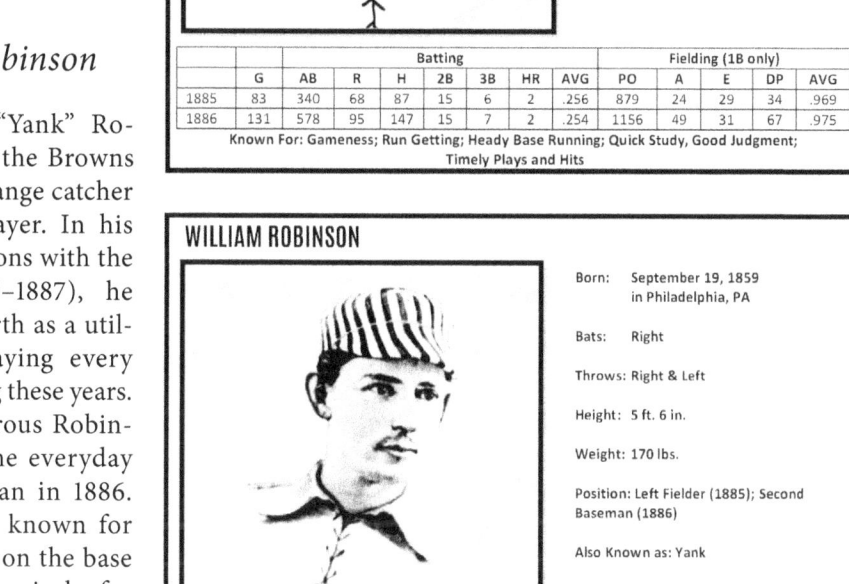

The images of Comiskey's and Robinson's baseball cards come from a team photograph entitled: "Champions. St. Louis Browns. American Association. 1886" (The Rucker Archive).

"base-getter,"[6] with an on-base average that was second-best on the team in 1885 and third-best in 1886.[7] In his first full season (1886), in addition to his 132 fair hits, he got on base 79 times on bases on balls (64) and being hit by a pitch (15).[8] Even more so than Latham, Robinson bothered pitchers by hitting foul balls, a strategy that frequently led to a walk and sometimes to a base on an error by a fielder who grew impatient or distracted as he waited for Robinson's time at bat to end. When needed, Robinson also was a proficient bunter, as illustrated in the final game of the 1886 world's championship.[9]

In the field, Robinson took chances, going after hard-hit balls into the gaps or hurrying throws to cut off advancing runners. In 1886, this risk-taking was likely responsible, at least in part, for both his Association-leading 95 errors and his unenviable fielding average of .888, which was second-lowest among Association second basemen with 200 or more chances. His throwing numbers were strong, second in the Association in double plays and fifth in assists. Robinson got batters and runners out, sometimes on routine plays and sometimes on plays no one expected him to make.

Robinson was Comiskey's kind of player: tough, edgy, and intense; capable of both taking and making chances; savvy at the bat, on the base paths, and in the field; and willing to do anything for the team. Although many anticipated that Robinson would have another good season in 1887, he exceeded these expectations by a considerable margin.

Walter Latham

Walter Arlington "Arlie" Latham joined the Browns in 1883 to play third base. By 1885, he had established himself as a "superb and dashing base runner,"[10] an excellent fielder, and an effective batsman. What stood out even more than his formidable performance on the field was a "natural exuberance of spirits and joyousness"[11] in the way he played the game, a disposition that found its fullest expression "as the witty and jovial master of the coaching lines."[12] With the exception of "The Dude," most of his nicknames came from his antics as a coach.

In recognition of Latham's history of run-making, in 1885, Comiskey made Latham the Browns' leadoff batsman. His "unmatched talent for base running"[13] was evident in the number of runs he scored and the number of bases he stole. From 1884 to 1886, he scored the most runs on the Browns. In 1886, his 152 runs scored led the Association.

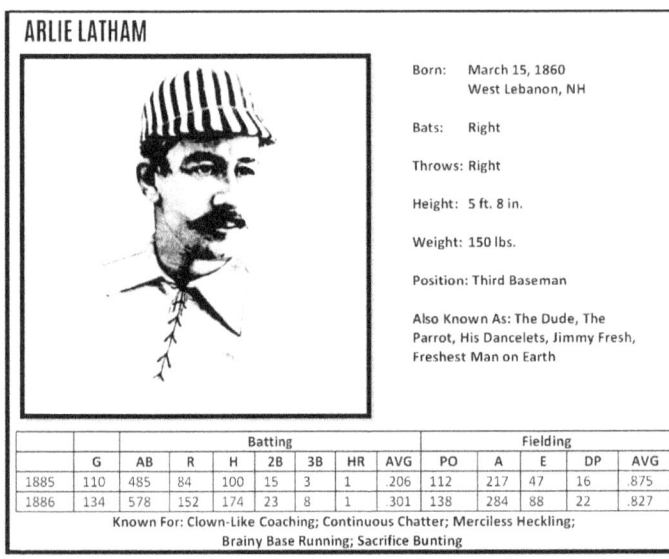

The image in Latham's baseball card comes from a team photograph entitled: "Champions. St. Louis Browns. American Association. 1886" (The Rucker Archive).

On the base paths, Latham put himself in position to score with his quickness afoot and calculated risks. He was an astute judge of when to steal. His audacious feints often drew errant throws that allowed him to advance a base. On a throw that beat Latham to the base, he would avoid what appeared to be a sure out by deftly eluding the tag through a headfirst or hook slide. As a result of his speed and maneuvers, Latham stole 60 bases in 1886, second-best in the Association.

After a disappointing year at the plate in 1885, Latham bounced back in

1886, recording a batting average of .301. Henry Chadwick called Latham "one of the most skillful men at the bat I know of." He continued: "He watches a pitcher like a cat, and it must be a pretty shrewd strategist who can get the best of him. He is not afraid of 'bunting' the ball, as too many batsmen are, and he does it very skillfully."[14] Latham was a versatile bunter, using it to get on base, to advance a runner (sacrifice bunt), or to frustrate a pitcher, repeatedly bunting a good pitch foul until the pitcher either walked him or threw a pitch that he punched for a base hit.[15]

In the early years with the Browns, Latham was often applauded for the way he played third base. Just as the 1884 season got underway, the *St. Louis Post-Dispatch* exclaimed that he "has but one or two who can be called equals in that position, and his clean picking up, sharp, accurate throwing across the diamond and generally brilliant work, have made him well known."[16] However, by 1886 Latham's work in the field was sometimes called into question as he led the Association's third basemen in errors (88) and had the third-lowest fielding average (.827) among the nine third basemen with 200 or more chances.

Latham began the 1887 season with the well-deserved reputation as a frenetic coach and base runner. He was "as quick on his feet as he was with his mouth."[17] At the plate, although he could be inconsistent from season to season and from game to game,[18] he worked pitchers as well as any player in the Association and kept the infield off-balance with his threat to bunt in almost any situation. In the field, Latham was still regarded as a better-than-average fielder, but not with the same dependability that marked his first three years with the Browns.

William Gleason

Along with Comiskey, Bill Gleason was one of the two core players on the field whose tenure with the Browns began in 1882, the first year of the American Association. He was a loyal lieutenant to Comiskey and dedicated to doing what was best for the team, and, as a result, was the first person Comiskey turned to when he needed someone to assist him with coaching. Together, Comiskey, Gleason, and Latham became an infamous trio of cacophonous coaches, the scourge of the American Association.

Born in St. Louis, "Brudder Bill"[19] was a "local-boy-makes-good" story. For many,

The image in Gleason's baseball card comes from a team photograph entitled: "Champions. St. Louis Browns. American Association. 1886" (The Rucker Archive).

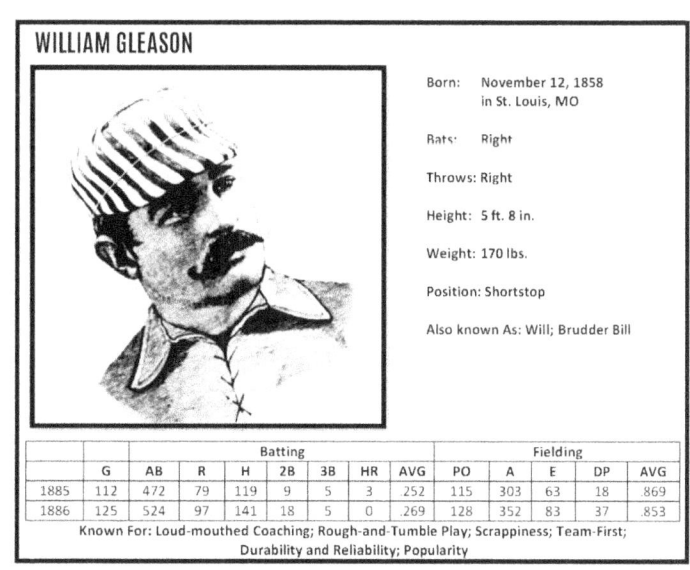

WILLIAM GLEASON

Born: November 12, 1858 in St. Louis, MO
Bats: Right
Throws: Right
Height: 5 ft. 8 in.
Weight: 170 lbs.
Position: Shortstop
Also known As: Will; Brudder Bill

	Batting								Fielding				
	G	AB	R	H	2B	3B	HR	AVG	PO	A	E	DP	AVG
1885	112	472	79	119	9	5	3	.252	115	303	63	18	.869
1886	125	524	97	141	18	5	0	.269	128	352	83	37	.853

Known For: Loud-mouthed Coaching; Rough-and-Tumble Play; Scrappiness; Team-First; Durability and Reliability; Popularity he played the game like it should be played, with grit, pluck, determination, and fortitude. Gleason saw baseball as a contact sport that, from time to time, required him as a runner to collide with baseman on close plays; as a fielder, to bump opposing runners as they rounded second base; and as a batsman, to lean in so that a pitch would hit him, which usually allowed him to take his base.

After his first two years (1882 and 1883), Gleason was in the top three in the major defensive categories among Association shortstops, leading in assists and double plays, and second or third in putouts and fielding average. However, between 1884 and 1886, though his defensive numbers remained relatively the same, he was rarely in the top five in the Association in any major defensive category. Gleason was as reliable as always and still more savvy than most, at least in terms of how Comiskey wanted the infielders to play. However, there were other shortstops in the Association who were playing with fewer errors and greater efficiency.

For the first three years (1882–1884), in recognition of his offensive contribution to the Browns, Gleason batted first in the order.[20] In subsequent years, as his batting average fell closer to the team average, he resorted to other means of getting on base, specifically through an increase in base on balls (29 walks in 1885 and 43 walks in 1886) and hit by pitches (12 times in 1884 and an Association-leading 15 times in 1885). Comiskey was confident that his seasoned warrior was an adroit batsman who could adjust his approach at the plate to advance runners with a well-timed bunt or sacrifice hit.

As the 1887 season neared, Comiskey looked to Gleason as a veteran who could provide leadership through his coaching on a team that, despite their championships, was still relatively inexperienced. He was a known and valued contributor in the batter's box and on the base paths. In the field, Gleason had lost a step or two at shortstop and thus did not always get to balls he routinely retrieved in previous years, but he more than made up for it in his positional play and quick defensive reactions to sudden changes in the game. And he was still a bruiser in his style of play, a pit bull on the coaching lines, and an aggressive competitor.

Curtis Welch

Curt Welch began his three-year stint as the Browns' center fielder in 1885. He was cut from the same cloth as Comiskey, Latham, Gleason, and Robinson: "a virulent member of Comiskey's umpire-baiting club,"[21] more belligerent in his rough play than either Gleason or Robinson, and more menacing than most in close offensive or defensive encounters. In reflecting back to Welch's days with the Browns, Alfred Spink observed: "Welch at this time was one of the most enthusiastic and aggressive players in the business. In fierce and offensive play, he had no superiors."[22]

Welch led all Association outfielders in fielding average in 1885 and 1886. In his profile of nineteenth-century stars, Bob Tiemann described the remarkable fly-catching abilities that Welch exhibited in his three years with the Browns: "As soon as a long drive was hit, he was off and running. Never looking back, he would invariably run to the spot where the ball came down … and he was adept at making headlong, diving catches of sinking line drives."[23] Welch roamed far and wide, grabbing deep fly balls that might have otherwise been better caught by the left or right fielder and short pop ups that, on first call, could have easily been more the responsibility of the shortstop or second baseman.

In most cases, the fielders yielded to the charging Welch, usually to good result.

At the plate, Welch was one of the leading batsmen on the Browns. His .271 average in 1885 was second-best on the team. In 1886, he led the team in doubles and was second in extra-base hits. Like Robinson, he crowded the plate and held his ground on inside pitches with the hope that he would get a base after being hit by a pitched ball, a tactic for which he would become even more famous in the years after he left the Browns. Welch, like Comiskey, Latham, and Robinson, was also adept at bunting to advance a runner.

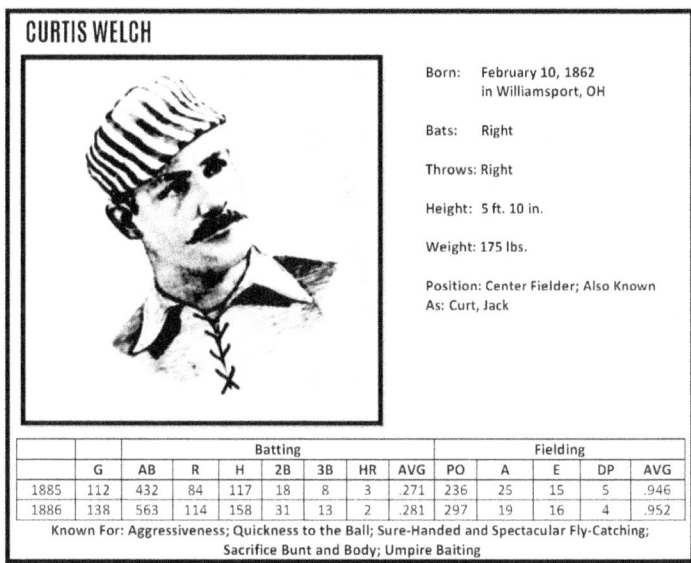

				Batting						Fielding			
	G	AB	R	H	2B	3B	HR	AVG	PO	A	E	DP	AVG
1885	112	432	84	117	18	8	3	.271	236	25	15	5	.946
1886	138	563	114	158	31	13	2	.281	297	19	16	4	.952

Known For: Aggressiveness; Quickness to the Ball; Sure-Handed and Spectacular Fly-Catching; Sacrifice Bunt and Body; Umpire Baiting

The image in Welch's baseball card comes from a team photograph entitled: "Champions. St. Louis Browns. American Association. 1886" (The Rucker Archive).

On the base paths, Welch was second only to Latham in run-scoring in 1886. He, like Robinson, intimidated opposing basemen with his hard slides into the bag. Welch would not let anyone get in his way when he drove for a base or chased down a runner.

Game after game, Welch dazzled the Browns with sparkling defensive play, hustle, tenacity, and a fiery determination to win. He was a multi-faceted offensive threat, hitting for both average and power and running with a desperation that unhinged opposing players. Welch entered the 1887 season as the Association's premier outfielder and as a leading actor in the dirty play that would make the Browns an object of contempt for most of the year.

Robert Caruthers

"Parisian Bob"[24] Caruthers signed as a pitcher with the Browns in the last month of the 1884 season. In the box, he quickly developed a reputation for his headwork and his pinpoint control. Caruthers posted a 40–13 win-loss record in 1885, leading the Association in games won, winning percentage (.755), and earned run average (2.07). He continued his dominance in 1886 with a 30–13 win-loss record (.682) and an earned run average of 2.32.

Caruthers pitched with a studied calmness, taking the time to assess each batsman for weak points that he could exploit. His two pitches were a fastball with some pace and a "hard-thrown in-shoot which seemed to ride the air,"[25] what today we would call a slider. With the aid of his catcher, Doc Bushong, Caruthers learned to vary the speed and the location of both pitches according to their assessment of what the batsman would least expect or would be least likely to hit with any power or consequence. Caruthers had

ROBERT CARUTHERS

Born: January 5, 1864 in Memphis, TN
Bats: Left and Right
Throws: Right
Height: 5 ft. 7 in.
Weight: 138 lbs.
Position: Pitcher; Outfielder
Also Known As: Parisian Bob; Green Baize Bob

	W-L	W-L %	R	ER	K	H	BB	HBP	WP
1885	40-13	.778	196	111	190	430	57	19	25
Per Game			3.70	2.09	3.58	8.11	1.08	0.358	0.472
1886	30-14	.755	164	100	166	323	86	7	15
Per Game			3.73	2.27	3.77	7.34	1.95	0.159	0.341

	Batting							Fielding (OF only)			
	G	AB	R	H	2B	3B	HR	AVG	PO	A	E	DP	AVG
1885	60	222	37	50	10	2	1	.225	9	2	4	0	.733
1886	87	317	91	107	21	14	4	.338	42	10	9	3	.852

Known For: Wily Delivery; Kicker on Called Pitches; Plucky and Patient Batsman; Speedy Runner; Confident Player

DAVID FOUTZ

Born: September 7, 1856 in Carroll County, MD
Bats: Right
Throws: Right
Height: 6 ft. 2 in.
Weight: 161 lbs.
Positions: Pitcher; Outfielder; First Baseman
Also Known As: Scissors, His Needles, String Beans, His Reachlets

Pitching	W-L	W-L %	R	ER	K	H	BB	HBP	WP
1885	33-14	.714	200	119	147	351	92	18	20
Per Game			4.26	2.63	3.13	7.47	1.96	0.383	0.426
1886	41-16	.719	216	118	283	418	144	10	23
Per Game			3.79	2.11	4.96	7.33	2.53	0.175	0.404

	Batting							Fielding (1B-1885 & OF-1886)				
	G	AB	R	H	2B	3B	HR	AVG	PO	A	E	DP	AVG
1885	65	238	66	116	26	13	4	.280	160	5	6	12	.965
1886	102	414	79	151	20	13	3	.357	57	7	7	0	.901

Known For: Unflappability, Calmness; Craftiness in the Box; Versatility, All-Round Player; Gentleman, Fair-Mindedness, Kindness

The images of Caruthers' and Foutz's baseball cards come from a team photograph entitled: "Champions. St. Louis Browns. American Association. 1886" (The Rucker Archive).

a delivery that was deceptive in its simplicity. His windup was neither exaggerated nor forced. He used none of the tricks of other pitchers (e.g., dancing from side to side in the box; starting with his back turned away from the plate to hide the ball). His movement across the box and his release appeared effortless, even indifferent, a motion that usually disarmed the batsman so that his swing was ill-timed and his hit readily handled by a fielder for an out.

Caruthers was also one of the Browns' most talented all-round players."[26] He was an effective batsman, a "brilliant outfielder,"[27] and "the best base-running pitcher in the profession."[28] By 1886, he was all but an everyday player, playing right field when Foutz was pitching, with Foutz doing the same when Caruthers was pitching. Caruthers would continue this pitching-right field assignment into 1887, a year in which he excelled in all facets of the game.

David Foutz

Dave Foutz began his almost four-year stint with the Browns in late July 1884. In an article on the unique style of pitchers, the *St. Louis Globe-Democrat* observed: "Foutz's great effectiveness is his change of pace and a good down-shoot. His slow ball is probably his best, and when he can command it, he is never hit hard."²⁹ While he could rear back and fire a fastball with considerable velocity, his ability to alter the pace of each pitch made his periodic speedy pitches all the more effective. Foutz also used his six-foot, two-inch frame and sidearm delivery to good effect, varying the angle at which the ball travelled toward the plate.

Although Caruthers led the way in 1885, Foutz was not far behind, posting a 33–14 win-loss record, good enough for second in the Association in winning percentage (.702) and third in wins. He was also fifth in earned run average (2.63). In 1886, it was Foutz's turn to take the spotlight, with 41 wins and 16 losses, the only season he won 40 or more games. He led the Association in wins, winning percentage (.719), and earned run average (2.18), and was second in shutouts (11) and fourth in strikeouts (283).

Between 1885 and 1887, Foutz proved equally versatile as Caruthers, playing with considerable defensive finesse and savvy in right field or at first base when he was not in the pitcher's box.³⁰ By late 1887, Comiskey articulated what he had appreciated for some time, that is the wide-ranging skills that Foutz brought to the Browns: "Dave Foutz comes near to being the best general player in the Association, and the most valuable man possessed by any club when his batting, fielding and base-running ability is considered along with his pitching skill, disposition and willingness."³¹ In demeanor, he was a calming influence on a team that was prone to turbulence. Spink recalled: "As a thoroughly gentlemanly player Foutz had few equals on the diamond. In his whole career, no one ever saw him lose his temper or heard him speak a harsh word to his most formidable opponent."³²

Albert Bushong

Albert "Doc" Bushong, a dentist by profession (hence the nickname Doc), came to the Browns in 1885 after six years in the National League. By reputation, Bushong was known as "one of the best and most reliable back-stops in the business, his style of work being neat, clean and effective, he ranking as one of the best League catchers."³³ Although his offensive skills were less impressive,³⁴ his heady and skilled play behind the plate was invaluable to the Browns.

In a position known for injuries, Bushong had remarkable durability. He played more games than other catchers, leading the Association with 85 games in 1885 (24 games more than the catcher with the second-most games) and 106 games in 1886 (30 games more than the runner-

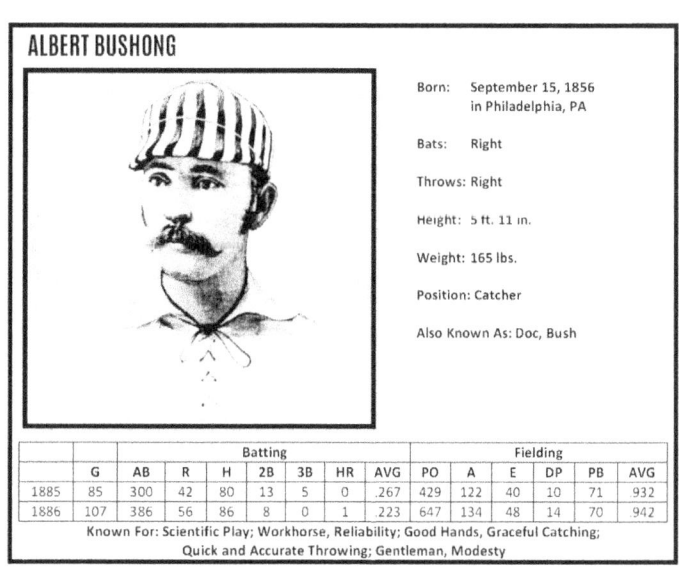

ALBERT BUSHONG

Born: September 15, 1856 in Philadelphia, PA
Bats: Right
Throws: Right
Height: 5 ft. 11 in.
Weight: 165 lbs.
Position: Catcher
Also Known As: Doc, Bush

	Batting								Fielding					
	G	AB	R	H	2B	3B	HR	AVG	PO	A	E	DP	PB	AVG
1885	85	300	42	80	13	5	0	.267	429	122	40	10	71	932
1886	107	386	56	86	8	0	1	.223	647	134	48	14	70	942

Known For: Scientific Play; Workhorse; Reliability; Good Hands, Graceful Catching; Quick and Accurate Throwing; Gentleman, Modesty

The image in Bushong's baseball card comes from a team photograph entitled: "Champions. St. Louis Browns. American Association. 1886" (The Rucker Archive).

up). Bushong led the Association in both years in putouts. He was third in fielding average in 1885 and first in 1886, first in assists in 1885 and third in 1886, and second in double plays in 1885 and first in 1886. In short, Bushong was not only durable but also someone who could be counted on to play at a high level from one game to the next.

Three things distinguished Bushong's style of catching. First, he was one of the first to catch much of the time in a crouched position close to the plate, which enabled him to shield signals that he sent to the pitcher, to set a better target for a pitch,[35] and to be more effective in the receipt of a low pitch.[36] Second, this crouch allowed him to catch the ball with his fingers pointing downwards—which he turned upwards on a high pitch—his left palm curled in a cupped position ready to take the initial force of the throw and his right hand poised to follow a split second later to the side of the ball to secure the catch. Once the ball made contact with his hands, Bushong would permit his hands to swing back slightly to neutralize the possible sting of the catch and, if necessary, to transfer the ball to the right hand for a possible throw, should there be a runner attempting to steal a base. Third, with a runner on base, he would rise from his haunches, reposition his feet, and quickly unleash a rifle-like throw to gun down or pick off a runner. Although caught-stealing statistics were not kept in the nineteenth century, game reports document that Bushong threw out numerous runners with his quick release and hard, accurate throws.

Bushong, Caruthers and Foutz formed the best battery combinations in the American Association and, to many, in all of baseball. Any mention of his weak batting was quickly overwhelmed by praise for his heady and skilled play behind the plate. With Bushong in place for 1887, a third championship for the Browns seemed destined.

In 1885 and 1886, the core players had worked hard to perfect their craft. Though still a young team, the Browns were confident in their game. They played as a team with skill and headwork and with a tenacious drive to win. In fact, as the next chapter illuminates, the Browns would do "anything to win."

4

"Anything to Win"[1]

As a unit, the core players were: daring and fearless; unflappable and relentless; bold and inventive; skilled in every facet of the game; and quick on their feet, that is, both speedy in their play and savvy in their decisions on the field. Joe Pritchard, the St. Louis correspondent for *Sporting Life*, described their game as follows:

> These boys play ball to win, and they are workers from start to finish. Every member of the team is always on the alert to take advantage of an error or careless play of an opposing team. They work together like a clock and to this may be attributed to the watchful eye of Captain Comiskey. Every person in the country who has watched this crack club play ball can join with me in saying that the great success of the Browns has been their casting of individual records to the four winds and going on the field with the full determination to do or die. They take the most desperate chances in all their work of any team that was ever on a ball field, and the way in which they run the bases, and their lightning-like fieldwork is enough to scare the determination to win out of an opposing team.[2]

There are three things to note in the above quotation. First, this was Comiskey's team. He was the architect, guardian, and exemplar of the Browns' style of play. Second, the expression "work together like a clock" highlighted the machine-like quality of the Browns' play, with each player doing his part in the service of whatever it took to win. The coordinated effort of the team in the pursuit of victory was the only thing that mattered, not the records of individuals, which in the quote are "cast to the four winds."[3] The Browns combined their numerous skills and knowledge or "headwork"[4] to work as a team, adeptly and smartly to achieve their goal of victory.[5]

Third, the quotation points to an intensity that enveloped the Browns' drive to "play ball to win," a style of play that seemed to include, yet go beyond, the effective application of skills and headwork. The references to "do or die," the press to be "ready to take advantage of an error or careless play," the exhortation to "take the most desperate chances in all their work," and the prediction that their actions would be "enough to scare the determination to win out of the opposing team," suggest the second dimension in their style of play, one that adopted a no-holds-barred approach to glory. Comiskey urged his charges to "work every advantage to win … to get there by fair means or foul or in any way possible so long as they get there … to hesitate at nothing, no matter how desperate, if it is necessary to win the game."[6] Comiskey expected the Browns to "turn a trick every time they got a chance … it is not so much in taking advantage of your opponents as it is getting away with it."[7] The Browns' drive to do anything to win thus also embraced a rowdy brand of baseball that some saw as "dirty ball."[8]

The St. Louis nine adopted a style of play that encompassed skills and headwork as well as aggression and determination. They relied on offensive (base running and batting) and defensive (fielding and pitching) skills and headwork and on various forms of dirty ball, specifically noisy coaching, incessant kicking, tricks, and rough play. Their ability to win depended on their capacity to do almost "anything to win."

Much of the Browns' offense turned on their running game. In most cases, the first priority of a batsman was to become a base runner. Once on the base path, a runner had the responsibility, sometimes in concert with the batter and sometimes on his own, to advance from base to base and to score runs. The Browns were second in the Association in runs scored in 1885, and in 1886 led in runs scored and stolen bases. Although there was no official record kept on stolen bases in 1885, the Browns established their dominance on the base paths in this season. The *St. Louis Post-Dispatch* reproduced the following excerpt from the *Cincinnati Enquirer* on the Browns' 1885 running record: "The St. Louis team owes its fine position in the race entirely to the base running abilities of its members. As sluggers and fielders, they do not rank at the top, but nearly every base hit they have made this season has meant a run."[9] Game-by-game reports and end-of-year reviews left no doubt about the Browns' "superior base running."[10]

In 1886, official scorers were required to report stolen bases, which included not only bases stolen on the pitcher but also any extra base a runner made in the course of play.[11] The Browns led the Association with a total of 336 stolen bases, or 2.4 per game. Four players on the Browns were ranked in the top seven base stealers in the Association (Latham, Welch, Robinson, Comiskey).

Base running combined both skill and headwork. A sportswriter in the *St. Louis Post-Dispatch* summarized the multifaceted proficiency of the Browns' base running:

> It is not only fleetness of foot and a knack of diving between the legs of the baseman that makes a successful base runner. It is also good judgment, ability to lead the pitcher and the catcher on into injudicious plays; the faculty of

EVERYTHING IS FAIR IN BASEBALL.

The *National Police Gazette* commented on the "scrapping matches" in the American Association, with a particular reference to Comiskey and the St. Louis Browns: "The St. Louis boys have been instructed to win at all hazards no matter how badly they may cripple or injure their opponents." The cartoon shows a St. Louis runner sliding into a base so as to upend the baseman and thus prevent him from catching the ball and applying a tag (*National Police Gazette*, May 25, 1887).

grasping at a glance complicated situations and arguing out the line of play necessary to be undergone and taking advantage thereof.[12]

Once on base, it was up to the runner to make things happen. He frequently could depend on the batsman to advance him one or more bases with a hit, but just as often the runner took things into his own hands and, early in the count, bolted from first to steal second base. At other times, he forced the play by taking a long lead to draw a throw before the pitch from the pitcher or after the pitch from the catcher, in each case calculating that, in their rush to pick him off, the throw would be wild to the base, enabling him to advance safely.

As the runner hustled to steal a base, he often had to slide to elude the tag applied by a baseman. After repeatedly observing Comiskey fearlessly lunging "headforemost into bases,"[13] many of the Browns, especially Latham, Welch, Robinson, Caruthers, and Hugh Nicol, made the headfirst slide their slide of choice. The feet-first hook slide was also executed with some frequency by Comiskey, Gleason, Latham, and Welch. Few resorted to the old-fashioned feet-first slide on a regular basis, although it could be effective as both a diversion and a surprise, especially if the runner went in hard with the spikes high.[14]

WALTER A. LATHAM.

Opposite the sketch of Walter A. Latham poised to steal a base, the 1888 *Reach's Guide* included an article on "Base Running." Latham was one of the "best representatives" of the "rapid class of base runners." In the article, Latham advised runners to get a good lead, take off at the first motion of the pitcher, and "slide head first every time" (National Baseball Hall of Fame Library, Cooperstown, New York).

Every runner was expected to move to third base as soon as possible. When on third, the runner had numerous opportunities to score. Sometimes he ran for home on a passed ball, a wild pitch, a slow-hit ball to the infield, or an error. In the mid–1880s, the Browns could expect in each game that the opposing fielders would make four or more errors and that the pitcher and catcher would combine for two or more passed balls or wild pitches. With less than two out, the runner usually tagged up on a fly out and scurried home. If the fly ball was too shallow to tag and run to the plate, the runner edged off the base after the tag and then raced for home if the throw-in from the outfield was wild or if the outfielder hesitated on the throw or momentarily bobbled the ball. Or with men on first and third base, the runners executed a delayed double steal, with the man on first breaking for second but running at a pace that enticed the catcher to throw to second, at which point the runner on third broke for home in an attempt to score a run. The possibility of any one of these missteps by the opposing team was therefore high enough for a runner to take a chance on scoring from third.

The opposing teams were always on guard, sometimes to the point of distraction, forever wondering when the Browns would next try to take an extra base. The Browns thus used their running, or the threat of running, to their advantage, at times to take control of and eventually to win the game.

The Browns' base running clearly ignited their offense, especially in 1885. That season, they were not one of the better batting teams. Their .246 batting average was fifth-best among the eight teams, a percentage that exactly matched the Association average. They did not fare much better on hits or total bases, the latter an indication of their limited power. The Browns were a different batting team in 1886. They leapt to a team average of .273, well ahead of the other seven teams and significantly higher than the Association average of .243. They led the Association in hits and total bases, thanks to an increase of 105 extra-base hits. St. Louis had established itself as a leading team at the plate, one that could hit for average and for power. Their emerging batting prowess combined with their effectiveness on the base paths made the Browns the most formidable offensive force in the American Association.

Comiskey recognized that certain approaches to batting increased the likelihood of getting on base, advancing runners, or scoring runs. He valued a batsman who could: put the ball in play (contact hitter); hit to all fields or to a gap created by the positioning of the opposing fielders (place hitter); and swing for a single or double and not for a triple or home run (hitting for average). These approaches enabled the batter to respond more effectively to the changing conditions he faced each time at bat.

With less than two out and one or more runners on base, Comiskey wanted the batsman to locate a hit or a bunt that would move a runner into scoring position, a strategy that usually resulted in the batsman being out on the play.[15] Such sacrifice hits put the team first, an orientation that was at the heart of an anything-to-win approach to the game. O'Neill, Comiskey, Gleason, and Latham were the leading sacrifice batters on the team.

By the end of 1886, the Browns blossomed into a more offensive-minded team. Their running game still set the tone for their offense. On the base paths, they took chances, forced the play, and advanced one or more bases willfully, often at will, so much so that their thefts sometimes became the deciding factor in the outcome of a game. St. Louis could explode for five or more runs in an inning. Its batsmen were adept in advancing base runners through hits, sacrifice hits, or simply putting the ball into play, a style of play that was very much cued by their teamwork and headwork.

The Browns also were a formidable defensive club, with well-coordinated and skilled fielding and high-caliber pitching. In 1885, the Browns had the highest fielding percentage and made the fewest errors of any team in the American Association. In the following year, though they registered similar numbers, they were edged out in both categories by Pittsburgh.[16] The Browns also had four perfect fielding games, a relatively rare defensive feat distinguished by no fielding errors and no battery errors (wild pitches, passed balls). The Browns won all four perfect fielding games, two of them by shutout.[17]

The Browns could also be quite bold in the way they fielded the ball, seemingly unafraid to make errors in the service of Comiskey's maxim of doing anything to win. As in base running, the players used their quick reflexes and foot speed to take chances in the field. They went after hits that were too hot to handle, slightly out of reach, or risky if missed (e.g., a fielder diving to catch or block a ball hit into the outfield could result in the ball getting by him for extra bases). For the Browns, it was better to make an error on a risky defensive play than to pull up on a fly ball or to let a hard-hit ball go through the infield. As Comiskey reflected some years later, an error on a daring defensive effort was accepted, even encouraged: "No one was afraid to take chances. No one cared for errors, not if he knew that he attempted to make the play the right way."[18] There were nonetheless some limits to when and under what conditions a fielder took chances.

Playing it safe went hand in hand with taking risks. Comiskey explained: "I am a great believer in a safe ball but as that it is the knowledge when to make a daring play or turn a clever trick that makes the great ball players and the winning teams, and I think our old St. Louis Browns knew about as well as anybody."[19] The challenge was to know when to be "daring" and when to be "clever," a judgment that depended on headwork on the defensive side of the ball.

Certain rules governed the positioning of infielders. Comiskey wanted infielders to play deep and away from the base. The first and third basemen should play back and close to the line to guard against the troublesome hit along the foul lines. The third baseman should not play as deep as the first baseman, in part to be ready for a bunt and in part to accommodate the long throw to first needed on a ground ball. The first baseman should field a ball hit in his direction whenever possible, which often required the pitcher to cover first base. With the first and third basemen close to the line, the second baseman and shortstop should play deep and away from second base. The Browns rarely deviated from this deep positioning.[20]

Following what Comiskey called the "science of team play," he set guidelines to differentiate between when the Browns would play for the batter and when they would play for the base runner:

> My general rule is to play for the batter unless the score is very close. In other words, do not try so much to recover from harm already done as to prevent more harm. So, unless the score is very close and it is near the end of the game, I never pull in my infielders for a possible play at the plate, but rather play for the base runner.[21]

In most scenarios, Comiskey preferred his players to get the batter out first. On balls hit to third or first, the play usually was to first to get one out. When there were men on first and third and two out, the play was to first base unless an easy force-out presented itself.[22] However, with less than two out and a man on first, the play on a ball hit to the shortstop or second baseman was to try for a double play.

The outfielders, with the exception of Welch, who preferred to play shallow, also tended to play deep, situating themselves to complement the location of the infielders, but varying their position according to the batter and game conditions. In the case of the right fielder, his deeper positioning was linked to how Comiskey roamed the field: "Comiskey plays first base different from any other first baseman, standing farther out in right field than any baseman in the country. He does this to capture flies in short right field. And permitting his right fielder to play a deeper field."[23] The outfielders needed to be ready to back up fellow outfielders on hard-hit balls and infielders on throws to nearby bases (e.g., left fielder on throws to third base, center fielder on throws to second base). Once they caught or retrieved a ball hit to the outfield, the outfielders had to return it to the infield as quickly as possible, to an infielder who was in the best position to prevent the advancement of runners.

Bushong and Comiskey devised a system of signals that they could use at key points in the game to inform the fielders how the Browns' pitcher would approach a batter (e.g., type of pitch, inside-outside, high-low). They also signaled to the fielders when the catcher or pitcher was about to pick off a runner. With this advanced information, the fielders could adjust their position according to where they expected a ball, if hit, might go. In the case of a throw to pick off a runner, they could be ready to back up the play.

Notwithstanding Comiskey's strong commitment to playing deep and getting the batter out first, he advocated one rule that superseded all others, namely that "situations can alter any rule."[24] Comiskey was first and foremost a student of the game and, in his emphasis on headwork, wanted his players to learn how to adapt to situations and to take into account such things as: the score of the game and the circumstances of the moment (e.g., number of men on base, who was at bat); the moves that their own battery would adopt (e.g., how the Browns' pitcher and catcher would pitch the batter; how they would check the runners under different circumstances); the offensive strategies that the opposing team would likely use; and what adjustments the Browns as a team would make.[25] In the field, the Browns opted for the safe out as a rule, but gambled on a riskier play when the situation presented itself. In fielding, skill was clearly in the service of headwork, as it was with pitching, the other arm of the Browns' defense.

Foutz and Caruthers were the Browns' leading pitchers, and indeed the premier pitchers of the American Association in the mid-1880s. Together they started 99 of 112 games in 1885 and 100 of 139 games in 1886. Their combined win-loss record was 144-57 (.716), with their 144 wins accounting for 84 percent of the Browns' total in these two years. The Browns' pitching staff as a whole led in most of the statistical categories. For example, in both seasons, the pitchers were almost a full run lower than the Association average in earned runs per game.[26] The Browns had, in Foutz and Caruthers, two pitchers who possessed considerable skill and who, with the guidance of Bushong and Comiskey, developed into strategically crafty hurlers. They had good command of their pitches and kept batters off-balance through changes in delivery, speed, and type of pitch.

Bushong, the "model coaching catcher,"[27] was known for his headwork. Like Comiskey, he studied the batters on the opposing teams. He developed a knowledge of each batter's habits, strengths, and weaknesses, and used these insights to work with his pitchers to determine a pitching strategy for every batter they faced.

Through 1885 and 1886, the Browns continued to refine and extend their highly-developed skills in base running, batting, fielding, and pitching. Over his first two seasons as captain and manager of the Browns, Comiskey coached his players on how best to deploy their skills to play smartly, as a team, and for the win. Whether on offense (base runner, batsman) or on defense (fielder, pitcher, catcher), they relied on their strategic wisdom to figure out what to do in each situation. The Browns entered the 1887 season well prepared to play with the kind of headwork espoused by their leader.

The anything-to-win brand of Browns baseball involved more than skills and headwork. It also compelled an aggressive style of play that pushed players to win by whatever means and at whatever cost. Although many commended the Browns on their baseball skills and savvy, most condemned them for their rowdiness or dirty ball. The Browns were called "hooligans, roughs, toughs, and a number of other choice pet names, and [were] accused … of bulldozing and with being always either anxious for a fight or actually engaged in one."[28] After Jimmy Williams, the manager of Cleveland and the former manager of the Browns in 1884, criticized the Browns' rough work, Comiskey defiantly responded: "All's fair in war and base ball … anything to win a game, so long as there is no danger of being declared out, should be resorted to and that if he were allowed to tie a man up by the thumbs to prevent him from reaching a base the man would be tied up."²⁹ Unperturbed by these accusations, the Browns were relentless in their drive to win. Whether verbally assertive in coaching and kicking or physically aggressive through tricks and rough play, the players combined elements of surprise, distraction, deception, and intimidation to confuse, overwhelm, or disrupt the rhythm and concentration of their opponents and sometimes the umpire. Their various aggressive tactics were designed to cause their opponents to make mistakes—a missed catch, an errant throw, a hesitation in play-making, a passed ball, a pitch gone awry—small gains to be sure, but possibly enough to give the Browns an edge that might ultimately affect the outcome of the game. In short, the Browns invested heavily in what others saw as dirty ball.

Of the many sounds of a baseball game in the mid–1880s, the disquieting noises of the coaches³⁰ reverberated around the ball field. Comiskey, Latham, and Gleason were the dominant coachers, while Robinson, Foutz, and Welch were sometimes recruited to this role, as needed. With his booming "foghorn voice" and taut, combustible demeanor, Comiskey set the tone for the other coachers. Latham was known more for his continuous banter and favorite expressions (e.g., "Whoo-ah, that's the way"; "Be lively boys, be lively"), his clown-like antics, and his piercing wit. Gleason had a "mealy voice with a touch of rough in it." He relied more on menacing gestures and sudden bursts on to the field. More often than not, he followed the coaching lead of Comiskey or Latham.³¹ Officially on the line to cheer, encourage or guide their teammates, the Browns' coachers devoted more time to rattling the opposition or, in Latham's case, providing entertainment.

Even when cheering on a teammate, a coacher hoped to distract the opposition by the loudness and chant-like persistence of his encouragements. In an article on famous coachers, the *St. Louis Post-Dispatch* included a vignette of Comiskey on the coaching lines in a game in which Robinson was on first:

> Comiskey's charm is in his voice, and he uses it with wonderful effect. His gradations would make jealous a grand opera artist. Standing in his cage at third base, his hands on his hips, he leans over and gets his vocal chords in swing. Here's the way he does it:
> "Go on now, Robbie, go on, go on, h-o-o-o, go back, go on, h-o-o-o-o, go on."
> Robbie gets his chance and goes on as fast as his legs can carry him. From the time he leaves the base until he arrives at his destination, Comiskey indulges in one long protracted yell or whoop, beginning on a low note and increasing in its volume and raising it in tone. The note swells and goes up as the man runs and when he touches the object base Comiskey's whoop blossoms out like the burst of a waterfall in an indescribable sound, half yell and half scream, as though some terrible calamity had fallen on its utterer. Then the storm subsides and all is quiet until the play goes on again.³²

Such distractions were of a different kind when Latham was on the coaching line. His coaching brought "the stands down on him every time he opens his head. Lath only smiles at their hoots and hisses. He is the one player in the profession who doesn't care a fig for the ridicule of the spectators and newspaper comments."³³ Latham worked the crowd as much as he did the opposition and the umpire. He specialized in the farcical gesture, the stock-in-trade of a diamond jester. He traded barbs with the cranks, turned somersaults or danced after a good play or a win, and jumped about wildly when a call went against the Browns. Intent on having fun as much as making fun of others, Latham's coaching was also laced with wit and repartee. Such antics were used to get opposing players to pay more attention to him, with the hope that during their lapse in concentration, the Browns might benefit—perhaps a runner edges one step closer to a base he wants to steal or a batter reaches base on a misplay on a batted ball. What seemed like a desire to amuse became an act of subterfuge. While his coaching was amusing, zany, and entertaining, Latham coached to win. And the Browns won, to the delight and entertainment of the fans.[34]

Sometimes coachers used a more aggressive approach to putting the opposition off its game. For example, Comiskey periodically used his foghorn voice to bellow insults at the other team's pitcher or catcher. On one occasion, Comiskey and Gleason stood on either side of an opposing catcher and commented on his "breeding, personal habits, skill as a receiver, or rather lack thereof, until the unlucky backstop was unable to tell whether one or half a dozen balls were coming his way."[35] Much more than a distraction, such aggressive rattling was designed to belittle and intimidate their adversaries.

By June 1886, many of the owners in the American Association were frustrated by the roaming, noisy, and aggressive coaching perpetuated largely but not exclusively by the Browns' coachers and, consequently, passed new rules that limited the actions of coachers. In the new rules, the ground reserved for the coachers had clearer and more confined boundaries. They were required to locate themselves in a space defined by lines 75 feet from the catcher's lines and 15 feet from and parallel to the foul lines. They had to restrict their verbal efforts to base runners. They were not to address batsmen, except to provide cautions. They were to refrain from any direct comments to the opposing pitcher or catcher. Furthermore, only the captain was permitted to question an umpire's decision, and only then on questions about a possible incorrect application of a rule. With their characteristic bravado, the Browns found ways around these rule changes. Both coachers and players continued to kick as they had done ever since Comiskey took charge of the Browns.[36]

The other noise heard most often during Browns games came from the incessant kicking against the umpire. Though kicking could come from all quarters, players and fans alike, the kicks came most often from Comiskey. For example, after a 6–5 loss to the Browns in an 1886 game filled with kicking, Secretary Caylor of the Cincinnati club exclaimed: "As a royal, three-ply, copper-bottomed skilled kicker, he stands at the top. Charley comes from Kickersville."[37] Kicking was a key component of Comiskey's anything-to-win orientation: "I go in and kick because I believe that unless you kick you stand a good chance of losing every game that you play, and because I believe that kicking is half the game."[38]

Comiskey, as the captain of the team, was quick to challenge anything that he perceived to be an unfair decision by the umpire. Sometimes he kicked to point out a missed call or to overturn an incorrect decision. Other times he kicked to instill a sense of guilt or debt in the umpire so that he would make up for his error in judgment by ruling in the Browns' favor on a close or crucial play later in the game. As the "sole and absolute judge of play,"[39] the one umpire assigned to each game[40] frequently had his hands full keeping up with the many things happening on the field at any given moment, especially when there were men on base. Furthermore, he often had to make calls when he was not in position to observe the play clearly. Comiskey understood the likelihood of error in umpire judgment that may arise under these conditions and was ready to challenge if not exploit the vulnerable position in which the umpire was placed.

In virtually every game, Comiskey as the boss kicker found fault with the decisions of the umpire. He challenged calls on close plays at a base when a Browns' runner was called out or when an opposing team's runner was called safe.[41] He kicked about any tactics by the opposing team that jeopardized the Browns' chances to win. For example, an opposing team sometimes would take steps to delay the game so that the umpire would be forced to call the game on account of darkness, with the winner the team in the lead at the end of the last completed inning. When this reversion to the score at the end of the previous inning might result in a loss for the Browns, Comiskey was quick to remind the umpire that such dishonest and manipulative tactics were against the rules.[42] He also defended his players when the umpire ruled against them for tricks or rough plays.

In some cases, Comiskey's kicking turned into a formal protest,[43] and a few times he was so furious at a call that he took his team off the field. To pull his men off the field following a perceived unjust ruling by the umpire was an act all the more brazen or foolhardy, because the rules required the umpire to declare a forfeited game in favor of the club still on the field when one of the teams refused to continue playing.[44]

The St. Louis Browns lost the second game of the 1885 world championship series against Chicago by forfeit on a disputed call by umpire Dave Sullivan, who initially ruled that a slow-rolling ball off the bat of Ned Williamson, the Chicago third baseman, was a foul hit. However, the ball ended up in fair territory, so Sullivan changed his call to a fair hit. Comiskey exploded and demanded that the umpire hold to his original ruling of a foul hit. A number of St. Louis fans poured onto the field to join in the dispute over the call. The game was suspended, and, later that evening from the safety of his hotel room, Sullivan declared a forfeited game in favor of Chicago. Comiskey and Anson, the two captains of the teams, agreed that the game would be a draw. The teams had tied the first game. Thus, when the Browns won three of the last five games, they regarded themselves as the new champions of the world. Albert Spalding, the president of the Chicago club, insisted that Chicago won Game Two by forfeit, and thus the championship series should end in a draw with three games apiece and one game tied, which was the eventual decision. In this ultimate form of kicking, Comiskey paid a steep price, denying his team a possible chance at the undisputed 1885 world title.[45]

Although Comiskey led the way in kicking, he had willing collaborators. His fellow coaches, Latham and Gleason, often protested calls or even threatened the umpire.[46] Robinson and Welch also challenged the decisions of umpires, especially when called out on attempted steals or censored and fined for rough play.[47] Caruthers "sulked" in the pitcher's box and even "sassed" the umpire to show his displeasure at his inconsistent and poorly gauged calls on balls and strikes.[48] A number of times each season, the Browns as a team erupted in protest. They left the bench, surrounded the umpire, and strenuously voiced their outrage about a decision. O'Neill readily joined the chorus in these team kicks. However, when he was personally displeased with a call, he did not verbally confront an umpire on his own behalf at any point in 1885 or 1886. At most, he displayed his frustration at a call through a grimace or a groan or, if it was on a called third strike, by tossing his bat.

One marker of the extent to which the Browns engaged in aggressive play was reflected in the fines incurred for infractions of the playing rules. For the 1886 season, the *Cincinnati Enquirer* reported that the St. Louis Browns had $515 in fines, with most of the fines given for kicking. Comiskey had more than two-thirds of the fines allocated to the Browns in 1886. Chris Von der Ahe initially called the fines unjust but nonetheless paid Comiskey's fines shortly thereafter.[49] Comiskey and Von der Ahe no doubt found the fines worth the aggravation. It was part of the price of doing business, which in the case of the Browns meant doing whatever it took to win the game. To protest the call and then challenge the fairness of the fine and, on occasion, even to petition for the suspension of the umpire who made the alleged bad calls, were all part of a style of play that pushed the boundaries of the rules. It was a strategy, for the most part, that they followed with impunity. On balance, the Browns were fined fewer times than the number of kicking and coaching infractions reported in game accounts. In other words, when Comiskey bulldozed the umpires, it seemed to pay off in that the Browns got away with more than they were fined for and thus gained the advantages they sought with their aggressive tactics.[50] The Browns also usually avoided censure or sanction when they employed tricks and rough play.

Turning a trick was typically based on catching opponents off-guard. A successful trick required deception, surprise, and precise timing. It often involved either pushing the limits of the playing rules or breaking the rules altogether. As such, a trick also had to be done when the umpire was busy with another play or was not looking or aware of what was about to happen. The Browns, especially Latham, Robinson, Welch, Comiskey, and Gleason, found ways to turn tricks as part of their efforts to get on base, to steal bases or score runs, and to prevent opposing runners from stealing bases or scoring runs.

The return of bunting in the mid–1880s was not without controversy. For many, the manliness of a batsman was defined by the crack of a well-stroked hit, preferably to the outfield, and not by the plop of a gently tapped bunt that rolled a few feet from the plate. The critics dubbed bunts as "baby hits," nothing more than "infantile tricks" by weak batters desperate to get on base.[51] Unconcerned by public criticism, Latham and Comiskey frequently dropped down a surprise bunt to get on base or to advance a runner.[52]

The Browns' tricksters also focused on tactics that would increase their chances of getting to first base without a hit. From 1884 onwards, the American Association allowed a batsman to take first when hit by a pitched ball. Welch and Robinson soon began to crowd or lean over the plate, daring the pitcher to throw at them. On an inside pitch, they would either not move at all, step into the pitch, or feign an attempt to get out of the way of the pitch, only to be hit by the ball and usually be awarded first base.[53]

Another way to get on base was with a base on balls, which occurred when the umpire called seven balls in 1885 and six balls in 1886. A player had to devise ways to induce the pitcher to throw more called balls. Crowding the plate sometimes caused pitchers to throw outside and off the plate. Occasionally, Latham, in an effort to disrupt a pitcher's rhythm, jumped sideways or forward in the batter's box just as the pitcher was about to release his pitch. Latham also used a fouling trick to wear down the pitcher until he eventually got his base on balls. A foul hit did not count as a strike or a ball. Thus, a batter could repeatedly foul off pitches that would otherwise be called strikes because they were simply ruled a foul hit. After a series of foul hits on good pitches, the pitcher could become frustrated, lose his control, and start to throw more called balls until the batsman earned a walk.

The Browns relied on various tricks to obstruct throws or catches that might threaten a teammate's efforts to reach base safely, to steal a base, or to score a run. With a man on first, Comiskey wanted the batsman to protect the runner when he tried to steal second base. Welch once fulfilled his obligation to the runner by stepping in front of the catcher to block his throw to second. Welch was declared out for obstruction.[54] On another occasion, there were Browns on first and third, with Welch standing in for Comiskey as the third base coacher. The opposing first baseman had the ball when Welch suddenly ran along the captain's lines as if he were trying to score a run. The first baseman mistook Welch for the runner on third base and threw the ball home, which in turn allowed the man on first to move up to second.[55] Two other unlikely obstructers, O'Neill, in an 1886 game that the Browns lost, 7–3, to Cincinnati, and Foutz, in a 7–2 losing cause to Baltimore, were each running to third as the batter hit a ground ball toward the same base. They ran in front of the third baseman just as he reached down to pick up the ground ball. Both O'Neill and Foutz were declared out for obstruction, though in Tip's case, the decision was reversed after considerable kicking on the part of the Browns.[56]

When it came to preventing opposing runners from stealing bases or scoring runs, the Browns resorted to various defensive tricks. In a 7–2 loss to Baltimore, on a steal of second base by one of the Baltimore players, Bushong, the St. Louis catcher, was unable to catch the pitched ball and so did not throw to second. However, Robinson, the St. Louis second baseman, motioned as if he had caught a ball thrown by Bushong, so the runner did not try to go to third on the passed ball.[57] Robinson was at it again in a 12–1 win against New York, this time with a hidden ball trick. Dave Orr, the New York Metropolitans' first baseman, hit a single to center field. It was promptly returned to Robinson at second base, who held on to it as Foutz, the pitcher, a ready accomplice in the hidden ball ruse, looked to home plate as if he was about to deliver the ball. As Orr took a lead off first base, Robinson swiftly fired the ball to Comiskey, who tagged Orr for the out.[58] Robinson was always ready to take advantage of an opposing player's miscue or lapse in concentration.

Like trickery, rough plays relied on deception, surprise, and precise timing. They were often aided by a fist or shoulder. In executing rough plays, the main protagonists—Welch, Robinson, Comiskey, Latham, and Gleason—did not just bend the rules, they broke them boldly, with a level of physical aggression that confronted and provoked their opponents. The Browns were convinced that they had to play a "rough-and-tumble game" to win.[59] Rough plays usually occurred on the base paths, offensively, in the course of players trying to steal a base or to score a run and, defensively, in their determination to prevent an opposing player from doing the same.

By 1886, the ongoing criticism of the Browns' noisy coaching and kicking expanded to include strong objections to their rough play:

> Since they have been away every newspaper throughout the East had not a single word of commendation for the Browns, but on the contrary, they have been attacked on all sides and the most violent and even vulgar adjectives have graced or disgraced the diction of their critics. The critics say the members of the club are ruffianly, unmanly and brutal. That their conduct on the ball field both in word and act is a disgrace to the profession. That they fight among themselves and that they fight their opponents. That they abuse everybody they collide with and in fact nothing is of too mean a nature for them to stoop to. That most of them are blackguards and some of them are drunkards.[60]

The infielders of the opposing teams were wary of what the Browns might do when they got on base. The Browns had a deserved reputation for sliding hard into a base and for running down basemen who got in their way. In a 2–1 loss to Pittsburgh in 1885, Comiskey broke up a double play when he "deliberately and wantonly ran into him [the second baseman] jostling him back several feet and preventing him from throwing to first."[61] In the first inning of a 5–2 loss against New York in mid–June of 1885, O'Neill also tried to foil a double play. O'Neill injured his leg in a collision with the second baseman and had to retire from the field. He missed almost half of the season. Subsequently, the *St. Louis Post-Dispatch* reported that O'Neill was likely a casualty of the expectation of Comiskey and Von der Ahe that all base runners must "run into fielders when they can make a point by it."[62]

On defense, the infielders, especially Gleason and Robinson, periodically blocked the path of a base runner, held a runner on the ground after he slid into a base, or struck him with a fist as he rounded the bag. Welch would sometimes creep in from center field for a pick-off play at second, occasionally bowling over the unsuspecting base runner in the process. By 1887, these acts of intimidation had become more frequent and consequently the focus of still further calls for retribution and sanction of the Browns by the press and the other American Association owners.

In December 1886, at the evening dinner of the annual meeting of the American Association, the Browns were toasted as the champions of the world. They were also celebrated by each of the American Association teams in the first away series of the 1887 season. As much as the Browns' world championship was appreciated and heralded by the American Association as proof that its teams were equal to the those in the National League, the owners nonetheless remained circumspect about the aggressive style of play that the Browns relentlessly pursued without compromise or apology. The 1887 season quickly became a year of kicking against the Browns and their dirty ball, even as some of the other American Association teams, notably Cincinnati and Baltimore, further embraced an aggressive style of play in an effort to beat the Browns at their own game.

As for O'Neill, in his first two years as the full-time left fielder (1885–1886), he enacted Comiskey's anything-to-win style of play through his efforts as an accomplished batsman and a dependable fielder. A heavy batsman[63] who struck the ball with considerable force, he hit for average and, increasingly, for power. In terms of headwork at the plate, he worked the pitcher to his advantage. He also fit in well with Comiskey's scientific approach to team batting. With his skill as a contact hitter, O'Neill could hit to all fields, a valuable skill for advancing runners through well-placed or sacrifice hits. As savvy as he was as a batsman, once he hit the ball and turned to base running, O'Neill became unsure of himself, seemingly incapable of sound judgment on the fly. On offense then, he was a productive and strategic leader in the batter's box but unpredictable and confused on the base paths.

O'Neill's 1886 fielding numbers, especially his fielding average and putouts, were among the best in the American Association. Although a few observers still grumbled about his slowness in going after the ball, once he got a bead on it, he could run down fly balls with the best of them and make the catch, spectacular or routine, on a regular basis.[64] Thanks to the coaching of Comiskey, O'Neill had the head for fielding. He knew how to alter his positioning for different batters or situations and was both quick and astute in getting the ball back to the infield to forestall the advancement of runners.[65] Even his throwing, despite the diminished capacity of his right arm, had improved. O'Neill was now a full-fledged contributor on defense.

Tip supported the more aggressive style of play advocated by Comiskey in spirit but rarely displayed this dirty ball on the field. He was not involved in the noisy coaching, individual kicking, tricks, or rough play that defined the Browns' drive to win, at least not to the degree enacted by Comiskey, Latham, Welch, Robinson, Gleason, and Caruthers. He readily joined in team kicks. The trickiest he got was on the base paths when he ran in front of a ground ball with the hope of disrupting the timing of an opposing infielder. On the few times he tried this trick, he was usually called out for obstruction. His rough play was confined to two times when he ran into a baseman on close plays at first and second base, the latter incident resulting in an injury that kept him out of most of the second half of the 1885 season. Any other bumps with opposing players were inconsequential and seemed more accidental than by design. Tip reserved his aggression, albeit in a quieter and more subtle manner than was the case with the rough plays and kicks of most of his teammates, for times at the plate where he did "everything to win" as a prolific batsman.

5

October 24, 1886, to April 15, 1887: Off-Season

In the off-season, players often got away from the game, enjoyed some well-deserved down time with family and friends, and, in some cases, found other jobs to sustain life between seasons. The 1886–1887 off-season for the Browns still had some of these elements, but it was different this time around. The Browns were the undisputed champions of the city, the American Association, and the world. The off-season was a time to bask in their success, to enjoy the attention afforded to champions, and even to swagger into the next season as the team to beat.

Tributes to the Browns began at season's end. O'Neill and Comiskey were honored during the last game of the season with medals from the E. Jaccard Jewelry Company, O'Neill for the best batting average on the team and Comiskey for the best fielding average.[1] At a banquet sponsored by a local doctor in recognition of the Browns' second straight American Association championship, the players contributed to the merriment with a number of songs, including solos by O'Neill, Latham, and Bushong.[2] Following the post-game celebrations of the Browns' dramatic, Game Six victory over Chicago for the world championship, the city of St. Louis was in a state of perpetual revelry, saluting their Browns in the press and through various community events. The Browns were warmly received at the St. Louis Merchants' Exchange, where the players were heartily applauded as each took his turn to thank the members for their support and to comment on the team's championship play.[3] A week later, the Elk Club showed their appreciation with a banquet and gifts of elegant jeweled scarf pins for each player.[4] That same week, the citizens of St. Louis presented the players with gold medals that were "set with nine diamonds, surmounted with a hand of white gold holding a ball of the same metal," and personally engraved, in Tip's case, reading: "Presented to J. E. O'Neill as a token of their esteem by the Citizens of St. Louis."[5] True to his word, Chris Von der Ahe shared the proceeds from the post-season matches, with each player receiving $530.51 from the world championship and $56.68 from the series with the St. Louis Maroons for the city championship.[6] Tip returned home to Woodstock, Ontario, a few days later to a welcome-back reception organized by family and friends. The *Woodstock Sentinel-Review* hailed Tip as "the finest left fielder and batter combined in the world" and wished him further success in the future: "More power to you 'Tip,' and may you go on and do better, if possible, next season!"[7] Tip had been thoroughly feted and rewarded in his two homes, St. Louis and Woodstock, for his part in the championship run of the Browns.

Although Tip O'Neill emerged as one of the more popular players during the 1886 season, his stellar batting performance in the Browns' world championship win against Chicago brought him even greater fame and acclaim. Tip was a bachelor who was adored for his good looks, "a really handsome fellow, with a splendid physique and … well fitted to be a good athlete."[8] *The Sporting News* added: "According to the St. Louis damsels, O'Neill, the Canadian, is the most graceful man on the diamond."[9] Others praised his character, especially his gentlemanly demeanor, his politeness, and his friendly and pleasing disposition. Compared to some of his more blustery and outspoken teammates, Tip was reserved, even quiet. At the same time, when queried on various topics, Tip was thoughtful and well-spoken in his remarks. He had the stolid and confident comportment of someone who was in control. Although not easily swayed or flustered, he could be forthright and assertive when the occasion called for directness or decisive action. O'Neill was a player of considerable interest to the fans and thus a newsworthy figure for the press. The St. Louis newspapers and the weeklies, especially *The Sporting News* and *Sporting Life*, fostered Tip's newly found status as a local hero.[10]

O'Neill was frequently in the news during the off-season, with stories or clips that sometimes seemed more exaggerated or invented than based on investigative journalism or direct contact with him. For example, on Tip's whereabouts over the winter months, newspapers at various points reported that he was involved with the following: touring with the McNish, Johnson and Slavin Minstrels[11]; in Woodstock hovering over a hot stove[12]; helping his father run a hotel[13]; keeping in shape by ice skating and tobogganing[14]; and chopping down trees to make bats for the new season.[15] Other reports focused on the coming season, with predictions that O'Neill would lead the Browns to another championship, and, in so doing, break the batting record of the American Association. *The Sporting News*, like many other newspapers, forecasted great things for him in 1887:

> Speaking of Tip O'Neill, recalls his great slugging record of last season, when he came within an ace of capturing the leading honor as the champion American Association Batsman. Look out for him this season. He has brought a cord of Canadian wood with him, and will have it cut up in bats, which to be about his size, will closely resemble young trees. Tip is in superb form, and will it is predicted, play the game of his career with the World's Champions this season. There are no better left fielders than he, and Muldoon will be badly mistaken, if he does not lead them all.[16]

Closer to the time that O'Neill was expected to report to St. Louis for pre-season training, the other storyline that dominated the press was less about his winter habits or upcoming feats on the diamond and more about why he was slow to return to St. Louis. Tip was in New York city with a "guiding star,"[17] a sweetheart to whom he was engaged, or so was the scoop by one newspaper,[18] "and cannot tear himself away." Eventually Tip arrived in St. Louis, unwilling to comment on speculations about his engagement. With no marital news to report, the press turned its attention to his "blooming mustache"[19] and the stir that this unexpected change in his appearance would likely cause:

> Tip O'Neill, tall handsome Tip, is with us again as bright, and smiling as his happy disposition always makes him appear. He has been dividing his time the past winter in the romantic Canadian woods, one day doing the "Snaggs" act at the Woodstock hotel, and the next, and for the last month or so, enjoying Gotham life. Tip is very much enamored of a dashing New York belle. That she is handsome, attractive and possesses all the charms by which the fair sex sways the world, goes without saying. Tip lingered by her side until "duty called him westward." He comes back a changed man. Some of his old friends have failed to recognize him. He will have to be reintroduced around the circle. The cause of this transformation is Tip's mustache. It is like its owner. It is a daisy. Tip looks very "swell" behind it. It improves his appearance greatly, and he ought to be very proud of it.[20]

Amidst this swirl of news about Tip's life back in Canada, his bride-to-be-or-not-to-be story in New York, and his return to St. Louis with a face adorned with fetching whiskers, there were important changes being made in how the game of baseball would be played in 1887, ones that would affect O'Neill's batting. Frustrated by three years of low-scoring games, anemic batting, and confusion or abuse of the rules of play, the National League and American Association struck a Joint Committee to establish a common set of playing rules that would significantly improve the game. Both leagues approved the new playing rules at their annual meetings in November (National League) and December (American Association). The changes were numerous and far-reaching, especially those that affected the pitcher and the batsman.[21]

Most of the rule changes seemed to favor the batsman, with one exception. Prior to 1887, a batter had the right to call for a high or low pitch. In 1887, a batsman could no longer call for a high or low pitch. Furthermore, a fair ball or strike was defined as a pitch over the plate between the knees and shoulders. These two changes gave the pitcher a bigger strike zone and the element of surprise, in that the batter could no longer count on a pitch thrown at the height he requested. Loyal St. Louis writers assured their readers that O'Neill, a notorious low-ball hitter, would have no trouble adjusting to high pitches or to the new strike zone.

The strategic advantage gained by the pitcher by the larger strike zone was offset by a number of advantages given to the batsman, the greatest of which were in the new rules governing balls and strikes and a base on balls. The number of unfair balls required for a base on balls was reduced from six (seven in the National League) to five. A base on balls was scored as a base hit and a time at bat. The number of fair balls required before a batsman is called out on strikes was increased from three to four. While O'Neill, like all players, would have to face both low and high balls, with the extra strike, he was less likely to strike out and had more time to wait for a pitch he preferred. He also had a better chance to get on base with a hit that now would be awarded on either a fair hit or a base on balls.[22]

The new rules also pushed the pitching distance further back. The front of the pitcher's box was still 50 feet from the plate, but the box itself was reduced from four feet wide by seven feet long to four feet wide by five and one-half feet long. The pitcher also had to start with one foot on the back line of the box and could not take more than one step before releasing the ball. In 1886 then, with a seven-foot-long box, the pitcher started 57 feet back of the plate. He initiated his delivery at or near the back of the box but was not restricted in the number of steps he could take before he released the pitch. Frequently he took two or more steps and did not release the pitch until he neared the front line of the box, which was 50 feet from home. In 1887, though the pitcher now started 55½ feet from the plate, with the one-step restriction, his release point was now between 51 and 53 feet from the plate, depending on the stride of the pitcher and the timing of his release. With a release point that was one to two feet further back than in 1886 and without the leverage gained by a multi-step run-up, the pitcher likely experienced a slight reduction in the speed of his fastball, possibly a greater break in his in- and out-shoots, and greater challenges in the control of these pitches, at least until he had fully adjusted to the distance and new rules. O'Neill thus had a bit more time to pick up the speed and spin of the ball, to judge whether it was a strike or a ball, and to determine if he wanted to swing at the pitch.

In addition to the restriction on the number of steps allowed in the box, the pitching rules stipulated that before each delivery, the pitcher had to return to the back line of the box and hold the ball "in front of his body and in sight of the Umpire,"[23] which also put the ball in full view of the batsman. In previous seasons, a pitcher could and often did try to trick the batsman by hiding the ball behind his back, beginning his delivery facing away from the batsman, pitching without a pause between pitches, or feigning a throw to a base and then twisting back to throw to the plate, all in one motion. With the pitcher required to pause and present the ball before he began his delivery, O'Neill had fewer distractions or deceptions to watch for. He could instead concentrate on the ball as it travelled from the pitcher's hand to the plate, especially with those pitchers who had previously depended on these tricks. The rulesmakers made changes that batsmen would take advantage of in 1887, O'Neill more than anyone.

Outside the rules affecting pitching and batting, the changes that most affected the Browns were those concerning coaching and kicking. The new rules were based on the provisional changes made by the American Association in June 1886.[24] The movement of coachers was now restricted to clearly demarcated coaching lines. Coachers could no longer challenge the rulings of the umpire or direct their comments to the opposing players or audience.[25] Such changes were intended to limit the intimidating tactics of coachers and captains and to reinforce the powers of the umpire to make final and uncontested decisions. Undeterred by the threat of fines for violation of these new guidelines on coaching, the 1887 Browns defied these rules by persisting with their noisy coaching and incessant kicking.

In the ensuing discussion about the new rules, there was much debate among players about how much these changes would significantly alter the way they played the game. Off the field, however, the players foresaw few if any changes in the control that owners had over their professional lives and careers. Many of the Browns had concerns about such issues as their freedom of movement (e.g., reserve rule), their inability to negotiate salary, and their lack of recourse on arbitrary or unfair discipline meted out by the owner and sometimes the manager (e.g., fines). By the end of 1886, a players' organization began to take up the cause of players on such issues.

The Brotherhood of Professional Baseball Players (hereafter referred to as the Brotherhood) had its first annual meeting of the Executive Council in November 1886.[26] At this meeting, they examined rules changes that they felt would improve the game. John Ward, the shortstop of the New York Giants (National League), in his capacity as president of the Brotherhood, was a member of the Joint Committee on rules. As the voice of the Brotherhood in 1887, Ward repeatedly raised questions about the welfare of players, especially when a player was sold, traded, or re-assigned.[27] The Brotherhood argued that a player had a right to be involved in any process that led to his movement to another team, and not simply be shuttled from one place to another as if he was "chattel."[28] Furthermore, in cases when a player was suspended or blacklisted for alleged misbehavior or when salaries were unfairly reduced, the Brotherhood also spoke out against the lack of due process or just treatment.[29]

Player unrest among the Browns concerning one or more of the above issues surfaced in various forms in late 1886 and periodically throughout 1887. In November 1886, Von der Ahe traded Hugh Nicol, the popular right fielder, to Cincinnati for John Boyle, a rookie catcher.[30] Moving a reserved player initially unsettled some of the core players and upset many of the St. Louis fans, but no further reactions followed. Albert Spalding, the owner of the Chicago club, still bothered by the recent defeat at the hands of the

Browns, in early December challenged St. Louis to another series of nine games for the world championship,[31] this time to be played with six games in April, prior to the opening of the 1887 season, and three games in October, after the season ended.[32] Von der Ahe accepted the challenge, a decision that was opposed by most of the players, with O'Neill, Caruthers, and Robinson publicly expressing their serious objections to the series.[33] Caruthers was especially pointed in his dissent, noting that nothing would be gained by beating a club that the Browns had already defeated. He argued that the "boys ought to insist on the right to go through the next season with their title as champions of the world as undisputed."[34]

Following their win in the world championship, many of the Browns were not in a hurry to sign their 1887 contracts. By December 26, only O'Neill, Comiskey, Robinson, and Boyle had signed. At various points, Caruthers,[35] Latham,[36] and Foutz[37] expressed their demands for higher salaries. Irked by his players' ungratefulness, Von der Ahe struck back by persuading the American Association in its March meeting to amend section 37 of the constitution to allow clubs to blacklist reserved players who "willfully hold off and refuse to sign a regular contract with the club … for the purpose of harassing the club or compelling it to increase his salary."[38] Robinson, in a comment consistent with the Brotherhood's stand on the rights of ballplayers, was quick to criticize both the amendment and Von der Ahe's role in its passage:

> It is time that ballplayers were treated other than like slaves. Ballplayers have grown tired of being driven around like so many dogs, and they will not stand it any longer.… That was a fine rule that was passed at the Cleveland meeting which permits the blacklisting of players for not signing with the club by which they are reserved whenever the manager or President says so. The rule was passed for the benefit of Von der Ahe and a few others who anticipate some trouble in obtaining the signatures of a few of their players. Such a rule is a disgrace to the American Association, and the first thing the Ball-Players' Association will do will be to break it up. We may be obliged to slave this season, but you can bet we won't be driven about with a lash next year.[39]

Doc Bushong signed before the March meeting, while others followed suit after the above amendment was passed. Welch, Gleason, and Foutz signed contracts in the middle of March, and Latham and Caruthers signed in early April. As a result, many of the core players were late in their return to St. Louis.

Von der Ahe did not anticipate that these players' issues would affect the extent to which he could count on them to beat Chicago again. Most of these holdouts were disappointed with the contracts they eventually signed and thus were not especially supportive of Von der Ahe's commitment to a high-stakes match before the 1887 season began. Only some of the players (Comiskey, Bushong, Gleason, Robinson) returned to St. Louis by March 10, the date requested by Von der Ahe so that the team could ready itself for the Chicago series and the season. O'Neill arrived in late March after his alleged romantic adventures in New York. Welch, Foutz, and Caruthers arrived after O'Neill. Latham was so late that he missed the first game against Chicago (April 7). The Browns thus never had their full complement on hand for any of the training sessions for the series and, as a consequence, the players were not equally fit for action at the start of their matches against Chicago.

In addition, O'Neill and Gleason were injured. A few days after O'Neill returned to St. Louis, in an exhibition game against Syracuse, he was hit by a wild pitch that split his thumb, making it difficult for him to catch the ball or hold the bat.[40] He was sidelined for most of the exhibition games leading up to the Chicago series. While "Tip and his mustache [were] missed by the ladies,"⁴¹ fans still expected him to return to the lineup for the Chicago series, fit and set to resume the slugging display he exhibited in the 1886 world championship. However, the effects of his injury continued through the six games against Chicago and into the first few games of the season. Gleason had a sore shoulder that reduced his ability to make hard, accurate throws from his shortstop position.

These problems notwithstanding, the Browns' anything-to-win spirit had carried them to victory before. Many believed that their toughness, determination, and ability to play hurt would help them to rise to the occasion once again. After losing the first game, 6–3, the Browns roared back to beat Chicago 7–4 in Game Two and 9–7 in Game Three. In Game Four, the Browns had a 9–6 lead after five innings when Caruthers badly damaged his middle finger trying to stop a hard-hit ball through the box.⁴² Foutz, who had been slated to start Game Six, replaced Caruthers in the sixth inning. Hampered by stiffness in his arm, Foutz was unable to maintain the lead, giving up 11 runs over the last three innings and losing the game by a score of 16–15. After a 6–3 loss to Chicago in Game Five, the Browns turned to the injured Caruthers to even the series at three wins apiece. For six innings, the Browns rallied behind Caruthers' blood-stained heroics in the box, his finger bleeding most of the game. With a 6–5 lead in the seventh, Caruthers was visibly weakened, unable to throw with the speed or spin of previous innings. Chicago exploded for 14 runs and a 19–9 win to conclude the spring leg of their nine-game series with a four-games-to-two lead.⁴³ The Browns, especially in their last three losses, had not been able to summon that gritty, win-at-all-costs spirit.⁴⁴

The six-game spring series also provided a ready comparison between baseball under the old rules, which governed the six-game series for the world championship that the Browns played against Chicago in October 1886, and baseball under the new rules, which were in force during their six games in April 1887. When the numbers from both teams are combined, the statistics in the six games in 1887 were quite different from those in 1886, with significant increases in runs (1887–103 runs; 1886–56 runs), earned runs (1887–60; 1886–20), and hits (1887–173; 1886–86), and a significant decrease in strikeouts (1887–14; 1886–56). The Browns' team batting average rose from .262 in the 1886 series to .323 in the 1887 series, while Chicago's jumped from .195 in 1886 to .343 in 1887. If these numbers were predictive of the effect of the new rules, fans could look forward to an 1887 season of higher-scoring games, freer hitting, more batters putting the ball in play, fewer strikeouts as a result of the four-strike rule, and consequently more fieldwork.

After leading all batsman in the October 1886 series, O'Neill was hobbled by his injured hand and thus unable to perform at the same level in the six games played in the spring of 1887. He batted a respectable .357, which was fourth-highest on the Browns, after Gleason with .481, Latham at .440, and Welch at .423, although bases on balls accounted for six of O'Neill's ten hits, three of which were in Game Two. His three walks prompted the following comment from the *St. Louis Globe-Democrat*: "O'Neill made three base hits yesterday before he touched the ball at all, going to base the first three times on balls. Another sample of the absurdity of the new rules."⁴⁵ The rule that counted "phantom hits" (bases as balls) as base hits would come under continuous criticism throughout the 1887 season.

Tip O'Neill was confident that he had turned a corner on batting, in part because his hand was feeling stronger and in part because he got rid of the Jonah⁴⁶ that impeded his recovery: "Tip O'Neill says since the departure of his mustache he has regained full use of his thumb, and has recovered his old-time stick wielding. This is a straight tip."[47] Whether or not shaving off his mustache was really the reason for his surge to the top of the American Association batting tables, O'Neill was nonetheless razor-sharp with the bat in 1887, especially in the first phase of the season.

6
April 16 to May 24: Batting for Average

Still hurting from their 19–9 loss to Chicago on April 14, the Browns turned their attention to their first game of the season in Louisville on April 16. On this opening day, I. D. Foulon, the editor of the *Musical Review* and an avid fan of the Browns, published the "Champion's March" in the *St. Louis Globe-Democrat*.[1] It was dedicated to "President Von der Ahe" and the "St. Louis Browns, Base Ball Champions of the World," in recognition of their success in 1886 and with the hope and wishes of a repeat performance in 1887. Unfortunately, this musical boost fell flat as the Browns suffered an 8–3 loss to Louisville. The champions marched on to win games two and three, a turnaround that the fans and press hoped would continue when they returned home for the next series.

Their home opener, the first of a four-game series against Cincinnati, was on April 22. The Browns, however, disappointed their fans, losing the first two games by scores of 5–2 and 6–5. Even though the season was young, the St. Louis press found a 2–3 record ill befitting a world champion. As reporters searched for reasons for this pedestrian beginning to the season, O'Neill also came under some scrutiny.

With O'Neill ever in the spotlight, the newspapers were quick to lament any downturn in his play. Like the Browns, O'Neill had a less-than-spectacular start to the season in these first two series, batting .344 on 11 hits in 32 times at bat, modest numbers in comparison to what followed in the next month. In his defense, Joe Pritchard reminded the readers of the "From St. Louis" column in *Sporting Life* that the pre-season injury of "handsome 'Tip'" still affected his batting and fielding.[2] On batting, Pritchard chastised his fellow journalists for their impatience:

> The papers in this neighborhood are howling about O'Neill's light stick work in the first few games. These reporters don't stop to think for a moment about Jim's sore finger, but they want to see him smash the ball in the nose, and hard, too, every time he steps to the plate. The fools are not yet all dead.[3]

O'Neill's struggles in the field also drew some criticism. He made five of the team's 20 errors in the first two series, all on fly balls. As with most fielders in the 1880s, O'Neill wore a thin, fingerless glove on his left hand. The glove afforded little or no protection either against or with an injury, only slightly softening the sting of a hard-hit ball. He did not like to stay out of the lineup for any length of time, and so quite probably returned to play before his finger had completely healed. On his errors, O'Neill got to the five fly balls but was not able to hold on to the sphere on contact, no doubt aggravating his injury on each failed attempt. After his strong season at the plate and in the field in 1886, commentators and fans alike wanted more of the same in 1887 from their favorite slugger, with or without an injury.

Before these doubts and criticisms surfaced, there was excitement throughout the American Association about the new season and about the Browns' successful post-season play in 1886. In Louisville, in honor of both the first game of the season and the Browns' win of the world championship, the home club organized a parade that included: mounted police; a 14-piece marching band; separate carriages for dignitaries from both teams, one of which was for Von der Ahe, who was bedecked with a "broad cloth, high silk hat and gorgeous button-hole bouquet"; other hacks for the Browns' players "in their handsome suits and flaming red jackets"[4]; and the Hecker Supply Company's carriage to display the Wiman Trophy, the prize awarded to the Browns as the 1886 champions of the American Association. A lavish luncheon at the Louisville Hotel followed the parade. In the Browns' first visit to each of the other seven American Association cities,[5] the host team organized various pre-game festivities to pay tribute to the world champions. All shared in the bragging rights now afforded to the American Association for the Browns' victory over Chicago, the champions of the National League.

In Louisville, the celebratory mood quickly changed after the first pitch was thrown and the Browns resumed their old habits of incessant kicking, noisy coaching, tricks, and rough play. Comiskey and Robinson found fault with a number of the calls, relentlessly pressing their point until the umpire grew angry and fined them for their outbursts. To Comiskey, umpire Al Bauer shot back: "Your conduct is ungentlemanly and unlawful on the diamond. I fine you $10 and will make it a $100 if you don't dry up immediately."[6] In addition to kicking, the "hoodlum" Robinson was guilty of various tricks and rough plays in games two and three. He tried to get on base by pretending he was hit by a pitched ball, writhing in pain on the ground until Toad Ramsey, the Louisville pitcher, mockingly said: "Get up baby, you are not hurt. You can't fool people in Kentucky. Quit your crying and take your seat like a man."[7] In the ninth inning of game two, Robinson pulled his old trick of cutting third base. He rounded second, cut across the diamond, by-passing third to pick up the base path from third to home several feet down the line, and sped across the plate to score the last of three runs in the Browns' come-from-behind, 9–7 win. Busy watching the play at first base, the umpire was unaware of Robinson's infraction and therefore was unable to disallow the run.[8] On defense, Robinson also resorted to rough play, intimidating the Louisville players by punching runners as they rounded second base. Such tactics by the Browns were common occurrences, especially in close games.

Latham, the court-jester coacher of the Browns, was a crowd favorite in Louisville. The fans enjoyed his antics and gleefully joined in the repartee as Latham verbally jostled with fans and opposing players alike. However, Latham roused the crowd's ire when, after Foutz threw a "vicious curve that threatened to decapitate him" (Phil Reccius, the Louisville right fielder), Latham shouted: "That's the way, Dave—keep him ducking."[9] In the final game of the series, Latham frustrated Guy Hecker, the Louisville pitcher, by "stooping and unnaturally lowering his shoulders," a tactic that led to four called balls and no strikes. On the fifth pitch, Latham leaned over the plate with the hope of getting another called ball so he could trot to first base with a base on balls. Hecker landed the pitch squarely in Latham's ribs, sending him to the ground in pain, much to the delight of the crowd.[10] Latham got the base he wanted, but not on a base-on-balls hit.

The Browns returned to Sportsman's Park in St. Louis to begin a 28-game home stand on April 22. A difficult team to beat at home, the Browns had previously compiled a 44–11 (.800) win-loss record at home and a 35–22 record away (.614) in 1885, and a 52–18 (.743) win-loss record at home and a 41–28 record away (.594) in 1886. In 1887, the Browns had an overall win-loss record of 95–40 (.704), with a 58–15 (.795) record at home and a 37–25 record away (.597). Clearly their favorite place to play was in St. Louis at Sportsman's Park.

The configuration of Sportsman's Park historically favored the batters.[11] It was 350 feet down the left field line and 285 feet down the right field line. The distances in the deeper parts of the park were 400 feet in left-center, 460 feet in center, and 330 feet in right-center.[12] Over the years, Von der Ahe invested significantly in the improvement of the facility. By 1886, the ballpark held 12,000 fans, with covered seats available under the pavilion and uncovered bleacher seats extended down both lines. The pavilion included an enclosed press box and a private box for the officers or directors of the Browns. With the larger crowds on weekend games, some fans arrived with their own seats as they watched the game in their horse-drawn carriages in the outer reaches of the outfield. Those admitted on standing-room-only tickets scattered to wherever they could find a place to watch the game: "Squeezed, jostled, and tightly packed, covering the roof of the grandstand, sitting astride the field fences, squatting in the outfield, this vast horde

OLD SPORTSMANS PARK FIELD AT ST. LOUIS.
On these grounds Comiskey, leading the St. Louis Browns, won four American Association and two World's Championships.

The photograph represents Sportsman's Park as it appeared when looking in from center field, likely near the scoreboard over 400 feet from home plate. On weekends when there were large crowds, many fans were admitted in carriages, viewing the game from this vantage point. O'Neill often hit balls to this part of the field, sometimes on a line drive and sometimes on the fly, sending those in the carriages scrambling to get out of the way of the ball (National Baseball Hall of Fame Library, Cooperstown, New York).

good-naturedly bore the inconveniences incident upon such occasion,"[13] as long as they could be at and hopefully see the game.

Pejoratively known as the Beer and Whiskey League,[14] the American Association actively promoted the sale of alcoholic beverages at games. Sportsman's Park had a beer garden in right field. Until 1888, a ball hit into the beer garden was considered in play. The ground rule stipulated that if a fielder retrieved the ball from the beer garden, he first had to return it to the pitcher before a play could be made on the runner. Waiters roamed parts of the grandstand and bleachers selling beer, soda, cider, sarsaparilla, and cigars. For those who wanted to eat at the game, the wiener wurst stand was popular.[15] The clubhouse and players' dressing rooms were behind the beer garden. Near the clubhouse, there were, at various points in time, a handball court, a lawn-bowling green, a ten-pin bowling alley, a room for a billiard table and a pool table, and a gymnasium.

On the large bulletin board in center field, park assistants posted the runs scored in each inning as well as the scores of other games being played that day in the American Association and the National League. The reporters in the press box and those who kept the out-of-town scores on the bulletin board up to date relied on information they received via telegraph or telephone. During the game, the runs scored and sometimes the plays in the Browns' game were regularly relayed to the Browns' downtown office, newspaper buildings, and select saloons and pool rooms, which in turn posted the updated score for fans who were unable to attend the game.[16] In the case of the pool rooms, the updates were used to settle existing bets or to stimulate further betting on the game.

The American Association welcomed one and all to their games, an invitation made possible by lowering the cost of a ticket for general admission to 25 cents—in the National League it was 50 cents—while those in the covered grandstand paid 50 cents. In an effort to make baseball more accessible to a wider audience, the Association also supported Sunday games. The diverse crowds were brought together by their mutual love of baseball and their shared loyalty to the Browns:

> What a curious impression comes over one when he first studiously sizes up the crowd in attendance. The banker, merchant, clerk, hod-carrier, dude, hoodlum, schoolboy—all are there, sitting side by side, chatting affably and intimately, as though they had been friends for years, and not a chance acquaintance of but the hour previous.
>
> Another curious feature which presents itself to the observant mind, is the fact that almost everyone, from the schoolboy to the gouty old gentleman, keeps a record of the progress of the game on his scorecard, being quick to score a good play and charge an error to some careless or indifferent player. The gray-headed old gentleman will enter into an animated discussion upon the merits of this or that play with the schoolboy. The hoodlum and the dude, deadly enemies except on the ballfield, will likewise engage in friendly discussion as to the probable chance of the home team carrying off the pennant. Even the banker and his clerk will enter into argument, on equal footing, concerning some disputed play or decision. All seem to throw aside their affectation, loftiness or dignity of manner, and become bonded together as one large family, intent upon one object—the game at issue.[17]

The fans' boisterous but good-natured demeanor, however, could turn quickly to howling at opposing players or to badgering the umpire. In his account of the 1886 world championship, Bill James called the Browns' cranks the "most notorious fans in the sporting world."[18] The St. Louis fans in the 1880s were quite willing to get involved in the game:

> Visiting players had no dugouts to hide in, only a bench, exposed to the hostile fans sitting close enough to be heard, close enough to hurl, close enough to reach out and touch… Many people felt you couldn't win in St. Louis; if the fans didn't get you, they'd get to the umpire.[19]

On a questionable call, the umpire could "be subject to a perfect avalanche of abuse, vile epithets and the most cutting sarcasm as to his competency for that exacting position."[20] The umpire sometimes called on the policemen on duty to eject particularly rowdy fans, but this did not necessarily ensure that such behavior would not erupt again either during or after the game.

Chris Von der Ahe led the way in public relations by "continually inventing ways of flaunting the name of the Boss team to the public."[21] He made the Browns the most famous and infamous team of the 1880s,[22] added "color and dazzle to the game,"[23] and expanded the fan base.[24] On the latter point, he made a concerted effort to increase the attendance of ladies at ball games, admitting escorted ladies for free to Tuesday, Thursday, and Saturday games. Most ladies sat in opera chairs with cushioned seats or on benches with comfortable backs, in a special section of the covered grandstand. Smoking was not permitted in this section. Uniformed ushers showed the ladies to their seats, and a "colored" woman attendant was available to assist in the bathroom. In the first game after a road trip or in games on holidays, the ladies often received a beautiful souvenir, as occurred in the first home game of the season:

> The design represents the champions in portraiture in satin. In the center of the satin design rests President Von der Ahe's portrait, gracefully entwined amid floral embellishment. A miniature representation of the diamond and field is prettily presented, together with emblematic features of the game. The satin design is held by silk cord to a folder of terra-cotta color, and the combination forms a very pretty souvenir. On the terra-cotta folder the home games and the names of the Browns are artistically arranged. The souvenir is enveloped and it will certainly prove a splendid memento of the gala event.[25]

The ladies' attendance, some argued, improved the behavior of those men who might otherwise be rowdy or vulgar. For Von der Ahe, adding ladies to the fan base was another step towards his desire to make baseball accessible to and enjoyable for everyone.

As a left fielder in Sportsman's Park and, indeed in most ballparks, Tip faced numerous challenges. He had a lot of territory to cover and long throws to make when he caught or retrieved a hit ball. All balls hit his way were in play except those that went over the left field fence. Thus, when a ball got by him through a hit over his head or in the gap or as a result of his error,

CHRISTIAN VON DER AHE

Born: October 7, 1851 in Hille, Germany

Position: Owner

Also Known as: Der Boss President

Known For: Shrewdness; Generosity; Ostentatiousness; Promotions, Pride; Order and Discipline; Mercurial and Rash Behavior

Chris Von der Ahe, the president of the St. Louis Browns, was one of the key figures in the development of the American Association. As the owner of the Browns, Von der Ahe often referred to himself as "Der Boss President." He was a flamboyant character, at times generous and gregarious and, at other times, insistent on order and discipline, rash in his decisions, and pugnacious in his relations with players. The image in Von der Ahe's baseball card comes from a team photograph entitled: "Champions. St. Louis Browns. American Association. 1886" (The Rucker Archive).

he had to chase it down sometimes through crowds, sometimes in between carriages or as the ball bounced off horses, and sometimes into or under the seats in left field. He had to be wary each time a fan touched the ball in case the umpire called a block.[26] With the larger crowds on weekend games, he had to contend with more horse-drawn carriages and more fans who stood closer to him along the left field foul line and in back of him in the deeper parts of left and left-center field. These fans were all too ready to commend or condemn his defensive efforts, or, in between pitches, just to engage in casual talk. Regardless of the purpose—an invitation to chat, a criticism, or a pat on the back—all were distractions Tip had to ignore, to respond to, or, in some form, to accommodate. In Sportsman's Park, there was more to playing left field than simply catching fly balls or grounders.

After losing the first two games to Cincinnati in their opening series at home, the Browns won games three and four.[27] The Browns' 6–1 win in game three of the series was the start of a 15-game win streak. The final game of the series featured the debut of Charles "Silver" King,[28] a newly signed pitcher who, with strong support from the St. Louis batsmen, handily beat Cincinnati, 19–6. With the return of Nat Hudson[29] uncertain, Von der Ahe signed the rookie to be the Browns' third man in the pitching rotation. The St. Louis native was 20 years old, six feet tall, and 174 pounds. He relied on a speedy fastball that likely had considerable movement as a result of his sidearm, crossfire delivery.[30] King proved to be a great addition, leading the Browns with 32 wins in 1887, a figure which surpassed both Caruthers, who won 29 games, and Foutz, who won 25.

Following the Cincinnati series, the Cincinnati newspapers, like their compatriots in the Louisville press, had something to say about the Browns' "dirty ball." The *Cincinnati Enquirer* condemned the Browns on their "desperate and reckless" style of play and advised their own players on how they should respond:

> In their extremity the Browns have hit upon another plan to cause consternation in the ranks of opposing teams. Von der Ahe's men are nothing if not original, and they are continually creating new features. Their last, but not a new one, is being pushed to the utmost limit. They are now playing what is known as "dirty ball." By "dirty ball" is meant that the Browns have been instructed to take every chance in stealing a base or making a point, and to hesitate at nothing, no matter how desperate, if it is necessary to win a game. It means that the Browns have been told to throw any baseman down that they can conveniently reach without being detected by the umpire. It means also that they will not hesitate to block off base-runners or to trip them up, or to close in with a man so that he cannot throw a ball, or get in the way of a pitched ball so as to make first base…. The writer is not complaining of the Browns, but simply takes this occasion to caution the players how to act when playing the St. Louis champions. It is a case of "fighting the devil with fire." When you are playing the Browns, play as the Browns do. If they play dirty ball, come back at him with the same kind, and there will no reason to complain.[31]

Cincinnati did just that, returning the "fire" of the St. Louis devils in the subsequent games they had against the Browns punch for punch, blocked runner for blocked runner, knocked-over baseman for knocked-over baseman.

Although Louisville and Cincinnati vehemently condemned the St. Louis club for their aggressive style of play, they agreed with the Browns' complaint about the ineptitude of Al Bauer, the umpire in the Louisville–St. Louis series and for the first two games of the Cincinnati–St. Louis series. Von der Ahe, with the support of representatives from both the Louisville and Cincinnati clubs, filed formal charges of incompetency against Bauer. On May 1, Bauer resigned, protesting to the end that he had been "unjustly censored and treated unfairly." The Browns, although fined by Bauer for their kicking against his calls, got in the last kick as they forced Bauer's dismissal.[32] Von der Ahe and Comiskey were instrumental in the firing of two other umpires later in the season.

As Tip went, so went the Browns, or so it often seemed. Whether he spearheaded or simply emulated the success of the Browns at home, for O'Neill there was no better place to brandish his bat than at Sportsman's Park. With the exception of 1888, O'Neill's batting average in his first five years as the Browns' full-time left fielder (1885–1889) was higher at home than away.[33] In 1887, O'Neill batted .535 at home and .434 "abroad."[34] For the 17 games that followed the Cincinnati series, O'Neill went on a batting tear, wielding his "little Canadian tree"[35] to grand effect, much to the delight of the fans who gathered in the congenial confines of Sportsman's Park.

Although Tip was taller and heavier than many of the major league players in the 1880s,[36] he used a wagon tongue bat[37] that was smaller than those preferred by most other batsmen.[38] He endured the teasing he received about his "little hickory,"[39] presumably because he intuitively understood, much ahead of his time, the importance of bat speed, something he could more effectively control and accelerate with a smaller bat. In contrast to the many batters who were like "nervous jacks-in-the-box who play a tattoo on the plate and prance all around the base while waiting for the ball,"[40] Tip calmly settled in before each pitch with an air of disinterest in what was about to be hurled his way:

> The Champion slugger of the world—Tip O'Neill's handsomely earned baseball title, fits him with becoming grace. Tip is a modest hitter. You wouldn't think he could touch a balloon, as he stands at the plate the personification of indifference, as though he didn't care whether school kept or not. But, ye gods: Appearances are deceitful. Tip spares no pain to send his terrific drives in every conceivable direction.[41]

Tip was an exemplar of the "erect batter," a term used to describe a hitter who stood "straight, with his feet close together,"[42] his bat resting on his shoulder, awaiting the delivery of the pitch. Once the ball left the pitcher's hand, in the split-second he had before it crossed the plate, Tip determined if it was a pitch at which he wanted to strike. If so, he readied his bat to swing, and then, with precise timing, unleashed his wagon tongue. In terms of footwork and body shifts, "[Tip] moves the left [foot] back and swings his body around so as to face third base. In this way, he gets a terrific swing to his bat, and he probably hits the ball harder than any man in the profession."[43] With this coil-like turn, Tip used his left leg as an axis, with his bat gaining speed and power based on the torque created by the rotation around the leg.

The fans grew to expect the frequent cracks that resonated from Tip's bat. He was a line-drive hitter who most times made solid contact. Even his outs made news, with credit going to the fielder who dared to snare one of Tip's rockets. And when a fair or sacrifice hit was needed, Tip was one of the best batsman to advance the runner:

> O'Neill is considered a natural batsman. He wields his bat gracefully as well as effectively. No matter how swift or deceptive the pitching, he always scores his share of clean hits. At critical points in a game, when a clean, hard hit means a victory, O'Neill is invariably the right man in the right place.[44]

With his steely glare, Tip defied pitchers to put their pitch by him. Neither fastball nor curve ball deterred Tip in his cause: "O'Neill was absolutely fearless of speed. Possibly not a pitcher lived who could force him away from the plate. All of them tried it but after a while they gave it up."[45] He rarely chased bad balls or was fooled by deceptive deliveries.[46]

With his tiny bat in hand, his unique stance and swing well-defined, and his hitting eye alert and focused, Tip embarked on a historic "week,"[47] rising to a level of slugging hitherto unseen at Sportsman's Park.

In an extraordinary baseball week—covering seven games between April 27 and May 7, four games against Cleveland and the first three games of the four-game Louisville series—O'Neill had 27 hits in 36 times at bat for a .750 average. Fourteen of his 27 hits went for extra bases: seven doubles, three triples, and four home runs. Thus, in this remarkable seven-day outburst, O'Neill hit not only for average but also for power.[48] He also hit for the cycle twice, in a six-hit performance on April 30 as part of the Browns' 28–11 win over Cleveland, and again on May 7, with a five-hit performance in the Browns' 12–7 win over Louisville.[49]

O'Neill's historic week began at the expense of the newest member of the American Association. The Cleveland club replaced Pittsburgh, which had finished second in the Association in the previous season but had chosen to move to the National League in 1887.[50] Unfortunately, Cleveland did not prove to be a worthy successor, finishing in last place in the Association with a 39–92 win-loss record. The Browns were not especially welcoming to Cleveland, beating the "Babes" in 18 of the 19 games they played in 1887. The die was cast in this first series. While two of the games were reasonably close—13–11 and 14–13 wins in games two and four respectively—the Browns spanked Cleveland 19–3 in game one and 28–11 in game three. The 28 runs in game three were both the most runs scored by the Browns and the most runs allowed by Cleveland all season.[51] O'Neill pummeled Cleveland pitchers over the four games, hammering out 17 hits including five doubles, two triples, and two home runs. In the last two games (April 30 and May 1), O'Neill got on base in ten consecutive times at bat, beginning with a base on balls and followed by nine fair hits. The *Cleveland Plain Dealer* proclaimed: "His work this season has been extraordinary, and should he keep it up he will stand at the head of the batting list, not only of the association but also ahead of the crack hitters of the league."[52]

O'Neill continued his historic week in the first three games of the Browns' four-game sweep of Louisville (May 4–8). Although he had a single and double in the Browns' rain-shortened, six-inning, 4–1 win in game one, he made two errors in judgment on the base paths. O'Neill was on third base when Comiskey, who was on first, initiated a delayed

In this cigarette card from the Old Judge series (N172), O'Neill is shown swinging at a pitch. The photograph illustrates how he choked up on the bat and used a split-hand grip. His feet are relatively close together, and his eyes are fixed on the ball. The front foot is turned out, which indicates that O'Neill is in the midst of twisting his body, generating bat speed as he uncoils his swing (The Jefferson R. Burdick Collection, Gift of Jefferson R. Burdick, The Metropolitan Museum of Art, New York, NY, USA. Image Source: Art Resource, NY, ART 491396).

double steal. Tip took off for home too late and only scored because the catcher dropped the ball. In a second running gaffe, after he hit a ground ball to the first baseman, in his disgust at making such a feeble hit, O'Neill sauntered to the players' bench, failing to notice that the first baseman had not stepped on first base but instead threw the ball to second. O'Neill belatedly scurried to first ahead of the return throw, in so doing escaping the rebuke that Comiskey was about to direct at him for his inattentive play. The umpire had not seen O'Neill's failure to run and so did not call him out, as he should, much to the protest of the Louisville players.[53]

In comparison to the three wins in which the Browns came from behind to beat Louisville by scores of 4–1 in game one, 12–7 in game three, and 6–4 in game four, the Browns' 10–3 win in game two was never in doubt. O'Neill made amends for his shaky base running in game one. The *St. Louis Republican* included O'Neill as an example of the "fleet-footed, head-sliding feats accomplished by the champions."[54] On a routine ground ball that the third baseman threw to first base for the out, Gleason scored from third while O'Neill hustled to score from second base. At the plate, O'Neill had three hits in five times at bat, one a home run that he slammed high over the left-center field fence, some 400 feet from the plate, a smash that was "probably the longest hit ever made on the grounds."[55] The *St. Louis Republican* lavished its praise on Tip's towering blast:

> Ramsey was not batted as bad as the score indicates as a good many of the Browns' hits were of the lucky order. Such was not the case however, with O'Neill's drive in the ninth. Perhaps it might be called lucky too—lucky that it didn't break a window in the house on the other side of Spring Avenue.... The hit was not merely a long one but it was high, so high that shorted-sighted spectators couldn't keep track of it, and the ball came down with frost on it.[56]

On May 7, in the third game of the series, O'Neill hit a second home run in as many days over the same fence, but this time on a line drive. This four-bagger was part of a five-hit game in which he also made a base on balls, single, double, and triple to complete his second cycle in five games. This Louisville-based cycle was also part of an 11-times on-base streak that began on May 4 in his last plate appearance in game one, continued on May 6 through game two, and ended on May 7 after his last time at bat in game three. The 11 times at bat started with two hits followed by a base on an error, and concluded with a string of eight hits in a row (seven fair hits plus a base on balls).[57] Game three ended O'Neill's extraordinary week. He had two other impressive seven-game batting exhibitions, one in late August and the other in early September, but these did not match the batting average, long hits, and on-base streaks of this historic run against Cleveland and Louisville.

The bubble burst in the final game of the Louisville series when O'Neill went hitless in five times to the plate, a disappointment for the small boys in attendance. They nonetheless had something to cheer about in the third inning when he chased a ball into the left field benches and threw it back to the infield to hold John Kerins, the Louisville catcher, to a triple. The thrill of seeing O'Neill unleash a hard throw from the outfield, however, was tainted by the fact that a fan, against the rules, had given O'Neill the ball when he neared the benches. Had the umpire seen that a fan handled the ball, he would have declared a block, which, according to the playing rules, would require O'Neill to return the ball to the pitcher in his box before the Browns could put the ball in play. In this game, no infraction was called by the umpire on the play at third, and no protest was made by Louisville.[58] O'Neill's strong throw prevented a run, momentarily at least, for Kerins scored from third on the next play.[59]

After a four-game sweep of Baltimore (May 10–14), the Browns travelled to Philadelphia for a four-game series (May 16–19), confident that, in game one, they would extend their winning streak to 15 games in a row. The Browns were up to the task, defeating Philadelphia, 7–2. However, in game two, the streak came to an end as Philadelphia defeated St. Louis in ten innings, 4–3.

Down 4–3 after seven innings of the third game, the Browns were in a closer battle than their eventual winning score of 12–4 suggested. Undaunted, they rallied with three runs in the eighth inning to take the lead, 6–4, and secured the victory with six more runs in the ninth. As was often the case in close contests, the Browns relied on their aggressive style to gain some advantage in the play. For example, despite a new rule that prevented coachers from directing any comments to the pitcher or any opposing player, in the eighth inning, as the Browns began their comeback, the coachers and many of the players yelled insults and taunts at Al Atkinson [Atkisson], the Philadelphia pitcher, with the hope of throwing him off his game. Apparently, it worked, as evidenced by the nine runs he allowed in the last two innings. After the game, the Philadelphia manager expressed his anger at the Browns' coaching: "Atkisson became rattled in the eighth inning through the non-enforcement of the coaching rules, the Browns all getting around the diamond shouting until Atkisson lost his head."[60] Taking advantage of a flustered Philadelphia club, in the ninth inning Robinson successfully executed a hidden ball trick. Jocko Milligan reached first base on a single to center field. When the ball came in to Robinson, he kept it instead of relaying it to the pitcher. When Jack Milligan, the Philadelphia first baseman, took a lead off first base, Robinson threw the ball to Comiskey, who tagged Milligan for the out.[61] Such antics and tactics, when combined with their daring running and timely hits, gave the Browns the edge that they needed to take control of the game in the late innings.

Prior to the final game of the series, which the Browns won 8–4, O'Neill promised to hit the hat sign on the top of the fence in left-center field in Sportsman's Park. In the first three weeks of the season, he had already had numerous long hits to left field, some that soared over the fence and some line-drive shots that violently caromed off the seats or the fence. Two of these blasts had come close to the hat sign, which read: "Hit Me for $5." In the current series with Philadelphia, he had pounded out two triples, one into the left field seats in game one as part of the Browns' 7–2 win and the other out to the bulletin board in center field as part of their 12–4 win in game three. Cocksure of his ability to achieve this tip of the hat, O'Neill hit two booming doubles in game four; one bounded towards the left field seats, and the second glanced off the bulletin board, but alas none tickled the hat sign. He had boldly called his shot but missed his mark. Many years later, Von der Ahe recalled that O'Neill was the only player who "ever earned the V."[62]

At the plate in the Philadelphia series, O'Neill had again hit well despite going hitless in game two. Amidst this rare lapse with the stick, Tip nonetheless "played a perfect game in the field,"[63] pulling down six fly balls. His game was clearly rounding into form: "Tip O'Neill is not only hitting the ball with unprecedented success, but he is fielding better than ever. Tip is playing in the best form of his career."[64]

On May 20, the Browns opened their four-game series against Brooklyn (May 20–24). This first game turned out to be the last that O'Neill played until June 6. In his first time at bat, O'Neill was hit on the right wrist by a pitched ball. The "lame-wristed slugger"[65] valiantly played on, contributing two singles and a triple to the Browns' 15–9 win. By the seventh inning, however, the pain in his wrist was too great to continue, and he was replaced by Lou Sylvester. The Browns won the series, three games to one. O'Neill missed 12 games in a row. The St. Louis newspapers were surprised by the length of time it took him to recover from a sore wrist. In a conversation with Pritchard, the St. Louis correspondent for *Sporting Life*, Tip commented on the discoloration of his wrist: "That's genuine black and blue, there's no funny business about that bruise. There's no arnica-iodine trick about that sore. Oh, no."[66] He could not play through this injury.

The May 20 game marked the end of the first phase of O'Neill's season. At this juncture, the Browns had a 20–4 record. By the end of this series with Brooklyn, their record improved to 22–5 to extend their hold on to first place, six games ahead of second-place Baltimore. O'Neill led the Association and the Browns with an average of .560. Foutz was second on the team at .479, followed by Gleason at .413, Comiskey at .412, and Latham at .403.[67]

Under the new rules, as predicted and intended, there was a significant increase in batting across the Association. In 1886, the Browns led all clubs with a team average of .273, while only seven Association batters hit .300 or better, including Caruthers and O'Neill. By May 16, 1887, the Browns once again were leading the Association in batting, but this time with a whopping average of .398. There were now 44 players in the Association with averages of .300 or higher, 20 of whom were hitting .400 or higher.[68] O'Neill stood at the head of a long list of batters who were enjoying the best start of a season they ever had.

Although O'Neill ended his first 24 games as he began the season, with a sore hand, in between these injuries, he threw down the gauntlet to batsmen near and far with his unprecedented triumphs against Association pitchers. The table below summarizes O'Neill's extraordinary batting record in his first 24 games. In each of his last five series—four four-game series against Cleveland, Louisville, Baltimore, and Philadelphia, and a fifth series cut short by injury to only one game against Brooklyn—he had hit better than .500. He won the battle against the opposing pitchers, going 17-for-23 or .739 against Cleveland hurlers, 10-for-18 or .556 against the Louisville rotation, 13-for-20 or .650 against the Baltimore staff, 11-for-19 or .579 against the Philadelphia aces, and 3-for-4 or .750 against the lone Brooklyn pitcher he faced. In a sport where the pitchers were the ones who usually got the batters out seven or eight times out of ten times at bat, O'Neill was changing the odds, at least in these five series, by getting a hit five or six times every ten times to the plate. Across the season, O'Neill batted .500 or better in 20 of the 41 series in which he played, accumulating a batting average of .628 on 182 hits in 290 times at bat in those series. O'Neill was the victor in the pitcher-batter duals more than six times out of every ten times he faced American Association hurlers.

Games	AB	R	H	BB	1B	2B	3B	HR	AVG	SB
24	116	41	65	12	27	15	6	5	.560	9

In terms of run-making, in addition to the 41 runs he scored, he had 31 runs batted in, and produced 67 runs (runs produced = R + RBI − HR).[69] Of these runs scored or batted in, 14 had a significant impact on the outcome of the game, ten of which either tied the game or put the Browns into the lead, and four of which were the winning run.[70] In 19 of the 24 games, he had two or more hits, with five or more hits in three games and five four-hit games. He went hitless in only two games. While the newspapers commented most on his groundbreaking .500-plus average, his slugging record was equally impressive. Twenty-six of his 53 fair hits were for extra bases. As O'Neill's batting average climbed, so did his number of long hits. For O'Neill, hitting for average included an increase in both the number of times he batted safely and the number of times he slugged the ball for a double, triple, or home run. In an era when the prevailing view was still critical of slugging, Tip demonstrated that a slugger could also hit for average, bat scientifically, and "play for the side."[71]

7

Two Cycles

As evident in the first phase of the season, O'Neill was at his batting best when he had multi-hit games that included at least one long hit. Multi-hit games favorably influenced his batting average, while a combination of one-base hits (single or base on balls) and long hits (doubles, triples, home runs) increased his total bases.[1] O'Neill's historic week, the seven games between April 27 and May 7, illustrated how these two batting feats contributed to the Browns' seven wins. In four of the seven games, O'Neill had four or more hits, at least two of which were long hits. His 27 hits in 36 times at bat (.750) improved his batting average from .344 to .521. The 13 one-base hits (ten singles plus three bases on balls), seven doubles, three triples, and four home runs amounted to 52 total bases. The concentration of hits and bases were directly related to O'Neill's overall run production. Across the seven games, Tip scored or drove in 35 of the 100 runs scored by the Browns in these seven games.

Hitting for the cycle was a single-game manifestation of O'Neill at his best—at least one single, one double, one triple, and one home run. Four or more hits positively affected his batting average, and the required distribution of hits assured him of ten total bases or more. O'Neill's two cycles also generated timely hits, extra bases, and significant runs.

In the history of the game, hitting for the cycle is a relatively rare feat. Between 1876 and 2016, only 312 players have hit a single, double, triple, and home run in the same game. Four players have hit three cycles in their careers: John Reilly (1883—two cycles, 1890), Babe Herman (1931—two cycles, 1933), Bob Meusel (1921, 1922, 1928), and Adrian Beltre (2008, 2012, 2015) and 27 players have hit two cycles in their careers, one of whom was O'Neill. Only four players ever hit two cycles in the same season: Reilly (1883), O'Neill (1887), Herman (1931), and Aaron Hill (2012). Reilly and O'Neill share the record for the fastest two cycles, both doing so in a five-game span. In 1887, there were five cycles, four in the American Association, two by O'Neill, one each by Bid McPhee and Dave Orr, and one in the National League by Fred Carroll.[2]

As prominent as cycles are in today's baseball lore and records, O'Neill never knew what a cycle was. Furthermore, most researchers and baseball enthusiasts for more than a century after the fact did not know that O'Neill hit for the cycle in 1887, not just once but twice. O'Neill was neither aware that he was on track to hit for the cycle nor conscious of those hits he still needed. O'Neill was simply building up as many hits and bases as he could to help the Browns win in each of these two games.

O'Neill first hit for the cycle in the Browns' 28–11 win against Cleveland on April 30 and then again in their 12–7 win against Louisville on May 7. As part of the lopsided victory over Cleveland, Tip pounded out six hits in seven times at bat, including a base on balls, a single, and four long hits—a double, a triple, and two home runs. His six-hit performance has also been recently recognized as a "quasi-cycle," a term coined by Herm Krabbenhoft to indicate when a player has "four long hits in a game with at least one double, at least one triple, and at least one homer." Krabbenhoft identified 87 players who hit quasi-cycles between 1876 and 2016. O'Neill is one of the 31 players who also hit a single and thus had both a cycle and a quasi-cycle in the same game.[3]

Krabbenhoft argues that the quasi-cycle is "technically better" than the cycle because the greater number of long hits increases the chances of scoring runs.[4] O'Neill's quasi-cycle on April 30 illustrates Krabbenhoft's claim about run production. For his quasi-cycle, Tip hit four long hits between the fifth and eighth innings. In the Browns' nine-run fifth inning, he drove in two runs on a home run and one on a triple. In the eight-run sixth inning, he hit a second home run, knocking in three runs. He also had a double, likely in the eighth inning, but did not score or drive in a run. With these four long hits, O'Neill completed his quasi-cycle, compiling 13 total bases and scoring or driving in six of the 17 runs tallied by the Browns. For his cycle, O'Neill scored a run on his single in the fourth inning, produced no runs on his double in the eighth inning, drove in a run on his triple in the fifth inning, and drove in three runs on his home run in the sixth inning. O'Neill completed his cycle, compiling ten total bases and scoring or driving in five of the 19 runs by the Browns. O'Neill reached more bases and produced more runs in the four long hits for his quasi-cycle than he did in the four hits for the cycle. In the six innings in which he had a turn at bat, O'Neill's combined cycle-quasi-cycle generated 15 total bases and contributed to eight of the 24 runs scored by the Browns in these innings.

His cycle on May 7 had an even greater impact on the outcome of the game. Unlike his first cycle, when the Browns walloped Cleveland by a score of 28–11, O'Neill's second cycle occurred in a match where the Browns, after trailing Louisville, 5–2, exploded for seven runs in the seventh inning and went on to a 12–7 win. The following summary of the five innings in which O'Neill was at bat documents how important Tip's four runs scored and four runs batted in were to the outcome of this game. The Browns scored their 12 runs in four of these innings.

In the first inning, Latham led off with a double, moved to third on Gleason's sacrifice, and scored on O'Neill's triple into the left field seats. O'Neill scored the Browns' second run when the left fielder dropped a fly ball hit by Comiskey. With two out in the third inning, O'Neill went to first on a base on balls and then was forced out at second base on Comiskey's ground ball to the third baseman. After three innings, the Browns led, 2–1.

Louisville scored four runs in the fourth inning to take a 5–2 lead. The Browns got two runs back in the fifth inning. With one out, Gleason reached second on an error by Pete Browning, the Louisville center fielder. Gleason went to third on O'Neill's infield hit to the shortstop and scored on Comiskey's groundout, also to shortstop Bill White, with O'Neill advancing to second on the play. On Foutz's single to left field, O'Neill crossed the plate with the Browns' fourth run, closing the gap to 5–4.

Following a scoreless sixth inning by both teams, the Browns erupted for seven runs in the seventh inning. Bushong reached first on an error by White, took second on a passed ball, and slipped to third as Latham's infield hit just eluded the pitcher. Latham stole second and scooted to third on Gleason's single to center field as Bushong scored to tie the game at five runs apiece. O'Neill hit a home run, driving in three runs. Ahead 8–5, the Browns added three more runs, the first on a single and a stolen base by Comiskey, and a single by Foutz that sent Comiskey home with the Browns' ninth run. Welch singled to left field, advancing Foutz, who in turn was forced out at third on Robinson's grounder to the shortstop. With Robinson on first on a fielder's choice, Bushong hit safely to center. Welch scored the tenth run as he hustled to beat the center fielder's desperate attempt to throw him out at the plate. With no play at home on Welch, the catcher turned and fired to second base with the hope of nailing Robinson as he rounded second base. The throw was wide of the base, and Robinson sped home to give the Browns an 11–5 advantage.

O'Neill doubled in the eighth inning and scored the 12th and final run two batters later on Foutz's fourth hit of the day, a double to right field. Louisville got two runs back in the ninth to close out the game, falling short in its comeback. The victory was the Browns' third win over Louisville in as many games.

In the four innings that constituted his cycle—single in the fifth, double in the eighth, triple in the first, and home run in the seventh—O'Neill was a key player in seven of the 12 runs scored by the Browns in these innings, scoring four himself and driving in four others.[5] His home run was particularly critical to the Browns' victory, giving the team a decisive lead, with the run he scored on his four-bagger proving to be the winner. The win itself was a pivotal moment for the team, because with this victory, the Browns took over first place in the American Association, a position they never relinquished for the rest of the season.

On O'Neill's critical seventh-inning strike, the *St. Louis Republican* paused long enough to differentiate that day's home run from his soaring blast on the day before: "The hit differed from O'Neill's drive over the same fence in the previous game, in that it was a line fly, and went so fast that it probably would not have stopped had it not struck the fence."[6] Although the home run in the Browns' 12–7 victory on May 7 was not heralded with the same awe as the one he hit the previous day, it was remarkable in its own right because the ball that he hit out of the park was in such bad condition. As the *St. Louis Republican* explained, the Louisville club was implicated in a ball-switching trick:

> One feature of the game that is worthy of mention is that the Browns did nearly all of their batting off an old ball. After the Browns had batted in the fourth inning, one of the Louisvilles managed to secrete one of the balls which was in play, in the hope that a new ball would be called into requisition that inning. It so happened that the visitors did some good batting in this inning, and presently, when a high foul was knocked over the grandstand, Valentine [umpire] discovered the absence of the other ball but refused to let the Louisvilles make their point and waited for the old ball to come back before play was resumed. He then compelled the teams to use the same ball all the remainder of the game, not even varying the rule when O'Neill would knock the balls over the left field fence.[7]

As the game progressed, O'Neill batted a ball that became softer and more damaged for each of the remaining three times that he went to bat. In effect, O'Neill propelled a dead ball on a line and for a distance well over 350 feet, a remarkable feat of bat speed and power, and certainly equal in stature to his more celebrated home run in the May 6 game.

In addition to his cycle-quasi-cycle on April 30, Tip came close to hitting for the cycle in seven other games in the 1887 season. The following table summarizes these "near-cycle" games:

Date	Games Home (H) or Away (A)	Hits–At-Bats	Singles–Bases on Balls	Long Hits Doubles (D)–Triples (T)–Home Runs (HR)	Total Bases	Runs	Runs Batted In	Missing
April 28	Beat CLE 13–11 (H)	4–5	1–1	D–T	7	3	1	HR
August 9	Beat CLE 11–8 (H)	5–5	2–1	D–T	8	4	1	HR
August 25	Beat BAL 14–8 (H)	3–5	1–0	D–T	6	2	1	HR
August 30	Beat BRO 7–4 (H)	4–5	1–0	D–2T	9	3	1	HR
September 2	Beat NY 12–4 (A)	5–5	3–0	D–T	8	2	4	HR
October 4	Beat LOU 13–9 (A)	3–5	1–0	D–T	6	3	0	HR
October 6	Beat LOU 11–5 (H)	5–5	2–1	T–HR	10	2	2	D
Totals	7 Wins—0	29–35	11–3	6D–8T–1HR	54	19	10	1D–6HR

BAL–Baltimore; BRO–Brooklyn; CLE–Cleveland; LOU–Louisville; NY– New York

In all of the near-cycle games except the one on October 6, O'Neill missed the cycle by failing to hit a home run. But like his cycles and quasi-cycle, these near-cycle games included at least two hits that went for extra-bases. The game on August 30 was a near cycle and one long-hit shy of a quasi-cycle. Across the seven games, O'Neill went 29-for-35 for a batting average of .829. He also had 15 (54 percent) of the Browns' 28 long hits. In each game, he led the team in total bases. O'Neill contributed to 28 (or 35 percent) of the 81 runs scored by the Browns. The Browns won all seven games to add further support to the belief that "as Tip goes, so go the Browns." As illustrated in his two cycles (one of which was a quasi-cycle) and seven near-cycles, more times than not O'Neill had his best games when he belted out two or more long hits, which often generated runs that had an impact on the outcome of the game.

With O'Neill unable to play for 12 games following his injury in the May 20 game against Brooklyn, the Browns found out that they could continue their winning ways without him in the lineup. June and July, however, proved to be less productive months for the Browns and for O'Neill. He had to wait until August to regain the form that he displayed in May. As he had done in the first phase of the season, in the fourth phase (August 12 to September 8), O'Neill combined batting for average and batting for power to lead the Browns to another offensive burst.

8

May 25 to July 11: Injury and Struggle

As in the first phase of the 1887 season, O'Neill began and ended the May 25–to–July 11 segment injured. O'Neill missed 12 games, the last three games against Brooklyn (May 21–24) in the previous period and the first nine games in this second phase.[1] He returned to active duty on June 6. Like many nineteenth century players, he came back before he had fully recovered, with the result that his lingering sore wrist hampered his performance for a few games. The injury, however, provided O'Neill with an opportunity to appear in an advertisement for Merrell's Penetrating Oil, extolling the virtues of this product during his recuperation. The advertisement included a sketch of O'Neill and read as follows:

> I was hit by a pitched ball on the wrist on Friday, May 20, by Terry, the Brooklyn pitcher. The pain was simply intense, and I was compelled to lay off for some time. MERRELL'S PENETRATING OIL afforded me great relief, and I am convinced that it is all that is claimed for it. J. E. O'NEILL.[2]

Near the end of this second phase in his season, in the first game of the Browns' doubleheader against New York on July 4, O'Neill injured a finger while catching a fly ball. While O'Neill only missed two games, when he returned to play on July 8, his injured finger continued to bother him during the next two series, first against Baltimore (July 8–11) and then against Brooklyn (July 12–14). O'Neill found it difficult to grip the bat and to pull down hard-hit balls in left field, and, as a result, played cautiously, forever worried about aggravating his injured hand.

Despite O'Neill's absence from the lineup, the Browns initially fared quite well, reeling off an 11–1 record, which included ten wins in a row (May 24 to June 4). On O'Neill's return on June 6, the Browns' record stood at 31 wins and five losses, which put them nine games ahead of second-place Baltimore. However, in the 30 games between June 6 and July 11, 21 of which were on the road, as Tip struggled, so struggled the Browns. Once outside the friendly confines of Sportsman's Park, the team stumbled to ten wins, ten losses, and one tie, a respectable road record to be sure,[3] but one that left the Browns with a 25–13 record (.658) in this period and an overall 47–18 record (.723), good enough for a 6 1/2-game lead over second-place Baltimore. After starting the season with 31 wins in their first 36 games (.861), the Browns, though still the leading club in the Association, no longer seemed invincible. They were on the wrong end of three high-scoring road games, losing 16–8 to Philadelphia on June 13, 15–12 to Baltimore on June 14, and 16–4 to Louisville on July 1.[4] They won seven of 11 series (three at home, four on the road), tied two (both on the road), and lost two (both on the road). As the Browns experienced more losses than in the early weeks of the season and got deeper into their first extended road trip, their aggressive style of play became more pronounced, more desperate, and dirtier, which brought to the team even greater scrutiny and attack, especially from the managers on other Association teams and the newspaper reporters in the Association cities which the Browns visited.

O'Neill played in 28 of the 39 scheduled games in this phase.[5] He had 53 hits in 125 times at bat for a .424 batting average, a drop of 126 points from the .560 batting average he recorded in the first phase in the season (April 16 to May 24). While O'Neill started the year hitting over .500 in five of the first seven series, in this second phase he managed to hit .500 or better in only two of the nine series. The most telling difference in this period was his lack of power at the plate, in 28 games hitting only seven doubles, no triples, and one "scratch-hit" home run.[6] By comparison, in the seven games of his historic week between April 27 and May 7, in 36 times at bat, he hit seven doubles, three triples, and four home runs. Without the long ball, O'Neill was still able to come up with timely hits, ones that either advanced runners or put himself in a position to score a significant run. Tip's impact on the base path was a different story.

Following a somewhat cautious year on the base paths in 1886,[7] O'Neill was determined to be a bolder and smarter base runner in 1887. He was better than anyone else on the team in his ability to fulfill the first obligation of a batsman, namely, to become a base runner. It was what he did or did not do when he got on base that was the problem, though in 1887, there were signs that O'Neill might be putting some of these past base-running issues behind him. He increased his stolen base total to 33, a significant improvement over his inconsequential record of nine stolen bases in 1886. More than half of O'Neill's stolen bases were on the pitcher, mostly going from first to second and always done without sliding, a skill he did not developed until 1888.[8] It took speed, precise timing, fearlessness, and considerable luck to steal every base standing up, but incredibly, in those cases in 1887 when he was successful in his attempt to steal a base, he did so without sliding. He also had some steals through hustling for an extra base on a hit, such as when he scored from second base on a single.

Remarkably, after a number of failed attempts at a delayed double steal in 1885 and 1886,[9] O'Neill finally got the hang of this strategy in 1887. The Browns successfully executed this delayed double steal at least six times during the 1887 season when O'Neill was the runner on third base. Within a span of two weeks in August, he stole home as part of three delayed double steals.[10] He was less dependable in other base-running situations.

Although O'Neill stole second around 15–20 times, took an extra base on a hit by a teammate at least 4–6 times, and stole home about 6–8 times as part of a delayed double steal, he had almost as many occasions when he was unsuccessful on the base path, often due to an error in judgment or a lapse in concentration.[11] O'Neill was caught stealing, napping, or trying for an extra base roughly 18–25 times. Aware of O'Neill's foibles on the base path, opposing teams frequently tried to catch him as he led off from the base (napping). Pop Corkhill, a Cincinnati outfielder, had Tip's number, throwing him out three times in 1887 as he tried for an extra base, twice when he sought to stretch a double into a triple,[12] and once when he tried to go from first to third after Corkhill muffed a fly ball by Caruthers.[13] Other times, O'Neill simply misread the situation. In a 10–8 loss to Philadelphia late in the season, he was on second when Caruthers hit a line drive towards the third baseman, who caught the ball at his bootstraps. Off at the crack of the bat, O'Neill froze in his tracks once he saw the catch made. The third baseman tagged Tip out for the unassisted double play.[14]

While the above miscues were sometimes excused if not accepted as part of what could happen in the Browns' daring, take-every-chance style of play, there was no room for a lack of hustle. As was the case with some of his lumbering efforts at chasing down fly balls, O'Neill could also be slow on the base path. For example, in a game against Baltimore in which St. Louis ultimately won, 8–1, in the fifth inning with the Browns ahead 4–1, O'Neill was on third base with two out when Caruthers hit a ground ball to the third baseman. Likely anticipating that Caruthers would be thrown out at first, O'Neill slowly trotted home. Caruthers beat the throw at first for an infield hit, but O'Neill was thrown out before he could touch the plate.[15] The *St. Louis Post-Dispatch* was especially upset by Tip's misjudgment:

> In the fifth inning O'Neill lost a golden opportunity to score on Caruthers' hit, thinking the batsman was out at first. The tall fielder walked in, giving the opposition time to return the ball to the plate. O'Neill, it seems, will never learn how to run from third base with anything that smacks of judgment.[16]

Another illustration of O'Neill's occasional lack of hustle occurred on June 19 as part of the one-sided, 23–4 win against Cincinnati. On a solidly struck single to right field, O'Neill casually tossed his bat to the side and ran at less than full speed to first base, confident that he would get to the base easily, make the turn, and ready himself to go to second if the throw from the outfield went awry. Hugh Nicol and John Reilly, two of O'Neill's former teammates,[17] were respectively quick to the ball and to the base, with Nicol throwing out Tip at first before he recognized that they were making a play on him. As O'Neill made a desperate but late dash to step on the bag ahead of the throw, he spiked Reilly, with the result that Tip and Reilly had a little wrestling match amidst an exchange of angry words.[18] For Chris Von der Ahe, such inconsistent effort by O'Neill on the base paths was tantamount to shirking his duties and thus deserved close attention if not sanction by Der Boss President.[19]

At times, O'Neill's failure to run hard or at all irked his captain and teammates. On June 29, in a game in which the Browns eventually defeated Louisville, 16–12, St. Louis was losing, 10–6, after six innings. The Browns roared back in the seventh inning, scoring nine runs to secure the victory. O'Neill came to bat twice in the inning. In his first at-bat, with Latham at third and Gleason at first and nobody out, Tip flied out to left field. Latham tagged up and scampered home with the Browns' first run. The Browns scored another eight runs without recording an out. O'Neill came up for as second time with Gleason on second. He hit the ball sharply to Bill White, the Louisville shortstop, who tagged Gleason for the second out and threw to first for the third out. Inexplicably, O'Neill had not run to first, which caused Comiskey to lecture his slugger on this transgression.

Comiskey generally avoided public admonishments of his players, but when confronted by such an obvious breach of the Browns' hustling style of play, he dressed down O'Neill immediately following his base-running gaffe. The *St. Louis Post-Dispatch* added its public reprimand: "O'Neill has a very bad habit of not running when he hits short, and in yesterday's game he saw the bad results of this carelessness. O'Neill is a good batter and all that, but he should take more interest in the game and sacrifice a little personal comfort to saving his life. By doing this he will make himself more popular."[20] No doubt in the post-game team meeting in the clubhouse, O'Neill came under further fire from his teammates.[21] The Browns could be rough on their own, not just on the opposition.

In 1887, O'Neill clearly made a greater contribution to the Browns' running game than he had in previous seasons. His 33 stolen bases, more than half of which were to second base, were the highest total of his ten-year career. He also became a fairly dependable partner in the delayed double steal, one of the Browns' favorite base-running strategies. That said, his many gaffes and lapses in base running—caught stealing second base, thrown out trying for an extra base, caught napping, or failing to hustle to first base or between bases—overshadowed the modest progress he made in stealing second base and executing the delayed double steal. Once on base, Tip was still less adept, less savvy, and less daring than most of his teammates. Fortunately, with such skilled base runners as Latham, Comiskey, Robinson, Welch, and Caruthers, the Browns did not have to rely on O'Neill's base-running abilities.

Between May 30 and July 3, the Browns went on their first extended road trip of the season for 23 games in a row, playing at Brooklyn, New York, Philadelphia, Baltimore, Cincinnati, and Cleveland. They returned briefly to St. Louis for a series against Louisville, followed by a series in Louisville and then back home on July 4 to begin a 12-game home stand. Although they managed to come away with a winning record on the road, with 15 wins, ten losses, and one tie game, the Browns had a rougher time of it. When their opponents were on their home turf, in front of their own boisterous fans and with the support of the local press, they seemed to battle harder against the Browns. Embroiled in more hard-fought and closer-scoring games, the Browns responded with an even rougher brand of their usual aggressive style of play.

Unflinching in their desire to win, the Browns demonstrated grit, determination, and a toughness to withstand whatever was thrown their way. While the Browns certainly suffered through adversity and injury, the other Association teams were more likely to argue that it was their players who were the victims of kicks, knockdowns, punches, and injuries inflicted by the Browns, rather than the other way around. In the games on the road during this period, the Browns, especially Latham, Robinson, and Welch, were more aggressive and rougher than at any other time in the season.

Latham's penchant for incessant chatter, his impish delight in pranks and practical jokes, and his relentless efforts to distract, rattle, or confuse the opposition were his stock-in-trade as a coacher and a player. He was exuberant in victory. On May 30, at the end of the first game of a doubleheader in Brooklyn, Comiskey won the game with a home run in the tenth inning. Prior to this walk-off home run, Latham shouted to Comiskey: "Now cap, we win the game right here—lift her for a home run."[22] As the ball soared over the fence, Latham danced the hornpipe and did somersaults to celebrate the dramatic win.[23] As with his exhortation to Comiskey to hit a home run, Latham also cheered on his teammates: "Only an old-time New York drive to the fence," "Eat 'em up, Jim," "Mister Caruthers, make a single and bring in those two runs," "Get ready, Doctor. Take my bat; it's a three-base hit bat."[24] While such expressions were not allowed under the new rules of coaching, they were rarely censored by umpires.[25] Much of the above was simply business, or funny business, as usual. However, there was a difference that surfaced in the 26 road games, an edge in Latham that was more aggressive and angrier than had been evident before or would be present after this time abroad.

Unlike Comiskey's confrontational style, Latham tended to question an umpire's decision through a quip or a humorous gesture, usually avoiding the fines that Comiskey regularly received for questioning calls. In this period, however, in a June 16 game in Baltimore that ended in an 8–8 tie, Latham "stepped out of the batter's box so as a let a pitched ball hit him ... [but instead] McQuaid called a strike on him." When Latham questioned the umpire's call, he was fined for "too much flippancy."[26] Two weeks later, in one of the Browns' worst losses of the year, a 16–4 shellacking at the hands of the Louisville club, Latham received a series of four $10 fines for his insulting remarks to the umpire. The *Louisville Courier Journal* described the escalating exchange between Latham and Ben Young, the umpire:

> The side feature of the game was the fining of Arlie Latham, the chipper third baseman of the Browns. In the eighth inning, after he had been called out at first on an attempt to bunt the ball, he became decidedly insulting in his remarks to the umpire.
>
> "Now wait, gentlemen, let Mr. Young adjust his spectacles before the game progresses. He is not responsible for what he does anyhow."
>
> "Fine him," yelled the crowd to Mr. Young.
>
> "I won't accept his dirty fine," rang out Latham.
>
> "That will cost your third baseman ten dollars," said Young, quietly addressing Capt. Comiskey.
>
> "Fine me again, old man. Keep up the music. I dare you."
>
> "Ten dollars more," said Young.
>
> "Double it, you heathen," called Latham.
>
> Young piled up fines until they reached $40, when Latham grew more quiet, but in an undertone gave Young what was evidently a scorching denunciation.[27]

To some fans at the game, Latham's more irascible demeanor on the field seemed out of character. At the same time, it was consistent with the overall increase in aggressive play adopted more and more as the Browns got further into their extended road trip. While Latham's belligerence was primarily manifested vocally in his kicking, others such as Robinson and Welch turned to more physical acts of aggression.

Robinson took his lead from the rough-and-tumble example set by Comiskey and Gleason. Whether at home or away, on offense he ran or slid hard into base, bowled over fielders in his way, and hustled for extra bases whenever the opportunity arose. On May 24, in the fourth inning of the Browns' 9–2 win against Brooklyn, Robinson got his base on balls, promptly stole second base and, shortly thereafter, attempted to steal third. Bob Clark, the Brooklyn catcher, threw to George Pinkney, the third baseman, to prevent the steal. Just as Pinkney caught the ball, "Robinson threw himself flat on the ground and slid right under him; then by an upward spring he sent Pinkney flying high in the air and he fell sprawling, the ball flying out of his hands. The same spring that knocked Pinkney down landed Robinson on the base," safe at third.[28]

On defense, he bumped or punched runners as they rounded second base and stood his ground, ready to tag vigorously any runner who attempted to take second on a steal or hit. Forever the trickster, Robinson looked for ways to dupe runners. On June 22, the Browns lost an away game to Cincinnati, 8–4. At the start of the ninth inning, Cincinnati had a 6–4 lead when McPhee, the second baseman, reached on an error by Gleason. Frank Fennelly, the Cincinnati shortstop, hit to right field. Caruthers fumbled the ball and then threw it wide of second base, enabling McPhee to score and Fennelly to go to second. The errant throw by Caruthers rolled to the pitcher's box, where Foutz picked it up and hurriedly tossed it toward Robinson at second with the hope of catching Fennelly as he made the turn. As Fennelly dove back to the bag, the throw by Foutz missed the mark, scooting deep into center field. Robinson acted as if he had caught the throw from

Foutz, falling on Fennelly as he applied the tag. He then pretended that the ball had been knocked loose. Gleason played along by scurrying after the imaginary, nearby ball as Robinson continued his act, waiting anxiously for Gleason's toss, all the while keeping Fennelly pinned to the ground. Hugh Nicol, the third base coach, quickly sussed out the hoax perpetrated by Robinson and Gleason. When he saw that Welch was still chasing down the ball in center, he left the coaching lines and ran to second to inform Fennelly about the deception and, running beside Fennelly, escorted him around third and to home, where Fennelly stepped on the plate for Cincinnati's eighth run.[29]

On July 9, in the 9–3 win against Baltimore, Robinson was involved in another bluff. With one out in the fifth inning, Sam Trott, the Baltimore catcher, singled and moved to second on a passed ball. Jack Boyle, the St. Louis catcher, tried to pick Trott off second, but the throw went wild, skipping well into center field. Again, the con was on, this time with Robinson tagging Trott as if he had the ball and triumphantly raising his glove to celebrate a well-timed out. Robinson yelled at the umpire to confirm the out while Trott, taking the bait, rose in defiance, arguing that he was safe. The rest of the Baltimore team shouted at Trott to run to third, but they could not be heard over the laughter of the crowd and the hot exchange between Trott and Robinson. Welch returned the ball to the infield before Trott discovered the ruse. The next two Baltimore batsmen failed to reach base, the second on a fly out to Robinson who "trotted" off the field to the approving applause of the spectators.[30] Robinson's defensive trickery invariably involved some degree of rough play as he held runners down, presumably to apply a ball-less tag, or bumped runners as he strained to catch a never-to-arrive throw.

Curt Welch took roughness to another level, with a number of incidents during the June segment of the road trip, with each episode bringing him both rebuke and sanction.

Welch was a hard-nosed, scrappy, and fearless warrior who went all-out on every play and was all-in on doing anything to increase the Browns' chances of a win. Citing the *Boston Globe,* David Nemec described Welch as a batsman who "had no fear of personal injury and would plunge headlong after a ball. At the plate, he would brave the fastest pitching. He frequently permitted the ball to hit him in order to secure a base."[31] On the base paths, like Robinson, Welch was like a runaway freight train going into a base, knocking over anyone who got in his way. In center field, he started after any ball hit out of the infield, no matter how far it was from him. Many of his teammates were only too happy to step aside as the charging, sure-catching Welch neared the falling sphere. He also insinuated himself into the action in the infield, frequently sneaking in from his shallow position in center field to surprise an unsuspecting runner on a pick-off play at second. At other times, with a man on first, if Robinson had to field a ball hit in the hole between first and second—or Gleason on a ball hit in the hole between shortstop and third—Welch would speed in to obstruct the runner as he rounded second base.

Two of Welch's many incidents of rough play occurred when he temporarily inserted himself into the infield. On June 4 in New York, in the ninth inning of a game that the Browns won, 1–0, Candy Nelson, the right fielder, took his lead off second base. Welch crept in from center field. Silver King, the St. Louis pitcher, spun and threw to second just as Welch reached the bag. Nelson's attempt to scramble back to the base was thwarted as "Welsh blocked the line and turned Nelson head over heels, at the same time touching him with the ball."[32] The umpire called Nelson safe, ruling that Welch had unfairly obstructed the runner's path back to the base. The St. Louis nine surrounded the umpire to protest the call but to no avail.

A second example of Welch's ventures into the infield going wrong occurred five days later as part of the Browns' 7–5 win in Philadelphia. In the fifth inning, Welch was at it again, this time hustling in from center field to block Gus Weyhing, the Philadelphia pitcher, as he neared second on his hit to left field. The *Philadelphia North American* was disgusted by Welch's "unmanly trick":

> In the fifth inning Weyhing made a line hit to the left field fence for two bases. There was no chance to put him out at second on a fair play, but that's not the kind of ball that the St. Louis team in general, and Curtis Welch in particular, are playing. The latter ran in from center and made an attempt to intercept Weyhing about six feet from the base, and failing, he deliberately hit the runner with his clenched fist. Of course, this thug-like act evoked a storm of hisses and hoots from the spectators, and a ten-dollar fine from Umpire Curry. Welch told Curry to go where ice melts, and Wesley slapped twenty-five dollars' worth more, which with the ten dollars that had been imposed upon him in the fourth for differing on balls and strikes decisions, made his total expenses for the afternoon's entertainment $45. There is no excuse for Welch's unmanly tricks."[33]

The Philadelphia Club submitted formal charges against both Welch and Comiskey to Wheeler Wikoff, the President and Secretary of the American Association. Welch was accused of "deliberately, maliciously, and without provocation, striking August Weyhing with his clenched fist, inflicting on said Weyhing much pain from the blow."[34] In addition, Welch and Comiskey were charged with the use of profane language as they passed by the ladies and gentlemen in the grandstand. Wikoff investigated the charges but did not impose further fines or sanctions. The most notorious rough play of the month occurred in the third game in the four-game series in Baltimore (June 14–17), also at second base, but this time while on offense when Welch was running from first to second.

The series against second-place Baltimore, as well as their three-game series in St. Louis (July 8–11), attracted large crowds, over 40,000 across four games in Baltimore and over 13,000 across three games in St. Louis.[35] As a showdown between the top two teams in the Association, the four games in June were the most important series of the season to date. Baltimore was in second place, just 5 1/2 games behind the Browns. Still smarting from a previous visit to St. Louis (May 10–14) when they were swept by the Browns in four games straight, the Baltimore club was anxious to avenge this earlier loss and to gain ground on the Association leaders. The Browns, however, refused to allow Baltimore to close the gap, winning both the hard-fought June series as well as the three-game set in St. Louis a few weeks later (July 8–11).

The two Baltimore series were the only ones in this phase in which O'Neill hit .500 or better. In the June 14–17 series, O'Neill had 11 hits in 19 times at-bats (.579), with two bases on balls, seven singles, and two doubles. For the three-game, July 8–11 series, he had seven hits in 14 trips to the plate (.500), on two bases on balls, three singles, and two doubles. For the most part, O'Neill played well in the field, making 15 putouts in the two series, with his catches featured in the newspapers in four of the seven games.

On the morning of the first game (June 14), the Baltimore club, in honor of the first appearance of the season of the reigning Association and world champions, welcomed the Browns with a parade through town. The managers and players of both teams rode in carriages, and the procession was led by a brass band. After the parade, the teams had a luncheon at the Eutaw House before heading to the grounds. Von der Ahe brought the Wiman Trophy, the prize awarded to the champion of the American Association, which was displayed in a window of a prominent shop in downtown Baltimore. He also provided two pennants, the American Association pennant that was flown atop the Eutaw House and the world championship flag that was "placed on *The American* building and given full sway to the breezes that sweep over this lofty structure."[36]

Mindful of the many incidents that the Browns had experienced in their games in New York and Philadelphia, Bill Barnie, the manager of the Baltimore Club, issued the following plea to the Baltimore fans:

> In view of the forthcoming contests between the Baltimore Base Ball Club and the "Brown Stockings" of St. Louis, champions of the world, the management of the home club trusts that the public will not be influenced by the violent attacks which have been made upon the visitors elsewhere, but will treat them in a fair, courteous and impartial manner, leaving all dispute of play to the respective captains of the opposing nines and the umpire for adjudication. From each member of the St. Louis team the Baltimore Club has always received the fairest treatment, and the management of the home team asks, on behalf of the visitors, a like fair, liberal and reasonable treatment—"nothing extenuate nor aught set down in malice." WM. BARNIE, Manager Balto. B. B. C.[37]

Estimates ranged from 12,000 to 15,000 fans in attendance at the first game, the largest crowd ever to see to see a baseball game played in Oriole Park. Worried about both getting to the grounds and getting into the game, fans headed to the park early, utilizing all manner of transportation to get there. While many travelled on the lines that went by or near the park, others made the journey by "handsome private coach and the hired hack, the dog-cart and the barrel wagon, the hansom and the swill-cart."[38] Still others made their way to the park on foot, choking on the dust stirred up by the many wagons and vehicles on the road. Once inside the park, fans then had to scramble for a seat or a spot to stand.

The grandstand and pavilion filled during the hour before the start of the game and, by game time, there were no seats left in the bleaching boards along the left field line. As more fans arrived, the police struggled to manage the onslaught of bodies as they found alternate routes into the grounds and, after gaining entry, rushed about looking for a place from which to view the game:

> They began coming into the field at the players' gate, and soon took up the extra chairs in front of the grand stand.... Next the people began to jump the barbed wire fence, and regardless of torn clothing or torn flesh, they came over by hundreds. The wagon gate was also scaled, but this did not last long; the gate gave way under the pressure, and the crowd poured in. Ropes had been stretched early in the day, extending from the east end of the grand stand along the left field fence, then along the lower fence across center field, up along the right field fence to the lower end of the pavilion. These ropes held the people in check until the posts were pulled out of the ground, and then it took the efforts of the city police, the county police and the specials to keep the crowd back. The game was played in a field surrounded by an animated picket of faces—a human hedgerow, as it were.[39]

Under such crowded conditions, a ground rule was added to deal with balls that went into the fans surrounding the field. Any fair hit into the crowd was automatically deemed a double. Furthermore, a base runner could only advance one base on a ball thrown into the crowd.[40] The fans who were nearest to the field of play were at some risk: "The ball frequently caromed on the heads and legs of the people, but they forgot their bruises in the general interest over the game."[41]

For those fans who could not go to the game, they could still gather outside one of the buildings of the two major Baltimore newspapers, the *American* and the *Sun,* to get inning-by-inning updates of the score and brief accounts of the key plays of the game.

The *Baltimore American* was particularly effective in these early "broadcasts." Although in game one, it started with simply posting the score on bulletin boards in the front of the *American* building, by game four there was more extensive coverage of the action. The *American* installed a private telegraph wire from the shed beside the Baltimore clubhouse in Oriole Park to an office in its building downtown. Outside the building, the *American* set up three stands, one to report the score after each half-inning, one with a diagram of the diamond to post the locations of players as the game progressed—for example, using a marker to indicate a runner on second base—and one to list short comments on key hits, errors, passed balls, injuries, and other incidents as they happened. To animate and explain what appeared on the bulletin boards at the three stands, the *American* appointed W. W. Breckenbaugh, a noted auctioneer, to convey the events of the game "as soon as the news was ticked off."[42] The combined information from the three stands and auctioneer endeavored to provide fans a rich and lively account of the game:

> All incidents of the game, questioned decisions, the actions and antics of different players, the coaching of Burns and Latham, and the comments of the knowing ones, were received in less time than it takes to write it.[43]
>
> Every fact which was likely to prove of interest to the assemblage was hastily given by a reporter of *The American* to the Western Union operator and transmitted by him with electric rapidity to this office and immediately posted. The crowd was virtually on the base-ball grounds. They knew who was at the bat, when a man reached the different bases, when he was put out, when a man was stealing from one base to the other, and in fact, the progress of the game was right there before their eyes.[44]

With the addition of the auctioneer, the game was also right there before their ears. In short, many more fans than the 40,000 in attendance in the park witnessed this four-game series.

The June series against Baltimore was noteworthy for many shifts in the style of play. What began as a celebration of the Browns as the world champions quickly turned to censure and rebuke. The captains and coachers oscillated between bouts of kicking, which occasionally escalated into vulgar outbursts, and periods of restraint, which in one game bordered on disengagement. On the field, for the first three games, there were numerous deceptive, combative, and rough tactics, primarily but not exclusively perpetuated by the Browns. Game three was stopped following a violent incident. In contrast, the fourth game was orderly, relatively quiet, and contact-free.

The first game set the stage for this topsy-turvy series, a high-scoring, lead-changing nail-biter. The Browns took a 3–2 lead after the first inning only to have Baltimore tie the game 3–3 after two. At the end of three innings, it was 5–4 in the Browns' favor, but at the close of five innings, Baltimore was ahead, 7–5. The Browns came back to tie the game after six innings, surging ahead to what seemed like a commanding 11–7 lead after seven. But Baltimore had other ideas, exploding with eight runs of their own in the eighth inning, vaulting them into a 15–11 lead. This eight-run outburst proved to be the knockout blow as Baltimore held on to defeat the Browns, 15–12.

Latham was in his usual form, chattering non-stop to the delight and amusement of the crowd. At one point, he took to calling strikes and outs: "Four strikes. Out," and "You're out at first." When the Browns had men on base, he rattled off various parrot-like expressions of encouragement: "Now, boys, take every opportunity. It only takes one to hit it. Who-o-up. Watch that box please. Play ball everybody."[45]

In terms of aggressive play, Baltimore, especially Oyster Burns, their captain and shortstop, and Tommy Tucker, their first baseman, gave as much as they got. In a throw by King to pick off Tucker at second, Gleason attempted to impede Tucker's efforts to get back to the bag, but Tucker shoved Gleason out of the way and returned to the base safely. At another point, in a close play at the plate, Matt Kilroy, the Baltimore pitcher, was covering home, poised to receive a throw from the second baseman to catch a charging Comiskey. Just as the ball arrived, Comiskey slammed against Kilroy's hand, preventing the pitcher from catching the ball. Throughout the game, the Browns drew some hissing from the crowd when they kicked, tried their tricks, or resorted to rough play. For the most part, the Baltimore players ignored such antics and tactics, enthralled by their first victory of the season against the Browns. At game's end, the fans rushed onto the field, cheering wildly as they ran helter-skelter, reveling in Baltimore's success. A few fans hoisted Kilroy on their shoulders and carried him around the field in a triumphant celebration of his heroic pitching. Most exuded unbridled confidence that Baltimore would win the series. Game two was a different story.

Anxious to end their three-game losing streak,[46] the Browns struck fast in game two, jumping to an 8–0 lead after three innings. Hopes of a repeat of yesterday's late-inning comeback were dashed as the Baltimore club could muster only two one-run innings in the latter stages of the game. The Browns won, 9–2. The domination of Foutz in the box and the Browns' eight runs in the first three innings discouraged the more spirited style of play that both teams had exhibited in game one. Comiskey and Burns, the captains and lead kickers on their respective teams, were relatively quiet most of the game. Latham prattled on, prodding the crowd into laughter if not retort. In a presumed concern for the ladies' safety, after a foul ball landed in their section, he yelled: "Now mind what I tell you, no more fouls up there."[47] He also initiated what the *Baltimore Sun* called a "daring but unsuccessful play,"[48] an attempted steal of home when Trott, the Baltimore catcher, stood at the plate holding the ball. Trott easily tagged Latham for the third out. Comiskey likely found this more foolhardy than bold. There were no egregious examples of rough play, which in hindsight was simply a lull before the storm in game three.

The Browns took an early lead in game three, scoring six runs in the second inning and two runs in the next inning for an 8–5 advantage after three. Baltimore tied the score, 8–8, in the fifth inning, which is where it stood going into the ninth. The first eight innings had a number of incidents and disputed calls that progressively increased the level of tension and agitation displayed by both teams. With each close call, the kicking became more pronounced and extended.

In the second inning, Tommy Tucker, the Baltimore first baseman, knocked over Bushong on a close play at the plate. Tucker was on third base and took off for home on a ball hit to Comiskey, who immediately fired the ball to Bushong. On the throw, "Bushong attempted to block Tucker but the stalwart possessor of first base turned him over amid great applause."[49] In the fifth inning, Joe Sommer, the Baltimore left fielder, was on third when Nat Hudson, the Browns' pitcher, threw a ball that got away from the catcher. Bushong, aware that Sommer was trying for home on the passed ball, quickly recovered the ball and tossed it to Hudson, covering the plate. Despite "several stabs at Sommer with the ball," most Baltimore loyalists, including the reporters from the two major newspapers, felt that Hudson failed to apply the tag. Nonetheless, the umpire called Sommer out, bringing another shower of jeers and catcalls down on his head. Three innings later, Jumbo Davis, the Baltimore third baseman, singled and attempted to steal second. He slid under Robinson, who had to stretch high for Bushong's throw before he could apply the tag. Davis lay sitting with his legs across the bag as Jack McQuaid rendered his decision, "Out!" The Baltimore faithful again booed as their manager complained in vain about the call.[50] Tempers frayed, the players on each team nonetheless readied themselves for what they hoped would be the final inning.

Baltimore failed to get a run in the top of the ninth, with only a base on balls to show for their efforts. This set the stage for a possible walk-off win by the Browns. After Welch's one-out single to center field, he took his lead from first, poised to steal second. The fans looked on anxiously, their eyes fixed on Welch, in anticipation of what might transpire. Similarly, the 2000–3000 disquieted cranks outside the *American* building, vicariously watching the game by bulletins and listening to the stream of announcements from the auctioneer, waited impatiently for the next updates by wire, which soon arrived in rapid succession to reveal the shocking events unfolding at Oriole Park. While one can only imagine what the auctioneer, "whose stentorian voice carried it squares away,"[51] told these downtown fans about what happened after Welch tried to steal second base, the following outline provides one version of what he might have reported[52]:

Welch runs to second—deliberately knocked down Greenwood, our second baseman

Greenwood is hurt—still on the ground—Welch called safe

[30-second pause to await the next message]

Burns and Comiskey kicking at each other—a possible fight?

Crowd is near riot—some fans are on the field—pushed back by police

[30-second pause to await the next message]

Welch arrested

Game stopped—declared a draw

By most reports, Bill Greenwood positioned himself on the side of the base in preparation to tag Welch as he slid. Instead of sliding, Welch veered off the line to plough into Greenwood. No one heard McQuaid rule on the play,[53] although later McQuaid said he called Welch out. The *Baltimore Sun* doubted this claim: "Nobody heard him [the umpire] if he did, and the subsequent actions of the players and their arguments with the umpire makes it doubtful whether he did so."[54] Worried by the deteriorating conditions—the bedlam among many of the fans, the wild wrangling among the players, and the potential fight between Comiskey and Burns—on the advice of Barnie, the Baltimore manager, the umpire suspended play and declared the game a draw, officially ending the game as an 8–8 tie at the end of the eighth inning. Meanwhile, the Baltimore mayor's secretary, distraught by what he had just witnessed, jumped onto the field and insisted to the police that Welch be arrested on assault charges. The police escorted Welch off the grounds and to the Waverly station-house, where he was formerly charged with assault and released on a $200 bond paid by Harry Von der Horst, one of the owners of the Baltimore club.

The St. Louis newspapers called the collision between Greenwood and Welch an accident. In a less serious note, the *St. Louis Sunday Sayings* quipped, "Curt Welch is the first ball player that has ever been arrested for stealing a base."[55] Von der Ahe, in an interview with a reporter from the *Baltimore Sun,* defiantly reminded the Baltimore fans that "in condemning Welch, [they] should remember that Tucker ran into and upset Gleason in the first game, and treated Bushong the same way in yesterday's game."[56] Tensions were high in anticipation of Welch's appearance in court.

WELCH ARRETED TO PREVENT A RIOT.

Like most of the baseball world, the *National Police Gazette* was appalled by the dirty trick played by Welch as he ran into the second baseman "with great force, knocking him down and hurting him very badly." It further reported that "it was only through the able efforts of the police that he escaped the wrath of the mob, who seemed bent on lynching him" (*National Police Gazette*, July 2, 1887).

On the next day, Welch met before the magistrate. Much to the puzzlement of John Ward, the prosecutor assigned to the case, Bill Greenwood testified that collisions of this kind were common, that the contact at second base was accidental, and that Welch had not assaulted him. Ward declared that "he could not understand why Greenwood would not prosecute Welch, as the assault had been outrageous, Welch having gone out of his way to violently knock him down."[57] The assault charge was dismissed. Welch was instead fined $1 for disorderly conduct plus $3.45 for court costs, both of which were paid by Von der Ahe. Afterwards, Welch confessed that he did run off the base path to knock the ball out of Greenwood's hand, but in doing so, he "did not want to hurt him."[58]

By the start of game four, all of the bad feelings from the previous day seemed to have gone. Both teams were cheered as they warmed up for the game. As promised by Von der Ahe, Welch did not play and in fact was nowhere near the grounds. At Comiskey's insistence, neither team used coaches. In the first inning, Latham momentarily forget himself and wandered to the third base coacher's box, proceeding to sing a song to O'Neill, who was on first after receiving a base on balls. Comiskey told Latham to sit down. Latham returned to the bench and refrained from his usual chatter and antics for the rest of the game. There was no kicking and "not a cross word spoken."[59] Although the Browns had 17 men reach base (three bases on balls, ten singles, two doubles, two on errors), not one of their players tried to steal a base. Instead "the two teams gamboled together on the green like lambs," a description never before or again used to characterize the Browns' style of play.[60] The Browns won the game, 7–3. They took the series with two wins, one loss, and a tie that would be replayed. As they left town, fans, players, management, and the press in both cities wondered if the troubles of game three would resurface when they met again on July 8–11, this time in front of the St. Louis fans.

After a swing through Ohio, where the Browns lost three of four games to Cincinnati and won all three games against Cleveland, they moved on to six games against Louisville, the first three in St. Louis (June 28–30) and the last three in Louisville (July 1–3). In their first game in Sportsman's Park since May 28, the Browns responded to the fans' enthusiastic welcome back with a 6–0 win. When Welch stepped to the plate for the first time, he was loudly applauded, a sign of unqualified support for his play in Baltimore. With the game paused for this ovation, while Welch repeatedly doffed his cap to the crowd, one of the fans presented him with a handsome bouquet. The game stopped again when he next stepped to the plate, this time to present him with an elegant diamond stud.[61] In honoring Welch with this gift, the Honorable Clay Sexton, one of the stakeholders of the St. Louis Club, made the following comments:

> Mr. Welch, I hold in my hand here a handsome diamond solitaire which comes from a number of your St. Louis admirers. The report reached St. Louis ahead of your return that you had run over a man in Baltimore in trying to reach second base, but we also heard that the man you ran over was on the line where he had no business to be. We do not approve of ruffianism on the ball field, but we do approve of your playing good, fair and square ball and we want to see you win. These friends present this stud to you on account of your gentlemanly conduct on the ball field. Take this stud and wear it, and may you never dim its lustre by any action on the field unbecoming a gentleman.[62]

The Browns opened the second leg of their six-game set with a 16–4 loss in Louisville. As much as they were bothered by this lopsided defeat, the Browns were even more concerned by the loss of Doc Bushong, their presumed injury-proof catcher, who had the little finger on his right hand broken by an in-shoot pitch, a break that kept him out of the lineup for several weeks.[63] Jack Boyle, the 20-year-old substitute catcher, replaced Bushong.[64]

The game also was a milestone of sorts for O'Neill. Unbeknownst to O'Neill or any of the sportswriters of the day, this game was the first time since May 1 that his accumulated batting average dropped below .500. O'Neill would never reach the .500 mark again in 1887.

The Browns bounced back with a convincing 10–3 win in game two but lost the third game by forfeit. After two innings in game three, Louisville had a commanding 7–1 lead. At that point, it started to rain. Umpire Ben Young called time and after the rain had all but ceased, ordered the teams to resume play. The *Louisville Courier Journal* reported that the rain was but a "faint drizzle."[65] The *St. Louis Globe-Democrat* concurred, describing the conditions as a "misting rain all the time ... a perceptible sprinkle, but not enough to wet much."[66] Comiskey disagreed and, in the ultimate kick, refused to allow his players to take their bat in the third inning. Young proceeded to declare first one, then two, and finally three batters out for failing to take their turn at bat and then announced: "Ladies and gentlemen, I am compelled to call this game forfeited by a score of 9–0 in favor of the Louisvilles."[67] The Louisville press was incensed, pouring a torrent of abuse on the heads of the Browns, describing their refusal to play on as: "a baby act"[68]; a "game of bulldoze and bluff"[69]; and an example of "rank cowardice," in violation of "all laws of courtesy, fairness and justice" by a band of "weak-kneed hoodlums."[70] Von der Ahe unsuccessfully protested the umpire's decision to call a forfeit. Comiskey and Von der Ahe initiated a petition for Young's dismissal. Young never umpired again.[71]

The Browns were likely relieved to head back to St. Louis for a 12-game homestand. On the road, they had endured much animosity: the hostile reception of fans; the bad calls and fines of umpires and a loss in Louisville when an umpire declared a forfeit; the criticism and outrage from the local press; and the howls and complaints from opposing managers and players about their aggressive style of play. Invigorated by the return to Sportsman's Park, the Browns celebrated their Fourth of July by overwhelming New York in both ends of a doubleheader, 15–2 and 20–3. While each of his teammates had three or four hits (except Latham, who had two hits), O'Neill could only manage one hit in six times to the plate. Even worse, in the eighth inning, he injured his finger on a fly ball. He tried to complete the game but could not take his last turn at bat: "Tip O'Neill is in hard luck this season. He was injured again on the Fourth, hurting a finger so badly that he refused to go to the bat and allowed the umpire to call him out."[72] Tip missed two games, the second game of the doubleheader and the game on July 6.

In the final three games of this phase in the season (July 8–11), St. Louis and Baltimore met for the first time since the June series in which Welch was arrested for knocking down Bill Greenwood. After the honors (tribute, diamond pin) bestowed on Welch in the Browns' first game at home after the 23-day road trip (June 28), a Baltimore newspaper ran the headline: "Welch Suits St. Louis—Rewarded for Rowdyness in Baltimore."[73] On the eve of the series, following the stories of gifts for Welch, there were concerns in Baltimore that they might get a "warm reception,"[74] especially by the rambunctious St. Louis fans. A few days before the start of the Baltimore–St. Louis series, Bill Barnie, the Baltimore manager, issued a warning, presumably to the St. Louis club and to their fans:

> If there are any rowdy demonstrations when my team reaches St. Louis, I will not allow the men to play until I am guaranteed police protection. The Baltimore club officials treated the members of the St. Louis Browns nicely when they were on our grounds and we want the same treatment when we reach theirs.

In response, the *St. Louis Republican* said: "Mr. Barnie need have no fears of rough treatment in St. Louis except from the St. Louis players, and then according to the strict code of rules adopted by the American Association."[75]

The two major Baltimore newspapers actively fed into the growing frenzy about the series with comments about the possible hostile crowds in St. Louis or the likely return to tricks and rough play by the Browns in their home park. The papers expanded their coverage of the series, the *Baltimore Sun* taking the unusual step of sending its own reporter to St. Louis, while the *Baltimore American* arranged to broadcast the game by "voice, paintbrush and diagram,"[76] securing a direct line from the scorer's box in Sportsman's Park to one almost a thousand miles away at the *American* building in Baltimore.[77] The Baltimore press stood on guard with their club and fans, ready to engage in combat by word and deed should any ill treatment come their way.

Baltimore entered the series still in second place, 5½ games behind the Browns. Barnie and his charges were determined both to end their two-game losing streak and, with a series win in St. Louis, to close the gap on the Browns. The pre-series worries about the St. Louis crowd were quickly dispelled as the Baltimore club received a ten-minute ovation before the game. The Browns fans also cheered throughout the game on Baltimore's good plays and wildly after the game on their exciting, come-from-behind victory. With one out and down 3–0 in the bottom of the ninth, Baltimore erupted for four runs and the walk-off win. It was a game that had only subdued and infrequent coaching, no kicking, no tricks, and no deliberate rough plays. O'Neill led the Browns at bat with a four-for-four game (two bases on balls, one single, one double). He had a hand in all three of the Browns' runs, in the first inning driving in the go-ahead run with a double, scoring the second run after his base on balls in the third, and, in the seventh inning, crossing home with the third run after getting on with a single. In addition, O'Neill also made four catches in the field, part of an all-around performance that prompted the *St. Louis Globe-Democrat* to feature him for both batting and fielding: "O'Neill, although suffering from a sore finger, did brilliant work both at the bat and in the field. Besides making four brilliant captures, he hit safe every time he went to bat."[78]

The Browns took games two and three by scores of 9–3 and 12–5, respectively. Both teams resumed some of their old habits, with the piercing sounds of coaching and kicking filling the air. Various efforts at deception, for the most part, were foiled before they had a chance to surprise or fool the opposition.

On July 10, game three was stopped by the police at the end of the first inning when Chris Von der Ahe was arrested for a violation of the Sunday law.[79] The 10,000 patrons at the game were issued what Pritchard, in *Sporting Life,* called "sun checks," a voucher that permitted the holder to attend any game of his or her choosing in the future. Von der Ahe was released on a $100 bond. While he awaited his appearance in court, game three was replayed the next day. A few days later, Judge Edward A. Noonan ruled that the St. Louis club was exempt from Missouri laws which prohibited business and some amusements on Sundays. The Browns could resume their practice of playing games on the Sabbath.[80]

The second phase of O'Neill's season was marred by injury. In addition to missing 12 games, he played hurt for many of the 28 games in which he was in the lineup. His injured hand forced him to adjust his grip on the bat, which in turn affected the speed and rhythm of his swing. In a gritty display of skill and determination, O'Neill managed to hit .424 in this phase, a remarkable achievement under the circumstances. While this represented a considerable drop from the torrid pace he set in phase one, when he soared to a .560 average, O'Neill experienced an even more dramatic decline in long hits.

The table below documents O'Neill's offensive output between May 25 and July 11. His total of eight long hits, including seven doubles and one home run, stands in stark contrast to the 26 extra-base hits that O'Neill smashed in 24 games in his first phase of the season (April 16 to May 24). In 17 of 28 games, he had two or more hits, a slight decrease from the 19 multi-hit games he had in phase one. However, O'Neill managed only three four-hit games and no games with five or more hits in phase two, compared to the three games with five or more hits and five four-hit games in the previous phase. Even with this fall-off in batting average and power, O'Neill still made an important contribution to the success of the Browns. Of the 30 runs he scored and the 22 runs he batted in, 14 had an impact on the game, nine of which either tied the score or put the Browns into the lead, and another five which represented the winning runs. These numbers compared favorably to O'Neill's runs in his more productive April 16-to-May 24 period, where 14 of his runs made a similar difference.[81]

	Games	AB	R	H	BB	1B	2B	3B	HR	AVG	SB
May 25–July 11	28	125	30	53	14	31	7	0	1	.424	6
April 16–July 11	52	241	71	118	26	58	22	6	6	.490	15

In any other season, hitting .424 for a 28-game period would be an outstanding achievement. Amazingly, in a season when a base on balls counted as a hit, O'Neill's .424 average seemed like a slump, especially when compared to the heights he reached in the first phase of the season. Even with this slump, on July 11, O'Neill remained atop the batting list with an overall average of .490. However, other Association batsmen were inching closer to the leader, based on batting records in phase two that exceeded his average.

Pete Browning, the Louisville slugger, was O'Neill's main challenger for batting supremacy in the American Association.[82] On May 24, Browning had a batting average of .458 (55 hits in 120 times at bat). He was 112 points behind O'Neill, a gap that he reduced to 14 points by the end of phase two. Between May 25 and July 11, Browning had 83 hits in 170 times at bat for an average of .488, increasing his season's average to .476. Throughout July, Browning continued to press O'Neill for the Association lead. And indeed, for the remainder of the season, Browning fixated on his rivalry with O'Neill, repeatedly commenting on their competition for the batting title.

On the Browns, by July 11 three of O'Neill's teammates were hitting over .400. Caruthers and Robinson had better batting averages than O'Neill in the May 25–to–July 11 period. Caruthers, a high ball hitter prior to 1887, had a slow start, hitting .338 in the first phase of the season. He finally adapted to the low pitches now permitted by the new rules, hitting .476 in phase two, raising his overall average by 90 points to .428. Similarly, Robinson hit .346 in the first phase of the season but jumped to .456 in the second phase, a 110–point increase that saw his overall batting average climb to .414. By mid–May, Foutz was hitting over .500, the only player on the team or in the Association who was close to O'Neill at that point in the season. By May 24, his average was .413. Foutz fell further off the pace, hitting .381 in phase two, which dropped his overall batting average to .403. In the third phase (July 12 to August 10), Tip continued to struggle, especially in July, but bounced back in early August, a prelude to his extraordinary batting feats in the fourth phase (August 12 to September 8) of his record-breaking season.

9
Featured Games: Batting and Fielding

In the more detailed accounts of each game, as part of their report, most of the major newspapers in the Association cities featured players on both teams who had distinguished themselves in batting, fielding, or pitching. Batsmen were highlighted for multiple hits, one or more long hits, or for key hits that turned around or won the game. For example, the Browns' 12–7 win over Louisville featured O'Neill's five-for-five batting performance:

> The one particular star was O'Neill, and the main feature of his work, and, in fact, of the game, was his home-run drive over the left field fence in the seventh inning, when the game was tied and, when he sent in two runs before him.... In addition to the above incident [home run], O'Neill made a triple, double, single, and base on balls.[1]

The newspapers commended one or more fielders for catching the most fly balls or putting out the most runners, for throws that caught a runner stealing or advancing a base, or for an outstanding catch. Although the Browns lost to New York on June 6, 5–1, the *New York Herald* applauded O'Neill on his remarkable seventh-inning catch: "Easterbrook drove a long high fly to the outfield that O'Neill caught grandly after a run to the end of the foul line."[2] In 1887, O'Neill's offensive and defensive play was featured in 65 (52 percent) of the 124 games he played, 47 times for batting.

Of the 65 games featured, the press highlighted both batting and fielding in seven games.[3] In their coverage of these double-featured games, reporters tended to give more attention to O'Neill's fielding feats. After duly noting his home run over the right field fence in the Browns' 8–3 win over Baltimore on May 14, the *St. Louis Globe-Democrat* was especially complimentary on O'Neill's fielding: "Jim dragged down three hard hits into his territory and is covering more territory than he ever has."[4] Similarly, as part of the Browns' 9–2 victory over New York on August 28, after acknowledging O'Neill, Latham, and Boyle as the most effective Browns at the plate,[5] most of the text concentrated on Tip's extraordinary game in left field, where he pulled in seven catches: "O'Neill's work in left field was the feature of the game. Some of 'Tip's' catches were marvelous."[6] The *St. Louis Republican* added: "The best fielding feature of the game was a catch by O'Neill of a drive from Jones' bat."[7] O'Neill had five other games in which he caught five or more fly balls, three of which were celebrated in the press.

O'Neill's six catches on May 17 in a game won by Philadelphia by a score of 4–3 was overshadowed by the fact that the loss ended the Browns' 15-game win streak. Later in the season, O'Neill once again hauled in six fly balls, this time on September 9 in an 8–3 win in Philadelphia. The *Philadelphia North American* observed: "The Browns fielded beautifully, O'Neill making several clever catches."[8] Two weeks later, on September 22 in a 6–0 loss to Cincinnati, while the Browns made 11 errors, their second-worst fielding game of the season, Tip played error-free with his second seven-catch game of the season, which was further enhanced by his one assist. The newspapers in both cities paid tribute to O'Neill's exceptional performance in left field:

> *Cincinnati Enquirer*: Tip O'Neill's work in left field has never been excelled in this city. He covered a wonderful amount of territory and pulled down what looked like home-run hits from Nicol and O'Reilly. He also made a one-hand side runner of a liner in the seventh inning that brought out loud and continuous applause. He took no less than seven flies, most all of which were difficult[9] ... three of them were of the circus order.[10]
>
> *Cincinnati Commercial Gazette*: He made several difficult catches, but his capture of Nicol's foul fly in the seventh inning, taking the ball with one hand on a hard run, was probably as fine a play as has been made on the grounds this season.[11]
>
> *St. Louis Republican*: The feature of the game was the magnificent fielding of O'Neill, who made seven difficult catches, each of them on a hard run.[12]
>
> *St. Louis Globe-Democrat*: O'Neill's hard catches were brilliant, one being with one hand on Nicol's hard fly.[13]

Based on both the number of catches made and the degree of difficulty of at least three of these catches, this game, albeit in a losing cause, was O'Neill's finest fielding performance of the year.[14]

The strengths in the field, and indeed the weaknesses, exhibited by O'Neill in 1887 were evident throughout his career. O'Neill was a durable fielder, a reliable fly catcher, and a savvy position player. He also had a weak arm, had difficulty with ground balls, and was slow to react to the ball off the bat. As a result, O'Neill could be both brilliant in the outfield as illustrated above, and disappointing, sometimes in the same game. First to his strengths.

In the years when O'Neill was a full-time outfielder (1885–1892),[15] he played the second-most games (953) of any outfielder in the major leagues, one back of Curt Welch, who played 954 games in the same period. He was also a durable outfielder in the American Association, finishing fifth all-time in games played among all outfielders in the league (1882–1891), and first was among the Association's left fielders. After 1885, O'Neill averaged 128 games per year for the last seven years of his career. He appeared in 124 of the 138 games played by the Browns in 1887, tenth-best among outfielders in the Association but second-best among left fielders.

O'Neill's reliability as a fly catcher was reflected in his number of putouts and, to some extent, in his fielding percentage, a measure that indicated that part of a player's defensive plays made without errors. In the 1885–1892 period, O'Neill ranked fifth in putouts (1,720) and 16th in fielding percentage (.923) among all outfielders in the major leagues. Over the life of the American Association (1882–1891), he was fifth in putouts (1,368) and eighth in fielding percentage (.916) among all Association outfielders, but first in both areas among left fielders. From 1886 onwards, O'Neill was generally regarded as a dependable fielder on balls hit on the fly to left field. An article by J. C. Kofoed published in 1913 in *Baseball Magazine* entitled "The Greatest Outfield" discussed who was best at picking up the arc of a fly ball. He focused on the 1894 Baltimore outfield of Willie Keeler, Steve Brodie, and Joe Kelley. However, as part of his analysis of the three outfielders, Kofoed referenced O'Neill: "Brodie, with the possible exception of Keeler and O'Neill, was the greatest judge of a fly ball that ever lived. His intuitive faculty was marvelous, and he could follow the flight of the ball over his head almost without looking."[16]

O'Neill's 247 putouts in 1887 were seventh-best among all Association outfielders who played in 100 or more games, and first among left fielders. However, his 1887 fielding percentage of .895, a record affected by his 31 errors, the most he ever made in one season, was the only time he fielded below .900 in the seven seasons in which he played 100 games or more (1886–1892). He finished well back of his fellow outfielders, placing 14th overall among those Association outfielders who played in 100 or more games, and fifth among the left fielders in this group.

While there was no statistic in 1887 to measure the savviness of an outfielder, under the tutelage of Comiskey, O'Neill learned how to adjust his position in the outfield based on the situation, the batsman, and the pitch selection of the hurler. O'Neill had a reputation for headwork, especially when it came to returning the ball to the infield after a hit into left field. Fred Pfeffer, the Chicago second baseman, in his 1889 book, *Scientific Ball,* wrote about the kind of split-second judgment that an outfielder must make after he retrieves a batted ball. He must instantly decide where to throw it. For example, with a runner on second, on a ground ball hit to left field, the fielder may feel that his first play is to throw the ball home to prevent the runner from scoring. However, if the fielder bobbles the ball on the pick-up, Pfeffer

"TIP" O'NEIL, HEAVY BATSMAN AND FIELDER OF THE ST. LOUIS

The above woodcut is based on the photograph of O'Neill in one of the cigarette cards from the Old Judge series (N172) produced in 1888. O'Neill was a reliable fielder on balls that he got under and caught with his hands over his head and his palms up (The Rucker Archive).

argued that he has lost his "margin of advantage,"[17] thus making a desperate throw to the plate would constitute an error in judgment since it would allow the batsman to get to second. On a bobbled ball, Pfeffer maintained that the throw should go to second. Pfeffer concluded that Tip O'Neill repeatedly demonstrated the kind of headwork needed in situations such as these:

> The strong point of a fielder is in knowing what to do with a ball after he gets it, and then acting promptly on this knowledge.... It is in the exercise of judgment at critical points like the one mentioned that a fielder exhibits his usefulness, and yet rarely is this appreciated by the average spectator.... I know one fielder, O'Neill, of the St. Louis Browns, who displays remarkable good judgment in disposing of a ball under the conditions named.[18]

Later in the book, Pfeffer explained that the aim of every good left fielder is to "catch and return a ball by almost one and the same motion" and "without premeditation, and almost without looking, [send] the ball where it [will do] the most good."[19] No longer blessed with a strong throwing arm, O'Neill, nonetheless, in 1887 and in numerous games played between 1885 and 1892, made accurate and quick throws back to the infield, to points that gave the Browns the greatest chance to thwart a run or to limit the advancement of runners.

These strengths notwithstanding, O'Neill also had three problems in the outfield, namely a weak throwing arm, difficulties in handling ground balls, and, on occasion, a hesitancy or slowness in running after fly balls. Although these problems plagued his entire career, in 1887 they were further exasperated by his three hand injuries,[20] ones that clearly affected his batting and especially his fielding. At bat, Tip altered his hand grip to take pressure off his sore fingers. He was able to hit but not as well and with diminished power. In the field, he at times seemed hesitant to go after some hard-hit balls or, with those he did attempt to catch, he was tentative in his handling of such shots for fear that his grip would fail him or that he might re-injure himself. As a result, until he had fully recovered, O'Neill was not as effective catching fly balls or line drives hit into left field.

O'Neill permanently damaged his throwing arm in 1884, his last season as a pitcher. As a consequence, when he moved to the outfield, he rarely tried to throw out a runner or to return the ball to the infield with a long or hard throw.[21] As noted above, while he was skilled and knowledgeable in his ability to return the ball to the infield, O'Neill was not a threat to throw out a runner. Year after year, he recorded few assists or double plays. In the 1885–1892 period, O'Neill's 74 assists and 15 double plays put him at 36th and 34th places respectively, rankings that placed him last in assists and near the bottom of the list in double plays among all outfielders in the major leagues who played in 500 or more games. He fared no better in the ten-year history of the American Association, finishing 21st in assists (59) and 18th in double plays (12) among all outfielders. O'Neill was fifth in assists and fourth in double plays among Association left fielders.[22] In 1887, O'Neill was 17th in assists (10) and 14th in double plays (3) out of 17 outfielders who played 100 or more games, and fifth on both categories among his fellow left fielders.

O'Neill's miscues in the field fluctuated from year to year. In his eight years in which he played full-time in left field, his 150 errors placed him 13th among all outfielders in the major leagues. He had the ninth-most errors (131) among outfielders in the American Association, but third most among left fielders. Tip had his most error-prone season in 1887, when his 31 errors were the second most among Association outfielders who played 100 games or more, and the highest number of errors for any left fielder.

O'Neill's second problem, his difficulty with ground balls, emerged when he converted from a pitcher to an outfielder in 1884. Of his 31 errors in 1887, 13 were made on fly balls, ten on grounders, four on errant throws, and four that were unspecified, that is listed in the box score but not described in game accounts. On his errors on ground balls hit into left field, O'Neill either fumbled them on the pick-up or missed them altogether, in both cases permitting runners to advance one or more bases.[23] He was never comfortable catching a ball in the palms-down, scooped position.[24] Furthermore, on the hard-hit ground balls that he fumbled or missed, he often was slow to get in front of the ball and thus did not have enough time to crouch down to pick up the ball or to go on one knee to field or block it. Tip struggled with ground balls in each of the five seasons that followed his 1887 campaign.

The third problem concerned O'Neill's apparent inability to react quickly to a fly ball hit into left field. In his first two years in the outfield (1884 and 1885), many attributed his slowness off the mark to his inexperience. As a novice outfielder, before he took chase after a fly hit to left field, he hesitated to pick up the flight of the ball, or so some believed. However, by 1887, this cautious approach was not always viewed as acceptable: "O'Neill is batting wonderfully but he does not take as many chances in the field as he might. He waits to see at what spot the ball is going to fall before starting for it."[25] When his slow start persisted, sometimes to the point that he did not break for the ball at all, some in the press labeled this listless play as fatigue or even laziness. In an 11–4 loss to Louisville, when O'Neill was slow to react to a ball that fell in between him and the center fielder, the *St. Louis Globe-Democrat* called this misjudgment "culpable negligence."[26] The *St. Louis Sunday Sayings* commented: "O'Neill doesn't improve in his fielding. The crowd is inclined to the belief that Tip is constitutionally tired. Appearances sometimes indicate that they are guessing about right."[27] Later in the season, the *St. Louis Chronicle* raised the possibility of slovenly play: "O'Neill made some wonderful catches in left field. 'Tip' always fields well, but he is l-a-z-y sometimes."[28] By 1888, the questioning of his fielding at times turned to unqualified criticism. Tip was occasionally chastised for playing a "lazy" or "sleepy game"[29] or for failing to try for a catch, with some of these miscues leading to the loss of a game.[30] The *St. Louis Post-Dispatch*, in its report on the Browns' 6–3 loss to Brooklyn on July 7, 1888, joined in the complaints against O'Neill's defensive play by including the following sketch of Tip asleep on a couch in left field.[31]

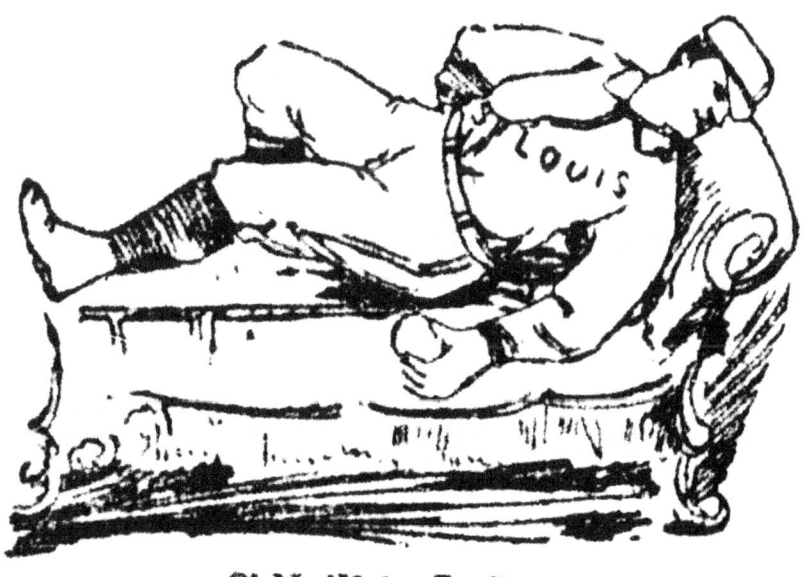

O'Neill in Left.

The press sometimes criticized O'Neill for his slowness in the field. He seemed to hesitate before he ran towards a fly ball or to lumber after those he did chase down. The above cartoon appeared in July 1888 in the *St. Louis Post-Dispatch* during a period when there were rumors that O'Neill's poor play in left field was intentional, with the hope that Von der Ahe would release him so he could sign with Brooklyn. O'Neill vehemently denied the rumor (*St. Louis Post-Dispatch,* July 8, 1888).

From 1888 to 1892, the negative comments on Tip's work in left field increased. Such criticism focused not only on his slowness but also on his indifferent play and sometimes on his limited capacity or unwillingness to cover his territory.

O'Neill's batting record in 1887 was frequently featured in game reports, usually for his multiple hits, long hits, or hits that turned around or won the game. Even in the games in which he did not hit so well, he was sometimes featured for hard hits that an opposing fielder miraculously caught, as if it were a feat that was not only extraordinary but rare. And when he struggled at the plate, it was still news, with most newspapers publishing notes on his temporary slump, on the possible reasons for his slugging draught, or on predictions about his imminent return to form.

O'Neill had his worst defensive year in 1887. He ranked among the worst outfielders in the major leagues and in the American Association in fielding percentage, errors, assists, and double plays. His only bright spot was his 247 putouts, the third-highest total of his career. Despite this drop in his defensive play, O'Neill was still featured for his fielding in 18 games, usually for catching the most fly balls or for making an outstanding catch. In seven of these games, Tip's performance was highlighted for both his batting and his play in the field.

For most of his eight-year career as a full-time left fielder (1885–1892), O'Neill was a dependable outfielder both in the number of games he played and in the number of fly balls he caught.[32] He was an excellent fly catcher who made a number of running catches, some of which were featured in one or more newspapers. Although O'Neill was not as quick to the ball or as inclined to throw a runner out, as was the case with Curt Welch, he nonetheless played his position smartly, adeptly, and with considerable range.[33] For the most part, his critics mistook his slow start to the ball and his loping strides for laziness, fatigue, or indifference. Most times, after his first few steps, O'Neill was in full chase after each hit ball, more times than not pulling it in for the catch. Over his last five years (1888–1892), on some days the press featured O'Neill for a good catch, and on other days, the newspapers highlighted an error, a miscue, or an inconsistent play. Despite the occasional criticism from the press, Tip's numbers, especially in the three subsequent years with the Browns (1888, 1889, 1891), were better than those in 1887, with higher fielding percentages, fewer errors, and a comparable number of putouts.[34]

In 1887, most newspapers highlighted O'Neill's bat-wielding skills and slugging prowess in one or more games almost every week. In each of his two best batting phases, April 16 to May 24 and August 12 to September 8, Tip was featured in 13 of the 24 games in which he played.[35] Though less frequent, O'Neill's fly-catching feats also garnered some praise, especially from April 16 to August 10, the first three phases of the season, where he was featured for his fielding in 15 of his 77 games.

10

July 12 to August 10: A Slow Return to Form

For most games between July 12 and August 10, O'Neill continued the slump[1] he had been in for most of phase two. Well into this third phase of his season, he hit new lows, first in a series against Brooklyn (July 24–26) when he had just two hits (single, base on balls) in ten times at bat, followed by a series against Baltimore (July 27–29) when he had only one hit (single) in 14 times at bat. In the final series of this phase, O'Neill decisively turned the corner, exploding for 15 hits in 19 times at bat in a four-game series against Cleveland (August 7–10), apparently living out the old adage, "Our greatest glory is not in never falling, but in rising every time we fall."[2] Tip rose from the ashes of a .125 batting average (3 hits in 24 times at bat) in the combined Brooklyn-Baltimore series in late July to the dizzy heights of a .789 average in the Cleveland series in early August.

Despite O'Neill's phoenix-like performance against Cleveland, his actual "return to form" was a tale that gradually unfolded in July and the first part of August. In the five series (15 games) completed in the July 12–29 period, including the one game played against Baltimore on July 19, O'Neill hit .318 (21 hits in 66 times at bat), while in the three series (ten games) completed in the August portion of this phase (July 30–August 10), he hit .581 (25 hits in 43 times at bat).[3] In the 25 games in phase three, he had only 14 multi-hit games, including one five-hit game and two four-hit games. However, he also had more pop in his bat, with 14 of his 46 hits going for extra bases (eight doubles, two triples, four home runs), again with more long hits coming in the ten games in August.[4] Some speculated on the causes of the downturn in his July performance: "Tip O'Neill fell off considerably in his batting just before leaving home. Whether it was because Tip thought it was too sultry to skin around the bases or whether he could not get his eagle eye on the ball is a problem that will have to be solved."[5] The *St. Louis Sunday Sayings* also noted O'Neill's aversion to hot-weather baseball: "Tip O'Neill suffers from the heat more than any of the champion men. He has been on the eve of pulling out of a game several times when the sun's rays have been at their hottest at Sportsman's Park."[6] However, O'Neill batted quite well in August under weather conditions not much different from the hot and humid days of July. It seems more likely that O'Neill's August resurgence was more related to being once again injury-free and back in the field he knew best, the hitter-friendly confines of Sportsman's Park.

While O'Neill tried to recover his rhythm in the batter's box, the Browns were winning games. Although they were on the road for 12 of the 25 games in this phase, the

Browns compiled an 18–5 win-loss record (.783), with two games tied. By August 10, they had 65 wins and 23 losses (.739), a record that extended their lead in the American Association to 14 games over second-place Louisville. With both runs and stolen bases harder to come by in this July 12–August 10 period,[7] the Browns relied more on their defensive skills and pitching prowess. They made two fielding errors or less in 16 of their 25 games.[8] In their 2–0 win over Brooklyn on July 13, the Browns registered a perfect fielding game (no fielding errors, passed balls, or wild pitches). The Browns pitchers allowed less than three earned runs in 15 of the 25 games.[9] Though it was more difficult for the Browns to score runs in this period, it was even tougher for their opposition to do so.

Notwithstanding O'Neill's struggles from July 12–29, the Browns had a 11–3 win-loss record with two ties. They swept two three-game series, one at home against Philadelphia (July 15–17) and a second in Baltimore (July 27–29). They beat Brooklyn two out of three games in two series, the first in St. Louis (July 12–14) and then in Brooklyn (July 24–26). The Browns also visited Baltimore (July 19) for a closely contested game that was called after 14 innings on account of darkness and declared a 2–2 draw. Their only series loss in this July segment occurred in a two-game stop in New York (July 20–22), where the Mets won one game and played the second to a 2–2 tie.

In the July segment of this phase, the Browns frequently won games on timely hits, strong pitching, and solid defense. They did so without the same level of offensive contribution from O'Neill as they had in the first phase of the season. In some games, the old Tip resurfaced, but for the most part, the press was both worried about his struggles at the plate and hopeful of a turnaround: "Tip has fallen off his batting recently. Wait till he strikes his gait again—he will break all standing records."[10] Following a three-game stretch in which he had only one hit, in the last two games of the Brooklyn series on July 13–14 and the first game of the Baltimore series on July 15, O'Neill helped the Browns to beat Philadelphia on July 17, 10–8. In this game, the lead changed hands four times. O'Neill had four hits in five times at bat (two bases on balls, single, triple) and scored three runs, two of which tied the game. In the ninth inning, with the Browns ahead, 10–8, Philadelphia had one out and a man on first when Denny Lyons, the third baseman, drove a ball into left field that O'Neill caught on the run and then wheeled and relayed it to Latham, who in turn threw out the runner at first for a game-ending double play.

The July version of the Browns retained the same level of noisy coaching and kicking that they exhibited throughout June. They were less involved in tricks and rough play. However, on occasion, when an opportunity to fool their opponents presented itself, Robinson, the Browns' master trickster, could not resist. On July 24, Brooklyn had a 3–0 lead on the visiting Browns after four innings. In the fifth inning, after the Browns tied the score, with one out and Robinson on second, Latham hit a ground ball to George Pinkney, the third baseman, who threw to Bill Phillips at first for the out. At the crack of the bat, Robinson initially bolted for third, but once Pinkney released his throw to first, he veered across the infield to bypass third base and headed home to score the Browns' fourth run. The *St. Louis Republican* applauded Robinson for "about the finest piece of ball-playing seen,"[11] while the *Brooklyn Citizen* cried foul on this "larceny":

> If, under the law, the robbery of the ball game were larceny, the St. Louis Browns and their accessory, Umpire Mitchell, would now be in Raymond Street Jail. The members of Mr. Von der Ahe's team are noted as speedy runners, but the police could catch up with them. In the fourth inning of the game at Ridgewood yesterday, Mitchell rendered one of the most outrageous decisions ever given on a ball

field.... Players and spectators saw the cheat. So plain was Robinson's failure to touch third that no effort was made to put him out at the home plate. Mr. Mitchell said Robinson had fairly scored.[12]

After Robinson was declared safe, Charlie Byrne, the Brooklyn manager, sat down on the Browns bench beside Robinson and, according to Von der Ahe, said: "That was a d_ _ _ dirty trick of you Robinson, to try to win a game that way." Robinson replied: "Are you hiring me?" Von der Ahe added: "Now look here, Byrne, you manage your men and I'll attend to mine. If the umpire didn't see the play, that was his fault not ours. Your men would cut a base, too. Now you get off our bench, and leave us alone, or I'll see that you do."[13] There was no further scoring. The Browns walked away with a come-from-behind 4–3 victory, with the winning run scored on Robinson's theft.

When Comiskey was not orchestrating tricks to prevent runners from advancing one or more bases, he took it upon himself to catch four-legged runaways. In a home game in which the Browns beat Philadelphia, 9–2 (July 16), Comiskey was the "hero of the hour,"[14] but not for anything he did at bat, on the bases, or in the field. He captured a runaway team of horses before any harm came to them or to those in their path. The *St. Louis Republican* described Comiskey's equine heroics:

> Just at the conclusion of the second inning, a runaway team, with a handsome brougham attached, dashed into the over-field from the carriageway and sped around the park at a terrific rate of speed. It began to look as if the carriage would be dashed to pieces, but, by a daring effort, Capt. Comiskey made a bold dash after the runaways and pluckily held on to them until they were quieted. His great catch was lustily cheered, and though an innovative feature at ball games, it proved an exciting struggle, more so than the Athletics' encounter with the champions.[15]

After sweeping Philadelphia in their final home series, the Browns departed for a 12-game road trip. The first stop was in Baltimore on July 19 to replay the game of June 16, a match in which the umpire suspended play and declared it an 8–8 draw. The suspension of play followed an aggressive act by Welch in the ninth inning when, during an attempted steal of second, he knocked over Bill Greenwood, the Baltimore second baseman. The crowd erupted. Some fans tried to storm the field. Welch was arrested for assault on the field and escorted to a nearby station-house. The next day, in the final game of the series, without Welch in the line-up, both teams played without incident, no coaching, no kicking, no contrary behavior whatsoever.

The contest on July 19 was the first home game for Baltimore against the Browns since the June series. It was also the first time that Welch was in the Browns' lineup in Oriole Park since he had been arrested. How would the Baltimore fans receive the Browns and, in particular, Welch, still the hooligan-at-large in the eyes of many?

Not to be outdone by the St. Louis cranks who had warmly received the Baltimore team in St. Louis earlier in the month (July 8–11), the Baltimore fans gave the Browns an enthusiastic reception as the team entered the grounds and continued to cheer at regular intervals throughout the game each time one of the Browns made a good play or got a hit. Welch "received the heartiest round"[16] of applause, a gesture that effectively put the bad memories of his rough play on June 16 behind at least most of the crowd. The game itself also quickly overwhelmed any thoughts of past misdeeds as the fans got swept up in what the *Baltimore American* described as the "greatest game played on the Huntingdon Avenue Grounds, and in science and skill has had no equal."[17]

The spectators were treated to a classic pitchers' duel between John "Phenomenal" Smith and "Parisian" Bob Caruthers. Supported by strong fielding by both teams, the pitchers had numerous three-up-three-down innings—Caruthers had seven, Smith four—while scattering a handful of hits over 14 innings after which the game was called on account of darkness. The final score was 2–2, with the only earned run as a result of O'Neill's home run in the fourth inning. O'Neill led the Browns at the plate with four hits in six times at bat, a home run, a single, and two bases on balls, one of which was an intentional walk.

In the fourth inning, with Baltimore leading, 1–0, O'Neill came to the plate with one out, determined to help the Browns even the score. He patiently "stood like a statue until he had four balls and three strikes called."[18] The fans in the stands rose to their feet, cheering for a fourth strike, while those gathered in downtown Baltimore outside the *American* building leaned forward, anxiously awaiting the click of the telegraph and the shout of the auctioneer for the breaking news of what O'Neill did on the next pitch. O'Neill blasted a line shot that "sailed majestically over Sommer's head,"[19] landing well over the fence in left-center field. The *American* exclaimed that the home run "was a daisy, probably the longest made on the grounds. It struck the houses on the near street."[20] Tip was loudly applauded in Oriole Park for his monstrous hit, while the crowd outside the *American* building, upon hearing the news of Tip's four-bagger, probably gasped and then groaned, disappointed that the game was now tied.

Baltimore took the lead in the fifth inning, and the Browns responded three innings later, knotting the score at two runs apiece. The "tug of war"[21] over the next five innings resulted in no runs by either team as Caruthers and Smith bore down on their respective opposing batters with the support of numerous brilliant plays in the field. The stage was set for the 14th and final inning, with both teams pressing for the win.

In the top of the 14th inning, Blondie Purcell, the Baltimore right fielder, went out on a fly to Welch. Oyster Burns, the shortstop, followed with a ground out to Latham, who made a "great stop on a hot ball."[22] Tommy Tucker singled and stole second on a wild throw by Boyle, with the ball skidding out to center field. On the overthrow, Robinson fell on the sliding Tucker and kept him pinned to the ground, preventing him from going to third. Sam Trott hit a short-field single that moved Tucker to third. Most observers believed that Tucker would have gone to third on the errant throw by Boyle if Robinson had not fallen on him and then would have scored on the subsequent hit by Trott.[23] Mike Griffin, the center fielder, ended the Baltimore half of the inning by grounding out to Robinson.

The Browns came up in the bottom half of the inning with their last chance to win the game. Gleason led off with a single. Caruthers, after two bunt attempts that went foul but were called strikes, successfully got his base on a bunt hit.[24] With runners on first and second, Foutz went out on a foul tip caught by Trott. O'Neill strolled to the plate, and "things looked cheerful for the Browns"[25] until it became apparent that he would not be "allowed another legitimate hit, however, but was presented with a phantom, and the bases were full and but one out."[26] The Browns squandered this golden opportunity as the next two batters flied out, Welch to shallow center field and Robinson to the third baseman. On Smith's decision to issue an intentional walk to O'Neill, the *Baltimore Sun* declared that he "showed his headwork when he gave O'Neill a five-ball hit, filling the bases, and taking his chances with the batters who were to follow."[27] Remembering Tip's earlier home run, the Baltimore press saw the wisdom in taking the bat out of his hands.

Three days later, in the second of two games in New York, O'Neill once again hit a home run, this time in the first inning of a match that, like the game in Baltimore, went into extra innings and ended in a 2–2 tie. His four-bagger was a solo shot, as was his home run in Baltimore, but this time stayed inside the park, giving the Browns a 1–0 lead. Unlike the ovation he received in Baltimore, O'Neill's New York home run agitated the crowd. Darby O'Brien, the New York left fielder, was badly hurt in his effort to catch the deep hit to left field:

> St. Louis took the lead in the first inning when O'Neill hit a long fly to O'Brien. The latter got the ball after a hard run, but, just as he was closing his hands, ran against the fence and dropped the ball, allowing the batter to clear the circuit of the bases. The force of the collision knocked O'Brien insensible, and a few minutes elapsed before he regained consciousness. He fell amid broken glass and his hands were badly cut.[28]

Some fans "thought O'Brien was entitled to the out and hooted the umpire during the rest of the match."[29] Furthermore, they would not have wanted O'Neill to receive a prize for a home run earned at the expense of an injured outfielder. Earlier in the season, the *New York World* announced that a bottle of *Pond's Extract* would be awarded to the player who made "the best batting and fielding average in the New York and Brooklyn Clubs, and to every player of the visiting club who makes a home run."[30] Tip likely left New York without his bottle of *Extract*.

After two ties and a loss in their last three games—tied Baltimore, 2–2, lost to New York, 10–6, and tied New York, 2–2—the Browns got back into the win column, victorious in five of the next six games. O'Neill contributed very little to the Browns' two wins and one loss against Brooklyn or to their three-game sweep of Baltimore, managing only three hits and one run batted in. He went hitless in four of the six games. In one barren, three-game stretch (July 26–28), O'Neill strolled to the plate 12 times in a row without a hit.[31] From this low point in his season, O'Neill began his return to form in the next three-game series as the Browns took two of three games in Philadelphia (July 30 to August 2). O'Neill had six hits in 12 times at bat in the series, including a home run over the left field fence in the Browns' 6–5 win in game one. He scored or drove in ten of the 21 runs scored by the Browns in their three games against Philadelphia. Ending their road trip with three series wins in a row, the Browns headed home, battle-weary but proud of their record abroad. There was no place like home, an adage that the Browns, especially Tip, would emphatically demonstrate in their prolonged August stand at Sportsman's Park.

In St. Louis, Tip, like many of the Browns who did not live year-round in St. Louis, roomed outside of Sportsman's Park in one of the apartment buildings owned by Von der Ahe, some of which were named after the players, and near a tavern, also owned by the Boss President. The bachelor Browns—Foutz, Robinson, Caruthers, Hudson, Boyle, King, and O'Neill[32]—and, on occasion, some of the married Browns—Bushong, Gleason, Welch, and Latham—took their meals at Comiskey's residence. The *St. Louis Republican* teased about the strategic genius of Comiskey that was likely at work in these meals:

> It has never before been brought out, but perhaps this explains the secret of Comiskey's wonderful command of his men. At the noon meal, he gives them instructions as to what is expected of them in the afternoon game, and in case any of them fail to toe the mark, he sends them home to bed without any supper.[33]

Months later, when asked about these meals, Comiskey replied that he "feeds them on eggs and beef, the former … to produce brain and the latter muscle."[34] The Browns seemed to eat, drink, and sleep baseball.

Tip O'Neill also returned to many of the routines and traditions that were part of playing at home. Prior to the game, he gathered with his teammates near the tavern for a parade along the streets and into Sportsman's Park. Young boys, possibly some who played on the Little O'Neills, a team organized for boys under 12 years of age,[35] surrounded Tip, vying for a chance to carry his bat bag in the procession. Befitting the occasion, the Browns emerged from their clubhouse and ran onto the field "in an entirely new and quite charming regalia—striped caps, blue blouses, white pantaloons and brown hose."[36] It was a homecoming, their first game back after a 14-day road trip, and as such, a time when fans lined the route of the parade and filled the seats of Sportsman's Park, all the while cheering their champion Browns.

The first home series was against Cincinnati. It opened on a Thursday (August 4), one of the days in the week formally acknowledged as Ladies Day. A large crowd was on hand, with the ladies filling the "lower stand ... one mass of bright dresses and waving fans."[37] The *St. Louis Republican* observed:

> A great crowd greeted the Browns yesterday on their return from the East and watched them toy for a brief time with the red-hosed heroes of Porkopolis. It was a jolly, good-natured crowd, who didn't mind the inconvenience of being packed in the grandstand like so many sardines in a box, for every seat was taken, and some of the seats were more than taken; but everyone looked red in the face and tried to entice gusts of fresh air by a vigorous use of his hat.... The remarkable feature of the attendance was the large number of ladies, it excelling, in fact, almost doubling, anything known before in the city. The grandstand looked like one grand bouquet, and it is no wonder that the players were inspired to greater efforts than usual.[38]

As was the case in the first home game of the season, to honor their attendance and to foster their continued support, the ladies received pins designed by a local jewelry company in the shape of a bat with a ball and cap at one end and a glove and mask at the other end.[39] Once the game began, the ladies "forgot all about their little treasures and did nothing but gaze at the handsome lads in uniform,"[40] especially Tip, "the handsomest man on the team."[41] Crammed in and revved up, the fans were poised to spur their lads on to victory. And O'Neill and the Browns were ready to reward the fans for their loyal and enthusiastic encouragement.

The fans did not have to wait long for something to cheer about. The Browns jumped out to a commanding lead, scoring five earned runs in the first inning. O'Neill drove in the first run with a single to center field and came around to score the third run on Foutz's triple. With a 5–1 lead in the fifth, O'Neill completed the scoring for the Browns with a two-run home run into the benches in left-center field. On this line shot, some of the ladies did more than admire from afar, politely clap their hands, or wave their fans in delight. On this long hit, the ladies earned an "assist": "The ladies in the center-field seats yesterday knew the rules of the game. When O'Neill's home run went into the seats they scrambled out of the way so as to let the ball go as far under the boards as possible."[42] The Browns followed this 7–2 win with a 5–0 loss in game two and a come-from-behind 3–2 win in game three. O'Neill finished the series with four hits (two singles, double, home run) in 12 times at bat, a modest output that gave little hint of the breakout performance that was to follow in the next series against Cleveland.

While fewer runs were scored in the four-game series against Cleveland (August 7–10) than in their first four-game-series in St. Louis (April 27 to May 1), the outcome was the same, namely a four-game sweep by the Browns.[43] O'Neill outdid himself in this series with a batting average of .789 (15 hits in 19 times at bat), exceeding his previous high of

.739 (17-for-23) achieved in the spring series. He hit with less power in this series, banging out five doubles and one triple in the four games, compared to five doubles, two triples, and two home runs in the four April games. He also had a lower number of runs and runs batted in, scoring 13 times but batting in only three runs in the four games in August. In the four games in the spring, he scored 11 times and drove in 11 runs. However, in the August series, O'Neill produced more runs. He figured in 16 of the 41 runs scored by the Browns (39 percent) whereas in the April 27–to–May 1 series, he was involved in only 19 of the 74 runs scored by the Browns (26 percent). Furthermore, between August 7 and 10, his runs had a greater impact on the eventual outcomes of the games; five of his runs scored either tied the game or put the Browns ahead. In game one, he crossed the plate with the winning run. In the end-of-April series against Cleveland, Tip created only two runs that had a similar effect, in that case, both on runs batted in, each of which put the Browns ahead.

In the Browns' 10–7 win in game one, O'Neill was featured for both his batting (three hits in five times at bat, two doubles and an intentional base on balls) and his fielding (four putouts). The Browns beat Cleveland, 8–4, in game two. From his first time at bat in game two to his first time at bat in game four, O'Neill got on base 11 times in a row, with ten hits to his credit, including six singles, two doubles, one triple, and one base on balls. O'Neill initiated his on-base streak with a four-hit effort, including singles in his first three times at the plate (first, third, and fifth innings), a hit-by-pitch in the sixth, and a double in the ninth inning. He contributed to four of the Browns' eight runs, scoring three and driving in one. Cleveland had an 8–5 lead after seven innings in game three, but the Browns rallied for three runs in each of the last two innings for the 11–8 win. O'Neill continued his streak with five hits in five times at bat: a single in the first, a base on balls in the third, a double in the sixth, a single in the eighth, and a triple in the ninth. He scored four runs and drove in another. In addition to sustaining his on-base streak, his single-double-triple tally constituted a near-cycle performance.[44] O'Neill's 11th and last time at bat in the streak occurred in the first inning of game four. He singled, advanced to second on a single by Comiskey, and came home on an error by Pete Hotaling, the Cleveland center fielder, on a towering fly hit by Foutz. In his next at bat, Tip grounded out to shortstop. He singled in the fourth inning and doubled in the sixth, scoring another run following each of these hits. The Browns won, 12–4. During the innings in which O'Neill was on his streak, he scored or drove in ten (or 48 percent) of the 21 runs scored by the Browns, a run production that was greater than the 12 (or 36 percent) of 36 runs scored or batted in during his streak in the April 27–May 1 series against Cleveland.

The local press celebrated the awakening of their previously slumbering slugger. *The Sporting News* exclaimed:

> Tip O'Neill is again slugging the ball in his old-time form. In the Cleveland games of Monday and Tuesday out of nine times at bat, he made nine safe hits, with two two-baggers and three-bagger included. Tip has marvelous hitting propensities, and certainly deserves to rank as the hardest hitter in the profession.[45]

Joining this jubilation about O'Neill's return to form, the *St. Louis Post-Dispatch* went further, foreshadowing his eventual batting championship: "Tip O'Neill has again located his optic on the ball and has taken a big jump for the lead in the champions' camp in batting. At his present rate, he will lead the Association at the end of the season."[46] Such bold claims or predictions had been made before, no doubt as an expression of local pride laced with some level of puffery, or perhaps as a counter to those in other Association cities making similar declarations on behalf of their leading batsman.

Tip O'Neill and Louisville's Pete Browning were both mired in their worst batting phases of the 1887 season. O'Neill entered phase three of the 1887 season with a batting average of .490, 14 points ahead of Browning's .476. Seventeen days later, O'Neill's lead had evaporated. In the six games between July 24 and 29, O'Neill had his worst week of the season, recording only three hits in 24 times at bat. As a result, O'Neill's average fell to .453, four points behind Browning's leading average of .457. It was the first time since the early days of the season that Tip was not at the head of the class of Association batsmen.

In this phase, the competition between O'Neill and Browning seemed less about which of the arch-rivals would leap into the lead in the batting race and more about which player would first stop his slide in batting. Between July 12 and August 6, O'Neill had only 31 hits in 90 times at bat for an average of .341. Tip's overall average had dropped 40 points to .450. Browning's average had also fallen in this period from .476 on July 12 to .453 on August 6. Browning was winning the race for whose batting average would fall the least. It would take an extraordinary performance by O'Neill in the last series of phase three not only to halt the slide but also to reverse it, and in so doing, regain the outright lead in the batting race.

O'Neill's dramatic surge in the Cleveland series gave him a much-needed boost over Browning. As the table below documents, his stellar performance in the Cleveland series increased his average for the phase to .422 and his overall average to .469, reducing his fall between phase two and three to 21 points. In his final series against Cincinnati, Browning had five hits in 12 times at bat, which increased his average over the July 12–August 10 period to .379 but decreased his overall average to .452. As he began phase four, Browning had fallen 24 points overall and was now 17 points behind O'Neill. In the race to stop the fallen averages, O'Neill had won.

	Games	*AB*	*R*	*H*	*BB*	*1B*	*2B*	*3B*	*HR*	*AVG*	*SB*
July 12–August 10	25	109	31	46	10	22	8	2	4	.422	3
April 16–August 10	77	350	102	164	36	80	30	8	10	.469	18

Browning, however, was a two-time batting champion in the Association (1882, 1885), had finished second twice (1883, 1886) and third once (1884), and was not about to concede the 1887 batting championship to O'Neill, a player who had never won a batting title. The *St. Louis Post-Dispatch* brought the alleged Browning obsession with beating O'Neill to the attention of its readers through a series of stories, some likely true, some embellished. The first *Post-Dispatch* story concerned a conversation Browning had with a reporter from *The Sporting News*:

> Now when I bat I watch the pitcher's eyes, and I can tell you just where's he's going to pitch the ball. It works first-rate. I'm lining the ball out for all it's worth, and the pitchers can't understand it. You can tell it to some of your friends in the League but don't give it away to Jim O'Neill or Dave Orr, because I want to lead the American Association in batting this year.[47]

The *St. Louis Post-Dispatch* followed the above interview with two other notes, the first on August 2 and the second on August 5:

> Pete Browning declares that "Tip" O'Neill must stand in with the official scorers. "Why," said Pete, "he hasn't made a hit in nine games and I've been hittin' the ball on the nose and yet he leads the Association."[48]

Tip O'Neill still leads the Association in batting. Pete Browning is a strong competitor for first honors in this department. While in New York recently, Pete met Tip. "Say, Tip, old man, I'll make you hustle before the season's over, I'm hittin' big."

Tip smiled and told Pete that he [Pete] was the greatest hitter in the land. He could discount all the big Association and League hitters, but he was playing in a little hard luck was the only reason why his average wasn't .600.

Just then John Kelly came along, and Pete blurts out: "Say, John, ain't I a hittin' though. I'll beat Tip yet." "Come off, you big baby! O'Neill can give you cards and spades and beat you out," was the king umpire's reply.[49]

Some days later, *The Sporting News* appeared exasperated by Browning's whining, easily siding with O'Neill as the better batsman and the better man:

> If the fight for the leadership in the official batting averages in the Association comes down between Tip O'Neill and the gladiatorial Browning, Tip will beat him out easy. Pete is constantly kicking about his batting not being recognized etc, while Tip goes quietly about his business, and pounds the life out of all opposing pitchers.[50]

The *St. Louis Republican* published its own quote from Browning about an upcoming series between Louisville and St. Louis (August 12–13): "Pete Browning says when he comes to St. Louis next Thursday he will fatten up his batting averages to such an extent that he will leave Tip O'Neill in the shade. This is as it should be, as no man wants to be in the sun this weather."[51] Browning stayed in the news, for better or worse, alternately fretting about his standing and confidently predicting his eventual victory over O'Neill by season's end. Tip remained silent on their rivalry.

Somewhat lost in this so-called tug of war between O'Neill and Browning was the fact that other Association batsmen had moved closer to both main protagonists. Denny Lyons, the Philadelphia third baseman, and Reddy Mack, the Louisville second baseman, were among the top five batsmen in the American Association. Other than O'Neill, Lyons was the only batsman who hit over .400 in each of the first three phases of the season: .420 between April 16 and May 24, .406 between May 25 and July 11, and .413 between July 12 and August 10, with an overall average of .412 on August 10. Reddy Mack's numbers for the first three phases were .434, .459, and .386, with an overall average of .429 at the end of phase three.

On the Browns, Robinson and Caruthers were two of only six Association batsmen still over .400. Robinson had a higher average than O'Neill in the last two phases, hitting .459 between May 25 and July 11 and .451 between July 12 and August 10. His .451 average in phase three was the best among the leading batsmen in the American Association, lifting his overall average to .425. Caruthers came in with an overall average of .418 despite his .386 performance in phase three. Foutz fell further back with a .387 average in this phase, dropping to an overall average of .398.[52]

With two phases in a row where O'Neill no longer appeared to stand apart or unchallenged as the batting leader in the American Association, there was reason to question whether O'Neill could retain his lead the rest of the season. Was O'Neill's extraordinary batting in the Cleveland series (August 7–10) a sign of things to come or a one-off performance against a last-place team? For some, his outstanding batting record in Cleveland was admittedly the exception in a string of unexceptional series stretching back to June 6. However, as he would soon show, these achievements in Cleveland marked the beginning of an exceptional run during which he returned to the slugging form he displayed in the first phase of the season.

11

Long Hits

In the 1880s, the expression "long hits" was used to describe extra-base hits, that is, doubles, triples, and home runs. The fans were increasingly thrilled by long hits, so much so that every time a slugger such as O'Neill stepped up to the plate, they cheered wildly with the hope that he would launch yet another blast, screaming deep into the field if not over the fence. Some observers and most managers, however, were less enamored of long hits, favoring instead scientific hitting, an orientation to batting that they argued better supported the team in its pursuit of victory. For Henry Chadwick, in this "batting-for-the-side"[1] approach, when a teammate was on base, the batsman devoted himself to the sole purpose of "doing his best to forward the runner round, if on first base, or in getting the runner home if the latter is on third.... In doing this he is just as ready to make a sacrifice hit as in any other way to give advantage to the team he is on."[2] Three years later, after witnessing the significant increase in the number of long hits in 1887, Chadwick, in the *Spalding's Official Base Ball Guide, 1888*, lamented: "Scientific batting—which is neither more nor less than doing team work at the bat such as in 'placing the ball,' making 'sacrifice hits,' studying the philosophy of handling the bat in proper form against strategic pitching—is as yet known only to a minority of batsmen."[3] He turned to a critique of home run hitting, the preferred choice of record players,[4] concluding that the "slugging style of batting" is a "drawback in progress toward scientific hitting and thorough team work at the bat."[5] According to observers such as Chadwick, short or "light," crisp hits such as well-placed singles or sacrifices constituted batting for the side, while most long hits privileged personal glory over the success of the team.[6]

Many newspapers, however, in their daily reports and notes featured the long hits made in each game. They heralded the sluggers for their power, and, in at least one case, questioned whether the system of tabulating a player's batting average fully recognized the contribution of these heavy hitters. The *St. Louis Post-Dispatch* argued that "computing a batter's average on his total bases" would both give the slugger his due and provide fans with a more complete and accurate measure of his batting performance:

> What they [the people] want is a batting average that will tell the correct story at once. No average can be a just one, the thinking man says, which makes no distinction between a home run and a single, between a grand three-bagger clearing the bases, and a little Latham bunt which the runner beats to first. Surely a batter should not get as much credit for a bunt as for a home run, and yet no distinction is made in the present system. The percentage is figured on the number of single hits in proportion to the times at bat. Therefore, if O'Neill twice at bat, makes two home runs, that is bats in two runs, at the least, and Latham, twice at bat, gets first on two bunts, the batting averages of the two men will be the same. If that is rewarding a player for superior batting, it is hard to see it.[7]

While the *Post-Dispatch's* proposal was not adopted,[8] it did draw even more attention to the importance of sluggers to the game and to the possible ways one could better recognize the value of long hits to an individual's and the team's record.

As the manager and captain of the Browns, Charlie Comiskey's offensive strategies were not dependent on or built around the long ball.[9] When asked about the *St. Louis Post-Dispatch* proposal to replace the current batting average with an average weighted to take into account the number of bases generated by a batsman's hits (total bases divided by times at bat), Comiskey gave a Chadwick-like response: "Capt. Comiskey of the Browns said no at once when the change was suggested to him. He declared it would practically stop sacrifice hitting and cause the batting of high flies, as, according to Comiskey, every little hitter would try to get in a big hit and raise his average."[10] He worried that such a change would encourage an increase in the long ball at the expense of the kind of strategic hitting that would better serve the Browns' capacity to manufacture runs by any and all means.

Many of the fans, of course, were not particularly concerned with baseball strategy. Nor were they especially bothered by condescending and disparaging remarks from commentators such as Chadwick, who sometimes ridiculed both fans and players for their shallow worship of the long hit:

> All batsmen who go for a record strive their utmost to make home runs. They are well aware of the fact that the majority of spectators at a match—especially in country towns—know little or nothing of what constitutes real skill in batting; the prevailing idea of the crowd being, that the best batsman is the "slugger," who manages to scratch a home run once out of every nine times at the bat. Hence the éclat attendant upon a dashing hit of the kind is too tempting to resist, and hence they throw team work in batting to the dogs, though it proves costly in the long run to the success of a team in taking the lead in a championship race.[11]

The fans enjoyed the offensive burst of 1887, especially the long hits. They got excited by the canon-like crack of the bat on a long hit, the blistering blur of the ball as it soared into the sky, and the frantic dash of the batsman as he rounded second, then third, and raced home. These sudden, unscripted, and heroic feats stirred the souls of those in the stands. They cheered wildly, their joy unbridled, their celebration frenzied and overflowing. What could the fans do but "long" for more, inviting their favorite slugger to wallop the ball again in his next at-bat.

When O'Neill strolled to the plate, the fans often greeted him with chants urging him to hit the ball over the fence. Similarly, when O'Neill was in left field, and especially in well-attended games when the fans lined the outfield, they engaged him in chatter about his play, again imploring him to hit a long ball their way in his next at-bat. Sometimes the temptation to respond to fans was too great and so, likely against his better judgment, he occasionally took up the crank challenge. In 1886, during the eighth game of the nine-game pre-season series against the St. Louis Maroons of the National League, as he came to bat, a fan yelled out: "Tip, put her over the fence and I'll buy you a new hat." Tip smiled, tipped his cap, and called back, "It's a go," and then smashed the ball over the left field fence.[12] Early in 1887, again inspired by the thirst for long hits by his admiring fans, O'Neill boldly declared that he would hit the hat sign in left-center field, a promise that he failed to make good, despite two doubles, one to the seats in left and the other to center field.[13] Tip was at it again on August 4 in the Browns' first game back at Sportsman's Park after an extended road trip. It was Thursday, Ladies Day, and the "grand stand was crowded with the youth and beauty of St. Louis, and even the bleaching boards contained a goodly portion of the precious load."[14] The Browns beat Cincinnati, 7–2, with O'Neill hitting a home run. Joe Pritchard, the St. Louis correspondent for *Sporting Life,* described what happened when Tip obliged a request from one of the young ladies in the left field seats:

> One fair beauty was sitting close to "Tip" O'Neill's pasture and asked him to knock a ball out to her when he was next at the bat so that she might "catch him out." The Browns' great slugger promised the young lady that he would give her a chance, and he was as good as his word. The sphere went sailing on a line from the home plate to the young lady, but instead of making an effort to catch it she attempted to get out of the way, and it struck her square in the—the—bustle. The young lady now takes her meals standing.[15]

Comiskey may not have liked the cockiness in these apparent fan-induced efforts to hit a home run, but he understood that O'Neill was a team player and could be counted on to respond dutifully when the captain wanted him to hit a ball to a particular side of the field or to advance a runner with a hit that would very likely ensure his own out. At the same time, Comiskey knew that O'Neill could hit for extra bases, which at certain points in the game was possibly more advantageous than a single or sacrifice hit. For most situations, Comiskey trusted that Tip would do the right thing.[16]

Less than a week after the *St Louis Post-Dispatch* published its proposal for a new batting average that would give sluggers their due, the *St. Louis Republican* put out a table entitled, "Long Hitters," showing the number of doubles, triples, and home runs made by about two-thirds of the Association players. Despite two phases in a row where his long-hit numbers were quite low (May 25 to August 10), on the strength of his power statistics in the first phase of the season (April 16 to May 24),[17] as of August 7 O'Neill led the Association in long hits and home runs. The following table[18] shows the top long hitters at this point in each of the three categories as well as the number of long hits when all three are combined:

Doubles		*Triples*	
Phillips (Brooklyn)	32	Davis (Baltimore)	16
O'Brien (New York)	28	Kerins (Louisville)	13
Latham (St. Louis)	28	Burns (Baltimore)	12
O'Neill (St. Louis)	27	McPhee (Cincinnati)	12
Lyons (Philadelphia)	27	Lyons (Philadelphia)	12
Browning (Louisville)	26	O'Neill (St. Louis)	8
Foutz (St. Louis)	26	(tied with 8 others in 14th place)	
Home Runs		*Total*	
O'Neill (St. Louis)	10	O'Neill (St. Louis)	45
Burns (Baltimore)	9	Burns (Baltimore)	44
Reilly (Cincinnati)	7	Lyons (Philadelphia)	43
Tucker (Baltimore)	6	Foutz (St. Louis)	40
Caruthers (St. Louis)	5	Phillips (Brooklyn)	40

Remarkably by season's end, O'Neill led the Association in doubles, triples and home runs, in front of all competitors by a significant margin in long hits, doubles, and home runs. His 52 doubles were nine better than Lyons, second with 43, and 19 more than the 35 registered by Pete Browning, Arlie Latham, and John Reilly. A definite "long shot" in the race for the most triples on August 7, O'Neill surged to the front by the last day of the season, winding up with 22 triples, ahead of five players—Oyster Burns, Jumbo Davis, Tom Poorman, John Kerins, and Bid McPhee—who were tied for second with 19 triples.[19] O'Neill and Reilly were the only two batters in double figures in home runs. O'Neill was first with 14 home runs, Reilly second with ten, and Burns third with nine. In total long hits, O'Neill, who had only one more extra-base hit than second-place Burns on August 7, finished the season with 88 long hits, an impressive 25 better than Lyons, the runner-up with 63. Tip dominated the Association in long hits over the last two phases of the season (August 12 to October 9).

Of O'Neill's 88 long hits, only five went over the fence, sometimes landing in the streets or near houses outside the park. The other 83 long hits were inside-the-park strokes to all fields, although 20 of the 29 triples and home runs described in some detail in game reports were line drives to left field or left center.[20] Sixty-four of his long hits— 38 doubles, 16 triples, and 10 home runs—came in Sportsman's Park. O'Neill also had 16 multi-long-hit games: one four-long-hit game, three three-long-hit-games, and 12 two-long-hit games. Thirteen of his 16 multi-long-hit games were in phases one (April 16 to May 24) and four (August 12 to September 8).[21]

O'Neill's longest shots in Sportsman's Park were often to center field on a line to the bulletin board, a distance well over 400 feet from the plate.[22] However, on some of his hard-hit, inside-the-park long balls, ones that had the promise of a triple or a home run, he was held to a double. For example, on May 19, in a game in which the Browns beat Philadelphia, 8–4, O'Neill came to the plate in the third inning with one man out, no one on base, and the score tied, 2–2. He drove the ball deep to center. The *St. Louis Chronicle* exclaimed: "O'Neill hit the bulletin board, making two bags, while the crowd yelled itself black in the face."[23] Amidst this unrestrained adulation, Harry Stovey, the fleet-footed center fielder for Philadelphia, as he had done in previous games, likely gathered the ball quickly and fired the ball back to the infield in time to halt O'Neill's progress. Sometimes O'Neill hit the ball so hard that it bounded off the wall that surrounded the bulletin board with a force that allowed the fielder to scoop it up and in one motion turn and throw it to the infield, again stopping Tip in his tracks. In inclement weather, a rain-soaked field occasionally slowed the ball, thus enabling the fielder to get to it sooner and consequently reduce O'Neill's aspirations from a triple or home run to a double. Or sometimes Tip misjudged the magnitude of his hit, surmising incorrectly that the speed with which the ball left the bat and the distance travelled by the ball gave him plenty of time to reach third or home.[24] Once he discovered this error in judgment, it was usually too late to advance any further than second. Regardless of the reason, a number of O'Neill's biggest hits turned out to be only good for a double.

Now and then an umpire applied a local ground rule[25] that limited O'Neill's long hit to a double. Most Association parks had some conditions or structures that affected such things as when a ball is in play (e.g., if it hits an obstacle) or considered to be out of bounds. In the 1880s, ground rules also could arise in response to the particular circumstances of a game, such as a large crowd, which required some fans to stand close to the foul lines and around the outfield, in some cases encroaching on the field of play. The umpire was obliged to consult with the captain of the home club to determine the ground rules in effect that game.[26] O'Neill played in a number of games where, because of the large crowd surrounding the field, any ball hit into the fans standing behind the outfielders was ruled a double. While it was possible that some of these balls lofted into the fans might have been caught by the fielder, some of O'Neill's hits into the crowds also might have gone for more than a double.[27]

One of the more unusual ground rules in the Association was instituted in the St. George Cricket Grounds on Staten Island, the home park of the New York Metropolitans.

The St. George Grounds was part of a multi-purpose amusement park that included a casino, a platform for a 60-piece band, tennis courts, an ice cream saloon, a picnic area, illuminated fountains, and areas for companies such as the Buffalo Bill's Wild West Show to perform. There was no fence to separate the Grounds from the rest of the amusement park, and so, on occasion, hits that got by the center and right fielders bounded into some of these other facilities. In 1887, the closest entertainment to the Grounds was an extravaganza known as "The Fall of Babylon," a theatrical spectacle that recreated the destruction of Babylon. The various props (e.g., lavish sets, panoramas, scenery), structures (e.g., turrets), and elaborate stage formed a border to the Grounds from center to right field.[28] Any ball hit into "The Fall of Babylon" entitled the batsman to two bases.[29]

On September 3, the Browns beat New York in the first game of a doubleheader by a score of 20–8. In the fifth inning, O'Neill "batted a ball over the Babylon scenery at center-field, the first time that feat had been done."[30] Days later, infused with the kind of light-hearted spirit befitting an amusement park, the *St. Louis Post-Dispatch* recounted the futile attempts of Charley Jones, the New York center fielder, to track down the ball launched by Tip over "Babylon's outer walls"[31]:

> A funny thing occurred at St. George's Grounds, Staten Island, during one of the St. Louis-Mets games. Tip O'Neill knocked a sky-scraper that looked like the POST-DISPATCH balloon miles away. It went sailing over the pinnacles of the Babylon scenery, and as Baby Jones ran up the ancient steps to watch its course the ball looked as though it had gone chasing an out-going steamer to the ocean. After a moment's deliberation Baby Jones, in the deep, stentorian voice of a Roman senator, yelled to Bob Ferguson: "Get a new ball, Bob, it's gone out to sea." Tip could have made two home runs on it.[32]

Of course, O'Neill did not make even one home run on this hit, because the ground rule provided for only a double on any ball hit into Babylon. Those who made the rule probably did not anticipate a batter hitting the ball over Babylon, but the umpire decided that he had no recourse but to apply the existing rule. On one of Tip's longest hits of the season, he stopped at second with a double.

O'Neill's 22 triples and 14 home runs attracted the most coverage in the newspapers. He hit 13 of his 14 home runs by August 29, his last home run not coming until October 6. By season's end, some observers were convinced that O'Neill was capable of hitting many more home runs if he played in more cavernous parks:

> O'Neill, although he has the best batting averages of any player in the country, does not lead in the matter of home runs. The reason for this fact is, that while he hits the ball hard he seldom sends it high in the air. He generally "lines them out," and unless playing on grounds like those at the Cincinnati Park, he seldom gets the full benefit of his hits. He has frequently sent the ball spinning against the short field fence at Sportsman Park, St. Louis, with such force that he would have difficulty in reaching second, while had the ball met no obstruction, he would have been sitting on the bench with a home run to his credit before it could be fielded in.[33]

While in the last six weeks of the season home runs were harder to come by, O'Neill nonetheless kept up his slugging with triples. From August 30 to October 6, he hit 12 three-baggers in a 29-game stretch, the final one of the season in the same game in which he hit his 14th home run. In addition to the five home runs that left the park, he hit another five home runs and two triples into the left field benches in Sportsman's Park.[34]

Among his 16 multi-long-hit games, O'Neill hit two triples in a game twice, both times against Brooklyn, the first on August 30, as part of a 7–4 win in St. Louis, and the second, on September 7, as part of a 14–9 victory in Brooklyn. Following his two-home-run performance in game two of the 1886 World Series against Chicago, O'Neill repeated this feat on April 30 as he hit for the cycle in a 28–11 win against Cleveland. He also had three games in which he hit a triple and a home run, twice as part of the cycle (April 30 and May 7), and, on October 6, in the second game of a doubleheader in St. Louis against Louisville.

After losing to Louisville, 12–10, in the first game, the Browns roared back to take the second game, 11–5. O'Neill led the way with five hits in five times at bat: "The feature of the game was O'Neill's batting. He went to bat six times, got his base on balls once, made two singles, a three-bagger, and two home runs, but one of the home runs was made in the ninth inning, which was not played out and does not count."[35] In his first at-bat, O'Neill hit a triple that drove in the Browns' second run. He scored the third run on Comiskey's sacrifice fly. In the seventh inning, O'Neill opened the inning with a home run into the left field benches, scoring the Browns' eighth run. The Browns went to bat in the ninth inning with an 11–5 lead. O'Neill hit another home run, driving in three runs to extend the Browns' lead to 17–5. However, at that point, the umpire called the game on account of darkness. Unable to complete the ninth inning, the umpire declared that the official record would show an 11–5 victory for the Browns at the end of eight innings. The six runs scored by the Browns in the top of the ninth did not count, nor did any of the individual performances of the Browns batsmen. The ruling thus expunged from the official records what would have been O'Neill's third two-home-run game in less than a year. The *St. Louis Republican* was livid about the stalling tactics used by Ice Box Chamberlain, the Louisville pitcher:

> After the Browns had pounded him [Chamberlain] around for sometime he quit trying and played lazily, and then in the ninth inning, after the Browns had pounded out six runs, he delayed the game until Connelly was compelled to call the game on account of darkness, although he should never have done so. It was a contemptible bit of work upon the part of Chamberlain and robs several of the Browns of well-earned hits. Had the game depended on his action, it would be viewed differently, but as it was there was no excuse for it and Connelly should have made him suffer for it.[36]

Through one ruling or another—a ground-rule double, a called game, blocking or fan interference, a forfeited game—sluggers such as O'Neill sometimes had a long hit either limited to a double when it might have been a triple or home run, or denied altogether. Such rulings nonetheless did little to detract from the fascination on the part of the fans and the press with the magic of the long ball. With 88 long hits in 1887, Tip was the master magician, driving balls with power and consequence to the delight and applause of baseball cranks and pundits in St. Louis and beyond.

O'Neill's 88 long hits were the most ever recorded in one season in the American Association (1882–1891) and stood as the major league record until Babe Ruth's 99 extra-base hits in 1920.[37] In the last two months of the season, it took an extraordinary long-hit outburst for O'Neill to lead the league in long hits and in each of the long-hit categories (double, triple, home run). With his slugging resurgence in the fourth phase of the season (August 12 to September 8), O'Neill established himself as the premier long hitter of 1887.

12

August 12 to September 8: Batting for Power

O'Neill's performance in phase four, like that of the Browns, was similar to the extraordinary record of the team and the slugger in the first phase of the season (April 16 to May 24). The Browns began the year with 22 wins and five losses, with a 19–5 record in games O'Neill played. They won six of seven series and had a 15-game winning streak. On the final day of phase one (May 24), the Browns had a six-game lead over second-place Baltimore. In phase four, they had a 19–5 win-loss record, won six of eight series, and had a 12-game winning streak. On the last day of phase four (September 8), the Browns had their biggest lead of the season, 19 games ahead of second-place Louisville and Cincinnati.

In the 24 games played in phase four (August 12 to September 8), within the batting lines[1] O'Neill wielded his little wagon tongue bat[2] with devastating power. As the table below illustrates, in this phase O'Neill matched or exceeded many of the numbers he put up in phase one. Tip won the battle between pitcher and batsman most of the time in both phases, hitting .500 or better in five of seven series in phase one and six of the eight series in phase four. In the April-May phase, he had two or more hits in 19 of 24 games, with five or more hits in three games and five four-hit games, and, in the August-September phase, he had two or more hits in 20 of the 24 games,[3] with five or more hits in three games and three four-hit games. O'Neill had 26 long hits and 107 total bases in each phase. He drove in 31 runs in phase one and 44 runs in phase four. Returning to the same dominating form that he displayed in phase one, O'Neill combined batting for power with batting for average.

	Games	*AB*	*R*	*H*	*BB*	*1B*	*2B*	*3B*	*HR*	*AVG*	*SB*
April 16 to May 24	24	116	41	65	12	27	15	6	5	.560	9
August 12 to September 8	24	115	44	66	10	30	14	9	3	.574	11

AB–At-Bats; R–Runs; H–Hits; BB–Base on Balls 1B–Single; 2B–Double; 3B–Triple; HR–Home Run; AVG.–Batting Average; SB–Stolen Bases

Notwithstanding the many similarities in his performances in the two phases, O'Neill's achievements in phase four still stood out in at least three ways. First, his batting average leapt 152 points from .422 in phase three to .574 in phase four, the largest increase from one phase to the next that O'Neill made all season.[4] Second, it was also the highest batting average of the five phases of his season, one that boosted his overall average to .495 on September 8, the closest O'Neill would come to the .500 plateau for the rest of the season.[5]

The third accomplishment that differentiated O'Neill's fourth phase was the extent to which his long hits and consequent runs and runs batted in mattered to the success of the Browns. In the August 12–September 8 period, the Browns scored fewer runs, 240, compared to 276 runs in phase one. They also had fewer hits, 390 hits in phase four and 439 hits in phase one, and fewer long hits, 75 long hits compared to 92. With O'Neill's numbers in runs, hits, and long hits about the same as those he recorded in phase one, his contributions to these three areas in phase four were thus proportionately greater. That is, he had 26 (38 percent) of the 75 extra-base hits made by the Browns in phase four compared to 26 (28 percent) of the Browns' 92 extra-base hits in phase one. Combining O'Neill's 44 runs and 38 runs batted in, he contributed to 79 (33 percent) of the 240 runs scored by the Browns in phase four, a significant increase from 67 (24 percent) of the 276 runs to which he contributed in phase one. O'Neill's timely long hits always put him in scoring position and often enabled his teammates to cross the plate.

In addition to the proportional increase in O'Neill's contribution to the runs scored by the Browns, he also distinguished himself in terms of the impact of these runs on the outcome of the game. O'Neill scored or drove in 19 runs in phase four that directly affected the course of the game, 12 runs that tied the game or put the Browns ahead and seven that represented the winning run. In phase one, O'Neill scored or drove in ten runs that tied the game or gave the Browns the lead and four that were the winning run. O'Neill's resurrection of his power game and his increase in run production bolstered a squad which, in the fourth phase of the season, was weakened by injury, illness, or personal circumstance.

At the start of the fourth phase, Doc Bushong had been sidelined for over a month with a broken finger, with no firm date set for his return to action. After taking sick on August 1 in the first inning of a game against Philadelphia,[6] Bob Caruthers was in Chicago, recovering from an illness variously reported as typhoid fever, heart disease, malaria fever, or cigarette smoking. By August 11, after one of the Chicago newspapers reported that Caruthers was feeling much better, Chris Von der Ahe sent a telegraph to Caruthers asking him when he planned to "report for duty." Receiving no reply, Von der Ahe scowled that "if Caruthers is 'playing off,' [I will] put a stop to it."[7] Nat Hudson, who last pitched on August 7 in a 10–7 win against Cleveland, was in Chicago to tend to his seriously ill mother.[8] The Browns thus entered phase four with Silver King and Dave Foutz as their only pitchers.

Two days into the fourth phase (August 14), Foutz suffered a dislocated thumb as a result of a line drive in the first inning against Cleveland. Silver King was now the only pitcher available. Caruthers returned on August 19 in right field, alternating with the sore-armed King until September 3. In early September, Von der Ahe signed Ed Knouff, a pitcher formerly with Baltimore, to be the third pitcher in the rotation. He pitched his first game in New York on September 3, winning the second game of a doubleheader, 7–4.

Among the position players, Lou Sylvester, the Browns' substitute outfielder, was hampered by a lame knee. He was released on August 20. Bushong unsuccessfully tried a comeback in two games against Cleveland (August 15–16). He did not return to the lineup until the final phase of the season.[9] Jack Boyle, the young catcher who replaced

Bushong, developed sore hands and was replaced by first Latham and then Robinson while Boyle's hands recovered.[10] By the end of August, Von der Ahe seemed more concerned about Comiskey, the "cripple" who had badly damaged his hand in the final game in a series against Brooklyn (August 31).[11] The *St. Louis Republican,* no doubt like many of the Browns fans, saw little to worry about in these maladies:

> The Browns yesterday won their eighth straight victory, which is considered quite a record for a broken-up club. The club has played with just nine men since Foutz was injured on August 14. They have had two pitchers and one catcher, and the extra pitcher has had to play right field. Their solitary catcher has been afflicted all the time with sore hands, and one of their pitchers has had a "sore" arm a good portion of the time, while the other got out of sick bed but a few weeks ago and has since met with an accident which would knock most men out. Notwithstanding all these adversities the team has kept winning against aggregations with plenty of extra men who take turns about at playing and resting up. Surely St. Louis base ball cranks are justified in boasting about their ball club and in declaring them the greatest aggregation of players in existence.[12]

Such resolve would be tested further in the first eight days of September.

The Browns opened their road trip on September 2 in New York. With only nine players, Comiskey expected everyone, including King, Boyle, Caruthers, and himself, to stay healthy, or at least, in the hard-nosed game advocated by the Browns, to remain in the lineup even if they were injured or ill. They did for two days, but on Sunday, September 4, in Monitor Park at Weehawken, New Jersey, in the replay of an earlier drawn game, another key player went down.[13] Curt Welch was accidentally hit in the nose by a bat thrown by O'Neill. He left the game in considerable pain.

Welch missed five games (September 5–9) and likely needed a few more days to recover from his injury. However, on September 10 against Philadelphia, Comiskey left the game with a broken thumb. With no substitute players on the roster, Welch was pressed into action.[14] Some newspapers predicted that Comiskey would be out for at least a month,[15] while others felt he would also miss the world championship series against Detroit.[16] Either way, phase four ended with Comiskey, Foutz, and Bushong out of the lineup, Welch reinstated when he was not ready, and Hudson still in Chicago, attending to family affairs following the death of his mother.[17]

Handicapped by the loss of key players and the injured state of some players who continued to play, the Browns' 19–5 record in the August 12–September 8 period was all the more impressive. It really did seem like the Browns could win under any conditions. Maybe the editors of the *Kansas City Journal* were right after all. In a show of state-level pride and loyalty to Missouri's leading baseball team, the paper commended the Browns on their fortitude:

> A St. Louis player may be kicked in the stomach, run over by a freight train, struck by a cyclone, have an eye knocked out, both legs broken or spine twisted in four ways, but he is always able to play ball and question the umpire's decisions.[18]

And, of course, win games.

The Browns won five games and lost three in the first three series in this phase, splitting a two-game series against Louisville (August 12–13) in St. Louis, winning all three games in Cleveland (August 14–16), and losing two out of three games at home against Philadelphia (August 19–21). In the first inning of the first game in the Cleveland series, Foutz left the game after he was struck on the thumb by a line drive off the bat of Ed McKean, the Cleveland shortstop. King, who had pitched the day before and who was starting in right field, the first time he had played in the outfield, was the only pitcher available, and so was summoned by Comiskey to take over from Foutz. King also pitched and won the last two games of the series. He also had been in the box for the last game of the previous series against Louisville. Thus, King had pitched four games in a row and could not go on without some time to rest his sore arm.

Von der Ahe was concerned about the enervated state of the Browns' pitching staff and, therefore, urgently wired Caruthers in Chicago to come back immediately. Caruthers returned for the first game of the Philadelphia series but played right field. Understandably, after pitching four games in a row, King got a well-deserved day off. Von der Ahe hastily arranged for Joe Murphy, the sporting editor of the *St. Louis Globe-Democrat,* to pitch the opening game. He won by a score of 22–8. The *St. Louis Post-Dispatch,* amused at the thought of an editor-as-pitcher reporting on his own game, commented: "Joe Murphy is the ideal base-ball editor. He steps into the pitcher's box, wins a game from the visiting club and comments on the whole business in his paper the next day. In such cases, however, Joe's opinion of the umpire might be well biased."[19] Murphy was pleased but understated in reporting on his own pitching performance: "For the Browns Joe Murphy pitched and, although hit freely, managed to keep the hits pretty well scattered, as the record of one earned run for the visitors will show."[20] King was in the box for the Browns' 10–2 loss in game two, and Caruthers pitched in the Browns' 5–1 loss to Philadelphia in game three.

In addition to the adjustments made in pitching, with only nine or ten players on their active roster during phase four, the Browns had to move their players to unfamiliar positions. For example, in the game when Boyle could not continue as catcher after the fourth inning (August 20), he moved to right field, Latham changed from third base to catcher, Caruthers moved from right to center field, Welch went from center field to second base, and Robinson vacated second to take up third base. Though their versatility and their commitment to team play enabled them to sustain their winning record, the Browns also experienced some challenges when their unfamiliarity with the position led to errors, misjudgments, or inaction.[21]

Arlie Latham, the Browns' third baseman, taking such changes in the lineup in his stride, was content to play his vocal, comic game from whatever location on the field he occupied. When Latham replaced Boyle behind the plate in game two of the Philadelphia series (August 20), he "created no end of merriment by his antics."[22] Two weeks later, a businessman recalled Latham's slapstick routine behind the plate:

> As a true bit of clowning it was a chef d'oeuvre. His business of bracing his heels very carefully into the earth before each ball pitched, his well-falsed quivering anxiety, the stolid look of awed surprise that followed the reception of each ball, his blusteringly aggressive, "Say how's that?" on balls three feet over the batsman's head, and a hundred tricks with the protector and mask kept players, umpire and audience screaming. At one time the laughter swelled into a cheer, and the clown had again and again to duck his cap.[23]

It is difficult to know how much King, the pitcher, enjoyed this buffoonery. However, Latham's comedic catching clearly distracted the crowd from feeling too bad about the 10–2 loss.

When he was not busy entertaining the fans, Latham, along with Yank Robinson, tested the limits of the new playing rules, especially the right of the umpire to call a strike on "any obvious attempt to make a foul hit."[24] Depending on the situation, Latham and Robinson resorted to this fouling tactic to tire and frustrate the pitcher, to keep the fielders off-balance, to wait for a pitch they could hit or bunt, or, in some cases, to work the pitcher for a base on balls.[25] Latham proudly described the strategic art of fouling:

> Whenever I want to make a foul I can do it as well by hitting the ball hard as I can by bunting it. Robinson does right along when three balls and no strikes are called. The way to do it is to stand back a little in the box and hit the ball before it comes to you. The result is that you knock it down toward third base, and often over the fence. A funny thing occurred to Robinson several times recently. To do this you have to hit it very hard. Well, Robbie hit her hard, and instead of going foul the ball went skimming along inside the line by third base and he got two bases on the hit. There is only one danger about the trick, and that is when you hit high you don't quite foul enough, and the third baseman captures it.[26]

Although periodically warned about their intentional fouls, Latham and Robinson persisted in their deliberate fouling. It was worth the occasional called strike if repeated foul balls disrupted the play of the opposing team or led to a base on a hit or a walk.

Always the opportunist, Robinson continued to employ some of his favorite tricks. In the Browns' 8–5 win over Louisville (August 12), Robinson was on second when Lou Sylvester hit a ball up the middle. Robinson veered across the diamond, hoping to cut third and score before a play could be made on him. As he neared the third base line, he glanced up to see that the umpire was on to his illegal shortcut. Robinson circled back to third base before the umpire could make a call. By that time, the ball had made its way into center field, where Pete Browning fumbled it, allowing Robinson to score "legally."[27] On defense, his tricks often entailed efforts to dupe the runner. In a game against Louisville that was stopped in the fourth inning on account of rain, Hub Collins, the left fielder, hit a double to Foutz in right field. Robinson went to the bag to await Foutz's throw. He stood passively, hands hanging to his side, showing no signs that the ball was on its way. Suddenly, as Collins reached second base, Robinson surprised him with a swift tag with the ball. The trick did not work this time; Collins was called safe.[28]

As the season headed into September, the press in most major league cities devoted more space to O'Neill's march to the batting title. In conversations about the leading sluggers in 1887, two opposing players were quick to single out O'Neill. Jack Milligan, one of the Philadelphia catchers, when asked, "Who do you think is the hardest hitter this season?" responded:

> Why O'Neill, most decidedly. I have stood up there behind the stick and watched his movements. He is so easy about everything. He fondles a bat and it looks to me at times like an impossibility for him to get his bat in position to hit the ball, but he generally gets the old stick in position just in the nick of time. In regard to fooling batters, I don't think there is a pitcher in the country that can fool O'Neill. He may be fooled on one or two balls, but that is about the limit. And then he hits so awful hard; it's a wonder to me that he don't kill an infielder once in a while.[29]

O'Neill had his usual strong series against Cleveland (August 14–16), batting out nine hits in 14 times at bat. Frank Brunell, the Cleveland correspondent in *Sporting Life*, remarked: "All the local twirlers proved 'berries' to Tip O'Neill. He hit out three basers on Crowell, four on Morrison, and seemed to want more."[30]

Amidst the folly and fervor of St. Louis Browns baseball, in the first eight games of phase four, O'Neill hit a respectable .405 on 15 hits in 37 times at bat. He had only two long hits, a triple against Louisville in the Browns' 13–3 loss on August 13 and a home run against Philadelphia, part of the Browns' 22–8 win in the first game of that series. His home run in the seventh inning drove in three runs, making up for a second-inning error on a fly ball with the bases loaded, a muff that resulted in three runs for Philadelphia.

Little did anyone know that O'Neill was about to go on a 16-game tear, with a display of slugging that grabbed the attention of many pundits and players. If the Cleveland hurlers were good to O'Neill by giving him singles, the "berries"[31] of the Baltimore, New York, and Brooklyn pitchers were all the more bountiful in the next 16 games (August 23 to September 8) as Tip slugged more long hits than singles in a memorable exhibition of power.

Over the last 16 games of phase four, the Browns had a 14–2 record, with a 12-game winning streak between August 23 and the second game of the doubleheader on September 3. Within this span, O'Neill had two outstanding batting weeks, one from August 24 to August 30 and the second from September 2 to September 8, both reminiscent of his historic week in the first phase of the season (April 27 to May 7). Like the earlier historic week, each included seven games. On average, O'Neill recorded at least three hits, one long hit, five total bases, and three runs scored and batted in per game. These two weeks in phase four were noteworthy, indeed near-historic exhibitions of hitting for both average and power.[32]

The opening game of the three-game series against Baltimore (August 23–25) offered few hints that this 8–1 victory was the start of a 12-game winning streak for the Browns or that O'Neill's single kicked off a 25-game hitting streak. In the unseasonably cold conditions, the hearty 2,000 fans who turned out for the game struggled to keep warm. Only the bases-clearing double by Robinson brought the cranks to their feet:

> Down in the grandstand the spectators pulled their coat collars up about their necks and sat dignifiedly through the game, withdrawing their hands from their pockets on but one occasion, and that was when Robinson drove the ball in dangerous proximity of the hat sign on the left field fence and sent in three runs and victory. On this occasion, the spectators, grandstand and all, rose up and howled a few moments, filled their lungs with fresh air and then sat down to quiet and contentment. On the bleaching boards, the boys played various tunes with their hands and feet between innings, and raised merry Cain generally, a pleasure which nobody begrudged them, for it admirably filled the place of overcoats.[33]

Part of the cheer that erupted on Robinson's blast was for Comiskey, Caruthers, and Welch, the three runners on base, as they crossed the plate "almost abreast,"[34] likely a mark of showmanship to sustain the crowd's applause.

Latham did his best to warm both the crowd and the opposing team. Following its headline, "Latham Furnishes the Entertainment on a Cold Day," the *Baltimore Sun* added:

> Latham amused the Baltimore players greatly by his ape-like cries and his South American capers, which he cut, not for the purpose of rattling the Oriole battery, but because, as he said himself: "It is a cold day, and we've got the park to ourselves." He singled out Purcell for his special victim, and that fielder was laughing at the dude during half the game.[35]

O'Neill offered the fans neither entertainment nor much reason to cheer, managing only one clean hit and two bases on balls. However, the cranks would have plenty to applaud over the next two days. The injury-ridden Browns dominated Baltimore in the last two games of the series. On August 24, the Browns jumped off to a 16–2 lead after four innings and coasted to a 24–6 win. O'Neill had a six-hit game (base on balls, two singles, three doubles), scoring five runs and knocking in another three. This game marked the start of his first noteworthy batting week (August 24 to August 30). His three doubles also kicked off a 12-game, long-hit streak.

Latham once again sought to amuse, though this time, Comiskey felt that his antics went a step too far. On a hit to third, Latham rolled the ball to first. The batter was safe and a run scored. Once the laughter died down, Latham faced a fine for his ill-advised roll. As explained by the *St. Louis Chronicle*, "Captain Comiskey shouted fine as soon as he saw what the witty third baseman had done and Umpire McQuaid promptly performed his duty."[36]

In game three (August 25), O'Neill had a single, double, and triple in the Browns' 14–8 win. Following his nine hits in the last two games, the *St. Louis Post-Dispatch* celebrated his historic season:

> Tip O'Neill's slugging abilities are simply marvelous. His average is near .500 up to date, including, of course, bases on balls. But his average on genuine hits is over .400 and exceeds any average ever made by any player since Nick Young was a youngster. This dates back to the early forties. Tip, therefore, is entitled to be known as the chief stick wielder in the land, and his handsome manly form will adorn the next guidebook of the American Association.[37]

For many, the highlight of the Browns' three-game sweep of New York (August 26–28) was the stolen-base contest in game two. Jennie Yeamans, a singer and an actress, was scheduled to play the first show of the 1887–1888 season at Pope's Theater in St. Louis. To bring further notice to her theatrical debut, Yeamans donated a gold medal to be awarded to the player who stole the greatest number of bases in the second game of the series (August 27), the same day that she opened at Pope's Theater.[38] With the exception of Welch, who refused to participate in the contest, the players "had on their running clothes,"[39] attempting to steal a base on almost every opportunity that arose. By game's end, the Browns had compiled 11 stolen bases to support their one-sided, 10–1 win. Although local betting in the pool rooms had Comiskey, Latham, and Robinson as co-favorites to win the stolen-base competition, Caruthers, "a rank outsider in the betting," won with four stolen bases on the day.[40] That night at Pope's Theater, with Von der Ahe, Comiskey, and their families in a lower box, and the Browns players in the front row, Caruthers was called on stage during the intermission prior to the final act to receive his medal.

After scoring an average of 13 runs per game in the Baltimore and New York series, the Browns could manage only seven runs in each of their first two wins against Brooklyn (August 29–30). Stolen bases were also hard to come by, and, in at least one case, the price paid for such a theft was too steep. In the eighth inning of the first game, which the Browns won, 7–5, O'Neill reached first on a single. Caruthers was at bat when O'Neill started for second. In an effort to support Tip in his attempt to steal a base, Caruthers leaned over the plate to obscure if not block Bob Clark, the Brooklyn catcher, in his throw to second. Clark's throw hit Caruthers in the back of the head, a blow that knocked Caruthers unconscious. He was carried to the bench and after a few minutes regained consciousness and resumed his time at bat, with O'Neill on second base with a stolen base to his credit. Caruthers flied out to right field. O'Neill moved to third on the out and then scored the Browns' seventh and final run on a double by Welch. Caruthers, playing right field, was wobbly for the rest of the game, complaining of severe head pains as he left Sportsman's Park. Fortunately, by the next day Caruthers showed no lingering side effects, holding the Brooklyn batsmen to eight hits to lead the Browns to a 7–4 win.

O'Neill distinguished himself in these two games, hitting his second home run in three games as part of the Browns' 7–5 win over Brooklyn in game one and completing his second near-cycle in five games in their 7–4 win in game two.[41] Following his seven hits in the New York series and another seven hits in nine times at bat in the first two games of the Brooklyn series, O'Neill ended his near-historic week (August 24–30) recording a batting average of .639, with 13 of his 23 hits for extra bases.

With no hits in his first three times at bat in the final game of the Brooklyn series, O'Neill's hitting and long-hit streaks were both in jeopardy. In the eighth inning, he came through with a double to extend his hitting streak to nine games and his long-hit streak to eight games. The two-bagger was the turning point in the game as the Browns went on to beat Brooklyn, 6–4. The Browns left the next day for New York to begin a series that opened on September 2, a game that initiated his second noteworthy week (September 2–8) in this phenomenal 16-game batting spurt.

In the first three games of the New York series, one on September 2 and a doubleheader on September 3, the Browns and O'Neill picked up where they had left off in St. Louis. The Browns beat New York, 12–4, 20–8, and 7–4, pushing their winning streak to 12 games. On September 2, O'Neill had five hits for the second time in the last eight games. His three singles, double, and triple constituted his third near-cycle in a week. Over the three games against New York, he had ten hits in 15 times at bat, including five long hits. At this point, O'Neill's hitting streak had reached 12 games, while his long-hit streak was at 11 games. He also completed a 12-times-on-base streak that started in his last time at bat in the Brooklyn series (August 31) and ended in his first time at bat in the second game on September 3. Seemingly unstoppable, neither the Browns nor O'Neill could have foreseen how a Sunday trip to New Jersey would affect their respective streaks.

By previous arrangement, New York and St. Louis agreed to replay the drawn game of July 22, which had been called on account of darkness after 11 innings with the score knotted at two runs apiece. The only date available was Sunday, September 4. It was illegal to play games on a Sunday in New York, so the "play-off"[42] was relocated to Monitor Park in Weehawken, New Jersey. While Brooklyn regularly moved from Washington Park to Ridgewood Park on Long Island to play games on a Sunday, this was the first time in 1887 that New York played a home game outside its regular grounds on Staten Island and on a Sunday. It was also the first time the Metropolitans used Monitor Park, a decision that proved inadequate, unsafe, and unprofitable:

> The experiment of playing baseball games in New Jersey on Sunday was tried yesterday by the Metropolitan and St. Louis teams, and judging from the obstacles encountered in the inaugural game, professional contests on the Sabbath in that section of the country will never prove a healthy or paying investment.[43]

Monitor Park had the capacity to house about 2,000 fans, around 500 in the grandstand and another 1,500 standing around the outside of the field. The organizers were totally unprepared for the over 6,000 fans who turned out for the game. Furthermore, the grounds had not been satisfactorily groomed and marked for a major league game. There had not been sufficient arrangements made for managing ticket sales or helping spectators to their seats or standing room areas. And, as stipulated in the "National Playing Rules," the New York club had failed to "furnish sufficient police force upon its own grounds to preserve order."[44] Under such appalling conditions, the game was destined to face challenges, the biggest of which were the size and nature of the crowd.

In their reports of the game, many of the newspapers' headlines succinctly captured the problems presented by the majority of the fans at the game:

> *New York Star:* Batters and Toughs. The St. Louis–Metropolitan Game Stopped by a Mob[45]
> *New York World:* Roughs at a Ball Game. An Unruly Mob Have Fun on the Weehawken Grounds[46]
> *The Sporting News:* A Riot in New York. The St. Louis Browns Tendered a Very Warm Reception at Weehawken[47]

St. Louis Chronicle: The Browns Mobbed. Weehawken Roughs Throw Rocks at the Champions[48]

St. Louis Republican: Won at Weehawken. The Browns Beat the Mets Among Untamed Jersey Natives[49]

Most of those in attendance were men and boys, some from "New York's toughest gangs,"[50] some con men and petty thieves, a significant number of whom "must have come from the alleys and byways of the worst quarters of the city, and who had ruffianly instincts developed to the highest degree."[51] These hooligans were as or more likely to turn on each other, though they also were ready to threaten the players should a reason arise, which it did.

Troubles began even before the game, first on the ferry on the way to Weehawken and then in the rush to find a seat or a place to stand once the fans entered Monitor Park. On the ferry, Captain Swipes, one of the gang leaders, insisted that a young man give him the cigarette he was smoking. When the young man refused to part with his cigarette, Swipes, aided by 12 of his compatriots, two who went by the names of "Mickey the Fish" and "Giblets," pounded the victim until they were "satisfied they had given the young man enough."[52]

As the fans arrived at the park, they soon realized that the grandstand was full and the only option left was to scurry about to find a place to stand. Some boys climbed nearby trees, while others made their way to the roof of the grandstand, which caused the roof to creak and sway, prompting those below to worry about buckling. The seated cranks screamed at those on the roof: "Get off! Get off! Get off the roof!" The persons overhead responded: "Let her go! Let her go! We're on top!"[53] With no seats available and no room on the grandstand roof, the remaining fans swarmed the field, jostling for spots where they could see the players. As the park rapidly filled, the fans who gathered near the foul lines started to encroach on to the field to the point that the umpire could not clearly see first or third base.[54] In the outfield, the throngs grew so large that they pushed the outfielders close to the infield such that once the game began, the left fielder and center fielder "were about four feet back of the bases and occasionally played second base, shortstop, and third base, as well as covering their own territory."[55] The game could not proceed until the crowd was no longer on the playing field. After appeals to the fans to move back failed, players armed with bats "shoved the fans outside the diamond lines."[56]

Although Bob Ferguson, the umpire, was reluctant to proceed with the game under such adverse conditions, he nonetheless agreed to call, "Play," with the ground rule that any ball hit into the crowd would be deemed a single. However, it soon became apparent that there was no way to keep the crowd off the field. At the request of both captains, Ferguson ended play after one inning and called the game a draw. The crowd erupted, shouting, "Play ball!" with some fans rushing to the ticket office to demand their money back and others surrounding the Browns as they tried to board their carriages to leave to park. Wanting the teams to resume play, the infuriated youths overturned Von der Ahe's carriage. With the players' carriages, they "began unhitching the horses and threatened to throw the vehicle over the cliff."[57] Fearing a riot, the teams decided to play the game. Deputies mounted two of the unhitched horses and trotted them into the crowds in an attempt to clear the diamond. "Play" was called once again, this time by Joe Battin, an International League player, who agreed to act as the umpire since Ferguson was nowhere to be found.

Much of the crowd welcomed the resumption of play. Other spectators were pleased with the extra time to play their own games. The *New York Times* described the shenanigans on the sidelines and in the stands:

> During the game all sorts of devices that are used to lessen the bank accounts of the gullible public were brought into execution. The young man with the "sweat" board was there; the young man who tells you to put your money "below, above, or on seven" was on hand; the young man with three innocent-looking shells was in attendance, and, in fact, the ground appeared to be a Mecca for the unemployed "fakirs" of New York and vicinity. Then there were the light-fingered gentlemen who rushed up against a person and made him keep his hands in his pockets, not that the weather warranted that act, but because if he didn't he probably would not be able to tell the time of day or pay his fare across the ferry.[58]

For some, the non-baseball "pitches, thefts, and hits"[59] of these games were likely more exciting than the baseball game that presumably had drawn them to Weehawken in the first place.

The game itself was variously described as a "farce with a bat and ball,"[60] "a very tiresome exhibition of the national sport,"[61] "a series of comic, tragic and rowdy features,"[62] and "a burlesque on base ball."[63] The game was called on account of darkness after six innings with the Browns in the lead, 16–6. Those watching the baseball game, in keeping with the ground rule that awarded a batsman one base for any ball hit into the crowd in the outfield, witnessed 34 singles in the six innings. Under normal circumstances, some of these singles would have been easy fly outs, while other balls that soared deep into the crowd would likely have gone for extra bases. Any ball hit into the crowd was not returned. On one time at bat, a player hit four balls into the crowd. Each of the balls was stolen by a fan.[64] The *New York Star* reported that O'Neill "did the heaviest batting,"[65] an observation that suggested that his three singles were among those that landed in the crowd well back of the diamond. In the end, the game did not count in the standings for the teams or in the individual statistics of the players. Unbeknownst to the fans and the press, at the beginning of the game, the teams recognized that "the ground was in such wretched condition and the enormous crowd encroached upon the playing ground to such an extent that a satisfactory game was out of the question." Accordingly, they agreed to continue the contest as an exhibition game.[66]

As frustrating as it was to endure such aggravating conditions for naught, the Browns were more upset by their inability to escape Weehawken without incurring further injury. In the fourth inning, O'Neill swung at a pitch and the bat slipped out of his hands, hitting Welch squarely on the nose while he was sitting on the bench. The force of the blow caused his nose to bleed profusely and, when he was taken to the clubhouse, the ensuing pain was so great that he blacked out. The preliminary assessment of the doctor was that Welch's nose was not broken, but, based on the damage and trauma of the blow, it would likely take several weeks before he could play again.[67] Although O'Neill was distraught by the sight of a teammate felled by a blow from his bat,[68] others were critical of his bat-throwing habits[69]:

> So "Tip" O'Neill accidentally smashed Welch in the nose with a bat. I was not surprised to hear that piece of news. I have been expecting that Tip would kill someone before the season was over. It's a common occurrence for him to throw a bat out toward the pitcher, up toward first base and back toward the Players' bench. But the boys have always been lucky enough to get out of the way of that flying sapling.[70]

The Browns returned to New York, limping into their final game of the series down yet another core player.

Without Welch for the next four games, the last game of the New York series (September 5) and the three-game series against Brooklyn (September 6–8), Comiskey rotated his three pitchers (Caruthers, King, and the newly acquired Ed Knouff) into the lineup, with one pitching and the other two playing in center and right field. The Browns lost the first two of these four games by scores of 6–5 to New York and 8–6 to Brooklyn. They roared back with decisive wins in the last two games of the series, beating Brooklyn, 14–8, in game two and 7–1 in game three. O'Neill did not get an extra-base hit in the first game of the Brooklyn series, thereby stopping his long-hit streak at 12 games. However, he continued his hitting streak with another nine hits in 14 times at bat in the three-game series against Brooklyn, highlighted in game two by his third five-hit performance in the last 13 games. The final game in the series completed his second near-historic week, seven days that featured a batting average over .600 and ten extra-base hits.

O'Neill's batting performance in phase four silenced those who had doubts about his capacity to return to the power hitting that they had enthusiastically celebrated in the first phase of the season. His .500-plus hitting, multiple batting streaks, long hits, and game-changing runs, most of which occurred in his two near-historic weeks, reminded Browns' followers of his early-season slugging. While not quite the historic week in phase one of the season (April 27 to May 7), these two noteworthy weeks nonetheless were significant in their own right. The following table compares the numbers for each of Tip's three incredible weeks:

	AB	R	H	BB	1B	2B	3B	HR	TB	RBI	AVG
April 27–May 7	36	20	27	3	10	7	3	4	52	19	.750
August 24–30	36	21	23	1	9	8	3	2	43	12	.639
September 2–8	33	11	21	2	9	5	5	0	36	14	.636

AB–At-Bats; R–Runs; H–Hits; BB–Base on Balls 1B–Single; 2B–Double; 3B–Triple; HR–Home Run; TB–Total Bases; RBI–Runs Batted In; AVG–Batting Average

With the exception of the 21 runs and eight doubles in the August 24–30 week and the five triples in the September 2–8 week, the historic week in phase one exceeded the other two weeks in every category, with his extraordinary .750 batting average standing out above all others. In each of the three weeks, O'Neill made a similar contribution in run production. O'Neill scored or batted in 35 percent of the Browns' runs in the April 27–May 7 week, 36 percent in the August 24–30 week, and 34 percent in the September 2–8 week. The only area where O'Neill's two noteworthy weeks in phase four were more prominent than the historic week in phase one was in the impact of his runs on the outcome of the game. In the April 27–May 7 week, O'Neill scored or drove in only four runs that directly influenced the course of the game, two runs that put the Browns ahead and two that created the winning runs. He had seven runs in the week of August 24–30 with a similar impact, with one that represented the winning run. In the week of September 2–8, O'Neill had six runs that made a difference in the outcome, scoring or driving in the winning run in three of the seven games. In ten of the 14 games in the two noteworthy weeks of phase four, O'Neill clearly delivered timely hits that led to consequential runs.

O'Neill's batting record in phase four also set him apart from the other leading batsmen in the Association. The following table compares the standing of O'Neill's batting average against the batting averages of five of his closest rivals:

	Phase Four: August 12 to September 8			Season: April 16 to September 8		
	At-Bats	Hits	Average	At-Bats	Hits	Average
Tip O'Neill, St. Louis	115	66	.574	465	230	.495
Pete Browning, Louisville	108	53	.491	493	227	.460

	At-Bats	Hits	Average	At-Bats	Hits	Average
Bob Caruthers, St. Louis	87	49	.563	338	154	.456
Yank Robinson, St. Louis	107	48	.449	474	204	.430
Reddy Mack, Louisville	113	43	.381	439	183	.417
Denny Lyons, Philadelphia	114	46	.404	502	206	.410

In the batting race, by the end of phase four, O'Neill had increased his lead over Browning from 19 points on August 10 to 35 points. Caruthers was the only player to gain on O'Neill by closing the gap from 51 points behind at the end of phase three (August 10) to 39 points at the end of phase four. Denny Lyons maintained the distinction of being the only player other than Tip to hit over .400 in each of the first four phases. In slugging, O'Neill had more than twice as many long hits as the other five batsmen: O'Neill—26 (14 doubles, nine triples, three home runs); Lyons—ten (nine doubles, one triple); Browning—ten (four doubles, five triples, one home run); Caruthers—eight (six doubles, one triple, one home run); Robinson—seven (five doubles, one triple, one home run); and Mack—seven (four doubles, two triples, one home run).

While Caruthers and Robinson trailed O'Neill in most batting categories, they were more versatile in getting on base and more effective on the base path. On his return to the lineup, Caruthers had his own notable week that began with a game (August 19) in which he had six hits in six times at bat (two bases on balls, three singles, home run). That week (ending August 26), Caruthers compiled 22 hits in 33 times at bat (11 bases on balls, eight singles, one double, one triple, one home run) for a .667 average. In this seven-game-run, he also scored 16 runs and stole seven bases. In the 19 games that he played in phase four, Caruthers had 26 hits through bases on balls, scored 27 runs, and stole 15 bases. Robinson had 17 hits through bases on balls, took first three times after being hit by a pitch, scored 22 runs, and stole 15 bases.

In spite of the fact that O'Neill increased his lead over Browning during the course of phase four, Browning remained determined to overtake him by season's end. However, for a short time, Browning seemed to lose his competitive edge. Whether he was bothered by his inability to gain ground on O'Neill or by his team's falling further behind the Association-leading Browns, as the phase wore on, Browning's play became erratic. In late August, he was fined for excessive drinking. The *St. Louis Post-Dispatch* reprinted a report published in the *Louisville Courier-Journal*:

> Pete Browning, who has been getting drunk again, was fined $50 at the conclusion of yesterday's game with the Athletics. Manager Kelly threatened to suspend him for the rest of the year if he did not improve his conduct.... Browning has been spreeing frequently, keeping irregular hours and indulging in bad company. Pete has not been playing up to his usual mark of late. He has taken a big drop in batting, and his work in center field has been marked by costly and flagrant errors.... Browning's playing yesterday was wretched. He had not entirely sobered up from a debauch on Tuesday night. In the first inning, he made such a feeble attempt to get under Robinson's fly ball that the latter made a home run on the hit, Browning falling twice in scrambling after the ball. At the bat Pete was worse than useless. He merely pecked at the ball, and made no unnecessary exertions to drive in a run, although he had several opportunities. Browning struck out three times and did not make a hit.[71]

Browning had only one hit in 14 times at bat in the Philadelphia series. However, he was quick to pay his fine and promised to stay sober and improve his game.

Browning made good on his promise, delivering his own notable batting week. From August 27 to September 4, Louisville won six of seven games, three against Brooklyn and three against New York. Browning batted .632 on 24 hits in 38 times at bat, which included four hits on bases on balls, 15 singles, two doubles and three triples. He also scored 15 runs and stole 14 bases. Browning clearly made amends for his prior inebriation: "The Gladiator has done some noble ball playing since he braced up."[72] Even with Browning's surge, however, some Louisville correspondents started to concede the batting title to Tip:

> Old "Petey" Browning is handling the bat again with great success. He may not be able to overtake Tip O'Neill, of the St. Louis Browns, but no man can oust him from second place. In the last five games the Gladiator has lined out nineteen hits. Last Sunday he made five hits off Porter, of the Brooklyns, and after the game Manager Kelly said:—"Just see, old boy, what you can do when you take care of yourself." "Yes," replied the tall center fielder, "old Petey is no slouch when he is in trim. He can make any of 'em hump, can't he Guy?"[73]

Although Browning showed no signs of conceding the batting title to O'Neill, he was frustrated by Tip's relentless slugging: "Pete Browning is said to take a duck-fit every morning when he reads in the papers the record of O'Neill, the long hitter of the Browns, who has been lining 'em out with great regularity."[74] But there were still 23 games left in the schedule, plenty of time for O'Neill to falter or for one or more batsmen to catch the leader.[75]

As the table below illustrates, O'Neill was once again, as he had been in the first phase of the season, at his best when he was batting for both average and power. While his lead for the batting honors was not as insurmountable as the Browns' lead in the American Association, he was strutting forward with an eye on the championship for his team and himself.

	Games	*AB*	*R*	*H*	*BB*	*1B*	*2B*	*3B*	*HR*	*AVG*	*SB*
August 12–September 8	24	115	44	66	10	30	14	9	3	.574	11
April 16–September 8	101	465	146	230	46	110	44	17	13	.495	29

AB–At-Bats; R–Runs; H–Hits; BB–Base on Balls; 1B–Single; 2B–Double; 3B–Triple; HR–Home Run; TB–Total Bases; AVG–Batting Average; SB–Stolen Bases

13

Batting Streaks

The Browns had three double-digit winning streaks in 1887: a 15-game streak from April 24 to May 16, a ten-game streak from May 24 to June 4, and a 12-game streak from August 23 to September 3. O'Neill also had various batting streaks, most of which occurred within or overlapped the Browns' 15-game and 12-game winning streaks.[1] Specifically, O'Neill's batting streaks consisted of consecutive times on base, including consecutive plate appearances with a hit within the same on-base streak[2]; consecutive games with a hit; and consecutive games with an extra-base or a long hit. In one stretch, O'Neill had two streaks (consecutive times on base and consecutive games with an extra-base hit) within a longer streak of consecutive games with a hit. While such feats, especially consecutive plate appearances with a hit, were heralded by the press as impressive accomplishments in their own right,[3] in O'Neill's case, each of his streaks also contributed to the outcome of the games and to the overall offensive record of the Browns.

In 1887, O'Neill had four significant on-base streaks, three of which are summarized in the following tables[4]:

Browns Beat Cleveland 28–11 (April 30) and 14–13 (May 1).
O'Neill was on base 10 times in a row.

Date	April 30						May 1			
Sequence	1	2	3	4	5	6	7	8	9	10
Inning–Hit	3–BB	4–1B	5–HR	5–3B	6–HR	8–2B	1–1B	2–2B	4–1B	6–2B
Run Production and Impact	O'Neill scored or drove in 13 (36 percent) of the 36 runs made by the Browns in those innings in which he came to bat. O'Neill drove in the first run on May 1, putting the Browns into the lead.									

Browns Beat Louisville 4–1 (May 4), 10–3 (May 6), and 12–7 (May 7).
O'Neill was on base 11 times in a row.

Date	May 4	May 6					May 7				
Sequence	1	2	3	4	5	6	7	8	9	10	11
Inning–Hit (or Error)	5–2B	1–1B	3–E	5–1B	6–1B	9–HR	1–3B	3–BB	5–1B	7–HR	8–2B
Run Production and Impact	O'Neill scored or drove in 15 (63 percent) of the 24 runs made by the Browns in those innings in which he came to bat. O'Neill scored the winning run on May 6 and drove in the winning run on May 7. He also drove in the first run on May 7, putting the Browns into the lead.										

Browns Beat Cleveland 8–4 (August 8), 11–8 (August 9), and 12–4 (August 10). O'Neill was on base 11 times in a row.

Date	August 8					August 9					Aug. 10
Sequence	1	2	3	4	5	6	7	8	9	10	11
Inning–Hit (or hit by a pitch)	1–1B	3–1B	5–1B	7–HP	9–2B	1–1B	3–BB	6–2B	8–1B	9–3B	1–1B
Run Production and Impact	O'Neill scored or drove in ten (48 percent) of the 21 runs made by the Browns in those innings in which he came to bat. O'Neill scored the first run in each of the games on August 8 and 10, giving the Browns the lead. He also scored a run on August 9 that tied the game.										

1B–Single; 2B–Double; 3B–Triple; HR–Home Run; BB–Base on Balls; HP–Hit by Pitch; E–Error

The ten-times on-base streak on April 30 and May 1 and the 11 times on base in the August 8–10 streak were similar in that for both O'Neill had ten hits in a row. The April 30–May 1 streak began with a walk followed by nine clean hits, while the August 8–10 streak had nine clean hits, a base on balls, and a hit by pitch.[5] In the 11 times on base in the May 4–7 streak, O'Neill had ten hits, counting one for his base on balls. However, on his third time at bat, he got his base on an error, an interruption that reduced his hit streak to eight in a row.[6]

Although O'Neill had fewer hits in a row in the May 4–7 streak than he did in the other streaks, he was involved in more than half of the runs (63 percent) scored by the Browns in the innings in which he batted. By comparison, in the August 8–10 streak, his runs produced constituted 48 percent of the runs scored by the Browns, and 36 percent during the April 30–May 1 streak. In addition, the May 4–7 streak was the only one of the three streaks described above that played a decisive role in scoring the winning run, on May 6, crossing the plate with the winning run after getting on base on an error, and, on May 7, scoring the winning run on his late-in-the-game home run. In the May 4–7 streak, getting on base by an error or a home run proved equally important to the outcome of the game.

On the same day that the Browns started a 12-game winning streak (August 23), O'Neill began a 25-game hitting streak that ended on September 21. Eight games after the completion of his streak, O'Neill initiated a second consecutive-game hitting streak, one that spanned 22 games across two seasons, from October 4, 1887, to May 10, 1888. Trent McCotter compiled a list of 24 players in the American Association who recorded 20 or more consecutive games with at least one hit. O'Neill's 25-game hitting streak was the longest of five streaks in 1887.[7] His 25-game streak ranks fifth in the Association's ten-year history (1882–1891).[8] O'Neill was the only player on McCotter's 24-player list who hit over .500 in his hitting streak, doing so twice, batting .565 (65 hits in 115 times at bat) in his 25-game hitting streak and .511 (46 hits in 90 times at bat) in his 22-game streak.

Within his 25-game hitting streak and overlapping most of the Browns' 12-game winning streak, O'Neill had a 12-game, long-hit streak (August 24 to September 5) that spanned four series, the first three at home against Baltimore, New York, and Brooklyn, and the last on the road at New York. His fourth on-base streak began in the last game at home against Brooklyn (August 31) and extended to the first three games in the New York series, ending on his first at bat in the second game of the doubleheader on September 3. In his 12-game, long-hit streak, O'Neill had a .610 batting average based on 36 hits in 59 times at bat. Twenty-one (58 percent) of his 36 hits went for extra bases, including 14 doubles, five triples, and two home runs. In the innings in which O'Neill had a long hit, he contributed to 28 (56 percent) of the 50 runs scored by the Browns.

The long-hit streak commenced during the last two games against Baltimore. In the second game of the three-game series (August 24), the Browns overwhelmed Baltimore, 24–6. O'Neill got the Browns off to a strong start in the first inning with a double to left field that drove in two runs. In the ninth inning, after his third double of the game, O'Neill scored the Browns' 24th and final run. On August 25, as part of the Browns' 14–8 win, O'Neill doubled in the first inning, driving in Gleason for the Browns' first run. He also tripled in the fourth inning and scored the team's fifth run a few moments later on Comiskey's single.

In the three-game sweep of New York (August 26–28), O'Neill's three doubles and one home run were part of an offensive surge that saw the Browns route the Mets by scores of 15–5, 10–1, and 9–2. In game one, the Browns had a 6–5 lead going into the sixth inning. O'Neill's two doubles contributed to three of the nine runs scored by the Browns in the sixth and seventh innings, an outburst that broke the game wide open. O'Neill's home run came in the second game with no one on base, increasing the Browns' lead to 4–1. His third double of the series came in the ninth inning of the third game, with the Browns in full command, ahead of New York, 8–1. O'Neill scored the Browns' ninth run on a single by Comiskey.

Although the Browns won all three of their games in the series against Brooklyn (August 29–31), in comparison to the Baltimore and New York series, the games were comparatively low-scoring, hard-fought contests whose outcome was in doubt until the late innings. In the sixth inning of game one, two out, and no one on base, O'Neill broke the 3–3 tie with "one of his customary home runs."[9] Stirred by Tip's blast, the Browns added two more runs to take a 6–3 lead, eventually winning, 7–5. On August 30, when the Browns beat Brooklyn, 7–4, O'Neill hit a double and scored the Browns' second run in the first inning, crossed the plate with the fourth run after lining a ball to right field for a triple in the fourth inning, and raced home for the seventh run after ripping his second triple to the left field fence in the ninth inning. His second triple proved too hot to handle for both the shortstop and left fielder, much to the chagrin of George Pinkney, the Brooklyn third baseman:

> Peebles was not anxious to emblazen his reputation as a shortstop yesterday. In the ninth inning O'Neill let one of his "peculiar" drives go at Jimmie, who nearly broke his neck getting out of the road of it. As the ball cut its way out to the left field fence Pinkney gave the new shortstop a look of intense disgust.[10]

Even though O'Neill was only five games into his long-hit streak, the press took notice of his slugging in recent games. Following his double and two triples against Brooklyn, the *St. Louis Republican* exclaimed:

> O'Neill's batting of late has been wonderful, and he certainly comes as near being a phenomenal batter as there is in the profession. He seldom misses a ball that he goes after, and when he hits it, it almost invariably goes out on a line. If it goes directly at a fielder he is deprived of a hit, but otherwise all the way from a single to a homer is the result.[11]

In the third game against Brooklyn, O'Neill was hitless in his first three times at the plate. The Browns came to bat in the eighth inning trailing Brooklyn, 4–2. With one out, Latham doubled and stole third base. Gleason struck a ball down the third base line, and Latham bolted for home. Pinkney, firing the ball home, forced Latham to turn back for third. As Latham darted back and forth between third and home in this rundown, Gleason moved up to second. Meanwhile, Latham wore down the third baseman and the catcher in their pursuit and landed on third base before either could apply a tag. O'Neill came to the plate for what would likely be his final turn at bat. On the first pitch, he lined the ball to center for a double, knocking in both runners to tie the game at 4–4.[12] O'Neill advanced to third on Comiskey's sacrifice. Caruthers walked and stole second. Bill McClellan, the Brooklyn second baseman, fumbled Welch's hit, and both O'Neill and Caruthers scored, securing the come-from-behind victory, with O'Neill scoring the winning run. O'Neill's double both kept his long-base streak alive and started his fourth and final on-base streak.

After a long train ride to New York, the Browns resumed play with a four-game series against the Mets (September 2–5). They won the first three games but lost game four, 6–5, thereby ending their winning streak at 12 games. In the first match against New York (September 2), O'Neill had five hits in five times at bat, including a triple in the second inning and a double in the fifth inning. The five hits extended his on-base streak, while the two extra-base hits prolonged his long-hit streak. In his first time at bat, O'Neill singled in the Browns' first run, which put them in the lead. Ahead 3–0 in the second inning, with one out and Gleason on second, O'Neill tripled to left field, scoring Gleason. O'Neill hustled home on Comiskey's groundout with the Browns' fifth and eventual winning run. He was one of two men left stranded after his single in the fourth inning. In the fifth inning, the Browns struck for five runs, increasing their lead to 10–1, with O'Neill's double driving in the ninth and tenth runs. Following his eighth-inning single, O'Neill went to second on a single by Comiskey and scored the Browns' 11th run on Welch's double.

The on-base and long-hit streaks continued on the next day (September 3) as the Browns won both ends of a doubleheader, 20–8 and 7–4. In the first game, O'Neill got on base in each of his five plate appearances, although not always on clean hits. He took first on a base on balls in the first inning, on an error to the third baseman in the second inning, and on an error in his second at-bat in the fourth inning, scoring three runs. In his first at-bat in the fourth, he led off the inning with a single and scored the Browns' ninth and winning run, advanced by successive singles by Comiskey and Caruthers. In the fifth inning, O'Neill launched his only long hit of the game, a towering ball that cleared the Babylon stage for a ground-rule double, driving in the Browns' 18th and 19th runs.[13]

In his first at-bat in game two of the doubleheader, his triple knocked in the Browns' first run. He scored their second run on a wild pitch. In his next at-bat in the third inning O'Neill grounded out, ending his on-base streak at 12. This streak is summarized below in the same tabular form as the three on-base streaks presented earlier in the chapter.

Browns Beat Brooklyn 6–4 (August 31) and then beat New York 12–4 (September 2), 20–8 (September 3-game one of doubleheader), and 7–4 (September 3-game two of double header). O'Neill was on base 12 times in a row.

Date	Aug. 31	September 2					September 3-Game One					Game Two
Sequence	1	2	3	4	5	6	7	8	9	10	11	12
Inning–Hit (or Error)	8–2B	1–1B	2–3B	4–1B	5–2B	8–1B	1–BB	2–E	4–1B	4–E	5–2B	1–3B

Run Production and Impact	O'Neill scored or drove in 16 (44 percent) of the 36 runs made by the Browns in those innings in which he came to bat. He scored the winning runs on August 31, September 2, and the first game on September 3. O'Neill also drove in two runs that

tied the score on August 31. He drove in two runs that gave the Browns the lead, one on September 2, and one in the second game on September 3.

1B–Single; 2B–Double; 3B–Triple; HR–Home Run; BB–Base on Balls; HP–Hit by Pitch; E–Error

In comparison to the other three on-base streaks, the August 31–September 3 streak had the fewest consecutive clean hits with six, seven counting his base on balls. Furthermore, O'Neill scored or drove in 16 (44 percent) of the 36 runs made by the Browns in those innings in which he came to bat, a run production that ranked third among the four on-base streaks. However, in terms of impact, O'Neill's hits in the August 31–September 3 streak were more significant to the outcomes of the four games than in the three previous streaks. After his double in the eighth inning on August 31, his triple in the second inning on September 2, and his single in the first at-bat in the fourth inning of the first game of the doubleheader on September 3, Tip scored the winning runs in each of these games. Moreover, he scored or drove in three other runs that tied the game or gave the Browns the lead. In these four streaks, while long hits could make a difference in a hurry, getting on base through any means, at the right time and under the right circumstances, could be as important in producing runs and winning games.

Although the 12-times on-base streak was broken in his second time at bat in the second game of the doubleheader, O'Neill's long-hit streak stayed alive with his triple in the first inning and his double in the fifth inning. The double drove in Gleason for the fifth run, yet another winning run, with O'Neill, three batters later, coming around to extend the Browns' lead to 6–2. The long-hit streak survived one more game, this time as part of a 6–5 loss to New York. Down 5–1 in the fourth inning, O'Neill lined a ball down the third base line for a double. He advanced to third on Comiskey's groundout and scored on a passed ball. The next day, the Browns shifted to Brooklyn for a three-game series (September 6–8). They suffered their second loss in as many days with Brooklyn taking the opening game of the series, 8–6. O'Neill managed one single in four times at bat. While his 12-game long-hit streak had ended, the accolades about his slugging continued. *Sporting Life* was one of many newspapers that marveled at Tip's batting, especially his recent fence-busting propensities:

> Tip O'Neill's St. Louis friends used to think he was a great batter, but they were mistaken. He didn't know how to hit the ball till this year. Under the new rules he seems to be at home with the stick, and in nearly every game he lines a few two-baggers, three-baggers, and home runs.[14]

For the 12 games in a row between August 24 and September 5, it did indeed seem that O'Neill churned out long hits at will. There is no report of an 1887 batsman, or for that matter of a batsman in any other season in the nineteenth century, who has matched or exceeded his 12-game, long-hit streak. O'Neill's record stood for 40 years until Paul Waner (Pittsburgh) in 1927 set the new mark at 14 consecutive games with an extra-base hit. It took another 79 years for another player to exceed O'Neill's streak. In 2006, Chipper Jones (Atlanta) matched Waner's record of 14 games.[15] O'Neill's 12-game streak still ranks as the third-highest with an extra-base hit.

After a game without a long hit (September 6), O'Neill recommenced his slugging. He had at least one long hit in each of his next five games (September 7–12), which, along with his streak, extended his record to an extra-base hit in 17 of 18 games. While this feat was no longer a streak, it was nonetheless an incredible slugging performance.[16] In the 12 games, O'Neill also had a 12-game runs-batted-in streak, driving in 23 runs.[17] In addition, he scored 31 runs, with a stretch of 14 consecutive games (August 23 to September

6) in which he scored one or more runs, which included all 12 games of his long-hit streak.[18] And, as previously noted, O'Neill's 12-game, long-hit streak was part of both a significant 12-times, on-base streak and a 25-game hitting streak. Taken together, the streaks-within-streaks that played out in this 12-game period were not only astounding individual achievements but also a critical part of the Browns' 12-game winning streak. O'Neill once again had made good on the maxim: As Tip goes, so go the Browns. Entering the final phase of the season (September 9 to October 9), the Browns had all but wrapped up the American Association championship, and Tip O'Neill was on track to win his first Association batting championship.

14

September 9 to October 9: American Association Champions

In this final phase of the season (September 9 to October 9), the Browns split their first two games in Philadelphia, winning 8–3 on Friday, September 9, and losing 5–4 in the second game on Saturday. The sting of defeat in game two was magnified by the injury of Comiskey, who broke his thumb, further hobbling an already weakened nine. Discouraged by the loss of their captain and manager, the players took some solace in the fact that the final game of the series was scheduled for Monday—Philadelphia did not play home games on a Sunday—giving them a day to recuperate and Von der Ahe a chance to figure out how best to replace Comiskey. Von der Ahe reminded the players that they had an exhibition game on Sunday at West Farms, New York, against the Cuban Giants, a "colored," professional team.[1]

Eight of the players were upset by the thought of yet another exhibition game, so much so that they concocted a plan to inform Von der Ahe of their refusal to play against the Cuban Giants. Rather than confront Von der Ahe in person with their protest, the players decided to draft a letter. Led by Latham and Gleason, with O'Neill as scribe, the eight players worked together to craft the wording of the letter.[2] O'Neill was also charged with delivering the letter to "Der Boss President." He found Von der Ahe at supper in the hotel dining room. He dropped the letter on the table and, without a word, made a hasty retreat. Von der Ahe opened the letter, which read as follows:

Philadelphia, Penn., Sept. 10
To Chris Von der Ahe, Esq.:
  Dear Sir: We, the undersigned members of the St. Louis Baseball Club, do not agree to play against the negroes tomorrow. We will cheerfully play against white people at any time, and think, by refusing to play, we are only doing what is right, taking everything into consideration and the shape the team is in at present.

W. A. Latham, John Boyle, J. E. O'Neill, R. L. Caruthers,
W. E. Gleason, W. H. Robinson, Charles King, Curt Welch.[3]

After reading the letter, Von der Ahe bolted from the dining room to find the players. He demanded an explanation. Hearing none, other than Latham's off-hand remark about the "black birds,"[4] Von der Ahe proceeded to threaten the players with fines, suspension, or releases. He paused and declared: "As it seems to be a matter of principle with you, you need not play tomorrow."[5] On Sunday morning, Von der Ahe ordered his secretary to send a telegram to John Bright, the manager of the Cuban Giants, to inform him that the Browns were too ill to play, with no mention of the players' letter. On Monday, Bright replied with the information that 7,000 people had showed up, expecting to see the world's championship club in action against the Cuban Giants. Instead they witnessed a match with the Danbury club, a last-minute replacement for the Browns. Angered by the Browns' no-show, the manager of the Cuban Giants expressed his intention to sue for damages.[6]

By Monday (September 12), the players' protest was national news. The *Times* in New York and Philadelphia broke the story on the front page under the headline: "A Color Line is Drawn in Baseball. The St. Louis Browns Refuse to Play with the Cuban Giants."[7] On the same day, newspapers in most of the cities with teams in the American Association and National League reported on this incident, in many cases running the same story as the one that appeared in the *Times*. Over the first two days, the stories focused on either the color line, the revolt of the players, or both, as reflected in the following sample of headlines:

Monday, September 12

St. Louis Republican: Rebellion in the Ranks. Von der Ahe's Men Draw the Color Line. They Flatly Refuse to Play the Famous Negro Team[8]

St. Louis Globe-Democrat: The Browns Refuse to Play[9]

St. Louis Chronicle: Base Ball Color Line. The Browns Draw It Very Plainly[10]

New York Evening Telegram: The Revolt of the Players. Why the Browns Failed to Play the Cuban Giants[11]

Tuesday, September 13

St. Louis Post-Dispatch: That Revolt. A Dramatic Account of the Mutiny Among the World's Champions[12]

St. Louis Globe-Democrat: The Browns' Color Line[13]

New York Evening Sun: Color Line in Base Ball[14]

New York Sun: The Browns Go on Strike. They Refuse to Come to New York to Play the Cuban Giants[15]

The players were surprised and "displeased that ... so much publicity had been given to their actions in drawing the color line in baseball, and they were evidently sorry for their hasty conduct."[16] But, like their reluctance to talk to Von der Ahe when he challenged them about the letter, the players, other than the occasional retort from Latham, were similarly reticent to speak to the press. They just wanted the story and the attention that it brought to go away.

Although drawing the color line was featured in the headline when the story broke, many reporters doubted that color had much to do with the players' refusal to play the Cuban Giants. In one of the more considered and progressive comments on the color line, the *New York Evening Sun* both chastised the players for not being honest about their objections to playing the Cuban Giants and argued for the inclusion of colored players in the major leagues:

> The color line has been drawn in and across and around pretty much everything else in the United States, and at length it has been drawn on the base ball field. The Cuban Giants is the name of a base ball nine composed of colored men, which started in New Jersey a year or two ago, and has played in various towns near New York. The Cuban Giants have played with such clubs as the Detroits, Chicagos, Louisvilles, and Athletics, nor was any objection made to them on account of their color until the other day, when a game had been arranged between them and the St. Louis Browns. President Von der Ahe had prepared for the game, but his players informed him by letter that they did not agree to play against negroes.

> Unfortunately for the consistency of the St. Louis players, it seems that they have several times played against colored nines without making any objections. "I think some of the boys wanted a day to themselves," says Comiskey. That is a harmless want enough, but would it not have been more manly not to raise against the colored club an objection not really felt? It may be admitted that the emoluments and renown of a successful white base ball player may entitle him to his own estimation to look down upon his colored brother, yet base ball is a science in which no color line should be drawn save in the matter of uniforms. Indeed, if colored players of phenomenal skill should be found, Boston or Chicago or St. Louis would be glad to hire them. If a man is a good batter, fielder, or base runner, the crowd does not care whether he is green or yellow, white or black. His ability to "get there," and not his hue, is considered. Perhaps in a few years some of the big cities may be represented in the League by a colored nine.[17]

Most sportswriters accused the players of using the color line as a ruse to divert attention from their real reasons for refusing to play the Cuban Giants, namely to have a day away from exhibition games so they could pursue their own interests.[18]

As the story of the revolt hit the press, Von der Ahe had also learned of the real reason behind the players' refusal to play the Cuban Giants:

> If it was a question of principle with any of my players I would not say a word, but it isn't. Two or three had made arrangements to spend Sunday in Philadelphia, and this scheme was devised so they would not be disappointed. There are no players in the profession who receive as large salaries as my men and who are accorded so many privileges or are so well treated, but it has been my experience that a baseball player is the most unappreciative of any class. Of course, there are exceptions but these are few.[19]

By Monday, Von der Ahe began to strike back at the players for their insubordination. As the players finished their dinner prior to the final game with Philadelphia, they were told that they would board the train to Baltimore immediately following the game. This change in plans meant that the players had to take their baggage with them to the game so they could change into their street clothes before going to the train station. Some players had to cancel their arrangements to attend a theater performance that evening in Philadelphia. Another player noted: "We will get into Baltimore at about 11 o'clock and have to go without our supper."[20] Still peeved at his players, Von der Ahe had, in effect, sent them to their rooms (on the train) without supper.

Some newspapers also focused on another reason suggested in the letter, namely "the shape the team is in at present." With numerous players either out or playing hurt, in recent games the Browns had scrambled to fill the nine positions, often fielding a team with some players not in their regular positions. The strain of playing under these conditions was exacerbated by the ongoing commitment to exhibition games. The *New York Sun* opined: "Base ball men hereabouts think that the color of the players was only an excuse. They think that the members of the club have been overworked lately, and that they have become tired of exhibition games in addition to the regular championship games."[21] In the week before the fateful Cuban Giants game, the Browns twice got up at 3:00 AM to catch a train for exhibition games, one on the previous Sunday (September 4) to play New York at Weehawken, New Jersey,[22] and the second in mid-week (September 7) to travel from Brooklyn to play a team in Connecticut in the morning, only to turn around and rush back for a regularly-scheduled game against Brooklyn that same afternoon.[23] While clearly stress, fatigue, and injury were factors in the players' decision to refuse to play against the Cuban Giants, it was the refusal itself that stuck in the craw of most baseball observers.

For the most part, as time went on, the players escaped criticism for drawing the color line, as did Von der Ahe for implying that such an act was a "matter of principle."[24] Instead, the sportswriters concentrated on the open act of defiance on the part of the players. The revolt of the eight players was forever inscribed in the letter and enacted the next day in their refusal to travel to West Farms. Many sportswriters were quick to condemn the disloyal and contrary behavior of the players and their failure to make good on the commitment to their owner and his contractual obligation to the Cuban Giants. Some commentators worried about the precedent set by the rebellion of these eight players: "Now that Von der Ahe has once knuckled down to his team [in the Cuban Giants matter], how many more mutinies will he have to face in the future? History gives some pointed pictures of the rise and spread of insubordination."[25]

Within a few days of the publication of the front-page story on "The Color Line in Baseball" in the *New York Times,* the newspapers had moved on to other matters. There was no record of the Cuban Giants' manager doing more than threatening to sue for damages, though it seemed likely that Von der Ahe provided some compensation to the Giants for his team's failure to play the game at West Farms. For a time, Von der Ahe tried to find another date to play the Cuban Giants later in the fall but abandoned this effort when no mutually agreeable date could be found. Although reports surfaced of Latham being fined $100 for his part in the affair, neither Von der Ahe nor Latham would confirm this penalty.[26] None of the other seven players were subject to any form of discipline. As the month wore on, everyone appeared content to return to the business at hand. The Browns still had to complete the season, secure the American Association championship, and ready themselves for their third world championship series in the last three years. However, the final phase of the season was different from the first four phases, with distractions on and off the field and a record that did not augur well for success in the post-season.

The Browns entered the final phase of the season (September 9 to October 9) 19 games ahead of second-place Cincinnati and Louisville. After the Browns' impressive 19–5 record in phase four, most expected to see the team close the season in a similar fashion, but this was not to be. Although they won four of eight series, the Browns limped to the finish line with 11 wins and 12 losses, registering their only sub-.500 record in the five phases of 1887. Most of the St. Louis newspapers blamed the Browns' downturn on the cumulative effect of their injuries, a weakened state that most believed would pass in time for them to defend their world championship. An injured Comiskey was still confident about their chances:

> Though suffering considerably from a broken thumb, he looks at matters very philosophically, and is very sanguine as to a speedy recovery of the use of his injured member. He does not regard the present broken-up condition of the champions as detrimental to their work this fall in the world's championship series, but thinks the long rests Bushong and Foutz have had will be greatly to their benefit in their return to the diamond.[27]

The last three weeks of the season belied Comiskey's optimism. Injuries continued to sap their play on the field. And various distractions off the field, some of which may have been related to the chaotic swirl of events surrounding the Cuban Giants incident, seemed to affect the Browns' legendary will to win, a previously impenetrable force that many felt had driven them headlong into victory during most of the season to date.

Unlike the struggles of the Browns, O'Neill ended his season with a solid performance at the plate. In 23 games, he had 45 hits in 99 times at bat for an average of .455. Like his teammates', O'Neill's record dipped in the seven games with Cincinnati, where he hit only .300 on nine hits in 30 at-bats. However, in the other six series, O'Neill topped the .500 mark, with 36 hits in 69 times at bat for a .522 average. During this phase, O'Neill ended his 25-game hitting streak on September 21 and started another on October 4, a 22-game hit streak that carried over to the first 15 games of the 1888 season. O'Neill had two or more hits in 13 of the 23 games in this phase, with one five-hit game and two four-hit games. His consistency at the plate however, did not extend to long hits. His 14 extra-base hits—eight doubles, five triples, and one home run—were the second-lowest number he had in any phase, exceeding only his paltry output of eight long hits in phase two (May 25 to July 11).[28] Like the team, who scored fewer runs in the final phase than in any other, O'Neill's 21 runs scored and 14 runs batted in were his lowest totals in the five phases. Of the 13 runs that had an impact on the outcome of the game, O'Neill scored or drove in 12 runs that tied the game or put the Browns ahead. He crossed the plate with what turned out to be the winning run in only one game.

In the first three series of the fifth and final phase of the season, the Browns lost two out of three games in Philadelphia, won two out of three games in Baltimore, and beat Cleveland twice in a home series shortened by rain. Although O'Neill fell a bit below the torrid batting pace he set in his last 16 games in phase four, he still was an ongoing topic of interest and praise in the newspapers. After he put on yet another batting display against Cleveland, the *Cleveland Plain Dealer* declared: "Tip O'Neill of the St. Louis Browns is today the best batsman in America."[29] The local newspapers predicted that Tip's photograph would appear in the 1888 *Reach's Guide* as the 1887 champion batsman of the American Association: "Tip O'Neill's phiz will, no doubt, grace the Reach Guide-Book this season. Tip is a really handsome fellow, and handsome is as handsome does."[30] Celebrating Tip likely was a welcome digression from the newspapers' preoccupation with the health troubles of many other core Browns.

Charlie Comiskey was out indefinitely after he broke his thumb in a game in Philadelphia on September 10. Although not ready to return to active duty after being struck in the face by a bat that slipped out of O'Neill's hands in a game in Weehawken, New Jersey, Curt Welch was re-activated to fill the ninth spot on the roster.[31] He played with considerable pain for a few games, eventually getting back into shape in the last two series of the season.

In the first game against Baltimore (September 14), Yank Robinson, in an attempted steal, was spiked in the hand by Bill Greenwood, the Baltimore second baseman. With no replacement available, Robinson had to stay in the game. Unfortunately, he ignored his injury, playing another four games before he sought medical attention. His hand was now poisoned, and he was in danger of losing his finger.[32] Robinson missed five of the seven games against Cincinnati (September 21–October 2), playing in the last two games before missing the five games in the Louisville series (October 3–6). When he resumed his position at second base in the last series of the season against Cleveland, he had difficulty gripping the bat or catching hard-hit balls.

In recovery from a broken thumb since August 14, Dave Foutz returned as the starting pitcher in the Browns' first game against Cleveland (September 17). Although "he showed some want of practice,"[33] Foutz pitched the Browns to an 11–inning, 9–7 victory. However, in the last 18 games played by the Browns, Foutz started just six games, compiling a disappointing 2–4 record. He had difficulty applying the kind of pressure needed for his three pitches (fastball, change of pace, down-shoot). Some worried that he might not rebound in time for the world championship.

With the exception of a premature two-game return to the lineup in August, Doc Bushong had not played behind the plate since June 30. By mid–September, Bushong edged slowly back into his old job, catching five games down the stretch, as Comiskey stayed with Jack Boyle for the other 11 games.[34] It took time for Bushong to regain his form, to get his timing back on throwing out attempted steals, and simply to catch without worrying about reinjuring his finger. Comiskey wanted to give his veteran backstop every chance to rediscover the calm and assured stance behind the plate that had made him so invaluable to the Browns. In short, the Browns staggered into their seven-game test against Cincinnati, a team that was in the midst of its best month of the year and was ready to take down the champions.[35]

In consecutive series against Cincinnati, the Browns lost six of seven games, including four games in a row, their longest losing streak of the season. In the first two games (September 21–22), Cincinnati beat the Browns, 15–3, for their worst loss of the season,[36] and 6–0, only the second time all season that they had been Chicagoed.[37] The *Cincinnati Commercial Gazette* gleefully highlighted the win with the headline: "000000000=0. The Above Represents the Work of Von der Ahe's Men Yesterday."[38] Although O'Neill went hitless in four times at bat, he was celebrated in the local press for his seven catches, a defensive feat that stood in contrast to his team's 11 errors.

After their third consecutive loss in Cincinnati, the Browns were determined to turn the tables on the Reds as the series shifted to St. Louis. Miraculously, Comiskey returned to the lineup after only a two-week convalescence. However, the home field did not provide its usual advantage. Down 4–0, Cincinnati exploded for eight runs in the eighth inning to defeat the Browns, 8–4. Furthermore, injury struck again when Caruthers split his finger on a fly ball to center field and had to leave the game. Four days later (September 29), Caruthers beat Cincinnati, 8–2, allowing only one clean hit in the first eight innings. In the final game of the series (October 2), he was in the box for another 8–2 score, this time taking the loss. Caruthers pitched only one of the last eight games of the season, a less strenuous schedule, in the hope that his finger would be in good shape for the world championship series against Detroit.

Delighted by the success of the Cincinnati pitchers against O'Neill, the local reporters repeatedly commented on how he floundered at the plate: "O'Neill, the champion slugger, failed to connect here. His hits were few and far between."[39] Elsewhere, most ignored the seven-game drop in O'Neill's production. In the midst of his downturn in Cincinnati, the *St. Louis Globe-Democrat* published the Association batting averages, noting the "good lead" O'Neill had over Pete Browning (.489 to Browning's .452).[40] The *St. Louis Post-Dispatch* observed: "Tip O'Neill still leads the Association, and in fact League, in batting. His average this season is unprecedented—with or without bases on balls."[41] Conceding the batting championship for 1887 to Tip, Browning and Hugh Nicol were already setting their sights on beating O'Neill in 1888.[42]

The Browns ended the season on a winning note, victorious in five of their final eight games. In a five-game set against Louisville (October 3–6), the Browns won two out of three games in Louisville and split a doubleheader in St. Louis on October 6. After scoring only 24 runs in seven games against Cincinnati, the Browns broke out for 47 runs in five games against Louisville. Held hitless in the first game of the series, O'Neill rallied for 13 hits in 19 times at bat in the last four games, including three doubles, two triples, and a home run. He had two near-cycles, the first on a single, double, and triple in the Browns' 13–9 win in game two. The second near-cycle was part of a five-hit performance, including a base on balls, two singles, a triple, and home run, in support of the Browns' 11–5 victory in the second game of the October 6 doubleheader.[43]

The final three-game series was in St. Louis against Cleveland.[44] With Robinson's return, the team was back at full strength, though there was some doubt whether every player was at full strength. In game one, the Browns beat Cleveland, 12–2, for their 94th win of the season, a new Association record. After winning 17 games in a row against Cleveland, the Browns set another mark by losing game two, 4–2, their first and only loss to the Babes in 1887. They closed out the regular schedule with a 6–2 win. With seven hits in 13 times at bat against Cleveland, O'Neill ended the season on a seven-game hitting streak, batting .556 on 20 hits in 36 times at bat. Many of the St. Louis faithful believed that the Browns, led by Tip O'Neill, the champion batsman of the Association, were rounding into form just in time for the world championship.

While the Browns clinched the American Association title by the middle of September, the National League champion was not decided until the last week of the season. Nonetheless, on September 17, with the Detroit Wolverines' 7½-game lead over their nearest rival,[45] Von der Ahe and Frederick Stearns, the President of the Detroit club, began a series of exchanges to determine the terms and conditions of the world championship series. As these negotiations proceeded, the St. Louis and Detroit press each waged a one-sided campaign to declare its club as the favorite to win the world championship. Von der Ahe liked the chances of his Browns:

> If my men are in good form when we begin the series, I have no fear of the result, and know we will win, hands down.... There has been a great deal of talk about the hard-hitting abilities of the Detroit players, but for the life of me I cannot see where they will have the advantage of the Browns on that score. There is no doubt but what we excel in fielding and base-running, and in spite of the popular clamor about Detroit hard-hitters, I think we are equally as good, if not better batters, than they are.... We have eight hitters that will out-bat any eight men on the Detroit team. O'Neill is a better slugger than big Brouthers. Big Thompson and Jim White are no better, if as good, with the stick as my two pitchers, Foutz and Caruthers. Besides these three star batters I have a quintet in Comiskey, Robinson, Welch, Gleason and Latham, who lay away over any five batters in the Detroit team, outside of the big four.[46]

Waiting until just before the series started, the *Detroit Free Press* responded to Von der Ahe's assessment:

> So much has been said in praise of the St. Louis Browns that their coming next Wednesday will be an event of great interest to base ball circles. The interest is greatly added to the desire of Detroit to see their own champions pitted against world beaters and compare their relative abilities. There is general belief in this vicinity that the superior batting prowess of the Wolverines, added to their splendid fielding, will win the day. The admirers of the Browns insist that they will hit just as hard as the Detroits, field as well, and run bases much better. Their base-running ability is admitted, ditto their fielding, but that they can bat with the Detroits will not be entertained for a minute.[47]

Fans on both sides looked forward to the match-up of the best batsmen in the country. The *St. Louis Sunday Sayings* expected big things from O'Neill: "O'Neill and Brouthers lead their respective associations as batters. Which of the two will do the best stick work in the world's championship series? As a side bet, O'Neill has the call, especially in the total bases."[48] Similarly the *St. Louis Globe-Democrat* anticipated a powerful display at the plate by both batsmen, with O'Neill leading the way: "It will be a rare sight to see the greatest hitters in the country, Tip O'Neill and Dan Brouthers, pitted against one another. Tip leads all batters in hitting this season, his average being at high-water mark—above

.490."[49] However, when the *Detroit Free Press* suggested that O'Neill, and indeed all of the Browns' batsmen, had inflated batting averages that they would not have made against pitchers in the National League,[50] the *Globe-Democrat* fired back:

> The *Detroit Free Press* claims that O'Neill would not have as large an average against League pitchers as he has against the Association twirlers. What rot! The Association twirlers are superior as a class to the League ones. Detroit's alleged sluggers were able to get but four hits off Shreve, an Association cast-off, a few weeks ago, yet the Browns knocked the pitcher out.[51]

Bats were drawn, with each club confident in the superiority of their leading slugger.[52]

Amidst this jousting between the newspapers in Detroit and St. Louis, Von der Ahe interspersed his confident predictions of the Browns' forthcoming victory in the world championship with his concerns about certain players. He implied or gave advance notice of his intent of trading or selling some of the core Browns. During the Cincinnati series, he suggested that he wanted to replace the veteran Bill Gleason next season.[53] Von der Ahe also expressed his willingness to part with Doc Bushong[54] and Bob Caruthers[55] as well as trade one of Dave Foutz, Silver King, or Nat Hudson.[56] A rumor also surfaced that Brooklyn wanted to buy Comiskey, Caruthers, and Yank Robinson.[57] And there were reports in numerous papers that the Boston club in the National League intended to offer St. Louis $5,500 to secure the services of O'Neill for the 1888 season.[58] Heading into the world championship, the Browns, for the first time in months, had all of their players on hand, ready to resume the level of team work and aggressive style of play that was at the heart of their success.[59] Statements or rumors of possible player moves likely served as distractions from the task at hand, namely to come together as a team to beat Detroit for the world title.

As the forthcoming championship series neared, the Browns' captain and manager, ever dedicated to victory by any and all means, was still mindful of what the team was up against:

> We are very badly crippled up, and I am afraid we will not be all right when we meet the Wolverines. They used to say that St. Louis had no bad luck, and could beat all the other clubs, because her players never got hurt, and the club was always at its full strength. Look what luck we have had this year. There never was a nine which had more severely injured players. Welch was almost killed by the bat that slipped from O'Neill's hands. Bushong had his finger broke and he was unable to play for half a season. His finger is nearly well now, but he has not yet recovered confidence and is always apprehensive of being hurt. Then Robinson was badly hurt. He can play ball now, but not in his best style. I broke my hand and I will hardly get into condition before the games commence. Foutz is in terribly bad shape. His arm is very lame, and he cannot do his accustomed work in the box. Caruthers is the only twirler in the club who is pitching good ball.
>
> "What seems to have been the trouble with the club this year?" The fight for first place has not been warm enough, and that has put even those who are not injured in bad shape. The boys, with a walkover, could not take a great interest in the game, and they played carelessly. The result is that they are out of trim, and it will require practice before they can play their accustomed good ball. We will make it hot for the Detroits anyhow, and if we do not win the series we will come mighty near it, I can tell you.[60]

The Browns finished the season with a 95–40 record for a .704 winning percentage. They were 14 games ahead of second-place Cincinnati. The Browns also led the Association in nine offensive categories: runs, hits, doubles, home runs, runs batted in, total bases, long hits, batting average, and stolen bases.[61] Their 1,131 runs scored were the highest in the Association, 160 more than their nearest rival. On a per game basis, the Browns scored 8.2 runs and allowed 5.5 runs for a run differential of 2.7 runs, all three figures the best in the Association.

The table below lists O'Neill's offensive output in this fifth and final phase as well as the totals in each of these offensive categories for the entire season. Like the Browns, O'Neill was also the leader in nine offensive categories, seven of which overlapped those categories in which the Browns led all teams, namely: runs, hits, doubles, runs batted in, total bases, long hits, and batting average. In addition, O'Neill was at the top of the lists in the American Association in triples and home runs.

	Games	AB	R	H	BB	1B	2B	3B	HR	AVG	SB
September 9–October 9	23	999	21	45	6	25	8	5	1	.455	4
April 16–October 9	124	564	167	275	52	135	52	22	14	.488	33

AB–At-Bats; R–Runs; H–Hits; BB–Base on Balls 1B–Single; 2B–Double; 3B–Triple; HR–Home Run; TB–Total Bases; AVG–Batting Average; SB–Stolen Bases

JAMES O'NEIL
Champion Base Ball Batter

At season's end, O'Neill led the Association with a .488 batting average. Pete Browning (Louisville) finished second at .459. Bob Caruthers followed (St. Louis) with .456. Yank Robinson (St. Louis) was fourth at .427, Denny Lyons (Philadelphia) was fifth at .415, and Mack (Louisville) was sixth at .410. Although the newspapers regularly commented on O'Neill's lead throughout the last phase of the season, there was no formal acknowledgment of his batting championship and percentage until November. It was not the time to celebrate individual achievements. The immediate test before the Browns was the defeat of Detroit for the world championship. Unfortunately for the fans, neither the team, the offensive juggernaut in the regular season, nor Tip O'Neill, the dominant offensive player in the Association, was up to the post-season challenge.

In 1888, the W. S. Kimball & Co's cigarettes released the series "Champions of Games and Sports." The series featured four baseball players: catcher, pitcher, batter, and fielder. O'Neill was included in the collection to represent the "Champion Base Ball Batter" (The Rucker Archive).

15

October 10 to October 26: St. Louis Loses to Detroit in the World Championship

One year earlier, after St. Louis beat Chicago, 4–3, in ten innings to win the world championship series, four games to two, the *St. Louis Republican* began its report of the Browns' win in the deciding game with the image of a rooster standing tall, chest extended, neck cocked, ready to bellow his majestic crow to announce the dawn of a new day. After the exclamation, "Had to Bring Out Our Rooster Again," the newspaper crowed the following headlines:

> He Crows for Our Browns First, Last and All the Time
> The Base Ball Champions of America and the World
> The Greatest Victory in the History of Base Ball
> The Chicagos Defeated and the Hippodrome Croakers Silenced
> Anson and Spalding Satisfied Now that Our Browns Can Play.[1]

On October 22, 1887, after their 13–3 win over the St. Louis Browns in Baltimore, the Detroit Wolverines were the new champion club of the world. It was the Wolverines' eighth and deciding win in the 15-game series. To this point in the series, the Browns had won only three games. Still flabbergasted and befuddled by how much Detroit dominated play in this series, the *St. Louis Republican* seemed angry and embarrassed by the loss. Their game report did not bring back the rooster. The elation and celebratory spirit were gone. With nothing to crow about, their 1887 headlines laid bare the stark facts as they saw them:

> Our Flag is Not There
> Detroit Knocked the Pole Down and Snatched the Gandy Rag
> The Browns Win by Magnificent Work in the Morning, But
> Play Like Boobies and Lose at Baltimore in the Afternoon.[2]

In "The Series That Went on Forever,"[3] the Browns and the Wolverines split the final four games, giving Detroit an overall record of ten wins and five losses.[4] Unlike the home-and-home series against Chicago in 1886, Frederick Stearns, the president of the Detroit club, and Chris Von der Ahe opted for a grand tour, a spectacle on wheels where the two teams would play ten of the 15 games in major centers in both leagues, with only three games in St. Louis and two games in Detroit. After the regular season, the two presidents, disappointed with the size of their home crowds but pleased with the numbers that attended their away games, expected that the turnout and thus the profits would be better on the road in the eight cities that they arranged for the series.⁵

For such an extravaganza, Von der Ahe contracted the Vandalia Railroad to provide a special train to get the teams from city to city on schedule and in a level of comfort befitting the world championship. The train included three Pullman sleeper cars, each with an adjoining drawing room, a car for the dining room, and, after the first match in Detroit (October 12), a baggage car with a safe to secure the profits from each game. The two clubs had their own sleepers, with banners that read "Detroit, League Champions for 1888" and "St. Louis, Association Champions for 1888," stretched along the side of the car to demarcate its occupants. The third sleeper car was reserved for the presidents and directors of each club as well as reporters from St. Louis and Detroit, with some representation from New York and Chicago newspapers.⁶ The entourage travelled over 4,000 miles, sometimes at rather breakneck speeds to ensure a timely arrival. In such hectic runs, "the cars rocked fearfully, and many of the party became quite ill, after the manner of seasickness. In the dining car, the dishes were rolling off the table, and those who had not passed through the experience of seasickness found the supper very unenjoyable."⁷ Under such conditions, the *St. Louis Post-Dispatch* marveled at the standard of play demonstrated by the two teams when they journeyed from St. Louis to Detroit for Game Three:

According to "This Game of Games," a blog dedicated to "St. Louis Baseball in the 19th Century," the image of the rooster appeared from time to time in nineteenth-century St. Louis newspapers after a significant victory by a St. Louis team. In 1886, the rooster was associated with boasting, gloating, and crowing. It strutted proudly, bellowing "cock-a-doodle-do" after the Browns won the world championship (*The Sporting News*, October 30, 1887).

> It is surprising indeed that the quality of base ball which both teams have played under the circumstances, has been as good as it is. Imagine a programme something like this and then fancy how fresh the men must have felt as they stepped on the ball field. On arriving in Detroit at 10:00 a.m. after breakfast on the dining car, dress in costume on car; parade through the principal streets with a brass band in front and a howling crowd on both side and to the rear; return to train for dinner, taken without a change of clothes; carriage for ball grounds; game of thirteen innings; wash; supper; leave at 8:30 for Pittsburgh, where the same programme is enacted, leaving for New York at 7:00 o'clock.⁸

The close proximity to the teams also afforded the reporters an opportunity to witness the ballplayers' pre- and post-game habits, an experience that did not always foster admiration, especially when the Browns did not play as well. Some members of the press blamed the Browns' subpar play on the players' late nights, gambling habits, drinking, and dissension, criticisms that they cultivated as travelling companions on the special train.⁹

Despite the claims by the Detroit and St. Louis press of their respective clubs' superiority, on paper the teams seemed evenly matched. The Wolverines led the National League and the Browns were first in the Association in runs, hits, long hits, and batting average. On defense, each team led the league in fielding average and made the fewest errors. In pitching, the Browns' staff had a slight edge, leading the Association with the fewest bases on balls and wild pitches, while second-best in earned run average and in fewest home runs allowed. However, after demonstrating some level of parity in the first three games of the series, the Browns were increasingly outmatched by the Wolverines.

In Game One (October 10), the Browns' 6–1 win, for some, removed any doubt about who was the best team. The *St. Louis Globe-Democrat* enjoyed the "sharp lesson" that the Browns gave to the Wolverines:

> After months of wordy arguments as to the relative strength of the Detroits and Browns, champions of the League and American Association respectively, the two teams at last came together on the ball field yesterday at Sportsman's Park to settle the much mooted question in actual battle. From yesterday's game it would seem that the local team is safe in its title of champions of the world.[10]

Surprised by how much its team was outplayed, the *Detroit Free Press* nonetheless gave credit to the Browns for their thorough drubbing of the Wolverines:

> They thrashed them out of shape, pounded them back into form again and finally stepped on them with both feet and crushed the Mound City Mud—outbatted, outfielded and outpitched, beatened, whipped, polished off, pulverized, demoralized, razzled-dazzled, subjugated. It was a defeat that would cause the most ardent admirer of the Wolverines to exclaim in the fervent language of the foreign poet, "O, rats what is the matter with us!" Whew, what a game those Browns did play! Fielding superb, sharp, accurate; not an error. Batting effective, tricky base running. Too fast, altogether too fast, and during the game constantly on the move. Lively as a cage of monkeys and as full of tricks, they play the most interesting game of any club in the country.[11]

In Game Two (October 11), Detroit came back to defeat the Browns, 5–3, thus splitting the two games in St. Louis. They then travelled 13 hours by train to Detroit, where in Game Three, (October 12) the Wolverines prevailed in a hard-fought, 13-inning contest, beating the Browns, 2–1. Over the next six days (October 13–19), Detroit won five of six games, two by shutouts, the first on October 13 in Pittsburgh, 8–0, and the second on October 15 in New York, 9–0.[12] The Wolverines scored 38 runs over the six games while holding the Browns to seven runs. At this point in the series, Detroit had seven wins and two losses, with just one more victory needed to dethrone the Browns for the world championship.

Although on October 16 Detroit only led St. Louis by a margin of four games to two, there was growing concern in St. Louis about the Browns' chances. In its assessment of the series to date, the *St. Louis Globe-Democrat* no longer gave the Browns the edge:

> The Brown enthusiasts have been not a little disappointed at the performances of the champions thus far in their contests with the League giants. There were a number of people in the city who really believed that the Association cracks were simply invincible.... They put up their money firmly convinced that it could not be lost, but the result of the series up to the present time has made them feel rather uncertain as to its safety. The most devoted admirers of the Browns are bound to acknowledge that they have met their match in the Detroits, and if they win the present series they will have done their very best to do so.[13]

At the start of the series, betting in the St. Louis poolrooms was brisk, with odds favoring Detroit by 12-to-10 to win the series. The odds changed to 10-to-9 after Game

Two, with most money still on Detroit to take the championship. After Game Three (Wolverines beat St. Louis, 2–1), the odds increased to 10-to-7 in Detroit's favor and then to 10-to-6 following the one-sided 8–0 victory by Detroit in Game Four. At that juncture, the St. Louis cranks turned cautious in their betting, worried that their money was in jeopardy.[14]

Perhaps as a way to inspire the Browns and to distract the increasingly distraught fans,[15] the *St. Louis Post-Dispatch* published a lengthy poem by Magoogin entitled, "The Last Game. A Metrical Forecast of the Detroit-Browns Series."[16] The summary beneath the title stated: "The Thrillsome Moment of the Final Contest—Suspense Knee-Deep All Over the Grounds—Everybody in Deep Perspiration—O'Neill Sends the Ball over the Fence and Hearts Resume Their Wonted Beating."[17] In this lyrical but imaginary story, the series was tied seven games apiece. The game was scoreless after 16 innings. Detroit failed to get a run in its half of the 17th inning. The following excerpt picks up the game as the Browns come to the plate:

> The Browns came rushing in
> To have a hack at the ball,
> And as the multitude's applause
> Grew loud and voluminous
> Monkey Latham clicked his heals
> And somebody yelled out "Who-oa!"
> As he lifted his laughing bat,
> And some one jeered,
> But Latham bunted the ball
> And beat it down to first,
> While Gleason, who came next,
> Stuck out his hip and struck the ball,
> And thus acquired a base hit.
> Latham was now on third
> When Tip O'Neil advanced
> And leaning o'er the plate
> Reach'd for the curving sphere,
> "Strike One!" The umpire cried
> And Gleason went to second.
>
> Once more the ball unto the catcher passed,
> "Ball One!" the umpire shrieked—
> And so it went: "Ball two!"
> "Strike two!" "Ball three!" "Strike three!"
> "Ball four!" until suspense
> Now seem'd so thick it might be shovel'd
> In tubs and tuns right off the grounds.
>
> A list'ning ear could catch the sound
> Of Von der Ahe's heart's wild beating,
> And Manager Stearns
> Look'd like the last hours of a condemn'd man,
> A solemn silence sat upon the throng.
> Bated breaths—
> Baited with beer, perhaps—
> And anxious haggard faces
> Possess'd the multitude.
> Only a single chance remained
> For all concerned.

> Pret. Getzein squeezed the ball
> And lifting high his leg in air
> Sock'd a swift inshoot
> At the unoffending batter.
> It might have been murder in the first degree,
> But Tip O'Neill
> Met the ball half way
> And sent it careening o'er the fence
> Into a passing baggage wagon.
>
> The vast throngs loosen'd up its lungs
> And shook the starry sphere
> With one mad howl of joy
> As Latham trotted home
> And scored the winning run.
> "Whoo-hoo-hoo-peeeeee!"
> "Rah for the Browns!"
> And other wild and discordant remarks
> Jarred on the Detroit's ears,
> And they silently shoulder'd their bats
> And sadly stole away.
>
> This settled the business.
> As anybody who knows anything about the game
> Can readily understand,
> Chris Von der Ahe was happy
> And the Browns—
> The batting, fielding, base-running
> Coaching, clowning Browns—
> Were champions of the world.
> Chestnuts![18]

While the poem may have lifted the spirits of the *Post-Dispatch* readers, it bore little resemblance to what happened. The Browns did win the 15th game by a score of 9–2. Having already lost ten games of the first 14 played, this was their fifth and final win of the Series. Since Detroit had already won the Series after game 11, the 15th game was also not the deciding game.

Perhaps O'Neill was stimulated by the poem's evocative account of his series-winning home run. In the game played one day after the publication of "The Last Game," O'Neill blasted his only home run of the Series. However, it was more of a face-saving blow, giving the Browns their only run in a 3–1 loss. The four-bagger allowed the Browns to escape their third shutout in four games at the hands of the Wolverines.[19] Sadly, for the Browns and the fans, he floundered at the plate for most of the Series.

In the 1887 world championship, O'Neill was not the same batsman who led the Browns to the 1886 world championship or who stood above his peers in the 124 games that he played in the regular season. He finished the 15 games with 13 hits in 65 times at bat for a pitiful .200 batting average.[20] At various points in the Series, the St. Louis newspapers wrote with some alarm about O'Neill's lack of hitting. When Detroit clinched the world championship (October 22), the *Globe-Democrat* was more forthright in its disappointment: "Those of whom much was expected realized the least. O'Neill was the weakest infant at the bat."[21]

Some fans were distressed by O'Neill's substandard record at the plate because of the wagers they placed on his batting in certain games or for the Series as a whole. In

Game One, someone bet $25 that O'Neill would not hit more than a single.[22] He hit a double. For Game Two, there were even odds that O'Neill would have more hits than Sam Thompson, Detroit's right fielder. Thompson had three hits and O'Neill had one hit.[23] At 3–2, Caruthers had the best odds to make the most hits in Game Three, with O'Neill and Thompson second with 7–5 odds. Welch was well back with 25–2 odds but was the best on the day with three hits.[24] O'Neill was hitless in six times at bat. Likely based on his Association-leading 167 runs in the regular season, the oddsmakers had O'Neill as the favorite at 7–5 to score the most runs in the Series. Latham, Hardy Richardson, and Jack Rowe tied with 12 runs apiece, while O'Neill scored seven. As the Series progressed, betting dwindled on the Browns and on their players. For the loyal St. Louis fans, it was bad enough to have their pride bruised by the loss of the world championship. For the betting public, it was likely even harder to have their pockets picked as they lost money on wagers placed on Tip's batting and run-getting, a seemingly sure thing that went terribly wrong.

O'Neill himself was upset and befuddled by his performance, or rather his lack thereof. In a subsection entitled "O'Neill Disgusted," the *St. Louis Post-Dispatch* reported on the conversation with Tip about his batting record to date:

> I thought I was going to slug when I started out on this trip, but I've disappointed myself. I've got a bat that weighs about a ton, not counting the rope wound around the handle, and I twist myself clean around in a way that's going to break my spine before the month's out, but I can't find the ball. I can knock home runs and three-baggers all day when we have a snap club, but would you believe that in these games when a base hit would win sure pop, I saw the air like a windmill and put the ball in the in-field as if I was playing roly poly. But this kind of thing ain't going to last.[25]

Unfortunately, O'Neill's slump did last for the rest of the Series. The pitching staff of the Wolverines fed him a diet of drop curves that disrupted O'Neill's capacity to make solid contact. As a result, O'Neill's characteristic line-drive hitting gave way to pop-ups or weak groundouts as he hit either over or under the ball.[26] On more than one occasion, his feeble outs were followed by throwing his bat as his frustration got the better of him.[27]

Though few and far between, O'Neill had some noteworthy moments in the 15-game series. In the Browns' 5–2 win in Brooklyn in Game Five (October 14), O'Neill drove in three of the five runs. After O'Neill's double in the first inning gave the Browns a 2–0 lead, the crowd erupted in applause and "the ladies smiled sweetly on Mr. O'Neill. Fortunate man!"[28] Over the Series, O'Neill tied Charlie Bennett, the catcher for Detroit, with nine runs batted in, the

H. D. S. and Company issued a set of 18 die-cut cards in honor of the 1887 World Championship Series between the St. Louis Browns and the Detroit Wolverines. The colored set featured the nine core players on the Browns (A. J. Bushong, R. L. Caruthers, Chas. Comiskey, David Foutz, Wm. Gleason, W. A. Latham, James O'Neill, Wm. Robinson, C. Welch) and nine players on the Wolverines (C. W. Bennett, Dan Brouthers, F. Dunlap, C. H. Getzien, Ed Hanlon, H. Richardson, J. C. Rowe, Sam Thompson, J. L. White) (The Rucker Archive).

most of any batsmen in the Series. Despite his few hits, O'Neill also scored or drove in 15 of the Browns' 54 runs, a rate that was about the same as his run production during the season.[29] Most observers overlooked such contributions. All they knew was that Tip O'Neill the slugger did not show up for the 1887 world championship.

Fortune shone on O'Neill in Game Six, this time on arguably the defensive play of the game. As the *St. Louis Post-Dispatch* noted, his running catch and subsequent throw to put out Fred Dunlap, the Detroit second baseman, was "the only thing to redeem the Browns' play in New York,"[30] as Detroit thumped St. Louis, 9–0. *The Post-Dispatch* described the catch and double play as follows:

> Bennett now picked up the ashen stick. He stood alongside the plate until Umpire Kelly announced three strikes and four balls. The next ball pitched was beautifully over the plate. Bennett hit at it. The ball struck the end of the bat and it went so far in the direction of left field that everybody arose to see it land beyond the outside surrounding line of spectators. O'Neill, however, who seems to know the batting peculiarities of every opponent, was in the crowd of spectators when the ball fell. He had had a hard run, but the ball did not pass through his hand. Dunlap, like everybody else, thought the hit was for a home run and speeded on his way. He had got half way to third base when O'Neill caught the ball. O'Neill did not dally. He threw the sphere on a line to Robinson and "Rob" sent it to first like a flash before Dunlap could get back within twenty feet of the base. This great play created applause, which lasted for several minutes.[31]

Other than the applause he got for the double play and the ovation he received for his ninth-inning home run in Game Seven (October 17), albeit in a losing cause, O'Neill heard few of the wild cheers that had followed him throughout most of the season.[32]

When the tenth game was rained out, the two presidents arranged for a doubleheader on the next day (October 20) in two cities, a morning game in Washington and an afternoon game in Baltimore. The Browns, mindful that the Wolverines needed only one more win to clinch the Series, denied Detroit their glory with a convincing 11–4 win in Washington. It was the Browns' best offensive game[33] and their largest margin of victory. The afternoon game was a different story. The Wolverines pounded Foutz for 18 hits, five of them for extra bases, and went on to defeat the Browns, 13–3.

Detroit was the new champion club of the world.

For days prior to Detroit's decisive win, the press searched for reasons why the Browns were not playing well. In addition to the criticism from reporters concerning the lack of discipline on the team manifested in such habits as staying up late, playing poker, and drinking, the press was bothered by "the Browns' lackadaisical attitude toward the series, their hostility toward Von der Ahe, and the tensions among [the players]."[34]

Rumors of dissension among the players surfaced in the fall and continued throughout the Series in reports of bickering, arguments, and the occasional fights among the players. When questioned on why they lost the Series, the players responded in much the same way, blaming some of their teammates: "They start out with a general proposition that the club as a body was playing poor ball, with the exception of the speaker himself. If a baseman, it was the fielder's and pitcher's fault; if a fielder, it was the pitcher's and basemen's fault; if a pitcher, it was because of a lack of support from the entire club."[35] The *St. Louis Republican* landed squarely on dissension as the debilitating force that precipitated the Browns' loss: "But the principal reason for the Browns' downfall is that there is dissension in the team and has been for months. The result is, they have lost that quality for which they were once so famous—namely team work."[36]

The animosity towards Chris Von der Ahe, simmering for most of the season, came to a boil in the protest against playing the Cuban Giants. As that incident subsided, the players resented Von der Ahe's lingering habit of criticizing certain players in the press, in some cases voicing his intent to sell or trade some of them immediately following the world championship series. Some players, such as Bushong,[37] countered by publicly declaring his desire for a release, while others, such as Caruthers and Gleason, asserted that under no circumstances would they play again for the Browns.[38] The players were also upset by Von der Ahe's parsimonious attitude concerning compensation for playing the 15-game Series.[39] Some observers wondered aloud if the players' less-than-stellar play was a deliberate act of protest against Von der Ahe's tightfistedness.[40] Whether the players' enmity for Von der Ahe played a role in the loss to Detroit, they were clearly livid for most of the off-season about the owner's failure to share some of the proceeds.

Others explained the downfall of the Browns, at least in part, on their string of injuries, which was an obstacle from which they never fully recovered, at least not in time to regain their form for the world championship.[41] Or when their defeat seemed inexplicable, some just put it down to hard luck.[42] However, in the end, most came around to the conclusion that the Browns on the day, or in this case, on the 15 days, were beaten by a better team. *The Sporting News* concluded that "Detroit has whipped us and whipped us fairly. That point is settled and excuses and crawfishing are now out of order.... Our Browns in most of these struggles played good ball but the Detroits played better.... But for the most part the games were won by good hard hitting, magnificent fielding and without any assistance whatever from Dame Fortune."[43] In most games, Detroit outplayed St. Louis at almost every turn.

With the series decided, the final four games were anticlimactic and of little interest to the fans. Attendance plummeted.[44] The game in Detroit drew 3,389 upbeat and festive fans, ready to welcome home their champions:

> Large crowds greeted the victors and the victims all along the route and the cheering was continuous. Arriving at the Russell House all dismounted and entered. Here the players and magnates held a levee, which was a grand crush. After the thousands of cranks had in a measure satisfied their curiosity, the stars of the diamond withdrew and took dinner together in the Russell. After dinner, the teams took carriages and paraded to the grounds.[45]

The game stopped on numerous occasions for presentations to individual players.[46] In the fourth inning, the game halted to honor Charlie Bennett, the Detroit catcher, who throughout the series had gunned down many of the Browns' would-be base stealers. A fife and drum entered the grounds accompanied by two men rolling a wheelbarrow towards home plate, filled with 520 shining silver dollars:

> "Come out here Charley," called the conspirators, and the king catcher was escorted towards the plate by some of his fellow players. Then Charley was informed that the coin shipment which he saw before him was intended for him. After a few other complimentary allusions three big policemen suddenly seized Bennett and informed him that unless he wheeled that sub-treasury around the bases they would be compelled to take him in. Charley accepted the situation and taking hold of the barrow rolled it slowly around, with one big policeman leading the way and one on each side of him to prevent escape. The band followed playing Yankee Doodle very artistically, and everybody got up and shouted themselves into hysterics. Charley scored an earned run.[47]

Although the day belonged to the Wolverines, the game broke briefly for some of Tip O'Neill's friends from Woodstock to present him with a bouquet of flowers. O'Neill bowed gracefully as the crowd, "in a yelling mood, yelled its loudest."[48] He stepped to the plate, likely determined to reward his friends with one of his screeching, line-drive hits. Instead he went out on a softly struck ground ball to the first baseman. Not even the presence of friendly faces could pull O'Neill out of his slump as he went hitless in four times at bat. His friends departed with no stories to tell back home, except possibly to regale his Woodstock family and fans about how hard O'Neill threw the bat when he failed to get a hit: "Baldwin's pitching was altogether too much for the Mound City men, and O'Neill's inability to hit the ball safely caused him considerable anguish of spirit judging from the manner in which he threw his bat around."[49]

O'Neill's astounding batting record in the regular season must have seemed like a distant memory. After hitting almost .500 in 124 games, he probably was dumbfounded by a drop of almost 300 points in the world championship. On the day that the newspapers reported that the Browns lost the eighth and deciding game of the 15-game series (October 22), *The Sporting News* released the official American Association batting averages.[50] The *St. Louis Republican* also published the same list of averages, highlighting Tip's accomplishment with the statement: "In batting O'Neill of the St. Louis Browns heads the list and breaks all previous records with an average of .495, and is justly entitled to the title of the champion batter of the world."[51] An article entitled, "The Work of the Two Clubs," appeared on the same page as the list of batting averages, criticizing O'Neill's poor performance in the world championship.[52] The *St. Louis Globe-Democrat, St. Louis Post-Dispatch, St. Louis Chronicle,* and *St. Louis Sunday Sayings* did not publish the Association averages or note that O'Neill had officially won the batting title. They continued to concentrate on the disappointing performance of the Browns and individual players, including O'Neill, in the world championship.

In previous years, it had been the custom to award prizes at the end of the season to those Browns who led the team in various offensive and defensive categories. The Mermod and Jaccard Jewelry Company planned to "give three medals to members of the St. Louis Browns excelling in hitting, base running and fielding."[53] This year's ceremony, scheduled for the Olympic Theater on October 29 following the last show of Sweatman, Rice and Fagan's Minstrels, was cancelled. While no explanation was given for the cancellation, some might have felt that it was too soon after the dismal play of the Browns in the world championship to celebrate the achievements of individual players.[54] Tip O'Neill would have to wait some time for this public recognition of his regular-season batting accomplishments.

By November 5, it became known that the previously announced official averages were neither "official" nor correct. The reported .495 average for O'Neill on October 22 was based on 117 games and not on the 124 games that he played in 1887.[55] O'Neill's official average was corrected to .492.[56] Within a few days, the St. Louis newspapers, and most other newspapers in National League and American Association cities, published either the list of batting, fielding, and pitching averages or a short note that acknowledged that O'Neill led the Association with an average of .492 and Browning was second at .471.[57] Although this was the first time that a player on the Browns had won the batting title, in the St. Louis press there were no congratulatory statements, no expressions of pride in one of their boys, no quote from Von der Ahe or Comiskey on the batting prowess of the Association's leading slugger,[58] and no further analysis of O'Neill's average or slugging. The Browns' failure to repeat as world champions left a long shadow over St. Louis for most of the winter. Fans and press alike were not able to celebrate O'Neill's remarkable batting achievements in the 1887 season until after he was featured in the *Reach's Official Base Ball Guide*, which was released in April 1888.[59] Prompted by the *Guide's* tribute to

O'Neill, the local newspapers joined in, lauding his unprecedented batting feats of the previous year. A few days later, on April 26, 1888, O'Neill received a pair of diamond sleeve buttons as the best batsman on the club.[60] Tip O'Neill's batting record in 1887 was indeed a memorable display of hitting for average and power, and, "perhaps the most dominant offensive season in history."[61]

16

A Season of Firsts

With the story of O'Neill's extraordinary 1887 season now told, I now pause to consider those batting achievements that set him apart from other batsmen. O'Neill's batting record included a wide range of remarkable feats. For example, he had numerous multi-hit games, two in which he hit for the cycle and 24 games in which he had four or more hits. O'Neill also put together different types of batting streaks: four with 10–12 consecutive times on base; one with at least one hit in 25 games in a row and another with 22 games in a row; and one stretch with one or more long hits in 12 successive games. In three separate weeks (April 27–May 7, August 24–30, September 2–8), O'Neill combined these special feats of multi-hit games, long hits, and batting streaks to hit over .600 and lead the Browns to victory in 20 of 21 games. Tip O'Neill indeed had a season filled with noteworthy batting feats.[1]

O'Neill's outstanding season, while centered on his batting average, encompassed much more than getting a hit every second time at bat. In compiling a .488 batting average, O'Neill also led the Browns, the American Association, and indeed the major leagues in most batting categories related to average and power, often with record-breaking performances. It was indeed "a season of firsts."

On the Browns, O'Neill was the leader in most of the batting categories.[2] His .488 average was 125 points ahead of the team average of .363. Caruthers was second with a .456 average and Robinson third at .427.[3] His 275 hits, 88 long hits, and 413 total bases were significantly higher than those of Latham, who finished second on the team in each of these categories with 243 hits, 47 long hits, and 304 total bases. In terms of runs production (runs scored plus runs batted in minus home runs), O'Neill contributed 278 runs, 43 more than Latham who again was second-best on the Browns.[4] Furthermore, 79 of O'Neill's runs had a direct impact on the outcome of games. He scored or drove in 60 runs that tied the game or put the Browns ahead, and 19 that were the winning runs. By any measure, Tip O'Neill was the dominant batsman on the 1887 Browns.

At the league level, O'Neill was also first in a number of batting categories in the American Association. In the following table, these firsts are listed in the column labeled, "First Place—1887-AA." O'Neill led in 11 batting categories,[5] six of which I previously reported in Chapter 14 (hits, doubles, triples, home runs, long hits,[6] and batting average). The other five statistics were total bases,[7] runs batted in, on-base percentage, slugging percentage, and on-base percentage plus slugging percentage. Although they were not official statistics required by the 1887 scoring rules,[8] they were calculations suggested or implied by various baseball commentators in the nineteenth century.[9]

In addition to leading in the 11 categories, these numbers or percentages established new records in many of the categories in the American Association and in the major leagues (National League and American Association). In the table, the first two columns under "Record-Breaking Performances," labeled "1887-AA" and "1887-ML," list those categories (marked with an "X") where O'Neill's achievement, in addition to being first-ranked, was also "first ever," that is, with the best record all-time. He set eight new records and tied two others (hits, home runs) in the American Association and eight new records (tied with Browning for the record in hits) in the major leagues.[10] As the next column, designated "1882–91-AA," indicates, the seven records that O'Neill set on his own in 1887 and the one tied with Browning still stood as all-time, single-season marks in the American Association when it ended in 1891.

Many of O'Neill's single-season records in 1887 also set new standards for all of baseball in the era in which he played (1876–1892). Gary Gillette and Pete Palmer, in *The ESPN Baseball Encyclopedia, Fifth Edition,* in the introduction to the section entitled, "The Glory of Their Times: The Lifetime Leaders," explain the importance of recognizing the leading performances by era:

> Some of the lists are divided by time period in order to more clearly highlight the standout performers of each era. Eight significant eras in baseball history have been defined for this purpose—each is distinguished by rule changes, by large changes in the number of leagues or teams, or by other important factors.[11]

Those who played between 1876 and 1892 lived through arguably the most rule changes of any era in the history of baseball. In the 17 years in this period, players often moved from team to team, and, in some cases, from league to league. Many played in two or more of the four major leagues of the era: National League (1876–1892), American Association (1882–1891), Union Association (1884), and Players' League (1890). It seems particularly important then to compare O'Neill's 1887 record to those fellow batsmen who experienced the same playing conditions, rules changes, and hitting challenges. The final column, under "Record-Breaking Performances," labeled 1876–92-ML," shows that the eight major league records that O'Neill set in 1887—hits (tied with Browning), doubles, long hits, total bases, on-base percentage, slugging percentage, on-base plus slugging percentage, and batting average—still stood as the all-time, single-season record in the major leagues until at least the end of the era (1892).

| Category | First Place 1887–AA | Record-Breaking Performances ||||
		1887–AA	1887–ML	1882–91–AA	1876–92–ML
Hits	275	Tied	Tied	Tied	Tied
Doubles	52	X	X	X	X
Triples	22	—	—	—	—
Home runs	14	Tied	—	—	—
Long Hits	88	X	X	X	X
Total Bases	413	X	X	X	X
Runs Batted In	125	X	—	X	—
On-Base %	.492	X	X	X	X
Slugging %	.732	X	X	X	X
On-Base Plus Slugging %	1.224	X	X	X	X
Batting Average	.488	X	X	X	X

After 1892, some of O'Neill's major league records in the above batting categories endured longer than others (see Appendix B). However, in the number of firsts, no other batsman has ever matched O'Neill for leading the league and the major leagues with the most record-breaking performances in batting categories in one season.

While some players have headed the list of sluggers in two of the three long-hit categories (doubles, triples, and home runs), only O'Neill has been the leader in the league in all three during the same season.[12] According to the Lifetime Topps Project, there have been "only eleven other players who have even led in doubles, triples, and home runs at different points in their career: Dan Brouthers, Roger Connor, Harry Stovey, Sam Thompson, Ed Delahanty, Sam Crawford, Ty Cobb, Rogers Hornsby, Lou Gehrig, Joe Medwick, Jim Bottomley."[13] Batting, however, encompasses more than slugging categories.

In 1971, in the last issue of *The Little Red Book of Major League Baseball,* just above the citation of O'Neill's record of leading the league in doubles, triples, and home runs in a single season, Seymour Siwoff included a record for "Leading in Most Batting Categories, Season."[14] Ty Cobb, the center fielder for the 1911 Detroit Tigers, Joe Medwick, the left fielder for the 1937 St. Louis Cardinals, and Stan Musial, the first baseman for the 1946 St. Louis Cardinals, tied for the record, each leading in 12 of 15 batting categories. The entry in each cell of the table below indicates the number or percentage achieved by the player in the category in which he led the league (two dashes note a category a player did not lead):

	G	AB	R	H	S	D	T	HR	RBI	LH	EB[15]	TB	SLG	BA	SB	Total
Cobb, 1911	—	—	147	248	168	47	24	—	127	79	119	367	.620	.419	83	12
Medwick, 1937	156	633	111	237	—	56	—	31	154	97	169	406	.641	.374	—	12
Musial, 1946	156	624	124	228	142	50	20	—	—	86	138	366	.587	.365	—	12

G–Games; AB–At-Bats; R–Runs; H–Hits; S–Singles; D–Double; T–Triples; HR–Home Runs; RBI–Runs Batted In; LH–Long Hits; EB–Extra Bases; TB–Total Bases; SLG–Slugging Percentage; BA–Batting Average; Stolen Bases

To compare O'Neill's number of batting firsts in 1887 to those of the three batsmen in the above table, I used an adapted version of two tables, the one above and the first table presented earlier in this chapter on O'Neill's batting performance in 1887 and in the 1876–1892 era. I added "singles" as another batting category. I dropped the category of "Extra Bases" because it is a statistic that no longer appears in official records. In order to focus solely on batting, I deleted four of the categories in the above table and added two further categories. In my view, a batting category should provide a measure, in the form of a number or a percentage, that explicitly and directly represents what happens when a player hits the ball (e.g., type of hit, total number of bases created by hits, frequency or percentage of getting on base). Accordingly, I added on-base percentages (OB) and on-base plus slugging percentages (OPS). I also omitted "Games," "At-Bats," "Runs Scored," and "Stolen Bases." The following table, I argue, offers a more concentrated and consistent profile of batsmen who led their leagues in the key batting statistics.[16]

After a review of batters with the highest batting average in the league or association, batters who have hit .400 or better,[17] sluggers (e.g., hitters with highest number of total bases, highest slugging percentage, etc.), and players who have earned the Triple Crown,[18] I expanded the list of Cobb, Medwick, and Musial to include nine batsmen who led in ten or more batting categories in a single season. Ty Cobb and Rogers Hornsby, the second baseman for the St. Louis Cardinals, each has two seasons in which he led in ten or more batting categories. The table thus provides the batting statistics for 11 seasons, including two seasons for Cobb and Hornsby (two dashes note the categories in which a player did not finish first)[19]:

	H	S	D	T	HR	RBI	LH	TB	OB	SLG	OPS	BA	Total
O'Neill, 1887	275	—	52	22	14	125	88	413	.492	.732	1.224	.488	11
Barnes, 1876	138	102	21	14	—	—	36	190	.462	.590	1.052	.429	10
Lajoie, 1901	232	156	48	—	14	125	76	350	.463	.643	1.106	.426	11
Wagner, 1908	201	—	39	19	—	109	68	308	.415	.542	.957	.354	10
Cobb, 1911	248	168	47	24	—	127	79	367	—	.621	1.086	.420	10
Cobb, 1917	225	151	44	24	—	—	74	335	.444	.570	1.014	.383	10
Hornsby, 1921	235	—	44	18	—	126	83	378	.458	.639	1.097	.397	10
Hornsby, 1922	250	—	46	—	42	152	102	450	.459	.722	1.181	.401	10
Klein, 1933	223	—	44	—	28	120	79	365	.422	.602	1.025	.368	10
Medwick, 1937	237	—	56	—	31	154	97	406	—	.641	1.056	.374	9
Musial, 1948	230	—	46	18	—	131	103	429	.450	.702	1.152	.376	10

H–Hits; S–Singles; D–Double; T–Triples; HR–Home Runs; RBI–Runs Batted In; LH–Long Hits; TB–Total Bases; OB–On-Base Percentage; SLG–Slugging Percentage; OPS–On-Base plus Slugging Percentage; BA–Batting Percentage

O'Neill and Nap Lajoie, the second baseman for the 1901 Philadelphia Athletics, led their respective leagues in 11 of the 12 batting categories, with O'Neill finishing sixth in the American Association in singles and Lajoie ranking eighth in the American League in triples. In the 11 seasons represented above, all nine batsmen dominated their leagues in hitting for power, as indicated by four of the long-hit categories: long hits, total bases, slugging percentage, and on-base plus slugging percentage. O'Neill, however, led in all seven long-hit categories: doubles, triples, home runs, long hits, total bases, slugging percentage, and on-base percentage plus slugging percentage (OPS).[20] In eight of 11 seasons, seven batsman led in six of the seven long-hit categories. Here is the year and category in which each was not first: Ross Barnes, the second baseman for the 1876 Chicago White Stockings (home runs); Honus Wagner, the shortstop for the 1908 Pittsburgh Pirates (home runs); Nap Lajoie (1901–triples); Ty Cobb (1911–home runs); Rogers Hornsby (1921–home runs; 1922–triples); Chuck Klein, the right fielder for the 1933 Philadelphia Phillies (triples), and Joe Medwick (1937–triples). Honus Wagner (1900–not home runs) and Ty Cobb (1909–home runs) also accomplished this feat in other years. Other sluggers have also led in six of seven long-hit batting categories, for example: Dan Brouthers (1886–not triples); Cy Seymour (1905–not home runs); Heinie Zimmerman (1912–not triples); Hank Greenberg (1940–not triples); Pete Reiser (1941–not home runs); Tommy Holmes (1945–not triples); Stan Musial (1946–not home runs); Ted Williams (1949–not triples); and Jim Rice (1978–not doubles).[21] James O'Neill stands alone as the first and only slugger ever to lead in all seven long-hit categories.

In terms of getting on base, O'Neill, like the other eight batsmen, led in batting average and hits. O'Neill also was first in on-base percentage, as were the batsmen in eight of the other 10 seasons. Cobb finished second in on-base percentage (American League, 1911) and Medwick was fourth (National League, 1937). Only three of the nine champions were first in their leagues in singles (Barnes in 1876, Lajoie in 1901, Cobb in 1911 and 1917). Most of these leaders also proved effective in driving in others who got on base, with only Barnes (tied for second in the National League in 1876) and Ty Cobb (second in the American League in 1917) failing to gain top spot in runs batted in.

O'Neill further differentiated himself from the other eight champions in the number of records he established, topping the list in ten of the 11 batting categories with record-setting performances in the American Association (tied the records for hits and home runs). O'Neill's 22 triples led the Association, but it did not break the record. Since Barnes (1876–National League) and Lajoie (1901–American League) were in the inaugural year of their respective leagues, they established records in every category in which they led. Lajoie thus set 11 batting records in the American League (did not lead in triples) and Barnes set ten records in the National League (did not lead in home runs and runs batted in). Only two other batsmen broke league records with their first-place ranking: Cobb in 1911 in the American League with five new marks and Hornsby in the National League with one league record in 1921 and five in 1922.[22]

O'Neill separated himself from the other single-season leaders in the above table in the eight major league records he set in 1887: hits (tied with Browning), doubles, long hits, total bases, on-base percentage, slugging percentage, on-base plus slugging percentage, and batting average. Cobb's record of 248 hits in 1911 was the only other major league mark established by the other eight batsmen in this elite group. None of the American League records set by Lajoie in 1901 were records in the majors.[23] In the number of single-season records set by his batting firsts, O'Neill led all others by a wide margin. When Association or League and Major League records are combined, he set 18 records (ten in the Association and eight in the Major Leagues). Lajoie followed with 11 American League records and then Barnes with ten National League records, both of whom set league records only. In 1911, Cobb established six records, five in the American League and one in the majors.

In summary, in his "season of firsts," James "Tip" O'Neill led the American Association in 11 categories, exceeding the mark of ten set by Ross Barnes in the National League in 1876. Nap Lajoie, in 1901, tied O'Neill for the record for leading in the most categories in one season. After Lajoie, five other Hall of Fame batsmen challenged but fell one short of the mark established by O'Neill and Lajoie: Honus Wagner (1908), Ty Cobb (1911, 1917), Rogers Hornsby (1921, 1922), Chuck Klein (1933), and Stan Musial (1948).[24]

O'Neill set records in ten of the 11 batting categories in which he led in the American Association. Eight of these 10 records were also all-time records in the major leagues. In comparison to the other batsmen who also had seasons in which they led in a similar number of batting categories in their respective leagues, O'Neill bested this elite group by a wide margin both in the number of single-season records he broke in the major leagues and in the number of records he established when number of records set in the Association and in the major leagues are added together. With the most first-ever batting performances in a season, Tip O'Neill was "first among equals."[25]

Epilogue

Tip O'Neill played five more years in the major leagues: two years with the Browns (1888–1889), one year with the Chicago Pirates in the Players' League (1890), back to the Browns (1891) for what turned out to be the final year of the American Association, and, for his last year, with Cincinnati in the National League (1892). In 1888, Gleason and Welch went to Philadelphia, while Caruthers, Foutz, and Bushong went to Brooklyn. Despite the departure of these five core players, the Browns captured their fourth American Association championship in a row. In the world championship series, they lost to the New York Giants, six games to four. O'Neill's Browns finished second to Brooklyn in 1889 and second to Boston in 1891. Although one of the favorites in 1890, the Chicago Pirates could only manage a fourth-place finish in the Players' League. Similarly, Cincinnati fell short of expectations in 1892, completing both halves of the season well back of the leaders.[1]

For 1888, the National League and American Association revoked the rule that counted a base on balls as a hit and a time at bat. The two leagues also reverted back to the three-strikes-and-out rule.[2] Batting averages plummeted, with the Association average falling to a record low of .238. In this difficult year for batsmen, only five players hit .300 or better, in contrast to the 66 batters who matched or exceeded the .300 mark in 1887. O'Neill hit .335 to win his second straight batting title.[3] In 1889, rule makers, in an effort to boost offensive numbers, adopted the four-balls, three-strikes ratio. The Association average jumped to .262, with 15 batsmen recording averages of .300 or higher. O'Neill finished second in the batting race at .335.[4]

In the 1887–1889 period, O'Neill established himself as the premier batsman in baseball.[5] When numbers and percentages are combined for these three years, O'Neill was first among the leading batsmen[6] in the American Association and in the major leagues (National League and American Association) in nine batting categories: hits, doubles, long hits, runs batted in, total bases, batting average, on-base percentage, slugging percentage, and on-base plus slugging percentage (OPS).[7] Despite later claims that O'Neill had only "one great season,"[8] most pundits in the late 1880s recognized that he was the preeminent hitter for at least three years if not more.

When I expanded the comparison to the first five years in which he was the full-time left fielder for the Browns (1885–1889), O'Neill led the American Association in seven categories: hits, runs batted in, total bases, on-base percentage, slugging percentage, on-base plus slugging percentage, and batting average. Harry Stovey, the first baseman and outfielder for Philadelphia, in this five-year period led in three categories: doubles, home runs, and long hits.[9]

Despite the sale of five of the nine core players, the 1888 St. Louis Browns won their fourth straight American Association championship with the team pictured above. In the top row, from left to right, Arlie Latham leans towards his son, Clifford, the team mascot, with James "Tip" O'Neill to the right of Latham's son. In the second row, from left to right: Bill White, Jim Devlin, William "Yank" Robinson, Tom McCarthy, Charles "Silver" King, and Joe Herr. In the third row, from left to right: Jack Boyle, Nat Hudson, Charles Comiskey, Jocko Milligan, and Tom Dolan. Sitting near Chris Von der Ahe's two dogs are Elton "Icebox" Chamberlain on the left and Harry Lyons on the right (National Baseball Hall of Fame Library, Cooperstown, New York).

In the Major Leagues, in this same five-year period, O'Neill had the best batting average with a cumulative five-year percentage of .370, ahead of Pete Browning (.360) and Dave Orr (.341), two of the leading batsmen in the American Association, and Dan Brouthers (.367), Cap Anson (.359), and Roger Connor (.344), three of the leading batsmen in the National League. O'Neill was in the top three in the majors in hits, runs batted in,[10] slugging percentage, and on-base plus slugging percentage, and fourth-best in total bases.[11]

After the 1889 season, O'Neill left the Browns. Over the next three years, he played on three different teams in three different leagues. In 1890, he joined the Chicago Pirates in the newly-formed Players' League. Tip hit .302, third on the team, and 18th overall in the league. For the only time in his career, he led the league with 137 games played (tied with his teammate Hugh Duffy). When the Players' League ended after only one year, he returned to the Browns for the 1891 season. In the familiar grounds of Sportsman's Park, O'Neill regained some of his old form, hitting .323, third-best in the American

Association.¹² After a ten-year run, the American Association folded. In 1892, O'Neill moved to Cincinnati in the National League for what proved to be his final season. His average fell to a career-low .251. He was still third among those on the team who played in 100 games or more and slightly better than the National League average of .245. Besides the steep drop in his batting average, the most telling change in these three years was the significant decrease in O'Neill's power. The following table documents this decline in slugging by comparing his numbers and percentages in seven long-hit batting categories in 1887–1889 to those in 1890–1892:

	G	D	T	HR	LH	TB	SLG	OPS
1887–89	388	109	40	28	177	904	.556	.987
1890–92	373	62	26	15	103	604	.400	.776

G–Games; D–Double; T–Triples; HR–Home Runs; LH–Long Hits; TB–Total Bases; SLG–Slugging Percentage; OPS–On-Base plus Slugging Percentage

At the beginning of the 1893 season, when few were certain when or if O'Neill would play again, *Sporting Life,* in the column, "Editorial Views, News and Comment," reflected: "Three years ago almost any club in the country would have had a line out for 'Tip' O'Neill, the hard-hitting batter of the St. Louis Browns. Now no one seems to want him."¹³ The Cincinnati fans and press expected more than what they got in 1892 from a batsman of O'Neill's stature.

For most of his last five years (1888–1892), O'Neill played under increasingly difficult conditions, some related to his health and others connected to the challenges of playing on teams rife with internal discord. Although O'Neill missed 60 games in 1885 after he hurt his leg in a collision at second base and 14 games in 1887 due to repeated hand injuries, in the 1888–1892 period he sat out fewer games because of injuries. However, he frequently played while not feeling well, staying in the lineup despite being weakened by illness, specifically malarial attacks and dysentery,¹⁴ especially in 1888, his best season in his final five years, and then again in 1892, his last and worst season. In his comment on the 1888 season, Joe Pritchard praised the Browns as a "team of stayers," who played with grit in the face of adversity. Of O'Neill, Pritchard added:

> At the opening of the season O'Neill was so full of malaria that he could not see a pitched ball nor a fly, and he was under the care of a doctor for some time, yet he played ball right along and stood the guying of a few newspaper men who were not aware of the great player's condition.¹⁵

O'Neill also struggled during most of the 1892 season. While he played in all but one of the first 100 games, he experienced regular bouts of abdominal pain.¹⁶ In late August, in a game against Philadelphia, O'Neill was injured going into third base. While he stayed in the game, he played with considerable pain in his ribs. By the end of August, Comiskey removed O'Neill from the lineup. His ill-health, injured ribs, and erratic play brought Tip O'Neill's season and career to an abrupt end.¹⁷

The climate of unrest that pervaded the Browns in 1888–1889 and again in 1891 affected all of the players, including O'Neill. Many of the tensions on the Browns were fueled by the erratic and aggressive behavior of the owner, Chris Von der Ahe. In the hotly-contested race for the American Association championship in 1888, Von der Ahe was quick to fine players for what he perceived as indifferent or poor play. For example, the owner became convinced that Tip's inconsistent play in late June was a ploy to get a release from the Browns so that he could join Doc Bushong on the Brooklyn club.¹⁸ Tip explained that his alleged bad play was because he had malarial fever. When Tip refused

In 1890, the inaugural and only year of the Players' League, many of the pundits picked the Chicago Pirates as one of the favorites to win the championship. Chicago finished a disappointing fourth. In the above diamond-shaped team photograph, the three players at home plate, from left to right, are: Dell Darling, Ned Williamson (with moustache), and Charles "Silver" King. Moving from home to first, after King, are Charles Bastian and Charles "Duke" Farrell (on first base). Going from first to second base are Arlie Latham, Hugh Duffy, and Charles Comiskey (on second base). From second to third base are Mark Baldwin, Jack Boyle, and James "Tip" O'Neill (on third base). Between third base and home is Charles Bartson (The Rucker Archive).

to go to Von der Ahe's doctor for treatment, preferring to visit his own doctor, he was suspended. In his own defense, Tip retorted:

> Everybody has been jumping on me … because I have not been playing as well as I did formerly. Well, I haven't; but it is not because I did not want to. I am sick and have been sick for some time. I believe that I must have malarial fever, because when a ball comes at me in the field my head swims, and when I look up at the sky it seems almost impossible for me to judge the ball as I should do to catch it…. Now, as for playing for my release, I want you to let me say a word. I do not deny that Bushong wrote me a letter. There was nothing in it beyond a simple mention of the matter. Certainly not enough to turn my head. I will give you that letter to publish if you want it. As for Byrne, he has not written to me. Besides, if Brooklyn was after me it is not likely I would play bad ball. I think that a man who plays for his release acts like a baby. I am satisfied to play in St. Louis and am not anxious to go elsewhere…. I will swear to you and pledge you my word that I have played as well as I could and will do the best I can in the future.[19]

Subsequent recurrences of alleged indifferent or bad play sometimes invoked suspicions that Tip might be playing for release or that he might be traded. It was likely difficult to concentrate on doing anything and everything to win in the swirl of reports of his imminent departure from St. Louis through one means or another.[20]

In 1889, Von der Ahe increased his penchant for fining and suspending players. He incurred the wrath of the entire team for one of his impetuous fines. Early in the season, during the warm-up prior to the start of the game, Yank Robinson had some problems with his uniform. After consulting Comiskey, Robinson elicited help from a boy attending the game, sending him to O'Neill's apartment to retrieve a new pair of trousers. Though the boy had a note from Robinson so that he could get back into the park, the elderly gatekeeper on duty refused to grant the boy re-admission. Robinson was forced to play in his soiled and badly torn pants. Between innings, Robinson scolded the gatekeeper for his refusal to let the boy bring him the pants. After the gatekeeper told Von der Ahe about the harsh words used by Robinson, Von der Ahe confronted Robinson on the players' bench, publicly reprimanding him for swearing at an elderly gatekeeper. When Robinson defended his actions, Von der Ahe fined him $25 for talking back. Once the game concluded, the Browns had to depart for Kansas City, the site of their next four-game series. Still angry about the humiliating rebuke from Von der Ahe, Robinson decided not to accompany the team on the road trip until his fine was remitted. Robinson's teammates were incensed by what they perceived as an unjust fine administered by Von der Ahe. In a show of solidarity, the players initially refused to get on the train to Kansas City. They eventually relented but not without a further display of defiance starting the next day. The players took their protest to the field, according to some accounts, deliberately losing the first three games against Kansas City.[21]

O'Neill was as much involved in the protest as any of the other players, especially in the outfield. In game one, he made two errors and was slow to get to two other balls hit his way, which appeared like intentional negligence to some reporters. Offended by these accusations, O'Neill spoke out in defense of the Browns:

> I think that charge made that the Browns threw the games at Kansas City is a most serious one and is certainly unjust. It is no trifling matter to charge a club with crookedness. We played miserable ball up there, it is true, but it could not be helped. We simply played in hard luck. It is such a streak as any team is apt to have, only we had ours at a most unfortunate time. The grounds up there are so bad that no club could do itself justice on them, but of course the home team has the advantage of being used to it. As Gaffney, the umpire remarked, if he thought there was any crooked ball playing there he would stop the game and report to the Association, as would be his duty. He was convinced, however, that we were doing our best. Of course the boys think Robinson has not been treated properly, and sympathize with him, but we played our best. We heard that we had all been fined $50 each, but do not know whether it is true. If we have it is certainly unjust, but I do not know what we can do about it, as Mr. Von der Ahe can hold it out of our salaries. Whether the members of the team would continue to play ball for him I do not know. They are all of an age, however, and ought to be able to act for themselves. The hits the Kansas Citys made were all scratches.[22]

Such conflicts did little to promote camaraderie or team work. These tensions were often distracting and sometimes divisive, sowing the seeds of dissension in the ranks.

O'Neill's move from St. Louis to Chicago in 1890 was in part motivated by his desire to leave the tensions and conflict of 1888–1889 behind him. Once the Players' League folded after only one year in operation, O'Neill reluctantly returned to St. Louis.[23] After a year of further turmoil with the Browns (1891), O'Neill left once again, this time for Cincinnati, ever searching for a team with few if any tensions. Unfortunately, the 1892 season was not only one of unrealized ambitions but also his final season in major league baseball.

O'Neill was the only member of the 1885–1887 core Browns who played under the managerial direction of Charles Comiskey every season between 1885 and 1892.[24] Shortly after Comiskey agreed to manage the Chicago Pirates in the Players' League in 1890, again in 1891 after Comiskey returned to the American Association to manage the Browns, and finally in 1892 after Comiskey moved to Cincinnati to pilot the Reds in the National League, O'Neill signed with each of these teams shortly thereafter. O'Neill understood and respected Comiskey's leadership style, and Comiskey valued the offensive punch that O'Neill brought to a team.

Although Comiskey often mediated the tensions with the players created by Von der Ahe's fines or suspensions, he was quite capable of meting out his own punishments when players lacked discipline or wavered from the style of play he expected. In this regard, O'Neill was not beyond reproach. In 1888, Comiskey reprimanded O'Neill on a number of occasions for not hustling after a fly ball or for not running hard on the base paths. At one point, Comiskey fined O'Neill $75 for not making an effort to catch a fly ball. O'Neill refused to pay the fine, threatening to sue if the fine was deducted from his salary.[25] The relationship with Comiskey remained strained for most of the 1888 season,[26] but improved in subsequent years. As long as O'Neill delivered at the bat, Comiskey would find ways to cope with his gaffes on the base path and occasional lapses in the field, or so it seemed. However, this unstated and mutual understanding between O'Neill and Comiskey broke down in 1892.

For most of the 1892 season, O'Neill struggled at the plate and was sluggish in the field and on the bases. Gone were the days of little boys waiting to carry his bat bag, ladies swooning in the stands as he took his place in left field, or fans greeting him with unbridled applause as he came to bat. The Cincinnati reporters grew tired of waiting for O'Neill's legendary bat to arrive and were angry at what they saw as his slovenly play in the field. They also increasingly questioned what seemed like Comiskey's blind loyalty to an old mate. On August 9, in the fourth inning of a game in Cleveland, the course of O'Neill's season and ultimately, his baseball career, would change forever.

With two men on base, O'Neill lost a fly ball in the sun. Once he located the ball after it fell to the ground, he was slow to retrieve and return it to the infield. As a result, Chief Zimmer, the Cleveland catcher, scored. Comiskey was furious,[27] or as the *Cleveland Leader* reported, "got wrathy"[28] and took O'Neill out of the game. After the game, O'Neill confronted Comiskey, a spat ensued, and O'Neill was ordered to return to Cincinnati and docked five days' pay for his insubordination.[29] Once back in Cincinnati, O'Neill was more reflective about the incident:

> This is the first rocky season I have had. There has been a clique crying for my release ever since spring. I have not been in good health and I have failed to slug the ball as I ought to, but I have played earnestly. Commie and I had a hot time of it, and we were both pretty free in our exchange of opinions. There is no use for me to cry. I will have to take it as it comes and hope that my streak of ill luck will break.[30]

Comiskey, on the other hand, hoped five days away from the game would stimulate O'Neill to do better upon his return, in the field, on the bases,[31] and especially at the plate: "I have been fighting big 'Tip' on the field for years and this little rest will only wake him up. There is no danger of my releasing him."[32] Comiskey needed O'Neill's batting to return to its former glory.

Many of the Cincinnati newspapers picked up on the fact that O'Neill was still sore about losing five days' pay,[33] allegedly sulking as if he had been unjustly treated.[34] In the spirit of reconciliation, the *Cincinnati Enquirer* looked forward to better times:

> Loafing around with nothing to do isn't to Tip's liking. He has been restless and ill at ease ever since he was sent home from Cleveland by Captain Comiskey. Tip showed a disinclination to obey orders, and a little tilt occurred between him and the Captain. Tip has been with Captain Comiskey long enough to know better. In spite of the fact that the big fielder has a few grumbles, he is a good ballplayer. He plays his field in good style, and when at himself is one of the greatest batters living. The breech between the Captain and the player will likely be healed when the team arrives today.[35]

O'Neill "did not report for duty" after his five-day, unpaid leave.[36] He returned to the lineup six games after he was sent home from Cleveland (August 17), with the extra game away a likely further protest of his suspension. On August 20, in a game in which Cincinnati beat Philadelphia, 3–0, O'Neill was knocked unconscious as he slid into third base. He later discovered that he had fractured two ribs.[37] He played the next eight games in constant pain and with limited mobility. In what would be O'Neill's final game in the major leagues (August 30), Comiskey replaced him after seven innings.[38] On September 4, when Cincinnati left on a ten-game road trip, O'Neill was left behind to recover from his rib injury. Possibly in frustration due to his continued bad luck, perhaps in anger over what he perceived as shabby treatment by Comiskey, or maybe because he saw no way to salvage what little remained of the season, O'Neill departed for his home in Woodstock, Ontario, to recuperate under the care of family and friends. Once he learned that O'Neill was in Canada, Comiskey laid him off without further pay. Months later, Comiskey recalled:

> It's funny about Tip. He left Cincinnati without permission and I haven't received a line from him since. If he can play ball for me as well as he did in St. Louis, I should like to have him. Last year Tip was in poor health and that is the reason I assigned for his weak stick work.[39]

In poor health, with sore ribs, and dragging a weak stick, Tip walked away from Comiskey, Cincinnati, and major league baseball, with no permission sought, no notice given, no line sent or received, and no glance back.

While the Cincinnati newspapers wondered or worried about O'Neill's possible return for the 1893 season,[40] he never gave any indication that he intended to rejoin the team or that he wanted his release from the Cincinnati club or to be traded so he could pursue opportunities to play baseball elsewhere.[41] Instead he devoted more time to some of his beloved pastimes. For example, over the winter of 1892–1893, he traveled to some of his favorite race tracks to bet on the horses.[42] In association with various members of his family, he also got involved in other ventures. He and his brother George became bookmakers for the summer season of 1893 at the Sheepshead Bay race track in New York.[43] Early in 1894, O'Neill went to Amsterdam, New York, with his brother, D'Arcy, and his brother-in-law, Max MacKay, to promote the development of their lucrative "Pug" cigar business.[44] O'Neill also flirted with the possibility of playing first base and managing an Amsterdam entry into the State League, but, in the end, rejected this offer because of the financial problems of the fledgling team and his need to devote time to his cigar business.[45] By the time Tip, his mother, his brother Joseph, and his sister Aggie (Agnes) moved to Montreal in the fall of 1894,[46] Tip was ready for a new, albeit non-playing, chapter in his baseball career.[47]

Before he even landed in Montreal in the fall of 1894, the *Montreal Gazette* published a note announcing that O'Neill would play in a charity game soon after his arrival.[48] While he did not play in the charity game, one month later it was announced that he would be the umpire of a forthcoming game, which he did do two days later.[49] For the next 20 years, O'Neill supported the development of baseball in Montreal and throughout the province of Quebec, usually behind the scenes and without much fanfare.

O'Neill's entry into Montreal baseball was orchestrated by Joe Page, a former teammate on the Detroit Hiawatha Grays in 1881.[50] Page, one of the most prominent figures in Quebec in the development of baseball,[51] readily understood the value of having a famous major league baseball player in their midst. With Page's encouragement and, on occasion, partnership, O'Neill got more involved. Over the years, he provided batting "tips" to players at all levels[52]; periodically served as a coach or manager[53]; and assisted in the organization and promotion of new teams or leagues.[54] When his brother George became first vice president and then president of the Montreal Royals in the Eastern League,[55] Tip worked with some of the Royals in their pre-season preparation. And whenever his brother sought advice on how best to manage a professional team, Tip likely was happy to oblige.

During his Montreal years (1894–1915), O'Neill's most frequent and, in one period (1897–1898), most concentrated engagement in baseball was as an umpire. O'Neill donned his umpire's garb a few times each year, sometimes on short notice, for local and regional games. When Montreal entered the Eastern League in mid-season of 1897, O'Neill was added to the umpire staff of the league. Over the two seasons in which he was a full-time umpire, O'Neill adjudicated over 130 games. Although umpires rarely pleased many of the fans or the writers, O'Neill seemed to be well accepted, as indicated by the fact that reporters rarely included any comments on his calls in their game reports. In an era when it was common to criticize or blame the umpire for poor judgment, silence from the press was indeed a compliment. Coinciding with the last game that O'Neill umpired in the Eastern League, in his Montreal column in *Sporting Life,* Joe Page published a tribute to two of the finest umpires he had observed: "Doescher and 'Tip' O'Neill have certainly on the whole umpired finely while here throughout the season and dealt in a fair manner to both visitors and home teams. Of course, they have made mistakes, but where they make one others make twenty."[56]

In addition to his local baseball activities, O'Neill maintained some connections with people he knew from his playing days. He reportedly served as an informal scout for some major league teams, contacting managers when he saw a promising young player.[57] From time to time, he travelled to cities with major league teams to participate in old timers' days.[58] These were occasions that afforded O'Neill time to visit with players who were retired from the game. And given the yearly reports in *Sporting Life* of O'Neill's post-career whereabouts and activities, he probably stayed in touch with those baseball writers who knew him when he was a major league outfielder.

O'Neill's most enduring link to the baseball world was through the fame of his nickname, a monicker he bore with pride. In his heyday with the Browns, Jim O'Neill was greatly admired and recognized by all as "Tip." It became a nickname that other ball players named O'Neill assumed. Tip himself sometimes teased about the popularity of his name. In a conversation with Joe Page, he "got a leg" on him with the following story:

> TIP: "I can always tell when a ball player by the name of O'Neill has been hitting the pipe."
> JOE: "How's that?"
> TIP: "He always calls himself 'Tip.'"[59]

However, over time his nickname also created some unexpected problems. O'Neill was less amused when he was mistaken for others who called themselves "Tip." After rumors circulated in 1897 that O'Neill was dying of consumption, he wrote to *Sporting Life* to correct this story.[60] A few months later, following yet another false citing, *Sporting Life* published a letter from Tip with the headline, "The Only Tip O'Neill Objects to Lightweights Appropriating His Famous Title":

> I notice in the week before last's issue of *Sporting Life* an article from a correspondent in Montgomery, Ala., that Tip O'Neill, formerly with the St. Louis Browns, had been secured as manager. It seems strange that every ball player who happens to be O'Neill should call himself Tip. One Tip died in London, Canada a few years ago, and when I would meet friends I had not met for some time, they would take me for a ghost. The *Chicago Record* last spring had me dying of consumption. Wishing you and the "Life" every success, I remain, sincerely, yours, James E. O'Neill (Tip).[61]

At his death and for years thereafter, references to O'Neill often identified him as the "first," "original," or "only" Tip.[62]

James O'Neill died in Montreal on December 31, 1915. He was 55 years old. As reported by the *Montreal Gazette*, his death was both unexpected and quick:

> Death came suddenly at noon yesterday on the corner of Bleury and St. Catherine streets to "Tip" O'Neill, an old-time baseball player and one of the best known men in town. He had just stepped off a Park Avenue car that had brought him downtown from his home in Esplanade Avenue when he staggered and fell to the sidewalk. It was thought at first that he had simply fainted and he was carried into Leduc's drug store, on the corner. When an ambulance from the general hospital arrived the physician, who accompanied it, said that life was extinct. Death was due to heart failure.[63]

Tip's brother, D'Arcy O'Neill, and his sister, Aggie (Agnes) O'Neill, took Tip's body to Woodstock, Ontario.[64] Tip was interred in the family plot in the St. Mary Cemetery outside Woodstock.[65]

In a gesture that no doubt would have pleased Tip, a number of the death announcements made a point of acknowledging in the title or in the text of the obituary that the player who died was indeed the "original" or "only" Tip.[66] Most death notices mentioned O'Neill's prowess as a hitter, as illustrated in the following statements in two of the St. Louis-based papers:

> *St. Louis Republic*
> O'Neill was a right-handed slugger and one of the great fence-busters the game produced. He was a giant in stature, a regular Apollo Belvedere in appearance, one of the handsomest men who ever donned the spangles.[67]

> *The Sporting News*
> James E. O'Neill, the original "Tip" and a member of the champion St. Louis Browns of the middle eighties, died suddenly in Montreal, Que., on January 1 of heart disease. O'Neill was one of the greatest batters the game has ever known and it was largely through his stickwork that the Browns under Charles Comiskey won the championship of the world.... He was a tremendously hard hitter and even his ground balls when the force of his bat was behind them are said to literally have carried infielders off their feet.[68]

Charles Comiskey, for nine years O'Neill's field boss in St. Louis, Chicago, and Cincinnati, highlighted Tip, the batsman, and Tip, the gentleman:

> Baseball lost one of its greatest exponents when "Tip" passed away. I am sorry to learn of his death, for in addition to being the equal of Anson as a natural batter, he always conducted himself in a gentlemanly manner, and for that reason was perhaps the most popular player the St. Louis public ever knew.[69]

Echoing Comiskey's recollections, Joe Page, after commenting on O'Neill's many batting achievements, remembered his old friend for the man he was: "And withal, as high as his general average was as a batsman, his average as a gentleman, sportsman, and friend in need was far greater."[70]

As I discussed in the Preface, for much of the twentieth century, numerous articles or record books most remembered O'Neill for his .492 batting average. To recap, the story of .492 began with its official recognition as the batting average of Tip O'Neill, the champion batsman of the American Association in 1887. For the next 80 years, despite challenges[71] and qualifications,[72] .492 still stood, albeit somewhat wobbly, as the highest all-time average in a single season in Major League Baseball.[73] In the late 1960s, two events altered the history of .492. First, in its development of "a code of rules governing record-keeping procedures," one of the decisions of the Special Baseball Records Committee was that "bases on balls shall always be treated as neither a time at bat nor a hit for a batter."[74] Second, Information Concepts Incorporated completed the most thorough study ever conducted into the batting statistics of nineteenth century players. Through this research, it generated the most comprehensive and, for many, definitive record of each player's performance, including that of O'Neill.[75] Subsequent to these two events, O'Neill's average was recalculated to .435 and, in 1969, published in the "Big Mac."[76] However, the story of .492 did not end there. In 2001, Jerome Holtzman, Major League Baseball's official historian, turned back the clock with his declaration: "If a walk was a hit in 1887 it should stand as a hit forevermore."[77] Based on the statistics on hits, bases on balls, and times at bat generated by Information Concepts Incorporated in the 1960s, O'Neill's average was adjusted to .485,[78] returning him to the top of the list with the best single-season average. Despite Holtzman's ruling, contemporary sources of baseball records continued to calculate batting records based on the same scoring rules for every season, which, in 1887, meant a walk would not be counted as a hit or a time at bat. Consequently, O'Neill's batting average is listed as .435. Either way, record-keepers conclude that O'Neill's average was .435 or, in a few cases, .485.[79] My finding of .488 (or .436 when bases on balls are excluded as hits and times and bat), while different from the average reported by most contemporary record-keepers, also closes the door on any further consideration of .492. Or does it?

Based on the rules of the day, two batting champions in 1887, Tip O'Neill in the American Association and Cap Anson[80] in the National League, won their respective titles based on averages determined by adding hits plus bases on balls and then dividing the total number of hits and walks by times at bat plus bases on balls. In effect, this is a nineteenth-century variation on the current formula for calculating on-base percentage. Thus, Tip O'Neill and Cap Anson shared the unique honor of being the only batsmen ever to win a batting title based on an on-base percentage.[81] The current formula for determining on-base percentage adds the number of times a batsman is hit by a pitch to the numerator and the number of times a batsman is hit by a pitch plus the number of sacrifice flies to the denominator, that is: (Hits + Walks + Hit by Pitch) / (At-Bats + Walks + Hit By Pitch + Sacrifice Flies). Scorers did not record sacrifice flies in 1887. Thus, applying the current formula (without sacrifice flies), O'Neill's on-base percentage was: (223 + 52 +5) / (512 +52 + 5) = .492. Alas, battered and bruised, .492 lives on to see another day, albeit in the guise of an on-base percentage, a statistic that was not officially recognized until 1984. In my view, .492 deserves some enduring, if not mythical, status as an average that is both historically accurate according to the computations of 1887 scorekeepers and retroactively defensible as an on-base batting title.

In the 1980s, almost a century after his record-breaking 1887 season, Tip O'Neill's career was rediscovered and his batting prowess more fully appreciated. By happenstance, the prominence of Thomas "Tip" O'Neill Jr., the Speaker of the United States House of Representatives between 1977 and 1987, contributed to some of the interest in the original Tip. As it turned out, O'Neill was the favorite player of the Speaker's father. Tom was called "Little Tip" as a young boy and, as time went on so did the nickname, with "Little" no longer attached.[82] Whenever the Speaker responded to the question, "How did you get your nickname?" he reminded others of the popularity and fame of Tip O'Neill, the St. Louis Browns batsman.

During the Speaker's term, the original Tip was also honored in his home country of Canada. The Canadian Baseball Hall of Fame and Museum began in Toronto in 1982.[83] O'Neill was in the first class of inductees in 1983.[84] In 1984, in his hometown of Woodstock, Ontario, one of the local baseball parks was renamed "Tip O'Neill Sportsfield."[85] He was also inducted into the Woodstock Sports Wall of Fame twice, the first time for his individual achievement in major league baseball[86] and the second for his part as a member of the Woodstock Actives, the Canadian Baseball Champions of 1878. In 1994, O'Neill was elected into Canada's Sport Hall of Fame,[87] and in 1997, he was elected into The Ontario Sports Hall of Fame.[88] As yet, he has not been inducted into the National Baseball Hall of Fame in Cooperstown, New York.[89]

If Tip O'Neill were alive today, I suspect he would be especially proud of the yearly award given in his name by the Canadian Baseball Hall of Fame and Museum. The James "Tip" O'Neill Award is "presented annually to the Canadian player judged to have excelled in individual achievement and team contribution while adhering to baseball ideals."[90] It was first awarded in 1984. Since its inception, Larry Walker has won the award nine times, three times with the Montreal Expos, five times with the Colorado Rockies, and once while in the minor leagues. Joey Votto has also won it seven times with the Cincinnati Reds (through 2017). Two others have won the award three times: Justin Mor-

The Tip O'Neill Award is awarded annually to the Canadian player who has excelled on the field, contributed to the team, supported community and charitable activities, and, beginning in 2017, been recognized by fan voting (The Canadian Baseball Hall of Fame and Museum, St. Marys, Ontario).

neau, twice with the Minnesota Twins and once with the Colorado Rockies; and Jason Bay, twice with the Pittsburgh Pirates and once with the Boston Red Sox.[91]

As this tale comes to an end, I want to highlight one last time the many batting feats documented in this book that define and animate Tip O'Neill's one-of-a-kind year at the plate in 1887. His batting average, multi-hit games, streaks, long hits, cycles, and Triple Crown were some of the triumphal moments that define the tapestry of his batting accomplishments. It is in the multi-faceted and interrelated stories of these various feats where the unique character of the man and his season truly lie. To bring closure to this narrative, I return to the latter-day amplifications of his nickname: the original Tip, Tip the First, and the Only Tip. First, James O'Neill was the "original" Tip by the very fact that he was the earliest batsman with this nickname. All others were but poor pretenders. Second, he was "Tip the First" in that he led the Association and the major leagues in more batting categories and with more record-breaking numbers or percentages in one season than any batsman in the history of the game. And, last but not least, "Only" Tip has ever recorded a batting average of .488, the highest single-season batting average in the major leagues since 1876.

Appendix A:
Resolution of Discrepancies in Game-Based Statistics

The determination of game-based statistics for each of the 124 games that O'Neill played in 1887 involved a comprehensive system of data-gathering, analysis, and evaluation. For most of the data, I relied on game reports published in newspapers and weeklies. In some game reports, I discovered gaps (e.g., little or no information on some of O'Neill's times at bat) and inconsistencies (e.g., sources reported different numbers and/or types of hits) in the information or statistics related to O'Neill's batting performance. Where possible, I sought additional sources to address these problems.

While I was unable to find information to fill in all of the gaps, I was able to compile additional data to assist me in the process of resolving inconsistencies or discrepancies. Two types of discrepancies were especially important to resolve, namely those related to O'Neill's batting average (at-bats, hits, base on balls) and to the distribution of his hits (bases on balls, singles, doubles, triples, home runs). I addressed these discrepancies twice. The first time occurred after I had completed three rounds of collecting game accounts. At this point, I had gathered sufficient sources to complete my own record of O'Neill's game-based statistics, including the resolution of problems in the information for some of his times at bat. The second time I addressed discrepancies occurred when I compared my records for each game with the game-by-game reports generated by Information Concepts Incorporated (ICI). The resolution of discrepancies between my statistics and those of ICI for eight games in the 1887 season enabled me to produce the final record of O'Neill's 1887 batting statistics.

The following sections describe the discrepancies I found between my game-based statistics and those of ICI in the number of at-bats, hits, and bases on balls, three statistics that affected the calculation of O'Neill's batting average, and in the number of triples that O'Neill hit. In the section below on batting average, I outline the three-stage process I used to review the game reports and the system I devised to rate the level of confidence in the information gathered on each game. I then examine the games where my records differed from those of ICI and describe how I resolved these discrepancies. I conclude with the application of these final game-based statistics to the calculation of O'Neill's batting average in 1887. Finally, in the section on triples, I provide a similar explanation about the discrepancies in the games where I listed O'Neill with a triple and ICI did not.

I end this section with a summary of the revised distribution of O'Neill's hits, that is, his total number of bases on balls, singles, doubles, triples, and home runs.

Batting Average

To determine the batting average of Tip O'Neill in 1887, I went through three stages. In the first stage, I collected and reviewed the game reports (box scores and descriptions) from nine to 16 newspapers for each of the 124 games that he played. I noted any gaps (e.g., time at bat not described in the text) or inconsistencies (e.g., different numbers for at-bats, hits, or bases on balls) in the batting data within each report and among reports from different newspapers.

In stage two, I devised a four-grade system (A, B, C, D) for rating my level of confidence (LoC) in the batting data for each game. For those games with a lower LoC rating (C or D), I re-read the game reports and, where possible, sought further game reports before making a decision on O'Neill's batting statistics for these C-rated and D-rated games.

In the third stage, I compared my game-based statistics for O'Neill with those generated by ICI and discovered that there were eight games where my numbers differed. Once again, I returned to the game reports to resolve these discrepancies. With these resolutions, I produced a final table of game-based statistics for all 124 games. Based on 1887 rules where bases on balls counted as hits and times at bat, O'Neill had 275 hits in 564 times at bat for a batting average of .488.

As I probed game reports in stage one, it soon became apparent that there was considerable variability in how newspapers described games. Most reports consisted of a box score and a short description of or comment on the game (typically five or six sentences), which I refer to as the "text" in my discussion below of the information on the eight games for which my numbers differ from those of the ICI. The box score included a tabular summary of individual statistics on batting and fielding, a list of team statistics related to batting, fielding, base running, and pitching (e.g., earned runs, total bases; which players hit doubles, triples, or home runs; which players received a base on balls; number of passed balls by each catcher), and a line score that displayed the number of runs scored in each inning. Sometimes the text described how each run was scored and how specific players contributed. However, few reports gave an inning-by-inning summary of what each player did in his time at bat.[1] While I had considerable statistical data on each game, I did not have consistent details about the play-by-play on the field. Despite amassing over 1,800 game reports, I have specific information on only 76 percent (435) of O'Neill's 569 plate appearances in 1887. I have details on most of his hits, bases on balls, and the five times when he was hit by a pitch. I have little or no information on some at-bats when he failed to reach base or when he got on base through a fielder's choice or an error.

Some game reports were incomplete or inconsistent. The tabular summary of individual statistics sometimes omitted the column for at-bats. In some newspapers, the team statistics below the table of individual statistics stated the number of walks allowed by each pitcher but not the names of those players who received their bases on balls. From time to time, the text and box score differed. For example, the text might describe a double hit by a certain player, but his name either did not appear below the individual table or was instead in the list of those who tripled. In the descriptions of key moments in the game, the writers occasionally used imprecise or vague language or omitted key details. The text might state that a batsman "got his base" but fail to clarify if the base was gained on a hit, a base on balls, or an error. Or it noted that a team scored three runs in the fourth inning on two hits, a base on balls, and three errors without an elaboration of which players got their base on a hit (and whether the hit was a single, double, triple, or home run), a walk, or an error, and how exactly these various batting events contributed to each of the four runs. Such gaps and inconsistencies were especially problematic if they surfaced in more than one of the nine to 16 newspapers I reviewed for each of the 124 games that O'Neill played. I needed a system that would help me to identify any problems in the game reports for each game and to differentiate among games according to the level of confidence I had in these records.

In stage two, I developed a four-part rating scale (A to D) on the level of confidence (LoC) I had in the information available on O'Neill's times at bat for each game. The following description of the four LoCs outlines the key conditions that define each level. Levels A and B are free of discrepancies but vary in the amount of detail or corroborating information:

LoC A—(1) Numbers outlined in box scores include consistent information on times at bat (AB), hits (H), and bases on balls (BB); and (2) At least one detailed account is available for every AB. Note: If the descriptions of O'Neill's ABs in the game are incomplete (e.g., no details on outs), an A rating can be given if the report includes details on each H and BB he had.

LoC B—(1) Numbers outlined in box scores include consistent information on the AB, H, and BB; and (2) While game reports do not include detailed accounts on all AB, H, or BB, there are no statements in the report that contradict the box scores (e.g., box score shows a triple but the game report notes a double).

A LoC rating of C or D indicates that there were discrepancies in the game reports on O'Neill's statistics. Games rated either C or D typically have fewer reports and accounts available. Furthermore, the accounts that are available were usually incomplete or had inconsistent information in the box scores, game descriptions, or both. A game rated LoC D has more discrepancies, including those in one or more of his AB, H, and BB, than was the case in a game rated LoC C.

LoC C—(1) Numbers outlined in box scores include consistent information in the AB, H, and BB in most of the reports; and (2) The box scores or game reports include one discrepancy in an area other than AB, H, or BB (e.g., type of hit, run batted in, strikeout, fielding, stolen bases, etc.).

LoC D—(1) Numbers outlined in box scores include discrepant information on at least one of AB, H, or BB; and (2) The box scores or game reports include two or more discrepancies in areas other than AB, H, or BB (e.g., type of hit, run batted in, strikeout, fielding, stolen bases, etc.).

After I had determined an LoC rating for the reports on each game, I engaged in further rounds of data-gathering with the intent of finding more detailed accounts of games with an LoC B rating. For those games with LoC ratings of C and D, I sought additional reports to address the discrepancies in the data and the lack of information on some of O'Neill's times at bat. Where warranted by the new evidence, I altered the LoC rating. In the end, there are 70 games with an LoC rating of A (56 percent), 41 games with an LoC rating of B (33 percent), 12 games with an LoC rating of C (10 percent), and one game with an LoC rating of D (1 percent). For the 13 games still with some discrepancies (those with LoC ratings of C and D), I made a final decision on their LoC ratings based on the preponderance of the evidence.[2]

In the calculation of O'Neill's batting average, it is important to have consistent reports on AB, H, and BB, especially in a season that counts a BB as a hit and a time at bat. As noted above, an LoC rating of A, B, or C includes reports with consistent information on AB, H, and BB.[3] Based on the above LoC ratings, I am confident in the AB, H, and BB statistics gleaned from 99 percent of the game accounts (with LoC A + B + C ratings). In the third stage, I compared my records for each game with the game-by-game reports generated by Information Concepts Incorporated.

As I noted towards the end of the Epilogue, the project conducted by Information Concepts Incorporated (ICI) in the late 1960s was "the most comprehensive study ever conducted into the batting statistics of nineteenth century players." In 1969, the Special Baseball Records Committee ruled that "bases on balls shall always be treated as neither a time at bat nor a hit for the batter." Accordingly, the ICI researchers reported the 1887 batting statistics as with any other season, that is, by not counting a base on balls as a hit or a time at bat. ICI concluded that O'Neill had 225 hits in 517 times at bat. He also had 50 bases on balls. Based on these numbers, O'Neill's batting average was calculated as .435.[4] In 2001, Jerome Holtzman, the official historian of Major League Baseball, declared that "if a walk was a hit in 1887 it should stand as a hit forevermore." Applying the 1887 rule for a base on balls to the above ICI numbers, O'Neill's batting average was adjusted to .485.[5] Regardless of how the numbers are applied, the ICI statistics for O'Neill in 1887—225 hits, 517 times at bat, 50 bases on balls—have been the numbers of record since the late 1960s.

In the third and final stage in the process of determining O'Neill's batting average, I used the ICI numbers as the primary reference point against which I assessed my results. The ICI statistics, also known as the "Day-by-Day Records," are available in microfilm at the National Baseball Hall of Fame Library.[6] The records are based on the 1969 ruling of the Special Baseball Records Committee and consequently do not count a base on balls as a hit or a time at bat. Thus, in a game where O'Neill had a base on balls and two singles in four plate appearances, the printout would show "1" in the base on balls column, "2" in the hit column, and "3" in the at-bat column (a base on balls not counting as a hit or time at bat). To facilitate the comparison between the ICI numbers and those that I generated as the primary reference point, I converted my game-by-game statistics to the rules that guided ICI. For example, using 1887 rules, for a game for which I recorded O'Neill's batting performance as four hits in six times at bat based on three singles, a base on balls, a fly out to center field, and a fielder's choice, I would change this to three hits in five times at bat, with one base on balls, to reflect how ICI would represent the same game. With this conversion, it became easier to compare the game-by-game statistics that I produced at the end of stage two with those reported by ICI. At this point in the process, the goal was to identify and resolve any discrepancies in the numbers (AB, H, BB). Once I had the final numbers, I could then use them to re-calculate O'Neill's batting average according to the rules of 1887.

My game-by-game statistics for times at bat, hits, and bases on balls were the same as the day-by-day records of ICI for 116 of the 124 games. To resolve the discrepancies in the remaining eight games, I re-reviewed the game reports. I concluded that the evidence supported my statistics for seven of the eight games. For the game on September

6, the evidence was incomplete or ambiguous, and, as such, did not unequivocally corroborate either my numbers or those of ICI. Without a clear resolution, I accepted the numbers produced by ICI for the game on September 6.

I summarize each of the eight games below. The summary includes: the score and location (HG-Home game; AG-away game) of the game; the nature of the discrepancy or discrepancies (AB, H, BB); a review of the evidence with a focus on those sources (newspapers) that best address the discrepancy or discrepancies; and a concluding comment on the resolution. Please note that once I introduce evidence from a newspaper, in subsequent citations, I identify the newspaper with an abbreviation (e.g., for the *St. Louis Republic,* I use *REP*).[7]

I begin with the seven games for which I believe that the evidence supports my numbers. In the first five games discussed below (May 4, May 20, September 3—first game of a doubleheader, September 5, September 9), ICI and I differ on O'Neill's number of times at bat. For the games on April 16 and July 25, ICI and I have different numbers for all three categories (AB, H, BB).

May 4: St. Louis beat Louisville, 4–1 (HG). ICI and I both listed O'Neill with two H and no BB. ICI had O'Neill with four AB while I recorded only three. The *St. Louis Republican* (*REP*) and the *St. Louis Globe-Democrat* (*G-D*) provided the most detailed accounts of the game.[8] Both of these St. Louis newspapers noted that the Browns were batting in the seventh inning when the game was called on account of rain. The *REP* indicated that before the game was called, the Browns had scored two runs on hits by Gleason and Comiskey and an error by the right fielder. O'Neill batted between Gleason and Comiskey and so, in what would have been his fourth time at bat, he either was out or got his base on an error or a fielder's choice. Since the game ended while the seventh inning was in progress, the final score of the game reverted back to the end of the sixth inning, and the AB of the seventh inning no longer counted as part of the official record. *G-D, REP*, three Louisville newspapers (*Louisville Courier Journal—LCJ, Louisville Commercial—LC, Louisville Evening Post—LEP*), and three weeklies (*The Sporting News—SN, Sporting Life—SL, New York Clipper—NYC*) all reported that O'Neill had two hits and no bases on balls in three at-bats. The evidence clearly supports three and not four times at bat.

May 20: St. Louis beat Brooklyn, 15–9 (HG). ICI and I both listed O'Neill with three H and no BB. ICI had O'Neill with three AB while I recorded four. The *REP* and the *G-D* provided the most detailed accounts of the game.[9] O'Neill was hit by a pitch in the first inning, singled in the third, tripled in the fifth inning, singled in the seventh, and then left the game, unable to continue because of his injured hand (as a result of the hit by pitch in the first inning). The Browns scored four runs in the fifth inning, three runs in the sixth inning, and three runs in the seventh inning. O'Neill batted third in the order. He was second at bat in the fifth, an inning which saw eight Browns go to the plate. Although there are no details on O'Neill's plate appearance in the sixth inning, he would have been the third player to bat. The two reports of the sixth inning described how the Browns scored their three runs:

> The Browns did their prettiest batting in the sixth inning, when they scored three runs. Latham, Gleason, and Comiskey made singles, and Foutz followed with a two-bagger. (*REP*)[10]
>
> In the sixth inning Latham hit to center for a base and advanced to third on Gleason's hit to left. Gleason stole second, and he and Latham scored on Comiskey's single to left. Comiskey stole second, and scored on Foutz's hit to left for two bases. (*G-D*)[11]

O'Neill thus likely registered an out in his time at bat in the sixth. In the seventh inning, he came up fifth and hit a single that moved Gleason to third base. After two plate appearances in the first three innings, O'Neill went to bat in three consecutive innings, for a total of four times at bat in the game (the hit by pitch did not count as a time at bat). The *REP, SL, New York Herald* (*NYH*), and *NYC* listed four times at bat in their box scores, while the *G-D* did not have an AB column in its box score but, like the *REP*, described four of the plate appearances and implied an out in his fifth time at bat in the sixth inning. The *St. Louis Chronicle* (*SLC*) confirmed O'Neill's first three plate appearances (First Inning: hit by pitch; Third Inning: single; Fifth Inning: triple). The other reports were brief, listed three hits, but did not have an AB column (*Brooklyn Eagle—BE, Brooklyn Citizen—BC, New York Times—NYT, New York World—NYW, New York Sun—NYS*). The only sources that either listed or described O'Neill's times at bat clearly supported four times at bat.

September 3—First Game of Doubleheader: St. Louis beat New York, 20–8 (AG). ICI and I both listed O'Neill with two H and one BB. ICI had O'Neill with five AB, while I recorded four. The *New York Evening Sun* (*NYES*) provided the only inning-by-inning account of the six-inning game.[12] Based on the *NYES* report, O'Neill came to the plate five times: First Inning: base on balls; Third Inning: took his base on an error by the third baseman; Fourth Inning: At bat twice—first time, a single; second time, no specific information, but based on the likelihood that he scored another run, he probably got his base either on a fielder's choice or on an error; and Fifth Inning: double. O'Neill did not have a time at bat in the sixth inning. All sources except *NYH* and *NYC*, which did not have a section below the box score that identified who received bases on balls, listed O'Neill with three hits, one of which was a base on balls (*NYES, NYT, New York Star—NYST, NYS, NYW, G-D, REP, SL, SN*). Four of the newspapers did not include an at-bat column (*NYT, NYST, NYW, NYS*). The most convincing evidence comes from the five sources (*G-D, REP, NYH, SL, SN*) that listed the number of times at bat in the box score and the one source that described O'Neill's plate appearances (*NYES*), all of which report that he had five times at bat. In short, in the only sources that either listed or described O'Neill's plate appearances, they represented five times at bat, one of which resulted in a base on balls. Thus, since ICI did not count a base on balls as a hit or a time at bat, its report should read two hits in four times at bat (and not five times at bat), with one base on balls.

September 5: St. Louis lost to New York, 6–5 (AG). ICI and I both listed O'Neill with two H and no BB. ICI had O'Neill with five AB, while I recorded four. As with the September 3 game above, the *NYES* provided the only inning-by-inning account of the game.[13] The *NYES* described all four of O'Neill's times at bat: First Inning: Ground out to second base; Fourth Inning: Double; Fifth Inning: Fly out to center field; and Seventh Inning: Double. O'Neill did not have another turn at bat. As noted by the *NYES*, Gleason was the last out for St. Louis in the ninth inning, with O'Neill waiting his turn on deck. Four of the newspapers did not include an at-bat column (*NYT, NYST, NYW, NYS*). Again, the most persuasive evidence was presented by the six sources (*G-D, REP, NYH, SL, SN, NYC*) that had a column for at-bats in the box score. Each of these papers listed O'Neill with four times at bat, while the *NYES* described his four times at bat.

September 9: St. Louis beat Philadelphia, 8–3 (AG). ICI and I both listed O'Neill with one H and no BB. ICI had him with five AB, while I recorded four. Four of the five

Philadelphia newspapers described how the runs were scored (*Philadelphia Record—PR, Philadelphia Inquirer—PI, Philadelphia Press—PP, Philadelphia Times—PTM*, but not the *Philadelphia North American—PNA*).[14] Since O'Neill did not score or drive in a run, his at-bats were not specifically described. However, it was possible to identify in which innings his three outs occurred (first, fifth, sixth). His one hit, a triple that was listed below the box score in all game reports, was either in the second or third inning. None of the Philadelphia newspapers included a column for AB in the box score. Three St. Louis–based newspapers (*G-D, REP, SN*), the *SL* (a weekly paper based in Philadelphia), and the *NYC* reported four AB in their box scores. In addition, in the box scores compiled by ICI, the game report showed O'Neill with four at-bats.[15] I support four at-bats based on the only sources that listed or described the times at bat.

July 25: St. Louis lost to Brooklyn, 4–2 (AG). ICI listed O'Neill with two H in four AB, with no BB. I determined that O'Neill had one H and one BB in three AB. Two local reports, by *NYES* and *BC*, provided inning-by-inning accounts of the game.[16] The *Brooklyn Eagle*, another local newspaper, offered a detailed report of the game with specific descriptions of innings one, two, seven, eight, and nine, and an abbreviated outline of the Browns' time at bat in the sixth inning. These three newspapers (*NYES, BC, BE*) noted that O'Neill had a base on balls in the sixth inning and a single in the eighth inning. They also reported four plate appearances. The *BC* and the *NYES* included the details of O'Neill's other two times at bat: O'Neill got on base on a fielder's choice in the first inning and flied out in the fourth inning. The *BC* and the *BE* were inconsistent in their report of O'Neill's statistics. Although *BC* listed O'Neill with two hits in four times at bat, which was consistent with 1887 rules and their description in the text of O'Neill's base on balls and hit, it only noted one base on balls for the Browns below the box. Caruthers was the only player named, even though in the account of the game, *BC* delineated two bases on balls for the Browns, one for O'Neill and the other for Caruthers. Although *BE* had also described a base on balls and a hit in the text, it listed O'Neill with only one hit in the box score. Below the tabular box score, it listed the Browns with two bases on balls but did not name those players who received a base on balls (presumably O'Neill and Caruthers). Like *BE*, the *NYC* noted that the Browns had two bases on balls but did not name the players. In their box scores, the *NYH* and *NYST* showed O'Neill with two hits, one of which was a base on balls. The *NYH* also listed O'Neill with four times at bat, while *NYST* did not have an AB column. Like *BC*, many of the newspapers listed O'Neill with one hit in four times at bat, with only Caruthers named as the player who received a base on balls (*Brooklyn Standard Union—BSU, Brooklyn Daily Times—BDT, NYT, NYS, NYW, SL, SN, G-D, REP*).[17]

I was unable to find any source that supported ICI's statistics of two hits in four times at bat, with no base on balls. In the end, despite some inconsistencies, I am most persuaded by the detailed reports of three local newspapers—*NYES, BC,* and *BE*—and the support of the box scores published in the *NYH* and the *NYST*. Among the numerous newspapers whose box scores showed O'Neill with one hit in four times at bat and no base on balls, there are few if any detailed accounts to explain how they arrived at these numbers. In short, the best evidence supports one hit in three times at bat, with one base on balls.

April 16: St. Louis lost to Louisville 4–2 (AG). ICI listed O'Neill with one H in four AB with no BBs. I had O'Neill with no H and one BB in three AB. There were no inning-by-inning accounts of this game. *LCJ, LC,* and *REP* provided accounts of the second inning, when the Browns scored three runs. O'Neill did not have a turn at bat in the second inning. The *Louisville Commercial* noted that in the first inning the Browns "went out without getting a man to first,"[18] which meant that O'Neill got out in his first time at bat. The *Louisville Commercial* also reported a rally by the Browns in the fifth inning that ended when Tip grounded out to the first baseman. There were no descriptions in the texts of the newspapers' game reports of O'Neill's other two times at bat. Most sources (*LC, LCJ, LEP, G-D, REP, Cincinnati Enquirer* [*CE*], *SL, SN, National Daily Baseball Gazette* [*NDBBG*]) listed O'Neill with one hit in four times at bat in the box score (*Cincinnati Commercial Gazette—CCG*—had O'Neill with one hit but its box score did not include an AB column). With the exception of the *REP, SN*, and *NDBBG*, these newspapers did not indicate whether his one hit was a base on balls or a base hit (single, double, triple, or home run). Two of the three local newspapers (*LC, LEP*) listed the Browns with one base on balls below the box score but did not name the player who got the base on balls. Furthermore, the three Louisville newspapers (*LCJ, LEP, LC*) did not mention a base on balls in their descriptive accounts of the Browns' runs and hits. The *REP* was the only newspaper that described the Browns' five hits in the text. It stated that the Browns had three hits in the second inning and that Latham had a hit to start the eighth inning. On the fifth hit, the *REP* stated: "The remaining hit was a base on balls by O'Neill."[19] The *REP* also listed O'Neill with the only base on balls for the Browns in the section on base on balls below the tabular box score, as did the *SN* and the *National Daily Baseball Gazette* (*NDBBG*). In most cases, in games where the Browns are the visiting team, I usually rely on the published accounts of local reporters who were at the game to provide information. I had hoped one of the Louisville newspapers would clarify whether O'Neill had a base on balls or a base hit but none of the Louisville newspapers included such details. Instead, Ed Sheridan, the sporting editor of the *St. Louis Republican,* became the best source of the Brown's play. Sheridan travelled to Louisville to cover the Browns' first game of the season.[20] He wired his report of the game to the *REP* for publication the next day. His report included more information on the offensive performance of the Browns than was the case with any of the Louisville newspapers. More importantly, since he was at the game, his account offers credible evidence that the only hit O'Neill managed that day was through a base on balls. Based on Sheridan's eyewitness account, I conclude that Tip had one BB in three AB.

The evidence for the eighth game (September 6) is incomplete and, in some sources, imprecise. In the following review of the game-based information, I compare the evidence that supports the ICI numbers and the evidence that supports my numbers. I was not able to resolve this discrepancy. As noted above, in this circumstance, I defer to the statistics reported by ICI.

September 6: St. Louis lost to Brooklyn 8–6 (AG). ICI and I both listed O'Neill with four AB and no BB. ICI had O'Neill with one hit while I listed 2H. The *NYES* provided the only inning-by-inning account of the game.[21] The *G-D, REP,* and *NYST* also published detailed accounts of selected innings.[22] O'Neill had a single in the first inning, grounded out in the third inning, reached his base in the fifth inning either on an error by Billy Otterson (shortstop) or on a base hit, and grounded out in the seventh inning. The discrepancy centered on the fifth inning and whether O'Neill was safe at first on an error or had a base hit. The majority of the reports noted only one hit for O'Neill (*BDT, BSU, NYT, NYH, NYS, NYST, G-D, REP, SL, SN*). Only *BE* and *NYC* had O'Neill with two hits. The *NYES* description of Tip's hit in the fifth inning stated: "O'Neill sent a hot one to

Otterson, who couldn't hold it."[23] Relying on the *NYES* account, the *G-D* observed: "O'Neill sent a ball too hot for Otterson to hold."[24] The *NYST* declared: "In the fifth inning, O'Neill got first on an error by Otterson."[25] The *REP* did not comment on the fifth-inning ball hit by O'Neill to Otterson. For Brooklyn games, I have found most *BE* reports to be detailed and reliable.[26] Despite the fact that *BE*'s report for this game was shorter than usual, I still sided with *BE*'s claim of two hits. However, the only descriptions of O'Neill's fifth-inning hit to Otterson were contradictory. The vague wording of the *NYES* and *G-D*, and the lack of explicitly calling it an error, stood in contrast with the *NYST*'s judgment that it was an error. Without further information to resolve this discrepancy, there is again insufficient evidence in this game to support my determination of two hits for O'Neill. ICI's statistics, one hit in four times at bat, with no base on balls, continue to be the numbers of record.

The following table summarizes the steps that I followed in stage three to determine O'Neill's final at-bat, hit, and base-on-balls statistics for 1887. I used the ICI statistics as shown in the first row of the table—517 times at bat, 225 hits, and 50 bases on balls — as the reference point in my final review of O'Neill's game-by-game statistics. Of the 124 game-by-game statistics that I examined, I discovered eight games in which there was a discrepancy between one or more of my AB, H, or BB numbers and those of ICI. After a re-review of the game reports, I concluded that there was sufficient evidence to support my numbers for seven of the eight games. The second row of the table documents the impact of these changes on the ICI statistics. In all seven games, I changed the number of times at bat. In six of the games, I reduced the number by one (April 16, May 4, July 25, September 3, September 5, September 9) and in one game, I increased the number by one time at bat (May 20), for a net reduction of five times at bat. The changes to April 16 and July 25 also led to a decrease of two base hits and an increase of two bases on balls. The second row in the table lists these changes from the seven games and the third row shows the changes in the overall ICI statistics once the five times at bat and the two base hits are subtracted from the ICI AB and H numbers, and the two bases on balls are added to the ICI number of BB. In the fourth row, I applied 1887 rules to these adjusted statistics by adding 52 bases on balls to the number of times at bat and to the number of hits and then dividing the new number of hits (275) by the new number of times at bat (564). O'Neill's batting average in 1887 was .4875, rounded up to .488.

	At-Bats	Hits	Bases on Balls	Batting Average
ICI Statistics (before resolutions)	517	225	50	.435
Changes—From Resolutions in 6 games	Minus 5	Minus 2	Plus 2	—
Adjusted ICI Statistics	512	223	52	.436
Final Statistics Based on 1887 Rules	564	275	52	.488

Triples

As part of the three-stage process outlined above, I also checked any differences in the type of hit recorded. While ICI and I had the same total for doubles (52) and home runs (14), we differed on the number of triples hit by O'Neill. Whereas ICI reported that O'Neill hit 19 triples, I found that he hit 22 triples. My review supported the 17 games identified by ICI where O'Neill hit 19 triples (O'Neill hit two on August 30 and September

7). However, I found three additional triples for O'Neill, one in the April 30 game in St. Louis against Cleveland and two in games in New York, one on September 2 and the other in the second game of a doubleheader on September 3.

April 30: St. Louis beat Cleveland, 28–11 (HG). ICI and I both listed O'Neill with five hits in six times at bat, with one base on balls. ICI reported two singles, one double, and two home runs, while I noted one single, one double, one triple, and two home runs. There are no inning-by-inning accounts in any of the newspapers. There was, however, information on six of O'Neill's seven plate appearances: First inning: out (three up three down, but no details on how he got out); Third Inning: base on balls; Fourth Inning: single; Fifth Inning: At bat twice—first time, O'Neill hit a home run, and the second time, he hit a double or triple; Sixth Inning: Home run; Seventh or Eighth Inning: At bat one more time, no information on which inning or what kind of hit he had to complete his five hits for the game. In the sections on extra-base hits below the tabular box score, all of the newspapers I consulted, with the exception the *G-D*, listed O'Neill with one double, one triple, and two home runs (*REP, Cleveland Plain Dealer—CPD, Cleveland Leader—CL, CCG, CE, NYT, LCJ, SL, SN*). The *G-D* listed O'Neill with a double and two home runs. In its account of the game, the *REP* confused things with the following report on the fifth and sixth innings:

> In the fifth inning he went to the bat twice. He lined out a home run, down back of the bulletin board and followed it with a beautiful two-bag drive to left. In the sixth inning he made another home run, sending the ball under the seats at the left-field fence, making in the two innings three hits with a total of eleven bases—something unprecedented.[27]

In their comments on the game, most of the newspapers, with the exception of the *NYC*, repeated this confusing statement from the *REP* (*CE, CCG, NYT, LCJ, SL*). For example, *SL* observed: "O'Neill distinguished himself by making two home runs and a two-bagger, a total of eleven bases on the fifth and sixth innings."[28] Only the *NYC* picked up on the fact that if O'Neill had 11 bases in the two innings, then he had to have two home runs and a triple. In the *NYC's* brief text that preceded its box score, it stated that O'Neill had "two home runs and a three-bagger in two innings."[29]

The fact that all but one newspaper (*G-D*) cited O'Neill with a triple below the tabular box score, or in the case of the *NYC* in the text of its game report, convinced me that he had a triple in the game. Notwithstanding the report of two home runs and a double for 11 bases, the repeated reference to 11 bases in the fifth and sixth innings persuaded me that O'Neill likely hit a triple in his second time at bat in the fifth inning. O'Neill probably had his double in the seventh or eighth inning. Although the *G-D* was a reliable source for most games in 1887, in this game, it seemed less careful in its reporting. For example, *G-D's* claim that O'Neill hit for 14 bases on the game did not match the hits it reported for O'Neill (two home runs, one double, two singles, plus a base on balls equals 13 bases). Furthermore, the *G-D* made another error in its calculation of total bases for the Browns. It indicated that the Browns had 54 bases in the game, whereas the batting information that they listed for the Browns worked out to 55 bases. Of course, had the *G-D* listed O'Neill's fifth hit as a triple instead of a single, the team total would have added to 57 bases, the total number of bases for the Browns reported by other newspapers and weeklies. In sum, the evidence most supports the conclusion that O'Neill hit a triple in this game. With the addition of a triple, O'Neill thus hit for the cycle (single, double, triple, home run).

September 2: St. Louis beat New York, 12–4 (AG). ICI and I both listed O'Neill with five hits in five times at bat, with no base on balls. ICI reported four singles and one double, while I had O'Neill with three singles one double, and one triple. The *NYES* provided the only inning-by-inning account of the game.[30] The *NYST* also published a lengthier report, with a more detailed summary of innings in which runs were scored. Based on the *NYES* and *NYST* reports, O'Neill had the following record in his five times at bat: First Inning: single; Second Inning: triple; Fourth Inning: single; Fifth Inning: double; and Eighth Inning: single. Of his hit in the second inning, the *NYES* stated: "O'Neill hit for three bases into the left field corner,"[31] while the *NYST* reported: "Then O'Neill's three-bagger brought Gleason home."[32] The *NYTR, NYS, NYT*, and the comments on the game by the *NYC* noted that O'Neill had a double and a triple.[33] The *G-D* and the *REP* published the game account of the *NYES* and thus described O'Neill's five hits, including his double in the fifth inning and his triple in the second inning. However, the *G-D* and the *REP* added a box score that listed only three hits for O'Neill, one of which was a double, with no triple identified in the section below the tabular box score.[34] Neither newspaper appeared to notice the inconsistency in their game account and box score. In addition to the *G-D* and the *REP*, four other newspapers cited only O'Neill's double below the tabular box score (*NYW, NYH, SL, SN*).

In my assessment, the evidence from the detailed reports of two local papers (*NYES, NYST*) and four other New York–based newspapers (*NYT, NYS, NYTR, NYC*) supports the conclusion that O'Neill hit a double and a triple in this game. The *G-D* and *REP* repeatedly relied on the *NYES* for game accounts of the New York and Brooklyn games against St. Louis. Their texts clearly showed that O'Neill hit a triple in the second inning. Their box scores tell a different story, one I find less credible since they had only three hits for O'Neill, while eight other sources list him with five hits.

September 3—Second Game of Doubleheader: St. Louis beat New York, 7–4 (AG). ICI and I both listed O'Neill with two hits in five times at bat, with no base on balls. ICI reported one single and one double, while I have O'Neill with one double and one triple. The *NYES* published an inning-by-inning account of the first five innings of the game, with summaries provided for the last four innings.[35] The *G-D* reprinted the *NYES* report on the game. The other game reports included box scores with some highlights in the brief accounts that preceded the box score (notably *NYST* and *REP*). From the *NYES* description, O'Neill tripled in the first inning, grounded out in the third inning, and doubled in the fifth inning. Although there are no details of O'Neill's other times at bat, he likely went to bat two more times, in both cases making an out or reaching base on an error or a fielder's choice. Of O'Neill's first-inning triple, the *NYES* stated: "Gleason hit a single and O'Neill sent him home on a hit to left field for three bases."[36] All of the newspapers that had sections on extra-base hits below the tabular box score listed O'Neill with a double and a triple (*NYT, NYH, NYS, NYW, NYST, New York Tribune—NYTR, G-D, REP, SL, SN*). The evidence, while limited in descriptive accounts, overwhelmingly supports the conclusion that O'Neill tripled in this game.

At 19 triples, O'Neill was tied for the most triples in the American Association with five other players (Tom Poorman, John Kerins, Oyster Burns, Jumbo Davis, Bid McPhee). The new total of 22 triples gives O'Neill the outright lead in this batting category. It also extends his lead in extra-base hits from 85 to 88. In addition, this change, along with those made in the six games above (at-bats, hits, bases on balls, batting average), results in a different distribution of hits made by O'Neill in 1887. The following table compares the hits identified in each category by ICI in the late 1960s (converted to 1887 rules with walks counted as hits) with those that I determined in the process outlined above:

	BB	1B	2B	3B	HR	Total Hits	Total Extra-Base Hits
ICI	50	140	52	19	14	275	85
Final Statistics	52	135	52	22	14	275	88

Appendix B:
Tip O'Neill—Single-Season
Batting Records and Feats in 1887

In the following outline, I list and briefly describe O'Neill's major single-season batting records and feats in 1887. I have already presented and discussed many of these records and feats in earlier chapters and in endnotes. While O'Neill was most known for his near–.500 batting average, he also set numerous records that endured for some time after 1887 and are still highly ranked on the all-time lists for numerous batting categories and accomplishments for one season.[1] In addition, there were a number of noteworthy feats which, along with his record-breaking performances, demonstrate the depth and breadth of O'Neill's prowess at the plate. The summary of these achievements in this appendix provides a handy reference to O'Neill's records and noteworthy feats in this extraordinary season. In parentheses at the end of most records and feats listed below, I include the chapter or chapters in which I provide further details of these accomplishments.

Records: Batting Categories

In 1887, O'Neill led the American Association and the major leagues with record-breaking performances in a number of individual batting categories. In this section, I review these batting-category records and how these records evolved over time.

Leading in Most Batting Categories, Season: 11. Nap Lajoie tied O'Neill's record in 1901. The following table displays the categories in which each batsman led:

	H	S	D	T	HR	RBI	LH	TB	OB	SLG	OPS	BA	Total
O'Neill 1887	275	—	52	22	14	125	88	413	.492	.732	1.224	.488	11
Lajoie 1901	232	156	48	—	14	125	76	350	.463	.643	1.106	.426	11

H–hits; S–singles; D–doubles; T–triples; HR–home runs; RBI–runs batted in; LH–long hits; TB–total bases; OB–on-base percentage; SLG–slugging percentage; OPS–on-base plus slugging percentage; BA–batting average; Total–number of categories in which player was the leader

Most Records in Batting Categories in League, Season: 10. Of the 11 batting categories in which O'Neill led, he broke or tied Association records in ten: hits (tied with Pete Browning, who like O'Neill had 275 hits), doubles, home runs (tied with Harry Stovey, who set the record in 1883), long or extra-base hits, total bases, runs batted in, on-base percentage, slugging percentage, on-base plus slugging percentage, and batting average. In 1889, Bug Holliday and Harry Stovey each hit 19 home runs to break the Association record. Although in 1887 O'Neill also led the Association in triples, he did not eclipse the record of 31 triples held by Dave Orr (1884). O'Neill also holds the all-time single-season records in nine categories in the American Association (1882–1891). (Chapter 16)

Most Records in Batting Categories in Major Leagues, Season: 8. In 1887, O'Neill set record in the major leagues (National League, American Association) in: hits, doubles, long or extra-base hits, total bases, on-base percentage, slugging percentage, on-base plus slugging percentage, and batting average. (Chapter 16)

Progressive Leaders and Records in Batting Categories in Major Leagues, Season: In the first table in Chapter 16, I list the 11 batting categories in which O'Neill led all players in the American Association in 1887 and those categories in which his performance established new records in the Association and in the major leagues. In the last two columns, I also note those categories in which O'Neill set all-time records for the Association (1882–1891) and those which were records in the major leagues that O'Neill still held at the end of the 1892 season, the last year in which he played. The table below begins with two columns: first the eight batting categories in which O'Neill held the record in the major leagues (Batting Category in Which Tip Set ML Record in 1887), second the number or percentage of each record (O'Neill's ML Record as of 1892). The table adds three columns: when a record was first broken, who broke the record, and in what year the new record was established (ML Record First Broken: New Record-Name-Year); the current record, who has it, and in what year it was set (Current ML Record: Record-Name-Year); and O'Neill's current ranking on the all-time leaders' list of the number or percentage that O'Neill achieved in 1887 (O'Neill's Current Ranking in 2018).

To illustrate the information in the table for one of O'Neill's records, I describe the columns for doubles. The first column indicates that in 1887, O'Neill established a new major league record for doubles in a season. The second column notes that O'Neill's mark of 52 doubles was still the record in 1892. The third column shows that his record was first broken when Ed Delahanty hit 55 doubles in 1899. The fourth column notes that the current record of 67 doubles was set by Earl Webb in 1931. The fifth and final column notes that O'Neill's 52 doubles are currently ranked 41st for doubles in a season (tied with 12 other batsmen).

As I declared in the Preface, in telling the story of O'Neill's batting performance in 1887, I honor "the conventionalist proclamation of Holtzman: 'If a walk was a hit in 1887 it shall stand as a hit forever.'" However, with the exception of the seventh and eighth editions of *Total Baseball,* most sources that cite baseball records have not adhered to this proclamation. These sources list O'Neill's records and rankings based on his recalculated statistics where bases on balls are not counted as hits or times at bat. Thus, to facilitate comparisons between O'Neill and those who subsequently broke his records, I include both his conventionalist numbers and rankings and, in parentheses, his revisionist numbers and rankings for those records affected by the base-on-balls scoring rule, that is, for hits, total bases, slugging percentage, on-base plus slugging percentage, and batting average. For example, his conventionalist slugging percentage of .732 for a season ranks 18th on the all-time list, while his revisionist slugging percentage of .706 ranks 31st. There is no difference in the two slugging percentages in terms of when the record was first broken or what the current record is.

Batting Category in Which O'Neill set a ML record in 1887	O'Neill's ML Record as of 1892	ML Record First Broken New Record-Name-Year	Current ML Record: Record-Name-Year	O'Neill's Current ML Ranking in 2017
Hits	275* (223)	Not Broken (237–Hugh Duffy–1894)	Not Broken (262–Ichiro Suzuki–2004)	1* (71)
Doubles	52	55–Ed Delahanty–1899	67–Earl Webb–1931	41
Long Hits	88	99–Babe Ruth–1920	119–Babe Ruth–1921	78
Total Bases	413 (361)	457–Babe Ruth–1921 (374–Hugh Duffy–1894)	457–Babe Ruth–1921 (457–Babe Ruth–1921)	15 (160)
On-Base %	.492	.521–Billy Hamilton–1894	.609–Barry Bonds–2004	27
Slugging %	.732 (.705)	.847–Babe Ruth–1920 (.847–Babe Ruth–1920)	.863–Barry Bonds–2001 (.863–Barry Bonds–2001)	18 (31)
On-Base Plus Slugging %	1.224 (1.197)	1.379–Babe Ruth–1920 (1.379–Babe Ruth–1920)	1.422–Barry Bonds–2004 (1.422–Barry Bonds–2004)	15 (21)
Batting Average	.488 (.436)	Not Broken (.440–Hugh Duffy–1894)	Not Broken (.440–Hugh Duffy–1894)	1 (2)

*Tied with Pete Browning

Leading League in Doubles, Triples, and Home runs, Season: 1. O'Neill is the only player who has ever led the league in all three extra-base-hit categories: doubles, triples, and home runs.[2] (Chapters 11 and 16)

Leading League in Most Extra-Base-Hit Batting Categories, Season: 7. I define extra-base-hit batting categories as those which are based solely or predominantly on long- or extra-base-hit figures, specifically: doubles, triples, home runs, long hits, total bases, slugging percentage, and on-base plus slugging percentage. O'Neill is the only player who has ever led the league in all seven extra-base-hit categories.

Records: Streaks, Cycles, Runs

The following records include three batting records, two from different types of streaks and one that follows from the number of times O'Neill hit for the cycle. The fourth record is for the number of runs scored, an important offensive statistic. However, as explained in Chapter 16, I do not consider scoring runs as a batting category.[3]

Consecutive Games with an Extra-Base Hit: 12 (August 24–September 5). O'Neill's record was broken in 1927 when Paul Waner had an extra-base hit in 14 consecutive games (June 3–19). Chipper Jones tied Waner's record in 2006 (June 26–July 16). O'Neill is tied with Rogers Hornsby (1928) at 12 consecutive games with a long hit, the third-longest streak ever recorded.[4] (Chapter 13)

Consecutive Times at Bat with a Hit: 10, which occurred twice in 1887 (April 30–May 1 and August 8–10). The current record of 12 was established in 1902 by Johnny Kling. It has been tied twice, first by Pinky Higgins in 1938 and then by Walt Dropo in 1952.

Both of O'Neill's ten consecutive plate appearances with a hit included a base on balls as one of the hits. If O'Neill's two streaks were adjusted to nine consecutive times at bat with a hit, then he tied a record established by Harry Stovey (June 3–4, 1886).[5] O'Neill's record, like those of Stovey (1886) and George Van Haltren, who had a streak of nine consecutive hits in 1891, was broken in 1893, when Jake Stenzel had ten hits in a row. O'Neill and Joe Kelley (1894, 1898) are the only players to complete two streaks of nine or more hits in a row. O'Neill is the only player to complete two nine-hit streaks (or ten-hit streaks based on 1887 rules) in the same season. (Chapters 6 and 13)

Cycles, Season: 2 (April 30, May 7). O'Neill's cycles tied a record established by John Reilly in 1883. Reilly hit for the cycle a third time in 1890, setting the record for the most cycles in a career. Through the 2017 season, three players have tied Reilly's career record of three cycles: Bob Muesel (1921, 1922, 1928), Babe Herman (1931—twice, 1933), and Adrian Beltre (2008, 2012, 2015). While four players have hit for the cycle twice in the same season (O'Neill, Reilly, Herman, Aaron Hill—2012), Reilly and O'Neill share the distinction of the fastest two cycles, completing the "double" in a five-game period. (Chapter 7)

Runs, Season: 167. O'Neill's record was broken in 1891, when Tom Brown scored 177 runs. Three years later (1894), Billy Hamilton established the all-time record with 198 runs. O'Neill is currently ranked fourth all-time, tied with Lou Gehrig. (Chapter 16).

Noteworthy Feats

Although the following accomplishments did not establish records, they are nonetheless noteworthy feats. They include: rare achievements (Triple Crown, hitting over .400); significant number of multi-hit games in the season, hits in consecutive games, or hits in a single game (e.g., O'Neill is ranked second for the most games with five or more hits in one season); impressive number of multi-extra-hit games in the season, extra-base hits in two consecutive games, and extra-base hits in a single game; prominent hitting streaks (e.g., 25-game hitting streak); and high ratios (e.g., 1.81 hits per game; 1.534 relative batting average).

Batting Triple Crown: O'Neill led the American Association in batting average, runs batted in, and home runs, and thus won the Triple Crown. Through 2017, 15 players have won 17 Triple Crowns (Rogers Hornsby and Ted Williams each won the Triple Crown twice). The only nineteenth century Triple Crown winners were Paul Hines (1878) and Tip O'Neill. Of the 17 Triple Crown seasons, O'Neill recorded the highest batting average with his conventionalist average of .488 and with his revisionist average of .436. Nap Lajoie was second with an average of .426 in 1901. O'Neill's .492 on-base percentage ranked second, with Ted Williams (1942, 1947) first with an on-base percentage of .499 in both years. Rogers Hornsby's OPS of 1.245 led all Triple Crown winners, followed by O'Neill's 1.197.

.400 Hitters: There have been 28 times when batsmen have batted .400 or higher. Of the 21 batsmen who achieved this, Rogers Hornsby, Ty Cobb, and Ed Delahanty each hit .400 three times, while George Sisler did it twice. O'Neill's .488 batting average is the highest in this .400 club, and his revised average of .436, when bases on balls are not counted as hits or times at bat, is the second-highest to Hugh Duffy's .440 average in 1894. Among the 28 .400–or–higher seasons, O'Neill had the highest average at home, .535 in Sportsman's Park, while his revisionist average was .479, without counting bases on balls as hits. Rogers Hornsby (1925) had the second-best, home-park batting average at .478, followed by George Sisler, who hit .473 at home in 1920. O'Neill was also one of only three players who hit .500 or better in two months in 1887 (May and August). Ross Barnes also hit over .500 in two months (June and July) as did Hugh Duffy (July and August).[6]

Relative Batting Average, Season: 1.416. The relative batting average (RBA) is a measure to normalize a player's batting average to the league average. It is calculated by dividing the player's average by the league's average.[7] Following the 1887 rules, *Total Baseball* listed O'Neill with a .485 batting average and the Association with a .330 average. In its section on single-season leaders, it indicates that O'Neill's RBA is 1.416, which ranks 41st all-time.[8] Using a revised batting average of .435 and an Association average of .273, the *ESPN Baseball Encyclopedia, Fifth Edition* reports that O'Neill's RBA is 1.564, second all-time to Ross Barnes, who in 1876 had an RBA of 1.608.[9]

Multi-Hit Games, Season: 84 (67.7 percent) games with two or more hits, 50 (40.3 percent) games with three or more hits, and 24 (19.4 percent) games with four or more hits. O'Neill's revised numbers, excluding bases on balls as hits or times at bat, are as follows: 69 (55.6 percent) games with two or more hits, 34 (27.4 percent) games with three or more hits, and 14 (11.3 percent) games with four or more hits. In comparison to the 28 seasons in which a batsman had a .400 or higher average (see last point), O'Neill had the tenth-best percentage for two or more hits (Ross Barnes had 69.7 percent in 1876), the third-best percentage for three or more hits (Ross Barnes had 37.9 percent in 1876 and Tuck Turner 29.3 percent in 1894), and the highest number but second-best percentage for four or more hits (Ross Barnes had 13.9 percent in 1876).[10] In a survey of 445 200-hit seasons since 1920, Jim Weigand determined that in 2009, Ichiro Suzuki established the modern-day (1952–2009) record of 73 (50.0 percent) games with two or more hits. He found nine batters in the 1920s and 1930s with percentages higher than Suzuki. Al Simmons had the best record in the 1920–1940 period, with 85 (55.6 percent) of the games in 1925 with two or more hits.[11] (Chapter 16)

Most Games with Five or More Hits, Season: 8 (including bases on balls as hits). Excluding bases on balls as hits, O'Neill had four games with five or more hits (April 30, August 24, September 2, September 7). Sam Thompson (1887) holds the record of five. Four others have had four games with five or more hits in a season: Ty Cobb (1922), Stan Musial (1948), Tony Gwynn (1993), and Ichiro Suzuki (2004).[12] (Chapters 6 and 12)

Most Hits in Seven, Six, Five, or Four Consecutive Games: Seven Games—24 hits (April 27 to May 7); Six Games—21 hits (April 28 to May 7); Five Games—18 hits (April 30 to May 7); and Four Games—15 hits (April 27 to May 1). O'Neill had what I called a historic week (April 27 to May 7), seven consecutive games in which he had 27 hits in 36 times at bat for a .750 batting average. He had two other noteworthy weeks. In seven consecutive games from August 24–30, he had 23 hits in 36 times at bat for a .639 average, and from September 2–8, he had 21 hits in 33 times at bat for an average of .636.

Trent McCotter described a "sensational week" by Jimmy Johnston in 1923, where in addition to his six consecutive games with three or more hits, Johnston also had impressive numbers in hits and times on base for seven, six, five, and four consecutive games. In the following tables, I compare Johnston's week with O'Neill's April 27–May 7 week (numbers revised to exclude bases on balls as either hits or times at bat) and the August 16–23 week in 1894 of Billy Hamilton.[13]

	Seven Games						Six Games					
Name	AB	H	BB	BA	OB (H+BB)	TB	AB	H	BB	BA	OB (H+BB)	TB
O'Neill	33	24	3	.727	27	49	27	21	3	.777	24	45
Johnston	30	24	5	.800	29	40	28	23	4	.821	27	38
Hamilton	37	25	7	.676	32	28	33	22	5	.667	27	25

FIVE GAMES							FOUR GAMES					
Name	AB	H	BB	BA	OB (H+BB)	TB	AB	H	BB	BA	OB (H+BBv)	TB
O'Neill	23	18	2	.783	20	39	21	15	2	.714	17	30
Johnston	24	19	4	.792	23	33	19	15	3	.789	18	28
Hamilton	27	18	4	.667	22	20	21	15	3	.714	18	16

AB–At-Bats; H–Hits; BB–Bases on Balls; BA–Batting Average; OB–Times on Bases; TB–Total Bases

While all three batsmen had impressive weeks, Johnston had the best numbers in hits (first in hits in six and five consecutive games, tied with Hamilton and O'Neill for the most hits in four consecutive games, tied with O'Neill and second to Hamilton, who had the most in seven consecutive games) and batting average (highest average for seven, six, five, and four consecutive games). Hamilton had the best on-base numbers (first in seven consecutive games, tied with O'Neill in six consecutive games, tied with Johnson for four consecutive games, and second to Johnson for five consecutive games). O'Neill had the best total-base numbers (first in seven, six, five, and four consecutive games) and was second-best in batting average to Johnston in seven, six, and five consecutive games (tied with Hamilton for the second-best batting average in four consecutive games). (Chapters 6 and 12)

Consecutive Games with One or More Hits: 25 (August 23–September 21). O'Neill also had a 22-game hitting streak that spanned two seasons (October 4, 1887–May 10, 1888). The 25-game hitting streak was the longest streak in the American Association in 1887. O'Neill's streaks were two of only 24 streaks of 20 hits or more recorded during the ten-year history of the American Association (1882–1891). Among the Association batsmen who had a batting streak of 20 or more games, O'Neill was the only one who hit over .500 during a streak of 20 or more, doing so in both streaks.[14] (Chapter 13)

Hits Per Game, Season: 2.22, based on 275 hits in 124 games. When re-calculated according to revisionist rules, O'Neill had 223 hits in 124 games, or 1.80 hits per game. Ichiro Suzuki, the all-time leader for hits in a season, had 262 hits in 161 games, or 1.63 hits per game. Among those who have hit .400 or better in a season (see above), O'Neill ranks sixth. Ross Barnes (1876) led with 2.12 hits per game. He was followed by Hugh Duffy (1894) with 1.90 hits per game, Willie Keeler (1897) with 1.85, and Sam Thompson (1894) and Fred Dunlap (1884) with 1.83 hits per game.

Most Games with Two or More Extra-Base Hits, Season: 18 (14.5 percent) of 124 games in which he played. Hugh Duffy had 85 extra-base hits in 1894. He had two or more extra-base hits in 19 (15.2 percent) of 125 games. Babe Ruth holds the record for the most extra-base hits, 119 in 1921, with two or more extra-base hits in 25 (16.4 percent) of 152 games.[15] (Chapter 11)

Most Extra-Base Hits in Two Consecutive Games: 6. On April 28, O'Neill hit a double and a triple, and on April 30, he hit a double, a triple, and two home runs. The record of seven extra-base hits in two consecutive games was set by Ed Delahanty in 1896 and subsequently matched by Earl Sheely (1926), Red Schoendienst (1954), Joe Adcock (1954), and Larry Walker (1996).[16] (Chapters 6 and 11)

Most Extra-Base Hits, Game: 4—double, triple, and two home runs (April 30). The record of five extra-base hits in one game was set by George Strief in 1885 and tied by George Gore two weeks later and then by Larry Twitchell in 1889. As of 2013, seven other batsmen have tied this record.[17] (Chapters 6 and 11)

Appendix C:
Tip O'Neill—Career Statistics

The following tables list O'Neill's batting, fielding, and pitching statistics by season and career. The numbers or percentages in **bold** indicate categories in which O'Neill led the league or association. O'Neill led in three categories in 1886 (H, 1B, RBI), 11 categories in 1887 (R, H, 2B, 3B, HR, RBI, BA, OBP, SLG, OPS, TB), three categories in 1888 (H, 1B, BA),[1] and one category in 1890 (G). He led in one pitching category in 1884 (W-L%). He was not the leader in any fielding category. Note that many of O'Neill's statistics are slightly different from those listed by Baseball Reference in batting in 1886 (AB, H, 2B, 3B, RBI, BA) and 1887 (H, 3B, RBI, SB, SO, BA, OBP, SLG, OPS, TB) and in fielding in 1887 (PO, A, E, FP, Fld%).[2]

Batting-Seasons

Year	Tm	Lg	G	AB	R	H	2B	3B	HR	RBI	SB	BB	SO	BA	OBP	SLG	OPS	TB
1883	NYG	NL	23	76	8	15	3	0	0	5	—	3	15	.197	.228	.237	.465	18
1884	STL	AA	78	297	49	82	13	11	3	54	—	12	—	.276	.309	.424	.733	126
1885	STL	AA	52	206	44	72	7	4	3	38	—	13	—	.350	.399	.466	.865	96
1886	STL	AA	138	574	106	**193**	29	15	3	**111**	9	47	—	.336	.393	.455	.848	261
1887	STL	AA	124	564	**167**	**275**	**52**	**22**	**14**	**125**	33	52	15	**.488**	**.492**	**.732**	**1.224**	**413**
1888	STL	AA	130	529	96	**177**	24	10	5	98	26	44	28	**.335**	.390	.446	.836	236
1889	STL	AA	134	534	123	179	33	8	9	110	28	72	37	.335	.419	.478	.897	255
1890	CHI	PL	**137**	577	112	174	20	16	3	75	29	65	36	.302	.377	.407	.784	235
1891	STL	AA	127	514	111	166	28	4	10	95	25	61	33	.323	.404	.451	.855	232
1892	CIN	NL	109	419	63	105	14	6	2	52	14	53	25	.251	.339	.327	.666	137

Tm–team (NYG–New York Giants; STL–St. Louis Browns; CHI–Chicago Pirates; CIN–Cincinnati Reds); Lg–league (NL–National League; AA–American Association; PL–Players' League); G–games; R–runs; H–hits; 2B–doubles; 3B–triples; HR–home runs; RBI–runs batted in; SB–stolen bases; BB–bases on balls; SO–strikeouts; BA–batting average; OBP–on-base percentage; SLG–slugging percentage; OPS–on-base percentage plus slugging percentage; TB–total bases

Batting-Career

G	AB	R	H	2B	3B	HR	RBI	SB	BB	SO	BA	OBP	SLG	OPS	TB
1052	4290	879	1438	223	96	52	759	163	421	194	.335	.400	.468	.868	2009

Batting-Postseason

Year	Tm	Series	Opp	AB	R	H	2B	3B	HR	RBI	SB	BB	SO	BA	OBP	SLG	OPS	TB
1885	NYG	WS	CHI	24	4	5	0	0	0	0	0	0	0	.208	.208	.208	.417	5
1886	STL	WS	CHI	20	4	8	0	2	2	5	2	4	5	.400	.500	.900	1.400	18
1887	STL	WS	DET	65	7	13	2	1	1	9	0	0	2	.200	.200	.308	.508	20
1888	STL	WS	NYG	37	8	9	1	0	2	11	0	6	3	.243	.349	.432	.781	16
				146	**23**	**35**	**3**	**3**	**5**	**25**	**2**	**10**	**10**	**.240**	**.288**	**.404**	**.693**	**59**

Series–WS (World Series); Tm–team (CHI–Chicago White Stockings; DET–Detroit Wolverines; NYG–New York Giants)

Fielding: Seasons

Year	Tm	Lg	Pos	G	Ch	PO	A	E	DP	Fld%	Lg Fld%
1883	NYG	NL	P	19	36	10	23	3	0	.917	.892
1883	NYG	NL	OF	7	10	7	1	2	0	.800	.849
1884	STL	AA	OF	64	90	67	6	17	1	.811	.847
1884	STL	AA	P	17	42	6	31	5	0	.881	.829
1884	STL	AA	1B	1	2	2	0	0	0	1.000	.960
1885	STL	AA	OF	52	101	83	6	12	1	.881	.879
1886	STL	AA	OF	138	316	279	14	23	4	.927	.877
1887	STL	AA	OF	124	285	249	10	31	3	.893	.898
1888	STL	AA	OF	130	255	231	8	16	1	.937	.907
1889	STL	AA	OF	134	295	264	12	19	3	.936	.903
1890	CHI	PL	OF	137	258	231	8	19	1	.926	.904
1891	STL	AA	OF	127	214	195	5	14	0	.935	.908
1892	CIN	NL	OF	109	218	188	13	17	3	.922	.912

Tm–team; Lg–league; Pos–Position (P–pitcher; OF–outfielder; 1B–first baseman); G–games; Ch–chances; PO–putouts; A–assists; E–errors; DP–double plays; Fld%–fielding percentage; Lf Fld%–league fielding percentage

Fielding: Career

	Pos	G	Ch	PO	A	E	DP	Fld%	Lg Fld%
10 Seasons	OF	1022	2042	1794	83	170	17	.917	.896
2 seasons	P	36	78	16	54	8	0	.897	.858
1 Season	1B	1	2	2	0	0	0	1.000	.960

Pitching

Year	Tm	Lg	G	W	L	W-L%	ERA	IP	H	R	ER	HR	BB	SO	HBP	WP
1883	NYG	NL	19	5	12	.294	4.07	148	182	129	67	5	64	55	—	33
1884	STL	AA	17	11	4	.733	2.68	141	125	95	42	3	51	36	4	14
			36	**16**	**16**	**.500**	**.3.39**	**289**	**307**	**224**	**109**	**8**	**115**	**91**	**4**	**47**

Tm–team; Lg–league; G–games; W–games won; L–games lost; W-L%–win-loss percentage; ERA–earned run average; IP–Innings Pitched; H–hits allowed; R–runs allowed; ER–earned runs allowed; HR–home runs allowed; BB–bases on balls; SO–strikeouts; HBP–times hit by pitch; WP–wild pitch

Chapter Notes

Preface

1. Alfred H. Spink, *The National Game. Second Edition* (1911; Reprinted Carbondale: Southern Illinois University Press, 2000), 250.

2. Mike Rogers, "The Greatest Season You Don't Know About," January 5, 2011. Accessed May 10, 2016, http://www.beyondtheboxscore.com.

3. In recent years, the number of published materials on baseball prior to the twentieth century has significantly increased. The members of the Nineteenth Century Research Committee of the Society for American Baseball Research (SABR) deserve special mention for their tireless efforts to promote research, discussion (conferences, symposia), and writing on a wide range of topics on baseball in the nineteenth century.

4. On notable exceptions—For a history of the American Association, I recommend David Nemec's *The Beer and Whiskey League: The Illustrated History of the American Association—Baseball's Renegade Major League* (Guilford, CT: Lyons, 2004). For an incisive historical analysis of the St. Louis Browns in the 1880s, see Jon David Cash, *Before They Were Cardinals: Major League Baseball in Nineteenth-Century St. Louis* (Columbia: University of Missouri Press, 2002), especially chapters 4–10. The recent biographies of some of the other members of the 1887 Browns provide helpful insights into the conditions under which the Browns played and into the many events, incidents, and issues they faced. On Arlie Latham, see L. M. Sutter, *Arlie Latham: A Baseball Biography of the Freshest Man on Earth*. (Jefferson, NC: McFarland, 2012). For Chris Von der Ahe, the owner of the Browns, see J. Thomas Hetrick, *Chris Von der Ahe and the St. Louis Browns* (Lanham, MD: Scarecrow, 1999). For Charles Comiskey, the Browns' manager, captain, and first baseman, see Tim Hornbaker, *Turning the Black Sox White: The Misunderstood Legacy of Charles A. Comiskey* (New York: Sports Publishing, 2014) and G.W. Axelson, *"Commy:" The Life Story of Charles A. Comiskey* (1919; Reprinted Jefferson, NC: McFarland, 2003).

5. See the following biographical chapters or sketches on O'Neill: Bob Elliott, "Of J. J., Tip and Friends," in *The Northern Game. Baseball the Canadian Way* (Toronto: Sport Classic Books, 2005), 55–63; Neil Munro and STATS, Inc., "James 'Tip' O'Neill 1883–1892" in Neil Munro and STATS, Inc., *Canadian Players Encyclopedia* (STATS Publishing, 1996), 47–50; Jim Shearon, "Tip O'Neill, Record Breaking Batter," in *Canada's Baseball Legends: True Stories of Canadians in the Big Leagues Since 1879* (Kanata: Malin Head Press, 1994), 14–17; Jim Shearon, "America's Champion Batsman Really Was a Proud Canadian," in *Over the Fence and Out! The Larry Walker Story and More of Canada's Baseball Legends* (Kanata: Malin Head Press, 2009), 76–79; and Doug M. Symons, "O'Neill, James Edward," in *Giants of Oxford: Women and Men Who Changed the World* (Woodstock, ON: Woodstock Historical Society, 2001), 64–67.

6. Regarding the 1887 rules governing when a batsman was out on strikes, Eric Miklich explained: "The batsman is out on strikes the moment the Umpire calls 'four strikes,' whenever first base is occupied and only one man is out, without regard to the catch of the ball from the fourth strike or not. In all other cases of four strikes being called, the ball on the fourth strike must be caught on the fly, or the batsman—then becoming a base runner—must be thrown out at first." Eric Miklich, *The Rules of the Game: A Compilation of the Rules of Baseball 1845–1900*. 19C Base Ball, www.19CBASEBALL.COM, 2005, 63.

7. I refer to the first position as "conventionalist" because it advocates the importance of following "conventions," which, in the case of the 1887 season, were those scoring rules that were in place, specifically the base-on-balls-as-a-hit rule. I call the second position "revisionist" because it wants to ensure that, as much as possible, the calculation of batting records in every season is based on the same scoring rules. Here revisionism is intended to ensure that the interpretation of batting records can be consistently done from one season to the next so that meaningful comparisons can be made between these records, which in the case of 1887 requires the reinterpretation or recalculation of the existing records.

8. *The Baseball Encyclopedia: The Complete and Official Record of Major League Baseball* (Toronto: Macmillan, 1969), 1310.

9. "Secretary Wikoff Pronounces Them the Only Official Figures," *The Sporting News*, November 5, 1887, 6.

10. To determine O'Neill's times at bat, I began with the formula for calculating his batting average based on the available 1887 numbers: 277/AB=492/1000, which resulted in 563.008 or, rounded out, 563 at-bats.

11. Note that the passage incorrectly cited O'Neill's batting average as .495. In the same *Guide*, in the section entitled, "Individual Batting Record," the official average of .492 was listed. "James E. O'Neill," *Reach's Official American Association Base Ball Guide 1888* (1888; Reprinted New York: Horton, 1989), page numbers not included in the reprint.

12. The term "phantom hit" was used in 1887 by sportswriters to denigrate the rule that counted a base on balls as a hit. Paul Dickson, *The Dickson Baseball Dictionary*, 3d ed. (New York: W.W. Norton, 2009), 632.

13. "Latham and O'Neill," *The Sporting News*, May 5, 1888, 5.

14. "The Season of 1887," *Sporting Life's Official Base Ball Guide 1891* (Philadelphia: Sporting Life, 1891), 50.

15. In 1914, Francis C. Richter had O'Neill first on a list of "Batsmen Who Have Made an Average of .400 or Better," and added "the highest average on record—but made in the year of the four-strike rule." Francis C. Richter, *Richter's History and Records of Base Ball, the American Nation's Chief Sport* (1914; Reprinted Jefferson, NC: McFarland, 2005), 231. In the *Little Red Book* published in 1932, under "Individual Batting Records—Highest Percentage," Hugh Duffy was listed with the highest percentage at .438, Rogers Hornsby with the highest percentage in the NL since 1900 at .424, and George Sisler with the highest percentage in the AL since 1900 at .420. In the final entry, it stated: "In 1887, when a base on balls was scored as a base hit, J. E. O'Neill, St. Louis AA, had a percentage of .492." Charles White, *The Little Red Book, Spalding's Official Base Ball Record* (New York: American Sports Publishing, 1932), 76. *The Sporting News*, in its 1975 record book, listed O'Neill in the section ".400 Hitters in the Majors—American Association" with a batting average of .492. In parentheses under the title, it noted: "Bases on ball counted as hits in 1887." Leonard Gettelson, *The Sporting News 1975 Official Baseball Record Book* (St. Louis: The Sporting News, 1975), 41.

16. F. C. Lane, "Who is the Greatest Player in the History of Baseball?" *Baseball Magazine*, VIII, no. 3 (1911), 27–34.

17. John Ward played for various National League teams (Providence, New York, Brooklyn) between 1878 and 1894. He was also the first president of the Brotherhood of Professional Baseball Players. He played with O'Neill on the 1883 New York Gothams and against him in the 1888 world championship series.

18. John J. Ward, "1887, the Black Sheep of Baseball Records," *Baseball Magazine*, XV, no. 2 (1915), 74.

19. Ernest J. Lanigan, *Baseball Cyclopedia* (1922; Reprinted Jefferson, NC: McFarland, 2005), 72, 74.

20. *Ibid.*, 71.

21. F. C. Lane, "One Batting Championship that Never was Deserved," *Baseball Magazine*, XXX, no. 6 (1923), 547.

22. *Ibid.*

23. *Ibid.*

24. *Ibid.*, 548.

25. *Ibid.* Lane argued that there were three games where Elias was able to determine the number of hits but not whether any came on a base on balls. Lane further noted that it was possible that O'Neill had more than 53 walks, which would in turn reduce his number of actual hits and drop his batting average to below .430.

26. *Ibid*, 547–548. In the article, Lane's revisionist stance was evident in his implicit argument for comparability, demonstrated through his desire to correct the statistics of 1887 by treating a base on balls as in every other season, that is neither as a hit nor as a time at bat. He commented on how a base on balls should be in "its proper niche." He remarked on the "damage" done to the records by the base-on-balls-as-a-hit rule. He also stated that O'Neill's 53 bases on balls were "no hits at all." And in recalculating O'Neill's batting average, he first subtracted 53 bases on balls from the number of hits and from his total times at bat, "which we should do," again as is the case in all other seasons.

27. Clifford Bloodgood, "Ted Williams vs. Tip O'Neill," *Baseball Magazine*, LXXX, no.6 (1948), 403.

28. John B. Foster, "The First Five Batters," *Baseball Magazine*, LXI, no. 2, (July 1938), 371.

29. O'Neill began with the Browns in 1884 as a pitcher. He developed a sore arm that "remained unimpaired," so he switched to left field, where he became the Browns' leading slugger. W. W. Aulick, "Tip O'Neill, Who Batted for .492 'After His Arm Gave Out,'" *New York Times*, 1911. Article in the clippings file of James Edward O'Neill, Baseball Hall of Fame, Cooperstown, New York.

30. G. W. Axelson, *"Commy:" The Life and Story of Charles A. Comiskey* (1919; Reprinted, Jefferson, NC: McFarland, 2003), 69–70.

31. In addition to the articles that directly challenged O'Neill's record in 1887 (such as those reviewed earlier by Ward, Lane, Lanigan, and Bloodgood), the questionability of his batting average was noted in more general articles about the St. Louis Browns, the world championships in the 1880s, or the rules in earlier seasons. For example, *The Sporting News* published a few articles that included comments that questioned O'Neill's 1887 batting record, such as: "Pennant-Winning Browns of the Atrocious 1880s," *The Sporting News*, July 4, 1940, 9; Frederick G. Lieb, "World's Series Foundation Laid in Unsanctioned Clash of 1882," *The Sporting News*, October 31, 1940, 9; J. Roy Stockton, "Antique Rules Helped Inflate Old-Time Marks," *The Sporting News*, May 3, 1961, 2, 4; and Frederick G. Lieb, "How Times Change! So Do Game's Rules, Feats. Walk Counted as Hit in '87; Ball Pepped Up in '20, '21," *The Sporting News*, November 16, 1963, 7–8. See also Harry Simmons, "The National League of 1887," *Baseball Magazine*, LXIX, no. 6, November 1942, 549.

32. *The Baseball Encyclopedia: The Complete and Official Record of Major League Baseball* (Toronto: Macmillan, 1969), 5.

33. *Ibid.*

34. *Ibid.*, 2327.

35. *Ibid.*, 2328.

36. The ICI data, when converted to the 1887 scoring rules, work out to 275 hits, based on 225 "actual" hits plus 50 bases on balls, two fewer than the 277 hits reported in 1887. Based on the 1887 statistics of 277 hits and a .492 batting average, O'Neill had 563 times at bat. The ICI data, when converted to the 1887 scoring rules, increased the times at bat to 567, based on 517 times at bat plus 50 times on bat from bases on balls, four fewer than the 563 calculated from the hits and average reported in 1887.

37. *Ibid.*, 1310.

38. At the end of the 1894 season, in the *Spalding Guide* and most record books before 1969, Duffy's average for 1894 was listed as .438. "The Official Averages for 1894," *Spalding's Official Base Ball Guide, 1894* (Chicago: A. G. Spalding and Bros., 1894), 131. The ICI research adjusted Duffy's average to .440, which was then published in *The Baseball Encyclopedia.* Since 1969, in most compendia and databases, Duffy's average for 1894 is listed as .440. John Thorn, Pete Palmer, and Joseph M. Wayman, "Evolution of Baseball Records," *Total Baseball: The Ultimate Baseball Encyclopedia,* 8th ed. (Toronto: SPORT Media, 2004), 2436.

39. David Voigt, "Denny Lyons' 52-Game Hitting Streak," *National Pastime: A Review of Baseball History* 13 (1993), 49. See also David Voigt, "Fie on Figure Filberts: Some Crimes Against Clio," Accessed May 13, 2017, from http://sabr.org/researchjournalarchives/BRJ-1983.

40. Jerome Holtzman, "An Important Change to the Official Record of Major League Baseball," Accessed on May 13, 2017, from https://ourgame.mlbblogs.com/why-is-the-national-association-not-a-major-league-and-other-record-issues.

41. In his announcement of changes to the official records, after noting that O'Neill was the batting champion in the American Association, at .492, Holtzman included the following in parentheses: "(As with Radford, an arithmetic correction reduces O'Neill's average to .485, still the all-time record)." The "correction" was discovered when the ICI-generated numbers were used to recalculate O'Neill's batting average of 1887, counting a base on balls as a hit and time at bat once again. Thus 50 walks were added to 225 hits and to 517 times at bat, giving 275 hits in 567 at-bats, which worked out to a .485 average. But what was being corrected? As worded, it seemed that .485 was a correction of the .492 batting average reported in 1887. However, strictly speaking, the .485 average was not a correction of .492. The implication in Holtzman's announcement seemed to be that Wikoff, the president and secretary of the American Association, who was responsible for the final determination of the official averages, made an arithmetic error in the calculation of O'Neill's average. But the game reports on which Wikoff relied to determine O'Neill's .492 average were no longer available. From what Wikoff reported, it appeared that he came up with different numbers, that is 277 hits and, as noted in note no. 10 above, 563 times at bat. Without an opportunity to review the game reports that Wikoff worked with and to re-do the tabulations he made based on these game-by-game numbers, it was not possible to check for errors that he might have made. The most that can be said, based on the evidence available, was that the batting average based on the ICI-generated numbers was different from the average presented by Wikoff. Many will side with the ICI-based .485 average because of the data collected by ICI and the rigorous process on which it was based. However, this is an evidentiary preference and not a correction.

42. John Thorn, Pete Palmer, and Michael Gershman, *Total Baseball: The Ultimate Baseball Encyclopedia,* 7th ed. (Toronto: SPORT Media, 2004), 551–52, 1066, 2065, 2326; and John Thorn, Phil Birnbaum, and Bill Deane, *Total Baseball: The Ultimate Baseball Encyclopedia,* 8th ed. (Toronto: SPORT Media, 2004), 38, 1512, 2438, 2459, 2485.

43. I took a photograph of the poster and copied the text during a visit to the National Baseball Hall of Fame on July 22, 2011.

44. In the first publication of its record book in 1972 (and before 1972 in its publications of *The Little Red Book of Baseball*), the Elias Sports Bureau reported O'Neill's average for 1887 as .492 with an asterisk and the following qualification in parentheses: (bases on balls considered hits in 1887). By the early 1980s, it listed O'Neill's average as .442. Seymour Siwoff, ed., *The Elias Book of Baseball Records, 2016 Edition* (New York: Elias Sports Bureau, 2016), 7.

45. Since the first publication of its record book in 1972 (and before 1972 in its publications of *The Little Red Book of Baseball*), the Elias Sports Bureau listed Hugh Duffy's 1894 average as .438. Seymour Siwoff, ed., *The Elias Book of Baseball Records, 2016 Edition* (New York: Elias Sports Bureau, 2016), 7.

46. In the final edition of *The Official Encyclopedia of Baseball,* in the section on "Four Hundred Batters," O'Neill was listed first among 1887 batters with an average of .492. Just below the list, a note explained that walks counted as hits that year. It further stated that, if walks were not counted as hits, just three batters would have hit over .400, with O'Neill still on top with an average of .442. See Hy Turkin and S. C. Thompson, Revisions by Pete Palmer. *The Official Encyclopedia of Baseball,* 10th ed. (Garden City, NY: Dolphin, 1979), 512.

47. In their chapter on the history of baseball statistics, Thorn, Palmer, and Wayman described the changes in relation to four stages: (1) The Origins, 1845–1875; (2) The Flowering, 1876–1920; (3) The Golden Age, 1920–1968; and (4) The Computer Age, 1969–. John Thorn, Pete Palmer, and Joseph M. Wayman, "The History of Major League Baseball Statistics," in John Thorn, Phil Birnbaum, and Bill Deane, *Total Baseball: The Ultimate Baseball Encyclopedia,* 8th ed., 951–962.

48. In the *Baseball Cyclopedia,* Lanigan produced lists of leaders in a number of batting categories, most of which included players in the National League and American Association in the last two decades of the nineteenth century. Though O'Neill's 167 runs scored and 277 hits in 1887 would have placed him near the top on both lists, his name only appeared well down the list of "Leading Manufacturers of Base Hits" for his 176 hits in 1888. Ernest J. Lanigan, *Baseball Cyclopedia* (1922; Reprinted Jefferson, NC: McFarland, 2005), 79–83.

49. F. C. Lane, ed., *The Little Red Book of Major League Baseball* (New York: Al Munro Elias Baseball Bureau, 1948), 15. Note that, unlike the conclusion in his 1923 article, where he argued that O'Neill's batting average was ".430 or possibly a shade less," not counting bases on balls as hits, Lane listed O'Neill's .492 average in 1887 in three places in the book, namely, in "Champion Batters in Major Leagues" (page 9), in parentheses at the end of the entry on "Individual Batting Records—Highest percentage (100 or more games), season" (11), and in "Major League Players Who Have Batted .400 or Better" (19).

50. Joseph G. Donner, "Hitting for the Cycle," *Baseball Research Journal* 10 (1981). Accessed on November 3, 2017, through SABR Research Journal Archives at http://research.sabr.org/hitting-for-the-cycle.

51. John Thorn, Pete Palmer, Michael Gershman, and David Pietrusza, *Total Baseball: The Official Encyclopedia of Major League Baseball*, 5th ed. (New York: Viking, 1997), 1512.

52. Gary Gillette and Pete Palmer, *The ESPN Baseball Encyclopedia*, 5th ed. (New York: Sterling, 2008), 1821.

53. Nemec, *The Beer and Whiskey League*, 128.

54. David Nemec, ed., "O'Neill, James Edward/'Tip,'" *Major League Baseball Profiles: 1871–1900, Volume 1*. (Lincoln: University of Nebraska Press, 2011), 589.

55. "Long hits" refer to extra-base hits, that is doubles, triples, or home runs. Dickson, *The Dickson Baseball Dictionary*, 514.

Chapter 1

1. The "crack" by Tip O'Neill described here occurred in Game Two of the 1886 World Championship Series between Chicago and St. Louis. The game was played in Chicago in the West Side Park. The Park was only 216 feet down each foul line but over 500 feet from the plate to center field. A ball hit to left-center then would be over 400 feet from home. Philip Lowry, *Green Cathedrals: The Ultimate Celebration of Major League and Negro League Ballparks* (New York: Walker, 2006), 49.

2. "Beer Beats Them. Chicago's Nine Receive the Season's Worst Defeat at the Hands of Von der Ahe's Players," *Chicago Inter Ocean*, October 20, 1886, 2.

3. "Kicking" was a term used to describe "protesting a decision made by the umpire." Paul Dickson, *The Dickson Baseball Dictionary*, 3d ed. (New York: W.W. Norton, 2009), 481.

4. "Browns Take Revenge. They Slaughter Anson's Helpless Infants Without Mercy," *Chicago Tribune*, October 20, 1886, 2.

5. In Games Two and Five, the two owners and presidents, Albert Spalding of Chicago and Chris Von der Ahe of St. Louis, decided to try a two-umpires-and-one-referee system. McQuaid, from the National League, umpired when the Browns were at bat, and Quest, an American Association umpire, was in charge when Chicago was at bat. Kelly, an American Association umpire, positioned himself behind the pitcher with no men on base and behind second with men on base. The umpire not on duty was the only person who could question a call of the on-duty umpire. If the second umpire disagreed with the call, the referee would be approached to make the final judgment on the play. See Peter Morris, *A Game of Inches: The Story Behind the Innovations That Shaped Baseball* (Chicago: Ivan R. Dee, 2010), 253–255.

6. "To guy" means to jeer or make fun of. Dickson, *The Dickson Baseball Dictionary*, 393.

7. By mutual consent, the game was called at the end of the eighth inning on account of darkness. "Hip, Hip, Hurrah! The Greatest Base Ball Victory of the Ages," *St. Louis Republican*, October 20, 1886, 6.

8. "Sporting: St. Louis 12; Chicago 0," *St. Louis Globe-Democrat*, October 20, 1886, 8.

9. "Hip, Hip, Hurrah!" 6.

10. Rule 55 (1) read as follows: "The base runner shall return to his base, and shall be entitled to so return without being put out, provided he do so on the run. (1) If the umpire declares a foul hit, and the ball be not legally caught by a fielder." "Playing Rules of the National League of Professional Base Ball Clubs of 1886," *Spalding's Base Ball Guide: Official League Book for 1886* (1886; Reprinted New York: Horton, 1989), 97.

11. "A Big Dose. St. Louis Gives Chicago Some of its Own Medicine," *Cincinnati Enquirer*, October 20, 1886, 2.

12. "Hip, Hip, Hurrah!" 6.

13. "Gossip of the Game," *Chicago Tribune*, October 20, 1886, 2.

14. A delayed double steal occurs with runners on first and third with less than two out. The man on first starts for second as if he is trying to steal the base. He either delays his takeoff or slows his pace between first and second, daring the catcher to throw him out. If the runner on first does draw a throw by the catcher to second, the runner at third has a better chance to score, especially if he edges down the line to increase his lead and can time his run for home to coincide with or quickly follow the release of the ball from the catcher's hand. Peter Morris, *A Game of Inches: The Story Behind the Innovations That Shaped Baseball* (Chicago: Ivan R. Dee, 2010), 180–181.

15. "All in a Heap. Chicago Champions do not Know What Struck Them," *St. Louis Post-Dispatch*, October 20, 1886, 7.

16. "Base Ball. St. Louis Turns the Tables on Chicago," *Cincinnati Commercial Gazette*, October 20, 1886.

17. The major Chicago newspapers did not report this incident (i.e., *Chicago Tribune, Chicago Inter Ocean, Chicago Daily News, Chicago Herald, Chicago Times*). The *St. Louis Globe-Democrat* and the *St. Louis Republican* did not mention Welch's arm hitting McCormick's arm.

18. "Hip, Hip, Hurrah!" 6.

19. In the nineteenth century, a "crank" was another word for a baseball fan. Dickson, *The Dickson Baseball Dictionary*, 223.

20. "Nine" refers to a baseball team. Dickson, *The Dickson Baseball Dictionary*, 580.

21. In its sub-heading, the *Boston Globe* declared: "Anson's Pets Chicagoed by the Browns," October 20, 1886, 2. The verb "to Chicago" means to shut out another team. Dickson, *The Dickson Baseball Dictionary*, 181–182.

22. "Base Ball. St. Louis Turns the Tables on Chicago," *Cincinnati Commercial Gazette*, October 20, 1886.

23. "The Lost Game," *St. Louis Post-Dispatch*, October 20, 1886, 7.

24. Jon Cash, *Before They Were Cardinals: Major League Baseball in Nineteenth-Century St. Louis* (Columbia: University of Missouri Press, 2002), 127. After the game, Comiskey expressed regret for the mistake in pitching Caruthers two games in a row, but in deference to Von der Ahe declined to say anything further. "Home Again. The Browns Arrive from the City by the Lake This Morning," *St. Louis Post-Dispatch*, October 21, 1886.

25. "Home Again," 7.

26. In 1886, when the team was at bat, often one coach stood in foul territory near third base and another was in foul territory near first base. Ostensibly coaches cheered on their own players, gave advice to runners on the base paths, and, on occasion, questioned the call of the umpire. Comiskey, Latham, and Gleason took turns coaching beside the two bases. They were known for their noisy coaching, kicking, and aggressive tactics. By 1887, the two leagues introduced rules to govern where coaches positioned themselves and what they were permitted to say or do. "The National Playing Rules," *Reach's Official American Association Base Ball*

Guide, 1887 (1887; Reprinted New York: Horton, 1989), 148–166.

27. "Chicago Wins," *Chicago Daily News,* October 18, 1886.

28. "Amusing Themselves. Chicago's Ball-Players Give the St. Louis Amateurs an Object-Lesson in Batting," *Chicago Times,* October 18, 1886.

29. "The Browns Massacred. Anson's Men Wipe up the Earth with the Pets," *Chicago Tribune,* October 19, 1886, 2.

30. "Editorial," *Chicago Daily News,* October 21, 1886.

31. The ground rules at Sportsman's Park in St. Louis stipulated that a fielder who retrieved a ball hit into the crowd in right field had first to return the ball to the pitcher before a play could be made on a runner. "Didn't We, Though? How We Did Give It to the Chicago Champs Yesterday!" *St. Louis Republican,* October 22, 1886, 6.

32. Clarkson insisted that the base on balls in the sixth inning was not intentional. He claimed that he was simply trying to pitch O'Neill carefully. Most other reports of the second base on balls argued or implied that it was not different from the deliberate or intentional walk issued in the fifth inning. "That's the Way! Capt. Anson Babies Have Nothing to Say About their Defeat," *St. Louis Post-Dispatch,* October 22, 1886, 7.

33. In the regular season, Williamson had pitched 3 innings and Ryan 23⅓ innings, all in relief.

34. "How to Bring Out Our Rooster Again. The Base Ball Champions of America and the World," *St. Louis Republican,* October 24, 1886, 14.

35. In a post-game interview, Kelly explained what happened on the final pitch and accepted the responsibility for the miscue as a passed ball. Some newspapers called it a wild pitch. For a recent account of the final game, see Bob Tiemann, "Curt Welch's Winning Slide," in Bill Felber, ed., *Inventing Baseball: The 100 Greatest Games of the Nineteenth Century* (Phoenix: SABR, 2013), 184–186.

36. For descriptions of the St. Louis celebration, see "As Seen from the Grand Stand," *St. Louis Republican,* October 24, 1886, 14; "Sporting. St. Louis 4; Chicago 3," *St. Louis Globe-Democrat,* October 24, 1886, 11.

37. "St. Louis Crazy," *Chicago Daily News,* October 23, 1886.

38. The Browns and Maroons agreed to play a nine-game series to determine the championship of St. Louis. The Browns beat the Maroons four straight times before the start of the series with Chicago. Their 6-5 victory was the Browns' fifth successive win over the Maroons and thus gave them the local championship. "Sporting: The Browns Again Victorious Over the Maroons," *St. Louis Republican,* October 25, 1886, 5.

39. *The Sporting News* summarized batting and fielding averages for the six-game series. The final column under batting was labeled "T.B. Ave." or Total Base Average, a forerunner of today's slugging percentage. "Figures," *The Sporting News,* October 30, 1886, 3.

Chapter 2

1. A number of players played right field during these three years. Hugh Nicol played right field in 111 of 112 games in 1885 and in 56 of 139 games in 1886. He was traded at the end of 1886 to Cincinnati. In 1886 and 1887, either Caruthers and Foutz played right field when they were not pitching. Caruthers was the right fielder for 42 games in 1886 and 50 games in 1887. Foutz was the right fielder for 34 games in 1886 and 50 games in 1887.

2. Most sources (e.g., *Baseball Reference, Retrosheet, Major League Baseball*) list O'Neill's date of birth as May 25, 1858. The Canadian Baseball Hall of Fame, based on a review of Canadian census reports, indicates that O'Neill's birth date was May 25, 1861. I located a record of O'Neill's baptism in the Archives of the Diocese of London in London, Ontario, in the *General Register of Ingersoll's Mission including Ingersoll, Woodstock, Norwich, and East Oxford 1850–1879.* The baptismal record lists O'Neill's birth date as June 15, 1860, the date I cite on the card. Most of the Canadian census records support 1860 as the year of his birth. In addition, in the many profiles of O'Neill in 1883-to-1892 newspapers in cities where he played, his reported age usually verified or suggested that 1860 was his year of birth. Of these various sources, other than the 1901 Canadian census which lists April 15 as his birth month and day, the baptismal record is the only source that includes the year, month, and day of his birth.

3. The eight O'Neill children were (with year of birth in parentheses): John (1857), James (Tip) (1860), George (1863), Clara (1867), Teresa (1869), Joseph (1872), D'Arcy (1875), and Agnes (1877).

4. Between 1860 and 1867, Tip's father was a hotelkeeper in the following villages or small towns near Woodstock (distance to Woodstock shown in parentheses): Springfield (27 miles), Norwich (15 miles), and Port Rowan (39 miles). In Woodstock, his father managed the International Hotel and the Market Hotel before he built the O'Neill House, which he owned and managed until his untimely death in 1883. Tip was used to living in hotels and to moving regularly from hotel to hotel, both experiences that would help him adjust to life as a baseball player.

5. Nancy Bouchier, *For the Love of the Game: Amateur Sport in Small-Town Ontario 1838–1895* (Montreal: McGill-Queen's University Press, 2003), 42.

6. Ibid. In 1866, the Young Canadians was the first baseball team of prominence in Woodstock. It beat Dundas, 98–50, in front of 1,500 fans. Two years later, the Young Canadians competed against the Ingersoll Victorias for the Silver Ball, the emblem of the Canadian baseball championship. William Humber observed: "Throughout the 1860s, Woodstock would be the best Canadian team." William Humber, *Diamonds of the North: A Concise History of Baseball in Canada* (Toronto: Oxford University Press, 1995), 26.

7. Brother George Morgan, *La Sallian Education: 150 Years in Toronto* (Toronto: Brothers of the Christian Schools, 2001), 22.

8. Doug M. Symons, "O'Neill, James Edward," in *Giants of Oxford: Women and Men Who Changed the World* (Woodstock: Woodstock Historical Society, 2001), 64–67.

9. Throughout O'Neill's career, newspapers usually misspelled his last name, typically leaving out the second "l", that is, "O'Neil," as it appears here, instead of the correct spelling of "O'Neill."

10. "Town and Country. Base Ball," *Woodstock Sentinel-Review,* March 29, 1878, 1.

11. The Canadian Baseball Association sent the team a streamer (24 feet long, eight feet wide) that read: "Actives of Woodstock, 1878, Champions of Canada." "Laurels," *Woodstock Sentinel-Review,* December 27, 1878, 1.

12. "Not True," *Woodstock Sentinel-Review*, June 20, 1879, 5.

13. An article that celebrated O'Neill's successful 1886 season and his batting feats in the World Championship Series began: "James E. O'Neill, better known to Woodstock people as 'Tip,' arrived home from St. Louis last evening after finishing the most successful season he has ever had." "One of the World-Beaters," *Woodstock Sentinel-Review*, November 11, 1886, 1.

14. "Our Browns," *St. Louis Post-Dispatch*, May 3, 1884, 9.

15. "St. Louis Siftings. Mac and Tip," *Sporting Life*, October 3, 1891, 8. Note that Campbell, the author of this article, did not identify the source of this explanation. He did not quote O'Neill or indicate that he had spoken with O'Neill or with someone from Woodstock who might have witnessed or heard about either O'Neill's poor performance in "Tip and Slasher" or confirmed the story of how his nickname was based on playing the role of Tip on stage. At the same time, it is possible that O'Neill might have taken to the stage for such a performance. He came from a family, notably his father and brother George, who told stories and sang at various occasions and celebrations in Woodstock. O'Neill himself had a "musical voice" and was "a splendid singer." Prior to the start of the 1886 world championship, as part of a banquet for the Browns at Furber's, a St. Louis restaurant, O'Neill was one of three players who sang a solo. After the 1886 season, he traveled for a brief time with the McNish, Johnson and Slavin Minstrels, singing and performing in skits with the troupe. "Diamond Dust," *St. Louis Globe-Democrat*, March 28, 1886, 9; "Base Ball Notes," *St. Louis Republican*, November 8, 1886, 3; "A Banquet to the Browns," *St. Louis Globe-Democrat*, October 13, 1886, 5. The *Sporting Life* article stated: "Jim never being possessed of a serious disposition suggested that the old farce, 'Tip and Slasher,' be put on." I did not find a nineteenth century farce entitled "Tip and Slasher." The source for Campbell's article may have gotten the title wrong. Or O'Neill and his fellow actors might have created their own farce or adapted it from a published farce. John Maddison Morton, an English dramatist, produced numerous one-act farces, one entitled "Slasher and Crasher," published in 1848, and another, "Who Stole the Pocket-Book, Or, A Dinner for Six," first published in 1857, with Mr. Tipthorpe as one of the characters. O'Neill and his fellow actors might have renamed and adapted one or more of Morton's farces for their purposes. John Maddison Morton, *Slasher and Crasher! An Original Farce* (New York: Samuel French, 1895) and John Maddison Morton, *Who Stole the Pocket-Book, Or, A Dinner for Six* (Boston: W. V. Spencer, 1857).

16. "Chris Von der Ahe, The Most Picturesque Figure in Baseball History," *St. Louis Post-Dispatch*, April 17, 1904, 40. When O'Neill was at the plate, he seemed relaxed, almost indifferent as he awaited the pitch. His swing was controlled and timed to meet the ball squarely as it crossed the plate. He was not given to excessive or exaggerated movements. O'Neill frequently made solid contact, driving the ball on a line into the field. In short, Von der Ahe's description of O'Neill's stance and swing captured how he hit the ball. However, I have found no references to this explanation as the basis of O'Neill's nickname during the years he played in St. Louis (1884–1889, 1891). It is puzzling that this nickname did not appear in St. Louis until late 1886, even though O'Neill's stance and slugging were well established in his first two years with the Browns (1884–1885). There is also no reference to this tip-the-ball explanation during the period following the first time that the nickname "Tip" appeared in press (1879) in the newspapers in Woodstock (1879–1881) or New York (1881–1883).

17. "Honoured Member. James O'Neill. Inducted in 1994." Accessed March 23, 2017, http://www.sportshall.ca. O'Neill was a patient batsman and did wait out a pitcher until he got a pitch he wanted. However, while the hitting-the-ball-foul explanation of the origin of his nickname also seems possible, many batsmen in the 1870s were reluctant to use such a strategy for fear that they might inadvertently hit a one-bounce foul ball that could be caught for an out (a rule in force at that time). Peter Morris, *A Game of Inches: The Story Behind the Innovations That Shaped Baseball* (Chicago: Ivan R. Dee, 2010), 59–63. Although this deliberate fouling strategy resurfaced in the mid-1880s, I have yet to find a game report in his Woodstock years (1877–1881) or in the years he played in the United States (1882–1892) where O'Neill used such a fouling strategy.

18. Along the way, O'Neill had brief stops with a number of semi-professional and professional clubs: Franklin Club of Chicago (1880); Detroit Club, just prior to the start of its first year in the National League (1881); Hiawathas, a barnstorming team out of Detroit (1881); and the Hartford Club, an independent professional team (1883). For a reference to the Chicago and Detroit teams, see "James E. O'Neil," *New York Clipper*, April 28, 1883, 85.

19. O'Neill's win-loss record was likely higher than 41–14. The reports on the games in the Woodstock newspapers and in most of the newspapers in the towns where the Actives played were brief, often without a box score, or if there was a box score, only outs and runs were listed. Sometimes a game was announced in the newspaper a few days ahead of when it was scheduled, but then was not mentioned again in a later issue. It could have been played but not reported or just cancelled. Since O'Neill was the only pitcher on the team and since the Actives won many of the games they played in these years, it seems reasonable to claim that both the team's and O'Neill's records would include more than 41 wins and 14 losses.

20. O'Neill's first no-hitter was a 1–0 win over Guelph. "Base Ball Notes. The Woodstock Actives Defeat the Leafs by a Score of 1 to 0," *Guelph Mercury*, August 23, 1878. The second no-hitter occurred the following year as part of a one-week, six-game tour of western New York State. Woodstock beat Batavia, 22–0. In addition to throwing the no-hitter, O'Neill had five hits. The Woodstock newspaper reprinted the report from the *Batavia New York Daily News*. "Our 'Actives' Abroad. How They Goose-Egged the Batavias," *Woodstock Sentinel-Review*, August 8, 1879, 1.

21. "James E. O'Neil," 85.

22. In O'Neill's first game in the box for the Hartford Club, he beat the West Ends, a "colored" team from Long Beach, New Jersey (newspapers of the time typically referred to black or Afro-Americans as "colored"). He struck out 15 batters. "Swinging the Ash. The Hartfords Beat the West Ends," *Hartford Times*, September 15, 1883. A few

days later, O'Neill pitched a no-hitter, beating a team from Holyoke, Massachusetts, 11–1. "The Holyokes O'Neiled. Nine Innings and Not a Base Hit," *Hartford Times*, October 2, 1883.

23. "The Metropolitans," *New York Clipper*, November 3, 1883, 543.

24. "Base Ball," *Woodstock Weekly Review*, June 14, 1878, 4; "Sporting Matters," *Detroit Free Press*, April 30, 1881, 1; "Baseball," *New York Clipper*, April 8, 1882, 39; "James E. O'Neil," 85; "Diamond Dust," *St. Louis Globe-Democrat*, March 25, 1884, 8; and "Our Browns," 9.

25. "Metropolitan vs. Princeton," *New York Clipper*, April 22, 1882, 73.

26. In 1880, the Chicago Franklins did not have a catcher who could cope with O'Neill's speed. "Baseball. A Canadian Player," *Toronto Mail*, April 28, 1881; Peter Morris, *Catcher: How the Man Behind the Plate Became an American Folk Hero* (Chicago, Ivan R. Dee, 2009), 133–134. That same season, when O'Neill returned to Woodstock, the Actives had lost twice in August to Guelph, their archrivals. Lew Brown, a Boston catcher who had been expelled from the National League that year for dissipation, joined the Actives in September. He was able to catch O'Neill more effectively than the local catcher. With Brown catching, O'Neill and the Actives beat Guelph twice, 17–2 and 1–0, the second game on a no-hitter. "Base Ball Match," *Woodstock Sentinel-Review*, September 3, 1880, 1; "Base Ball. The Actives Whitewash the Maple Leafs," *Woodstock Sentinel-Review*, September 10, 1880, 1. In 1881, O'Neill had a brief tryout with the Detroit club at the start of its first season in the National League. Frank Bancroft, the Detroit manager, reluctantly released O'Neill before the start of the 1881 season. Years later, he explained: "He is the fastest pitcher I have ever seen, but if he gets pitching wild it will take four men and a truck horse to stop his cannon shots." "Players with a Record," *Boston Globe*, October 17, 1887, 8. In both years in New York, John Clapp was the catcher most often assigned to form a battery with O'Neill. When O'Neill signed with the Browns in 1884, Jimmy Williams, the manager, noted that Clapp had never really mastered the skill of catching O'Neill. Buck Ewing, the first-string catcher of the 1883 New York Gothams, refused to catch him, apparently concerned that he might be injured by O'Neill's fastball. "His Ideas. Manager Williams Reviews the St. Louis Browns for '84," *St. Louis Post-Dispatch*, December 28, 1883, 5.

27. One example of O'Neill's wildness occurred in a game that he nonetheless won. The New York Gothams beat Philadelphia, 16–6, with the aid of a 13-run third inning. In this seven-inning game, O'Neill allowed ten hits, struck out three batters, walked six, and threw six wild pitches, while the two catchers—the starting catcher had to leave after two innings—had five passed balls. "Base Ball Hard Hitters. Decided Victory of the New York Nine over the Philadelphias," *New York Times*, September 9, 1883, 2.

28. "A felon on his right hand unfortunately prevented him from playing during the latter part of the season." "James E. O'Neil," 85.

29. In mid-June 1884, O'Neill, plagued by a sore arm, asked for time off to allow his arm to recover. Jimmy Williams agreed, but Von der Ahe wanted O'Neill to be examined by a physician in Baltimore. His diagnosis was inflammatory rheumatism, and his recommended treatment was "to exercise in warm weather." O'Neill strenuously disagreed with the recommendation, but Von der Ahe insisted that O'Neill continue to throw. Within two weeks, O'Neill was back in the rotation, the starter for games on June 17, 19, and 23. Despite one good start, it was apparent that his arm had not recovered and, as it turned out, his arm never did regain its old form for the rest of his career. After his three games in June, O'Neill started only three more games (July 6 and 12, August 30). He was re-assigned to left field. "A Chat with the Browns' President," *St. Louis Post-Dispatch*, June 20, 1884, 5.

30. With the limited information on games between 1877 and 1881, it is difficult to be precise about O'Neill's record as a batsman. O'Neill was often the leadoff batter, perhaps adhering to Chadwick's earlier advice: "Let your first striker be the coolest hand of the nine." Henry Chadwick, *Haney's Base Ball Player's Book of Reference for 1867* (New York, 1867), 83. Tip was once awarded $3.00 as the best batsman in the game. See "Dominion Day Celebration. The Base Ball Match," *Woodstock Weekly Review*, July 5, 1878, 1. In the reports of games that included a detailed box score and some comments on the game, O'Neill was frequently mentioned as the leader in runs scored and in the number of hits.

31. O'Neill saw action in 40 of the 162 games played by the New York Metropolitans in 1882 and in 23 of the 98 regular season games of the New York Gothams in 1883. "James E. O'Neil," 85. At the beginning of the 1884 season, O'Neill was also described as a "very hard batsman." "Our Browns," 9. His batting averages, .248 in 1882 with the Metropolitans and .197 in 1883 with the Gothams seemed far from the kind of numbers one might attribute to an "excellent" or "very heavy" hitter. However, Tip delivered more than was expected from someone who was a change pitcher. Furthermore, he had two or more hits in 12 of the 40 games he played in 1882 and, on occasion, hit for power.

32. "Batting Averages," *St. Louis Republican*, June 29, 1884.

33. O'Neill and his Woodstock teammates had often been described as gentlemanly. For example, they were represented as a "fine lot of well-behaved young gentlemen" in the report on the Woodstock Actives' 22–0 win over Batavia. "Our 'Actives' Abroad," 1. In 1883, he was again praised for his character: "He is moreover, an earnest and faithful worker, and his quiet and courteous demeanor, together with his acknowledged ability as a pitcher, has secured him widespread popularity." See "James E. O'Neil," 85.

34. "Our Browns," 9.

35. "A Disgraceful Performance," *Baltimore Sun*, July 3, 1884, 4.

36. "Disgrace to the Calling," *St. Louis Republican*, July 3, 1884, 6.

37. "Notes," *Baltimore American*, July 5, 1884.

38. "Diamond Dust," *St. Louis Globe-Democrat*, July 10, 1884, 8.

39. The *St. Louis Globe-Democrat* conveyed O'Neill's version of this incident: "Jim O'Neill claims that he had no connection with the trouble on Tuesday night and that the reports regarding him were unfounded." "Lewis Suspended," *St. Louis Globe-Democrat*, July 3, 1884, 8. O'Neill knew Emslie and so it seems likely that he would have gone out with him. Three newspapers were quite clear and specific in their account of how the disrup-

tion was started by O'Neill. I am inclined to believe the story of O'Neill's involvement and that he had the "street" smarts, given that he had grown up in hotels and saloons, to know how to escape before the police arrived.

40. "Lively Ball Talk," *St. Louis Sunday Sayings,* April 12, 1885.

41. There are different reports of the Batting Record of 1885. In the official record of the day, Browning (Louisville) had the highest average at .367. Dave Orr (New York) finished second at .366, and O'Neill and Harry Stovey (Philadelphia) were tied for third with .342. In the custom in effect in the American Association in 1885, any player made it to the "official" list if he played a minimum of five games. O'Neill was in the lineup in 52 of the 112 games played by the Browns, so he appeared on the official list as one of the leading batsmen of the Association. "Official Averages of the Players and Clubs of the American Association. Players Batting Record," *Reach's Official American Association Base Ball Guide 1886* (1886; Reprinted New York: Horton, 1989), 39. Following a thorough survey conducted in the 1960s by Information Concepts Incorporated of all available nineteenth century sources (mainly newspapers and weeklies), the batting averages were adjusted. In *The Baseball Encyclopedia* published in 1969, the top three batters listed were Browning at .362, Orr at .342, and Larkin at .329. O'Neill's batting average was recalculated to .350. However, he was not on the leaders list presumably because he did not reach the minimum number of plate appearances required for this list. *The Baseball Encyclopedia* (Toronto: Macmillan, 1969), 5–8, 115, 1309. The major databases today, for example, Baseball Reference, Retrosheet, or Fan Graphs, show the same leaders and batting averages as reported in *The Baseball Encyclopedia.* The databases use the 1957 rule to determine league leaders, namely, to be eligible for consideration, a player must have a minimum of 3.1 plate appearances per team game played. Based on this formula, O'Neill needed 347 plate appearances (3.1 × 112 games played by the Browns) before he could be considered for the list. He had only 223 plate appearances. In short, O'Neill was included on the list of official averages in 1885 and repeatedly reported as one of the leading batsmen in the press that year. He is not on the 1885 leader's list for batting average in contemporary databases, record books, and encyclopedia.

42. O'Neill played 138 games in 1886, the most he ever played in one season.

43. For much of the 1886 season and indeed well after the season ended, Munson, the official scorekeeper of the Browns, believed that O'Neill was ahead of Caruthers in batting average. "Under the New Rules," *St. Louis Sunday Sayings,* January 30, 1887.

44. "Sporting: St. Louis 8; Brooklyns 6," *St. Louis Globe-Democrat,* October 11, 1886, 6.

45. The official batting statistics of 1886 were published in the 1887 *Reach's Guide.* Dave Orr was declared the batting champion with an average of .346. In 1969, *The Baseball Encyclopedia* reported on the findings from the study conducted by Information Concepts Incorporated (ICI), which discovered that Guy Hecker won the batting title with an average of .341. The first two rows of the following table present the batting average of the first five batters in the *Reach's Guide* and *The Baseball Encyclopedia.* The third row includes the same averages for Hecker, Browning, and Orr as listed in *The Baseball Encyclopedia* and the averages I found for O'Neill and Caruthers after my review of the 1886 game reports. In each source, Caruthers had a better average than O'Neill.

46. Runs Batted In (RBI) were not recorded in the nineteenth century and did not become an official statistic in major league baseball until 1920. In the twentieth century, researchers calculated that O'Neill had 107 RBI, the highest number in the American Association in 1886. In my review of 1886, I list O'Neill with 111 RBI.

47. As the season unfolded, and as O'Neill became one of the leading batsman, the newspapers searched for more ways to describe his slugging prowess. For "heavy batsman," see "Gossip of the Game," *St. Louis Post-Dispatch,* June 5, 1886, 12; for "giant swing," see "Diamond Chips," *St. Louis Republican,* August 7, 1886, 6; for "hardest and surest batter in the American Association," a description that also included David Orr, New York, see "Notes," *Cincinnati Enquirer,* October 17, 1886, 10.

48. The soreness was so great in his right arm that O'Neill relayed the ball to the infield with an underhand throw. "Around the Bases," *St. Louis Sunday Sayings,* July 27, 1884. On at least one occasion, he also tossed the ball to the center fielder (Lewis) who, in this case, threw out the runner at third base. "Tit for Tat. Our Ball-Players Victorious in Cincinnati but Defeated at Home," *St. Louis Republican,* July 25, 1884, 6.

49. "Sporting: Atkisson and the Athletics Down Our Champions," *St. Louis Republican,* October 5, 1886, 6.

50. Fred Lewis was the Browns' center fielder in 1884, and Curt Welch was the center fielder from 1885 to 1887. Both sprinted towards a hit ball a split-second after they heard the crack of the bat. In the case of O'Neill, he initially paused

Source	First	Second	Third	Fourth	Fifth
Reach's Guide, 1886	Orr (NY), .346	Hecker (LOU), Caruthers (STL), .342	—	Browning (LOU), O'Neill (STL) .339	—
The Baseball Encyclopedia, 1969	Hecker (LOU), .341v	Browning (LOU), .340	Orr (NY), .338	Caruthers (STL), .334	O'Neill (STL), .328
Thiessen Calculations (O'Neill & Caruthers only), 2018	Hecker (LOU), .341	Browning (LOU), .340	Orr (NY), Caruthers (STL), .338	—	O'Neill (STL), 336

LOU–Louisville; NY–New York; STL–St. Louis

to locate the flight of the ball and, once he determined its path, only then did he start after the fly ball or ground ball. In comparison to these two center fielders, O'Neill's reaction time appeared slow, which to some observers was a sign of laziness. Occasionally the newspapers commented on O'Neill's slowness: "O'Neill ... has shown surprising 'get up and get' since the REPUBLICAN suggested a camp-stool in left field." "Diamond Chips," *St. Louis Republican*, July 26, 1884.

51. In the first inning of a 7–3 win against Brooklyn, the feature of the inning was "O'Neill's...running overhead catch of Smith's line drive to left." "Today's Games," *St. Louis Post-Dispatch*, July 5, 1886, 2. O'Neill also hustled on an infield hit as part of a 6–3 win over Cincinnati. On a hit to deep short, O'Neill got a "base-hit being earned by speedy running." "Our Bete Noir. The St. Louis Champions Again Victors," *Cincinnati Commercial Gazette*, August 26, 1886.

52. In 1886, the scoring rules credited the runner with a stolen base on the pitcher (e.g., going from first to second on a pitched ball) or on a hit ball (e.g., when he advanced more than one base on a single, such as going from first to third, or moved up a base after tagging up on a fly out). For a review of the changes in how to score a stolen base in 1886, see David Nemec, *The Official Rules of Baseball Illustrated* (Guilford, CT: Lyons, 2006), 163.

53. There was no report of O'Neill attempting a slide into a base until 1888, which he did as part of a 9–1 win over Cincinnati. "O'Neill surprised everyone by making two good slides in the fourth inning. He saved his life—but not his breeches." "Cincinnati Beaten," *St. Louis Republican*, June 16, 1888, 6.

54. "Sporting: St. Louis Browns, 9; Mets, 3," *St. Louis Globe-Democrat*, July 2, 1886, 8.

55. "Sporting: The Alleghenys Shut Out by the Browns," *St. Louis Republican*, June 14, 1886, 6.

56. "The Last Throws of Summer," *St. Louis Republican*, October 11, 1886, 4.

57. Dickson quoted from an 1889 definition of caught napping in the *Home Manual*: "When a player through carelessness or sleepy-headedness is caught off his base." Paul Dickson, *The Dickson Baseball Dictionary*, 3d ed. (New York: W.W. Norton, 2009), 170; Mrs. John A. Logan, *The Home Manual: Everybody's Guide in Social, Domestic and Business Life* (Philadelphia: H. J. Smith, 1889).

58. "Sporting: Browns Beat Philadelphia," *St. Louis Republican*, August 9, 1886, 3; "Brooklyn Shut Out," *St. Louis Republican*, July 4, 1886, 6.

59. "A Send-Off for 'Tip' O'Neill," *Woodstock Sentinel-Review*, November 1, 1886, 1. See also "One of the World-Beaters," 1.

60. "Sporting: The Browns Give Another Fine Exhibition of Ball Playing," *St. Louis Republican*, June 30, 1886, 6.

61. "From St. Louis. The Champion Browns' Work," *Sporting Life*, October 20, 1886, 2.

62. "Around the Bases," *The Sporting News*, March 12, 1887, 4.

63. "Caught on the Fly," *The Sporting News*, March 26, 1887, 7.

Chapter 3

1. Malcolm MacLean, "Anson to Comiskey to Chase," *Collier's*, September 20, 1913, 28.

2. Ibid., 29. Also see Hugh Weir, "The Real Comiskey," *Baseball Magazine*, XII, no. 4 (February 1914), 21.

3. Frederick Ivor-Campbell, Robert L. Tiemann, Mark Rucker, eds., *Baseball's First Stars* (Cleveland: The Society for American Baseball Research, 1996), 36.

4. Ted Sullivan, a former manager of Comiskey, argued that Comiskey was one of the best run-getters in the game. He combined "hitting, waiting, bunting, and base running" in ways that produced runs for his team. Ted Sullivan, "Base Ball Career of Charles A. Comiskey," *The Sporting News*, February 15, 1912, 5.

5. Charles A. Comiskey, "Thirty-Seven Years of Baseball," *Pearson's Magazine* 31, no. 3 (March 1914), 312; Hugh Fullerton, "Winning Baseball Pennants. Brains beat Hands and Feet in the Game," *Collier's*, September 11, 1909, 13.

6. A base-getter is "one who achieves a base and advances with regularity." Paul Dickson, *The Dickson Baseball Dictionary* 3d ed. (New York: W.W. Norton, 2009), 77.

7. On-base percentage (OBP) is a measure of the frequency that a batter gets on base. It is calculated by dividing hits plus bases on balls plus hit by pitches divided by the at-bats plus bases on balls plus hit by pitches plus sacrifice flies. It did not become an official statistic in major-league baseball until 1984. For 1885, baseball-reference.com lists O'Neill with the highest OBP on the Browns at .399, with Robinson second at .344. In 1886, Caruthers led the team with an OBP of .448, O'Neill was second at .385, and Robinson third at .377. Note that the OBP measures for the 1880s do not include sacrifice flies.

8. Although Curt Welch was better known for getting on base by deliberately letting a pitched ball hit him, in the three years that Robinson and Welch played together on the Browns (1885–1887), Robinson got on base after being hit by the pitcher 39 times and Welch 32 times.

9. As described in Chapter 1, Robinson, in the tenth inning of the deciding game of the World Championship Series against Chicago, laid down a sacrifice bunt that advanced Welch to third base, in position to score the winning run.

10. "Our Browns," *St. Louis Post-Dispatch*, May 3, 1884, 9.

11. Ibid.

12. Alfred H. Spink. *The National Game*, 2d ed. (1911; Reprinted, Carbondale: Southern Illinois University Press, 2000), 214.

13. L. M. Sutter, *Arlie Latham: A Baseball Biography of the Freshest Man on Earth*. (Jefferson, NC: McFarland, 2012), 238.

14. "Chadwick on the Browns," *St. Louis Post-Dispatch*, September 21, 1886, 11.

15. The rules in force in the 1880s allowed a batsman an unlimited number of foul balls without counting any of these as a strike. David Nemec, *The Official Rules of Baseball Illustrated* (Guilford, CT: Lyons, 2006), 27–28.

16. "Our Browns," 9.

17. J. Thomas Hetrick, *Chris Von der Ahe and the St. Louis Browns* (Lanham, MD: Scarecrow, 1999), 39.

18. In his first four years with St. Louis, Latham's batting average swung from .236 (1883) to .274 (1884) to .206 (1885) to .301 (1886). His variability on a game-to-game basis was also evident in 1886, when he hit .301 with 46 multi-hit games as well as 34 games with no hits.

19. The nickname "Brudder Bill" began in 1874 when, at 16 years of age, he joined a team on which his brother Jack played. In 1882,

Jack played for a short time on the St. Louis Browns alongside his brother, a period in which the nickname "Brudder Bill" surfaced again. David Nemec, ed., *Major League Baseball Profiles: 1871–1900. Volume 2.* (Lincoln: University of Nebraska Press, 2011), 314.

20. In batting average, Gleason was first on the team in 1882 (.288), second in 1883 (.287), and fourth in 1884 (.269).

21. Hetrick, *Chris Von der Ahe*, 39.

22. Spink. *The National Game*, 268.

23. Robert L. Tiemann, "Curt Welch," in Robert L. Tiemann and Mark Rucker, eds., *Nineteenth Century Stars, 2012 Edition* (Phoenix: The Society for American Baseball Research, 2012), 275.

24. After the 1885 season, Caruthers was concerned by the newly established salary maximum of $2,000. He insisted on a salary of $3,000. When Von der Ahe was not forthcoming with the salary that he wanted, Caruthers left for Europe. He continued negotiations by cable, and eventually Von der Ahe relented and gave Caruthers $3,200. For this escapade, he earned the nickname "Parisian Bob." Also see Hetrick, *Chris Von der Ahe*, 45.

25. "Great Pitchers and Their Peculiarities," *St. Louis Globe-Democrat*, August 27, 1887, 7.

26. Nemec claims that Caruthers was "arguably the game's most versatile player." David Nemec, *Beer & Whiskey League: The Illustrated History of the American Association—Baseball's Renegade League* (Guilford, CT: Lyons, 2004), 121.

27. "The World Beaters. They will be Seen at Detroit Next Wednesday," *Detroit Free Press*, October 9, 1887, 6.

28. "The Champions. Robert Caruthers," *Sporting Life*, October 14, 1885, 2.

29. "Great Pitchers," 7.

30. "David L. Foutz," *New York Clipper*, March 5, 1887; "Dave Foutz," *Cleveland Plain Dealer*, April 17, 1887.

31. "Notes," *Boston Globe*, September 5, 1887, 8.

32. Spink, *The National Game*, 130.

33. "Another Catcher," *St. Louis Republican*, January 17, 1885, 10.

34. "Base Ball," *The Sporting News*, December 4, 1886, 2.

35. In the crouched position, Bushong started with his hands about an inch from his kneecaps. This position would change, if he was sending a signal, to inside his knees. As the pitcher readied himself to deliver the ball, Bushong would move his hands again in front of him to set a target. From the target position, he could follow the ball as it was released. Brian McKenna, "Doc Bushong," *Baseball Biography Project*, Society for American Baseball Research. Accessed April 17, 2017, http//www.sabr.org. See also "King Catchers. Catching in the Olden Days and the New—Bushong and Bennett," *St. Louis Post-Dispatch*, August 14, 1886, 12.

36. Low pitches became even more common in 1887, the first year that batters no longer could call for a high or low pitch.

Chapter 4

1. "Anything to Win" summarized Comiskey's approach to the game. The expression is an abbreviated version of what he professed on numerous occasions. For example, when Manager Jimmy Williams criticized the Browns' rough work, Comiskey responded that "anything to win a game, so long as there is no danger of being declared out, should be resorted to and that if he were allowed to tie a man up by the thumbs to prevent him from reaching a base the man would be tied up." "Sixth to Second: The Browns Take a Big Jump in the Race," *St. Louis Post-Dispatch*, April 30, 1887, 12.

2. "From St. Louis," *Sporting Life*, October 20, 1886, 2.

3. In the nineteenth century, a "record player" was "more concerned about personal statistics than winning." Paul Dickson, *The Dickson Baseball Dictionary*, 3d ed. (New York: W.W. Norton, 2009), 693.

4. The term "headwork," also called brainwork, scientific baseball, or strategic play, referred to playing with good judgment. It often included such things as an understanding of strategy, a knowledge of positional play, and situational savvy. Dickson, *The Dickson Baseball Dictionary*, 405.

5. A number of players published books about the skills and headwork of the game: John F. Morrill and T. O'Keefe, *Batting and Pitching, Illustrated.* (Boston: Wright & Ditson, 1884); John Montgomery Ward, *Base-Ball: How to Become a Player* (1888; Reprint, Filiquarian Publishing, 2010); and N. Fred Pfeffer, *Scientific Ball* (Chicago: N. Fred Pfeffer, Publisher, 1889). Henry Chadwick and O. P. Caylor regularly commented on the skills and strategies of various teams in their weekly columns in *Sporting Life*. Chadwick published a number of articles and books, two of which were: *The Art of Batting* (Chicago and New York: A. G. Spalding & Bros., 1885) and *The Art of Pitching and Fielding* (Chicago and New York: A. G. Spalding & Bros., 1885).

6. Comiskey was frequently asked to explain or defend his anything-to-win orientation to the game. In this quotation, I combine his responses to this question about the Browns' style of play as reported in three different newspapers or weeklies, specifically in excerpts from: "The St. Louis Boys. Comiskey Talks about Players in General—The Browns Sized up by an Eastern Authority," *The Sporting News*, April 27, 1889, 2; "Editorial," *The Sporting News*, May 14, 1887, 4; "St. Louis Browns and 'Dirty Ball,'" *Cincinnati Enquirer*, May 8, 1887, 10.

7. "The St. Louis Boys," 10.

8. "St. Louis Browns and 'Dirty Ball,'" 10.

9. "Diamond Dust," *St. Louis Post-Dispatch*, August 10, 1885, 5.

10. In a report on the season's individual and club averages, it stated: "St. Louis ranked rather low in batting but excelled all in fielding and added thereto an important requisite for success, namely decidedly superior base running, and is therefore fairly entitled to premier position." "American Association. The Official Individual and Club Batting and Fielding Averages," *Sporting Life*, December 2, 1885, 3.

11. Although unlike today's definition of a stolen base (which was not adopted until 1898), the stolen base rule of 1886 provided a helpful measure for judging the effectiveness of the Browns' running game, which emphasized both stealing bases and advancing a base on any other opportunity to do so. For a further discussion of the evolution of the stolen base rule, see David Nemec, *The Official Rules of Baseball Illustrated* (Guilford, CT: Lyons, 2006), 162–163.

12. "Styles of Sliding: The Side and Full Slide—The Old-Fashioned Method," *St. Louis Post-Dispatch*, July 31, 1886, 12.

13. Robinson described the power of Comiskey's example:

"When we see our captain sliding headforemost into bases, at the risk of breaking his neck, we would be ashamed of ourselves not to follow his example." "Notes and Comments," *Sporting Life*, January 5, 1887, 3.

14. "Styles of Sliding," 12.

15. For references that illustrate Comiskey's commitment to sacrifice hitting, see "Comiskey and 'Little Nic,'" *St. Louis Post-Dispatch*, August 14, 1888, 8; "St. Louis Siftings. A Reliable Sacrifice Hitter," *Sporting Life*, September 5, 1888, 7.

16. In 1885, the Browns led the American Association with a fielding average of .920, a percentage that was slightly higher than the Association average of .909. Their 381 errors (3.4 errors per game) were the fewest in the Association, 53 lower than the Association average of 434 (3.9 per game). In 1886, the Browns' .915 fielding average was second to Pittsburgh's .917 and again ahead of the Association average of .906. Similarly, the Browns' 494 errors (3.5 per game) were second to the 487 (3.5 per game) made by Pittsburgh. The Association average in 1886 was 559 errors (4.0 per game).

17. On June 20, 1886, the Browns recorded a perfect fielding game. They beat Cincinnati, 8–0. "Sporting. The Cincinnatis Again Shut Out by the Champions. The Browns Play a Game Without Making a Single Fielding or Battery Error," *St. Louis Republican*, June 21, 1886, 5.

18. G. W. Axelrod, *"Commy:" The Life Story of Charles A. Comiskey*. (1919; Reprinted, Jefferson, NC: McFarland, 2003), 69.

19. Charles A. Comiskey, "How to Play the Infield," in Spink, *The National Game*, 395.

20. *Ibid.*

21. *Ibid.*

22. *Ibid.*

23. "Notes and Comments," *Sporting Life*, October 19, 1887, 3.

24. Charles A. Comiskey, "How to Play the Infield," 395.

25. Comiskey played an "open" game where he pulled fielders in, out, or over in response to the changing circumstances of the game and as a counter to the offensive strategies of the opposing team. G. W. Axelrod, *"Commy,"* 68.

26. The Browns' pitchers had a 2.44 earned run average per game in 1885 compared to the Association's average of 3.24, and, in 1886, had a 2.49 ERA compared to the Association's average of 3.44.

27. "Comments on the Catcher," *St. Louis Post-Dispatch*, July 13, 1887, 8.

28. "A Case of 'Sour Grapes,'" *St. Louis Sunday Sayings*, September 26, 1886.

29. "Sixth to Second. The Browns Take a Big Jump in the Race," *St. Louis Post-Dispatch*, April 30, 1887, 12.

30. "Coacher" was the common term in the nineteenth century for a first base or third base coach. Dickson, *The Dickson Baseball Dictionary*, 200.

31. "Some Famous Coachers. The Philosophy of Coaching and the Men Who Have Made it," *St. Louis Post-Dispatch*, July 24, 1886, 12.

32. *Ibid.*

33. "Bunched Hits," *St. Louis Sunday Sayings*, June 6, 1886.

34. L. M. Sutter, in the Epilogue of her recent biography of Latham, wrote: "Arlie Latham helped to popularize baseball and spread its appeal as entertainment. He was unique in his facility at weaving theater into sport to delight a restless American populace, one hungry for stimulation." L. M. Sutter, *Arlie Latham. A Baseball Biography of the Freshest Man on Earth* (Jefferson, NC: McFarland, 2012), 242. For an additional account of Latham's coaching style, see Robert Smith, "The Freshest Man on Earth," *Baseball: A Historical Narrative of the Game, the Men Who Played it, and its Place in American Life* (New York: Simon & Schuster, 1947), 109–114.

35. Axelrod, *"Commy,"* 52.

36. "Von der Ahe Paid the Fines," *St. Louis Republican*, June 10, 1886, 6; "The American Association Meeting," *St. Louis Globe-Democrat*, June 10, 1886, 5.

37. "My, How Sore!" *St. Louis Republican*, July 31, 1884.

38. "Those Fines. Comiskey Tells of the Beautiful Treatment the Browns Received in the East," *The Sporting News*, June 14, 1886, 5.

39. "Playing Rules of the American Association of Base Ball Clubs 1886," *Reach's Official American Association Base Ball Guide 1886* (1886; Reprinted New York: Horton, 1989), 142.

40. The stipulation that a game must have two umpires was not added to the rulebook until 1911. There were periodic attempts to use two umpires (e.g., the 1886 World's Series had two umpires and a referee; the 1887 World's Series used two umpires; the 1890 Players' League used a two-umpire system), but for most games in the 1880s and 1890s, only one umpire was on duty. Peter Morris, *A Game of Inches: The Story Behind the Innovations That Shaped Baseball*, (Chicago: Ivan R. Dee, 2010), 253–255.

41. On occasion the St. Louis newspapers did not support Comiskey's kicking. In one game report, the *St. Louis Globe-Democrat* stated that Comiskey's protests were "simply disgraceful" and his "performance was worthy of a corner-lot game between hoodlums." "Sporting. Pittsburgh 2; Browns 1," *St. Louis Globe-Democrat*, July 26, 1885, 8.

42. Comiskey recognized such delaying tactics because he himself had employed them when it was to the advantage of the Browns. For example, he was outwitted in a game which Baltimore led, 6–4, after six innings. When the Browns came to bat in the seventh inning, Jumbo McGinnis, the Baltimore pitcher, noticed it was getting dark and so threw the ball over the center of the plate to entice the batters to swing at will, to the point that they scored five runs without registering an out. The Baltimore players then complained to the umpire about the dark conditions, delaying the game for five minutes. The play resumed for two pitches only, and then the Baltimore players spent another five minutes arguing that the game should be called. In between the Baltimore stoppages, the Browns also complained to the umpire about the delaying tactics of Baltimore. About 20 minutes elapsed, and the Browns were still at bat. At that point, the umpire called the game on account of darkness with the Browns leading, 9–6. Unable to complete the seventh inning, the game was terminated after six innings, when Baltimore had the lead. The official score was recorded as 6–4 in favor of Baltimore. "St. Louis Outwitted. Baltimore Beats the Champions. A Game in which Darkness Played an Important Part," *Baltimore American*, September 21, 1886.

43. "Sporting. The Cincinnati Team Shut Out in Fine Style Yesterday," *St. Louis Republican*, July 24, 1884, 6.

44. Rule 39, section (2) read: "A Forfeited Game shall be declared by the Umpire in favor of the Club not in fault in the following cases: (2) If after the game has begun, one

side refuses or fails to continue playing, unless such game has been suspended or terminated by the Umpire." "Playing Rules of the American Association of Base Ball Clubs 1886," *Reach's Official American Association Base Ball Guide 1886* (1886; Reprinted New York: Horton, 1989), 120.

45. "Sporting. Sullivan's Umpiring Saves Chicago from Defeat. The Game Between Them and the Browns Ends in a Row," *St. Louis Republican*, October 16, 1885, 6. See also Nemec and Miklich, *Forfeits and Successfully Protested Games in Major League Baseball: A Complete Record, 1871–2013*, 39–40, and Jerry Lansche, *Glory Fades Away. The Nineteenth-Century World Series Rediscovered* (Dallas: Taylor, 1991), 61–66.

46. Latham was fined $10 for threatening to thump the ump. "Three Cheers for Young," *Louisville Courier-Journal*, April 26, 1886, 8. Gleason ended a prolonged protest of a call with a wish for a meeting with the umpire at season's end in a "twenty-four-foot ring with hard gloves, Queensberry rules, [that] would be a pleasure sweeter than honey." "Gleason and John Kelly," *St. Louis Post-Dispatch*, August 2, 1886, 5.

47. Robinson "got mad at Umpire York for calling him out at second base and talked back so loud and long that he was fined." "Browns 6; Athletics 1," *St. Louis Globe-Democrat*, September 22, 1886, 7.

48. "Diamond Dust," *St. Louis Globe-Democrat*, July 2, 1886, 8.

49. "Capt. Comiskey's Fines," *St. Louis Globe-Democrat*, May 31, 1886, 6.

50. When asked why so many American Association umpires allowed players to "dispute their decisions with such impunity as they did," Foghorn Bradley, one of the American Association umpires, responded as follows: "Fining them would not stop their kicking." He quoted Comiskey of the St. Louis team as an example: "Comiskey told me ... that I might go and fine him as much as I damned please, but that the fines would not be paid." Bradley further remarked that "when umpires fined players, the club to which the punished player belonged would not back up the umpire in inflicting the penalty but went against him by efforts to remove him from his position, and to save themselves umpires had to stop fining players, except in very aggravated cases." "Kickers and Kicking. Henry Chadwick Makes a Few Suggestions as to Remedies," *St. Louis Post-Dispatch*, August 31, 1886, 5.

51. Morris quotes the *Detroit Free Press*, May 9, 1886, when it criticized Art Irwin for bunting the ball, calling it a "babyish performance" and pointing out that "patrons object to such infantile tricks." Morris, *A Game of Inches*, 55.

52. "Shutout," *St. Louis Republican*, July 8, 1886, 6; "Bunched Hits," *St. Louis Sunday Sayings*, August 8, 1886.

53. "Sporting Matters. Cincinnati Wins a Great Game of Ball from the Browns," *St. Louis Republican*, May 17, 1886, 6.

54. "Browns 8; Baltimore 3," *St. Louis Globe-Democrat*, September 11, 1885, 5.

55. "Tricks of the Game. A Sample or Two of What a Man with Brains Can Accomplish," *St. Louis Post-Dispatch*, July 10, 1886, 12.

56. "Defeating the St. Louis Champions in a Marvelous Game," *Cincinnati Commercial Gazette*, May 14, 1886; "A Defeat for the Champions. Baltimore Shows Them How to Play Ball," *Baltimore American*, June 2, 1886.

57. "A Defeat for the Champions."

58. "The Daily Picnic of the Browns at Sportsman Park," *St. Louis Republican*, August 5, 1886, 6.

59. Comiskey and Gleason jointly endorse this "rough-and-tumble" style of play. "Notes and Comments," *Sporting Life*, August 12, 1885, 4.

60. "The Great Struggle," *St. Louis Post-Dispatch*, June 12, 1886, 12.

61. "Sporting. Pittsburgh 2; Browns 1," *St. Louis Globe-Democrat*, July 26, 1885, 8.

62. "Beaten by the Mets," *St. Louis Republican*, June 14, 1885; "Notes," *St. Louis Post-Dispatch*, August 15, 1885, 9.

63. "Gossip of the Game," *St. Louis Post-Dispatch*, June 5, 1886, 12.

64. J. C. Kofoed, "The Greatest Outfield," *Baseball Magazine*, XII, no. 2 (1913), 30.

65. Pfeffer, *Scientific Ball*, 38, 70.

Chapter 5

1. "Base Ball Gossip," *St. Louis Post-Dispatch*, October 11, 1886, 7.

2. "A Banquet to the Browns," *St. Louis Globe-Democrat*, October 13, 1886, 5.

3. "Sporting. The Browns Given an Ovation on 'Change," *St. Louis Republican*, October 26, 1886, 6.

4. "The Browns' Banquet," *St. Louis Globe-Democrat*, November 4, 1886, 8.

5. "The Browns' Medals," *St. Louis Post-Dispatch*, November 8, 1886, 7.

6. "From St. Louis," *Sporting Life*, November 10, 1886, 4.

7. "One of the World-Beaters: 'Tip' O'Neill of the St. Louis Browns Baseball Club Arrives Home," *Woodstock Sentinel-Review*, November 11, 1886, 1. See also "Diamond Dust," *St. Louis Globe-Democrat*, November 18, 1886, 5.

8. "The Bachelor Browns," *St. Louis Republican*, August 14, 1887, 4.

9. "Caught on the Fly," *The Sporting News*, December 4, 1886, 3.

10. Peter Golenbock, *The Spirit of St. Louis. A History of the St. Louis Cardinals and Browns* (New York: Harper Entertainment, 2000), 46.

11. "Base Ball Notes," *St. Louis Republican*, November 3, 1886.

12. "From St. Louis," *Sporting Life*, January 12, 1887, 2.

13. O'Neill's father died in 1883, so Tip was not helping his father in 1886 or 1887, as reported in the newspapers. He also did not manage the hotel, as noted in another newspaper; two of Tip's brothers ran the hotel. "World of Sports. Where and How the Ball-Players are Passing the Winter," *St. Louis Post-Dispatch*, January 1, 1887, 8.

14. "Base Ball Briefs," *St. Louis Republican*, February 17, 1887, 6.

15. "From St. Louis," *Sporting Life*, March 23, 1887, 3.

16. "Around the Bases," *The Sporting News*, April 2, 1887, 3.

17. "Base Ball Briefs," *St. Louis Republican*, March 17, 1887, 6.

18. "Diamond Dust," *St. Louis Globe-Democrat*, March 23, 1887, 5.

19. "Base Ball Briefs," *St. Louis Republican*, March 26, 1887, 10.

20. "Around the Bases," *The Sporting News*, April 2, 1887, 3.

21. Some of the more helpful articles on the 1887 rule changes include: O. P. Caylor, "New Rules. Radical Changes by the Joint Committee. The Game to Be almost Revolutionized in Pitching and Batting," *Sporting Life*, November 24, 1886, 1; "The New Rules for 1887," *New York Clipper*, December 18, 1886, 632; John Ward, "The New Rules," *Sporting Life*, February 9, 1887, 4; Henry Chadwick, "The

New Playing Rules of Base-Ball," *Outing*, X, no. 1 (April 1887), 77–78; Henry Chadwick, "The New Rules of Base-Ball," *Lippincott Magazine*, May 1887, 836–840.

22. From the outset, there was opposition to two of the changes: the rule that credited a base on balls with a base hit and the rule that required four fair pitches before a batsman could be called out on strikes. On May 14, at a special meeting in Cincinnati, the American Association decided to approach President Nicholas Young of the National League with a recommendation to revoke these two rules, effective immediately. "Secret CONFAB. A Special Meeting of the Association," *Sporting Life*, May 18, 1887, 1. Young responded that the National League supported the Association's resolution but did not want to make these changes until the end of the season. He noted that such changes should be officially endorsed at the annual meetings of the National League in November and the American Association in December. "The Rules will not be Changed," *Cleveland Plain Dealer*, June 18, 1887.

23. "The National Playing Rules," *Reach's Official American Association Base Ball Guide, 1887*, (1887; Reprinted New York: Horton, 1989), 108.

24. "Well done. Important Work at the Association Meeting. Increased Protection for Umpires," *Sporting Life*, June 16, 1886, 1.

25. For a further comment on the coaching rules, see Chapter 4. Also see Rules 7, 59, and 60(1). "The National Playing Rules," *Reach's Official American Association Base Ball Guide, 1887* (1887; Reprinted New York: Horton, 1989), 149, 161.

26. Nine players from the New York club in the National League quietly formed the Brotherhood of Professional Base Ball Players in 1885. The purpose of the Brotherhood was "to protect and benefit ourselves collectively and individually; to promote a high standard of professional conduct; [and] to foster and encourage the interests of Base Ball." Robert B. Ross, *The Great Baseball Revolt. The Rise and Fall of the 1890 Players League* (Lincoln: University of Nebraska Press, 2016), 52.

27. The Brotherhood also questioned the rationale for some trades or sales. For example, Chicago sold George Gore, Abner Dalrymple, and King Kelly in part because of their drinking and Jim McCormick for his failure to sign a contract. Such moves, to the Brotherhood, seemed arbitrary and without sufficient evidence. In the most high-profile sale, Chicago sold Kelly to Boston for $10,000, an amount that was more than twice the price ever paid for a player. This transaction came under considerable scrutiny and criticism from the Brotherhood.

28. John Ward, "Is the Base Ball Player a Chattel?" *Lippincott's Magazine*, XL (August 1887), 310–319.

29. Robert Burk. *Never Just a Game: Players, Owners, and American Baseball to 1920* (Chapel Hill: University of North Carolina Press, 1994), 94–99; Harold Seymour: *Baseball: The Early Years* (New York: Oxford University Press, 1960), 221–225; David Voigt. *American Baseball. Volume 1. From Gentleman's Sport to the Commissioner System.* (University Park: Pennsylvania State University Press, 1983), 154–160.

30. The deal was the first trade of reserved players between two major league clubs. "Good-bye 'Little Nic,'" *St. Louis Republican*, November 17, 1886.

31. In the 1880s, interleague play between teams in the National League and American Association, including the post-season series between the winners of both leagues, was organized as challenge matches. For the post-season challenges for the world championship, the two owners signed a contract that outlined the terms and conditions of the series. The arrangements for the world championships in the 1880s varied in number of games, game sites, financial rewards for the winner and loser, and the determination of umpires. The spring-fall challenge series of 1887, while understandable in the tradition of challenge matches—a challenge could be made at any time—nonetheless disrupted and confused the previous pattern of scheduling a series for the world championship at the end of the season. While both teams and the newspapers in each city commented as if the world championship was at stake in this spring-fall series, eventually some reported the contests as a series of exhibition games. In the fall of 1887, Detroit and St. Louis, the winners of the National League and American Association respectively, met for the world championship. Chicago and St. Louis did not play the final three games previously scheduled for the fall. "From St. Louis. Exhibition Games and Nothing More," *Sporting Life*, April 20, 1887, 4.

32. The first three games were scheduled in St. Louis, the next three in Louisville, Indianapolis, and Cincinnati, and the last three in Chicago. "The St. Louis-Chicago Games," *St. Louis Globe-Democrat*, March 6, 1887, 4.

33. "The World's Champions," *St. Louis Globe-Democrat*, December 25, 1886, 6.

34. "Caruthers and the Browns," *St. Louis Globe-Democrat*, December 24, 1886, 11.

35. *Ibid*.

36. "Brown Stockings and Swelled Heads," *St. Louis Sunday Sayings*, December 5, 1886, 8.

37. "In the World of Sports. The St. Louis Browns Still Without Foutz's Service," *Chicago Tribune*, February 26, 1887, 6.

38. Both Chris Von der Ahe (St. Louis) and Zach Phelps (Louisville) were dealing with players who refused to sign contracts. "Constitution of the American Association of Base Ball Clubs 1887," *Reach's Official American Association Base Ball Guide*, *1887*, 147.

39. "Sporting. Blacklisting Ball-Players," *St. Louis Globe-Democrat*, March 15, 1887, 8.

40. On his sore right hand, O'Neill held the bat with only three fingers. "Diamond Dust," *St. Louis Globe-Democrat*, April 10, 1887, 18; "Sporting. Great Game of Ball Between the Browns and Syracuse Stars," *St. Louis Republican*, April 4, 1887, 6.

41. "From St. Louis," *Sporting Life*, April 13, 1887, 9.

42. "The Crippled Browns," *St. Louis Post-Dispatch*, April 14, 1887, 5.

43. "Sporting. The Browns Again Defeated by the Chicagos," *St. Louis Republican*, April 15, 1887, 6.

44. "The Reasons Why: A Word of Explanation From the 'Champion Browns.' Where the Trouble Lay," *St. Louis Post-Dispatch*, April 15, 1887, 3.

45. "Sporting. Browns 7; Chicago 4," *St. Louis Globe-Democrat*, April 9, 1887, 7.

46. "Jonah" was a term commonly used in baseball circles in the last two decades of the nineteenth century to refer to "a person or thing that brings bad luck." Paul Dickson, *The Dickson Baseball Dictionary*, 3d ed. (New York: W.W. Norton, 2009), 471–72.

47. "Base Ball Notes," *St. Louis Republican,* April 22, 1887.

Chapter 6

1. I. D. Foulon, "Champion's March," *St. Louis Globe-Democrat,* April 16, 1887, 16.
2. "From St. Louis. Diamond Chiplets," *Sporting Life,* April 20, 1887, 4.
3. "From St. Louis. A Genuine Boom," *Sporting Life,* April 27, 1887, 10.
4. "The Parade of the Ball Clubs," *Louisville Evening Post,* April 16, 1887, 3.
5. The eight teams in the American Association were: in the west, St. Louis, Cincinnati, Louisville, and Cleveland; in the east, New York, Brooklyn, Philadelphia, and Baltimore.
6. "Won by St. Louis," *Louisville Courier-Journal,* April 20, 1887, 5.
7. Ibid.
8. Ibid.
9. Ibid.
10. In 1887, some pitchers, after they got behind in the count, with four called balls and no strikes, opted to put the batter on base by hitting him with the next pitch rather than risking a fifth called ball and thereby giving the batter his base on balls. Under the new rule where a base on ball counted as a hit, a walk would increase both the batter's batting average and the number of hits allowed by the pitcher, a statistical advantage for the batter and a mark against the pitcher. In this hit by pitch, while Hecker was clearly frustrated by Latham's attempts to get a walk, it was not clear that Hecker intentionally threw the ball into Latham's ribs to avoid giving him a phantom hit (base on balls). "Rubbed It In: St. Louis Succeeds in Winning Another Ball from the Kentucky Club," *Louisville Courier-Journal,* April 21, 1887, 2.
11. In 1887, the park factor for Sportsman's Park was 1.134, a rating that indicated a slight advantage for batters over pitchers. See retrosheet.org.
12. A ten-foot fence was added to the existing fence in 1887. Batters would have to hit a ball almost 300 feet down the right field line and close to 350 feet in right-center to clear the fence. "Sporting. The Browns Continue to Heap up Glory," *St. Louis Republican,* May 15, 1887,

15. For a description of the park, see Philip J. Lowry, *Green Cathedrals: The Ultimate Celebration of Major League and Negro League Ballparks* (New York: Walker, 2006), 198.
13. "Base Ball on the Brain. The Faces to be Seen at Sportsman's and Union Parks," *St. Louis Sunday Sayings,* June 8, 1884.
14. The owners of the teams in the National League frequently criticized or mocked the American Association for its sale of alcohol, its cheap seats, and its Sunday games. David Nemec, *The Beer and Whiskey League: The Illustrated History of the American Association—Baseball's Renegade Major League* (Guilford, CT: Lyons, 2004), 16.
15. Peter Morris, *A Game of Inches: The Story Behind the Innovations That Shaped Baseball* (Chicago: Ivan R. Dee, 2010), 416.
16. "1882. May 2," John Snyder, *Cardinals Journal: Year by Year and Day by Day with the St. Louis Cardinals Since 1882* (Cincinnati: Clerisy Press, 2010), 13.
17. A hod-carrier or hoddie was a laborer in the bricklaying industry. He carried 10–12 bricks at a time to where the bricks were being laid. "Base Ball on the Brain. The Faces to be Seen at Sportsman's and Union Parks," *St. Louis Sunday Sayings,* June 8, 1884.
18. Bill James, *The New Bill James Historical Abstract* (New York: Free Press, 2003), 47.
19. Ibid., 36.
20. "Base Ball on the Brain. The Faces to be Seen and Sportsman's and Union Parks," *St. Louis Sunday Sayings,* June 8, 1884.
21. Von der Ahe distributed banners, crockery, and blankets with the Browns name on them, named apartment buildings after some of the players, commissioned some pictures of the team or individual players, organized advertising where players endorsed particular drinks, cigars, or oils, etc. Robert Smith, "The King, the Captain, and the Boss," *Baseball: A Historical Narrative of the Game, the Men Who Played It, and its Place in American Life* (New York: Simon & Schuster, 1947), 104–105; J. Thomas Hetrick, *Chris Von der Ahe and the St. Louis Browns* (Lanham, MD: Scarecrow, 1999), 54–56.
22. In recognition of his contribution to the development of baseball in the nineteenth century, Von der Ahe was one of ten finalists on the Hall of Fame's Pre-Integration Committee's 2016 ballot. Von der

Ahe did not receive the requisite 75 percent of ballots cast to be enshrined in the Hall of Fame.
23. Edward Achorn, *The Summer of Beer and Whiskey: How Brewers, Barkeeps, Rowdies, Immigrants, and a Wild Pennant Fight Made Baseball America's Game* (New York: Public Affairs, 2013), 259.
24. Hetrick concluded: "His most lasting contribution was his belief that baseball is a sport for the masses." Hetrick, *Chris Von der Ahe,* 232.
25. "From St. Louis. The Souvenir—'Ladies' Day,'" *Sporting Life,* April 27, 1887, 10.
26. A blocked ball is a "batted or thrown ball that is stopped or handled by any person not engaged in a game." If a fan standing behind O'Neill in left field stopped a hit ball or threw or kicked the ball to O'Neill so that he could quickly throw it back to the infield, the umpire was supposed to call a "block," which required O'Neill to throw the ball to the pitcher in his box before any attempt could be made to put out a runner. "The National Playing Rules," *Reach's Official American Association Base Ball Guide 1887* (1887; Reprinted New York: Horton, 1989), 153, 160.
27. Cincinnati proved to be a formidable foe in 1887. They were the only team to win the season's series against the Browns with 12 wins against six losses.
28. Charles King was born Charles Koenig but changed his last name early in his baseball career to the more English-sounding King. He was nicknamed "Silver" because of the shiny gray tint of his blond hair. David Nemec, ed., *Major League Baseball Profiles: 1871–1900, Volume 1.* (Lincoln: University of Nebraska Press, 2011), 106.
29. Nat Hudson was a promising young pitcher who, in his rookie season (1886), had a 16–10 win-loss record. Before the start of the 1887 season, Hudson's father died at his home in Chicago. Hudson remained in Chicago to address some complications in his father's estate and to care for his ailing mother. His mother died in August. In 1887, Hudson missed the first part of the season, rejoining the Browns in early June. He returned to Chicago when his mother's condition worsened. As result of these family matters, in 1887, Hudson pitched in only nine games, with four wins to his credit. "Bunched Hits," *St. Louis Sunday Sayings,* April 3, 1887, and

David Nemec (Compiler and Editor), *Major League Baseball Profiles. 1871–1900. Volume 1.* (Lincoln: University of Nebraska Press, 2011), 94.

30. Ibid. For a further description of his pitching style, see "The Two Great Pitchers," *St. Louis Republican*, October 21, 1888, 15.

31. "St. Louis Browns and 'Dirty Ball,'" *Cincinnati Enquirer*, May 8, 1887, 10.

32. "Bauer Bounced," *St. Louis Globe-Democrat*, May 2, 1887, 3.

33. In 1885, O'Neill hit .398 at home and .310 away; in 1886, his average was .359 at home and .313 away; and in 1889, he hit .395 at home and .269 away. The exception was 1888, when O'Neill won his second batting title, with an average of .340 at home and .356 on the road.

34. "Abroad" was a term used to denote "playing away from one's field." Paul Dickson, *The Dickson Baseball Dictionary*, 3d ed. (New York: W.W. Norton, 2009), 4.

35. "Base Ball Briefs," *St. Louis Republican*, April 30, 1887, 6.

36. When O'Neill first signed with the Browns, Williams, the newly-appointed manager of the Browns, described Tip as follows: "He hails from Woodstock, Ontario and is as fine a specimen of physical manhood as one could wish to see. He stands over six feet in height and weighs about 180 pounds, is as straight as an arrow, and well proportioned, with a long arm, and tremendous sweep." "His Ideas: Manager Williams Reviews the St. Louis Browns for '84," *St. Louis Post-Dispatch*, December 28, 1883, 5.

37. A wagon tongue bat was made out of ash from the spokes or tongues of wagon wheels from horse-drawn carriages. Stuart Miller, *Good Wood: The Story of the Baseball Bat* (Chicago: ACTA, 2011), 113. On the back cover of the 1888 *Spalding's Guide*, there is a sketch of a wagon tongue bat in an ad by A. G. Spalding & Bros. offering a "liberal price ... for straight grained, well-seasoned, second growth Ash Sticks suitable for turning into Bats." The ad claimed that wagon tongue bats were "superior to anything in the way of a bat ever brought out, both as to quality of timber, models, and finish. Made as they are from such seasoned timber, an elasticity is given to them that makes the ball 'ring' when hit." *Spalding's Official Base Ball Guide 1888* (1888; Reprinted New York: Horton, 1989), back cover.

38. A bat-maker explained that the weight of most bats was between 33 and 40 ounces, with the average for professional players "to be about 34 ounces." "Grand Stand Chat," *St. Louis Post-Dispatch*, June 22, 1888, 8. Tip's bat probably weighed 29–31 ounces and was approximately 30–32 inches long. At this smaller size, the bat was likely about 2¼ inches in diameter, well below the maximum allowed of "two and one-half inches at the thickest part." "Playing Rules of the American Association of Base Ball Clubs 1887," *Reach's Official American Association Base Ball Guide 1887*, 151. The St. Louis Cardinals Hall of Fame and Museum has a replica of O'Neill's bat that was donated to the Museum by *The Sporting News* around 1968. The bat was made by the Hillerich & Bradsby Company in Louisville, Kentucky. The bat is 32¼ inches long, weighs around 29 ounces, and is about 2.65 inches in diameter. The length and weight of the bat are certainly plausible, but the thicker barrel is greater than the 2.5-inch diameter allowed in 1887. Furthermore, the tapered design of the bat, with a thin handle and a wide barrel, is not like the wagon tongue bat preferred by Tip, which was less tapered than the bat created for the Museum. Email communications, including a photo of the bat displaying its dimensions, from Paula Homan, Curator and Manager of the St. Louis Cardinals Hall of Fame and Museum, December 12, 2012, and January 16, 2013.

39. "Notes," *Cincinnati Enquirer*, October 9, 1887, 10.

40. "Attitude of Batters. The Right and the Wrong Way of Handling the Ash," *St. Louis Post-Dispatch*, July 24, 1886, 12.

41. "Bunched Hits," *St. Louis Sunday Sayings*, May 15, 1887, 8.

42. The other category was the "spraddled batter" who spread his legs far apart and, as a result of this wide stance, could only rely on his arms to activate his swing, which diminished the power he could generate. "Attitude of Batters," 12.

43. "How Big Batters Bat: Favorite Attitudes of Famous Hitters Striking at the Ball," *St. Louis Post-Dispatch*, September 6, 1888, 8.

44. "J. E. O'Neill," *The Sporting News*, February 22, 1890, 1.

45. "Telling the Story of the Original Giants," *The Sporting News*, February 22, 1923, 6.

46. John Milligan, the Louisville first baseman, described O'Neill as the "hardest hitter this season" and as a batter that no pitcher in the country could fool. "From St. Louis: The Browns' Jonah," *Sporting Life*, August 31, 1887, 4. Also see "A Fight to a Finish: Tip O'Neill," *The Sporting News*, March 22, 1890, 1.

47. The "week" here refers to the fact that he played seven games in a row. It does not indicate a calendar week since the seven games spanned 11 days.

48. Batting for average is when a batsman tries to get a base hit in order to improve his batting average. In contrast, a batsman who bats for power is less concerned with improving his average and more interested in hitting for extra bases (doubles, triples, home runs). Dickson, *The Dickson Baseball Dictionary*, 416.

49. A cycle involves hitting a single, double, triple, and home run in the same game. For a list of players who have hit for the cycle, see retrosheet.org.

50. At its winter meeting in November 1886, the National League formally admitted the Pittsburgh club. Pittsburgh became the first team ever to defect from one league to the other. Jon Cash, *Before They Were Cardinals: Major League Baseball in Nineteenth-Century St. Louis*. Columbia: University of Missouri Press, 151–153.

51. The Browns' combined total of 112 runs in four games as well as the accumulated 36-run margin of victory (Browns 76 runs, Cleveland 38) were early indicators of what could happen to run production under the new rules of 1887.

52. "J. E. O'Neill," *Cleveland Plain Dealer*, May 5, 1887.

53. "Base Ball Briefs," *St. Louis Republican*, May 6, 1887, 6.

54. "Sporting. Another Ball Game Won by the Browns," *St. Louis Republican*, May 7, 1887, 6.

55. "Browns 10; Louisvilles, 3," *St. Louis Globe-Democrat*, May 7, 1887, 7.

56. "Sporting. Another Ball Game Won by the Browns," 6.

57. The record for consecutive times at bat with a hit is 12, shared by three players, Pinky Higgins, Johnny Kling, and Walt Dropo. There are another 24 players with ten or 11 hits in a row and 30+ players with nine consecutive hits. While O'Neill had ten hits in a row (counting a base on balls as one of the hits), record-keepers only credit O'Neill with nine hits in a row.

O'Neill had a second streak of ten-adjusted-to-nine hits in a row in 1887 (see Chapter 13 for a further discussion of batting streaks and Appendix B for a further comment on O'Neill's streaks). O'Neill and Joe Kelley, a left fielder and third baseman with Baltimore, are the only players to have two streaks of nine or more hits in a row. O'Neill is the only player to have two nine-hit streaks in the same season (1887); Kelley had nine-hit streaks in 1894 and 1898. Gary Gillette & Pete Palmer, eds., *The ESPN Baseball Encyclopedia*, 4th ed. (New York: Sterling, 2007), 1820–1821. In 2015, Trott McCotter identified Johnny Kling as the third batter with 12 consecutive hits. "Johnny Kling's 12 Consecutive Hits," SABR Baseball Records Committee, April 2009. Accessed December 10, 2015, SABR-Baseball_Records_Cmte-2009-04.pdf.

58. "Sporting. Once More the Browns Defeat the Louisvilles," *St. Louis Republican*, May 9, 1887, 6.

59. On a similar play the day before, a ball hit into the left field benches was touched by a spectator. Hearing no call from the umpire that the ball was a block, O'Neill fired the ball to the plate, where Joe Werrick, the Louisville third baseman, was tagged out. The Louisvilles protested the out. The umpire, who had not seen the interference by the fan in left field, surprisingly reversed his decision, which in turn brought a vociferous kick by the Browns, but to no avail. "Sporting. The Browns Covering Themselves All with Glory," *St. Louis Republican*, May 8, 1887, 15.

60. "The Association. Atkisson Weakens in the Eighth Inning and St. Louis Pounds Out Victory," *Philadelphia Press*, May 18, 1887, 6.

61. "From St. Louis. The Athletics' Work in the Games with the Browns. Diamond Notes," *Sporting Life*, May 25, 1887, 9.

62. In the comment "the only player who ever earned the V," Von der Ahe was referring to the hat sign which said, "Hit Me for $5." The "V" was the $5 that O'Neill won when he eventually hit the hat sign. "Chris Von der Ahe, The Most Picturesque Figure in Baseball History," *St. Louis Post-Dispatch*, April 17, 1904, 40.

63. "Base-Ball and Athletics. Athletics, 4; Browns, 3," *St. Louis Globe-Democrat*, May 18, 1887, 8.

64. "Base Ball Notes," *St. Louis Republican*, May 16, 1887, 6.

65. "Great Slugging Match between Browns and Brooklyns," *St. Louis Republican*, May 21, 1887, 6.

66. "From St. Louis. Around the Bases," *Sporting Life*, June 1, 1887, 4.

67. I based O'Neill's batting average on my own research and the batting average of other players on the Browns on the statistics generated by the Information Concepts Incorporated (ICI) project in 1969. *American Association ICI. Statistics 1887* (Cooperstown: National Baseball Hall of Fame Library, 2002). The averages I cite for O'Neill, Foutz, Gleason, Comiskey, and Latham are consistent with those reported by the *St. Louis Post-Dispatch* and *The Sporting News*, which were "compiled from the official scores, just as they are sent to Secretary Wikoff of the Association." "The World's Champions. The Official Batting and Fielding Averages of the St. Louis Browns," *The Sporting News*, May 21, 1887, 2; "In Field and at Bat," *St. Louis Post-Dispatch*, May 21, 1887, 12.

68. Newspapers and weeklies published batting, fielding, and pitching statistics on an infrequent basis, usually just after the end of each month of the season. The report on the first month of the season, from April 16, Opening Day for most Association teams, to the games played on May 16, appeared in a number of newspapers in the third week in May. "Base-Ball and Athletics. How They Stand. American Association," *St. Louis Globe-Democrat*, May 22, 1887, 7.

69. I do not have a column in the table for runs batted in (RBI) because this statistic was not recorded in 1887. The RBI did not become an official statistic until 1920. I refer to RBI in various contexts throughout the book, in this chapter to provide a more detailed comment on O'Neill's contribution to the runs scored by the Browns. For a comment on the history of the RBI, see Nemec, *The Official Rules of Baseball Illustrated*, 159–160.

70. Runs Produced (RP) is a statistic that measures a player's contribution to run-making. It combines both scoring runs (R) and driving in runs (RBI). In the formula for calculating RP (R + RBI-HR), home runs are subtracted from the total number of runs and runs batted in so that home runs are not counted twice (as a run and a run batted in). While RP was not introduced until the middle of the twentieth century, I use RP in this book for two reasons. First, RP reflects the emphasis on run-making in the 1880s, evident in the strategic play of most teams and in the run-centered focus of most game reports in the newspapers (which usually describe how each run was scored). Second, it is a relatively straightforward calculation, in keeping with the statistics used at the late nineteenth century. "Runs Produced," Accessed July 30, 2015. http://baseball-reference.com. In addition to runs produced, I also discuss O'Neill's runs in terms of their impact (Run Impact). Specifically, I report the number of times that O'Neill's runs scored or batted in tied the game, put the Browns into the lead, or represented the winning run.

71. Henry Chadwick was one of the most ardent critics of players or teams who emphasized home run hitting. He argued that sluggers did not support teamwork and strategic or scientific play. According to Chadwick, the slugger was less likely to hit singles or sacrifice hits or to get on base. See Henry Chadwick, *The Art of Baseball Batting* (1885; Reprinted Indiana: Repressed Publishing, 2012), 43–46.

Chapter 7

1. In most cases, a player who hits for the cycle has four to six times at bat in a nine-inning game. Thus, the batsman would have a game average between .667 and 1.000 (e.g., 4 hits in 6 at-bats, 4 hits in 5 at-bats, 4 hits in 4 at-bats), a level that would increase his batting average. In terms of total bases, the minimum requirements of a cycle would produce ten bases (single—1 base, double—2 bases, triple—3 bases, home run—4 bases).

2. For the list of players who have hit for cycles, see Retrosheet.com.

3. Joe DiMaggio had two quasi-cycles. Herm Krabbenhoft, "Quasi-cycles—Better than Cycles?" *Baseball Research Journal*, 46, no. 2 (Fall 2017), 108.

4. *Ibid.*

5. On May 7, O'Neill had four runs and four runs batted in, which translates into to a creation of seven runs produced of the twelve runs scored by the Browns (after subtracting one for the home run, to avoid double-counting it as a run and as an RBI).

6. "Sporting. The Browns Cov-

ering Themselves All Over with Glory," *St. Louis Republican,* May 8, 1887, 15.

7. Ibid.

Chapter 8

1. O'Neill returned briefly in game one of the doubleheader against Brooklyn on May 30. He reinjured his hand on a fly ball to left field and left the game after one-half inning. Although he did not take a turn at bat, the game counts as one of his 124 games played in 1887. I include it as part of the 12 games he missed due to his injury.

2. Comiskey arranged for each of the Browns to appear in an advertisement for Merrell's Penetrating Oil at different points in the season. For O'Neill's advertisement, see "James E. O'Neill—Left Fielder," *The Sporting News,* July 23, 1887, 2. Comiskey's advertisement for Merrell's Penetrating Oil also appeared on the back cover of the 1888 Reach's Guide. *Reach's Official American Association Base Ball Guide 1888* (1888; Reprinted New York: Horton, 1989).

3. In the American Association, by season's end only St. Louis and Cincinnati had posted winning records on the road.

4. In 1887, the most runs allowed by the Browns in a game was 16, which occurred twice, the first time on June 13 against Philadelphia and again on July 1 against Louisville. The biggest margin of defeat was 12 runs. The Browns lost to Louisville, 16–4, on July 1 and to Cincinnati, 15–3, on September 21.

5. O'Neill started in two other games in which he had no recorded times at bat. He was in the lineup for a game on May 30 (see Note 1 above) that counted as a game played. He had one putout and no times at bat. The second game was against Louisville on July 3. Louisville was awarded the game by forfeit in the third inning when Comiskey refused to let his players go to bat. In a forfeit, the game counted as a win for Louisville and a loss for St. Louis. The statistics of individual players in a forfeited game did not count (e.g., time at bat, hits, fly outs, etc.).

6. O'Neill hit his lone home run in this second phase on June 22 as part of an 8–4 loss to Cincinnati. On what appeared to be a single to left field, the ball took an awkward bounce that alluded George Tebeau, the left fielder, and rolled to the picket fence, which gave O'Neill enough time to make the circuit for a home run. The *Cincinnati Times-Star* called it a "scratch safe hit." "'Our Charm prevailed.' Cincinnati Again Defeats the Champions," *Cincinnati Times-Star,* June 23, 1887, 6.

7. The following quote from a game against Pittsburgh noted the cautious approach that O'Neill took to base running: "Even the Pittsburghers were obliged to smile when Latham would shout out, 'That's right Jim, go to second on this ball,' this to Jim O'Neill, when everybody knew that Jim could not get to second unless the ball got past the catcher." "From St. Louis. Latham's Coaching," *Sporting Life,* June 23, 1886, 5.

8. O'Neill never developed the skill of sliding for which so many of the Browns were known (Latham, Comiskey, Welch, Robinson, Caruthers). From 1888 onwards, he did slide, but infrequently and usually awkwardly.

9. For two examples of O'Neill's failed attempts in 1885 and 1886 at a delayed double steal, see: "A Terrible Drubbing: That Administered to the Louisville Nine by the Browns Yesterday," *St. Louis Republican,* April 25, 1885, 6; "Sporting. Won, Of Course," *St. Louis Republican,* October 8, 1886, 6.

10. "Notes of the Game," *Cleveland Plain Dealer,* August 17, 1887, 4; "Browns, 15; Metropolitans, 6," *St. Louis Globe-Democrat,* August 27, 1887, 7; "Browns, 7; Brooklyns, 4," *St. Louis Globe-Democrat,* August 31, 1887, 8.

11. Although the official scorekeepers were required to keep a record of the bases stolen, the newspaper reports of the games did not always include a column in the box score for stolen bases, nor did they note each instance of a stolen base in the account of the game. Consequently, I use qualifiers such as "around," "about," "at least," or "likely" when citing the number of stolen bases or other base running statistics because it is difficult to be precise with most of these figures. When I cite a range (e.g., 6–8 times where O'Neill stole home as part of a delayed double steal), I have information to support the lower number. The higher number is my estimate of what seemed likely but not always verifiable from my review of the records of the full season.

12. "Cincinnati, 5; St. Louis, 2," *St. Louis Globe-Democrat,* April 23, 1887, 7; "Browns Shut Out," *St. Louis Republican,* August 6, 1887, 6.

13. "St. Louis, 8; Cincinnati, 2," *St. Louis Globe-Democrat,* September 29, 1887, 8.

14. "The Association. The Athletics Play to Win, and as a Result St. Louis Loses," *Philadelphia Press,* September 13, 1887, 6.

15. "Base Ball Notes," *St. Louis Republican,* August 24, 1887, 6.

16. "Notes of the Game," *St. Louis Post-Dispatch,* August 24, 1887, 8.

17. O'Neill played with Nicol when he was with the Browns from 1884 to 1886 and with Reilly on the New York Metropolitans in 1882. Both players would be familiar with O'Neill's base-running habits, including his inclination not to run to first at full speed on every hit.

18. "Base Ball. Cincinnati's Badly Beaten by Champions," *Cincinnati Commercial Gazette,* June 20, 1887, 3; "Notes," *Cincinnati Enquirer,* June 20, 1887, 2.

19. "Gossip of the Diamond. The Result of the Visit of St. Louis—Notes About the Games," *Baltimore American,* June 17, 1887, 4.

20. "Diamond Sparks," *St. Louis Post-Dispatch,* June 30, 1887, 8.

21. Comiskey regularly had post-game meetings to review the Browns' performance. After Comiskey expressed his views on particular plays or incidents, he invited the players to add their comments. The players were often direct in their criticisms of unacceptable play (e.g., failure to run) and would sometimes ride the offending player until he corrected or improved his game. In 1888, a reporter from the *St. Louis Post-Dispatch* eavesdropped outside the clubhouse door on a spirited post-game discussion following a loss in the 11th inning on a fly ball that most felt O'Neill should have caught. Comiskey began his harangue at O'Neill. After a "series of 'cuss words' which would exhaust the supply of dashes," O'Neill walked out of the room. Those remaining in the room then turned on Harry Lyons, the diminutive and mild-mannered center fielder, who had failed to bunt a ball when ordered to do so. He was "abused and brow-beaten by the whole crowd," unable to fight back like O'Neill, who could use his "fists and weight" to temper if not stop any verbal onslaught. "The Browns Have War: An Exciting Scene After

Yesterday's Game," *St. Louis Post-Dispatch*, June 20, 1888, 8.

22. "Caylor's Comments. Reflections Caused by Work of Two Great Clubs. The St. Louis Browns' Violation of the Coaching Rules," *Sporting Life*, June 8, 1887, 3.

23. "Two Big Games Lost by Brooklyn to the St. Louis Browns Yesterday," *Brooklyn Citizen*, May 31, 1887, 3.

24. For a sample of Latham's expressions, see: "From St. Louis. Chips from the Diamond," *Sporting Life*, May 11, 1887, 4; "I am a Dude," *The Sporting News*, June 18, 1887, 1; and "From Cincinnati. A Pen Picture of Latham," *Sporting Life*, June 29, 1887, 2.

25. Rule 59 stated: "The Captains and Coachers are restricted in coaching to the base runners only, and not allowed to address any remarks except to the Base Runner and then only in words of necessary direction." "Playing Rules of the American Association of Base Ball Clubs 1887," *Reach's Official American Association Base Ball Guide 1887* (1886; Reprinted New York: Horton, 1989), 161.

26. "A Drawn Game. Broken Up by Fielder Welch," *Baltimore Sun*, June 17, 1887, 1.

27. "Smashed the Ball. The Way the Louisvilles Won Yesterday's Game from the Champions," *Louisville Courier-Journal*, July 2, 1887, 2.

28. "Three Defeats. The Brooklyn Team's Poor Record in St. Louis," *Brooklyn Eagle*, May 25, 1887, 1.

29. "Three Straight. The Browns Take Another Tumble," *Cincinnati Enquirer*, June 23, 1887, 2.

30. "Our Oysters. The Browns Get Away with the Baltimore Brand," *St. Louis Republican*, July 10, 1887, 14.

31. David Nemec, ed., *Major League Baseball Profiles: 1871–1900, Volume 1*. (Lincoln: University of Nebraska Press, 2011), 625.

32. "Heroes of the Diamond. The Browns Scalp the Indians—Brooklyn Drubs Cleveland," *New York Herald*, June 5, 1887, 15.

33. "Welch's Ruffianly Trick. A Thug Who Should be Forever Barred from Honest Ball-Playing," *Philadelphia North American*, June 10, 1887, 1.

34. "In Trouble. Charges Against Two St. Louis Players. The Athletics Endeavoring to Have Comiskey and Welch Disciplined," *Sporting Life*, June 15, 1887, 1.

35. Attendance figures were not always reported and, when they were, sources sometimes differed on the numbers. For the series in Baltimore, the *Baltimore American* indicated that the paid attendance for the four games was 37,000, but when the ladies (who did not pay) were added, the total was over 40,000. "Gossip of the Diamond. Over 37,000 at the St. Louis Games," *Baltimore American*, June 18, 1887, 5. The *St. Louis Republican* stated that 6,000 fans attended game one of the July 8–11 series in St. Louis but did not provide figures for the other two games. The only other comment from the St. Louis press on the size of the crowd at each game was in the *St. Louis Globe-Democrat*, which indicated that 5,000 fans attended game one and "large crowds" were present in games two and three. "Baltimore, 4; St. Louis, 3," *St. Louis Globe-Democrat*, July 9, 1887, 6; "St. Louis, 9; Baltimore, 3," *St. Louis Globe-Democrat*, July 10, 1887, 11; "St. Louis, 12; Baltimore, 5," *St. Louis Globe-Democrat*, July 12, 1887, 8. The *Baltimore American* reported attendance numbers in St. Louis of 6,000, over 4,500, and 4,000. "It was a Big Surprise: St. Louis Counted on a Shut-out," *Baltimore American*, July 9, 1887, 1; "Loss by Lack of Nerve. Baltimore Could Have Done Better," *Baltimore American*, July 10, 1887, 4; "Hit Hard in St. Louis. The Champions Pound the Kid," *Baltimore American*, July 12, 1887, 6.

36. "Gossip of the Diamond. Arrival of the St. Louis Champions—A Great Game Today," *Baltimore American*, June 14, 1887, 4.

37. Ibid.

38. "Getting to the Grounds," *Baltimore American*, June 15, 1887, 4.

39. "A Game from St. Louis. The Overflow," *Baltimore Sun*, June 15, 1887, 1.

40. Ibid. Some of the hits ruled as doubles, without the ground rule, may have been triples or home runs. Others may have been retrieved quickly and the batsman held to single. Or still others might have been a fly out if the fielder had been able to get back quickly, which he was not always able to do because of the closeness of the crowd.

41. Ibid.

42. "The Game Played in Town. Novel Arrangements The American Had for Giving Out the News," *Baltimore American*, June 18, 1887, 5.

43. "The News in the City. The American Tells the People All About the Second Game," *Baltimore American*, June 16, 1887, 4.

44. "In Front of 'The American.' Thousands of People Watch the Game by Bulletins—A Special Wire," *Baltimore American*, June 17, 1887, 4.

45. "A Game from St. Louis. Latham's Coaching," *Baltimore Sun*, June 15, 1887, 1.

46. The Browns lost the last two games in Philadelphia (8–4 and 16–8) and the first game against Baltimore (15–12). The only other times in 1887 that the Browns lost more than two games in a row were against Cincinnati, when they lost three consecutive games from June 20–22 and four consecutive games from September 21–25.

47. "Notes of the Game," *Baltimore Sun*, June 16, 1887, 5.

48. "Won by St. Louis. The Baltimores Fail to Bat and Narrowly Escape a Shutout," *Baltimore Sun*, June 16, 1887, 5.

49. "Welch's Life in Danger. He Causes the Game to Stop," *Baltimore American*, June 17, 1887, 4.

50. Ibid.

51. "The Game Played in Town," 5.

52. I have no information about how the fans outside *The American* building were specifically told about the sequence of events that happened after Welch attempted to steal second base. However, the people who were responsible for updating the bulletin boards and for telling the audience about what was happening at the park did pass on a number of announcements to those gathered around the building. The events listed as telegraphed messages actually occurred. I have no knowledge of the contents of the telegraphed messages or of what was printed on the bulletin boards or orally told to the audience. As for who told the crowd about the information in the telegraphed messages, an auctioneer was not used until game four. In games one and two, those manning the bulletin boards periodically yelled out what was happening as they posted this same information on the boards. In short, my outline of reported messages from an auctioneer has to be considered historical fiction, though I would hasten to add, based on events as they were reported in newspaper accounts. For a description of how game three was "broadcasted," see "In Front of 'The American.' Thousands of People Watched the Game by Bulletins—A Special Wire," *Baltimore American*, June 17, 1887, 4.

53. In the initial excitement and uproar after Welch knocked over Greenwood, no one heard the umpire make a call, so most people assumed that the silence meant that Welch was safe. In the list of telegraphed messages, I surmised that the telegraph operator at the park, not hearing the umpire shout "Out!," would assume a safe call and send a message to this effect.

54. "A Drawn Game," 1.

55. "Bunched Hits," *St. Louis Sunday Sayings,* June 19, 1887.

56. "A Drawn Game," 1.

57. "Trial of Curtis Welch. Charges Made by Citizens—Greenwood Says He was not Assaulted," *Baltimore Sun,* June 18, 1887, 6.

58. "What Welch Says. He Knocked Down Greenwood Down Purposely So as to Make the Winning Run," *Baltimore Sun,* June 18, 1887, 6.

59. "St. Louis Wins the Odd Game. Effective Pitching by Caruthers—A Game Without Any Coaching," *Baltimore Sun,* June 18, 1887, 6.

60. Ibid.

61. "Gifts and Goose-eggs. Medals for Chris, Diamond for Curt, Shutout for Louisville," *St. Louis Republican,* June 29, 1887, 6.

62. "From St. Louis. Welch Remembered," *Sporting Life,* July 6, 1887, 5.

63. "Bad Luck for the Browns. Bushong's Finger Broken, Latham Fined, and a Game Lost," *St. Louis Republican,* July 2, 1887, 6.

64. Jack Boyle was acquired in late 1886 in a trade that sent Hugh Nicol to Cincinnati. He proved to be an excellent replacement for Bushong, catching 44 games in a row before he was relieved from duty. Like Bushong, Boyle rarely complained about sore hands or fingers. However, with limited major league experience—he caught only one game in Cincinnati—Boyle did not have the knowledge or savvy of Bushong. Nonetheless, he had many defensive skills. Blessed with a strong arm, he quickly established a reputation for throwing out aspiring base stealers. He was a sure catch and could "handle the swiftest and wildest pitching." And, at six feet four inches, Boyle was the tallest catcher in the nineteenth century, which, on occasion, enabled him to stand his ground against runners who tried to knock him over on close plays at home. Offensively, he was a weak batsman and base runner. In 88 games in 1887, Boyle hit .189 and stole seven bases. His batting average was the lowest of all Association batters who had 350 or more times at bat and well behind the core players on the Browns. The major contribution of Boyle to the team was clearly behind the plate. "Notes and Comments," *Sporting Life,* August 31, 1887, 5; "John Boyle," *New York Clipper,* March 21, 1891, 29; "Boyle, John Anthony/'Jack'" David Nemec, ed., *Major League Baseball Profiles: 1871–1900, Volume 2.* (Lincoln: University of Nebraska Press, 2011), 308.

65. "Nine to Nothing," *Louisville Courier-Journal,* July 4, 1887, 4.

66. "Louisvilles, 9; Browns, 0," *St. Louis Globe-Democrat,* July 4, 1887, 3.

67. "Nine to Nothing," 4.

68. "On the Diamond. Sunday," *Louisville Evening Post,* July 4, 1887, 3.

69. "Kicked Themselves Out. The Unique Spectacle Presented by St. Louis Base Ball Club," *Louisville Commercial,* July 4, 1887, 5.

70. "Notes of the Game," *Louisville Courier-Journal,* July 4, 1887, 4.

71. David Nemec and Eric Miklich, *Forfeits and Successfully Protested Games in Major League Baseball: A Complete Record, 1871–2013.* (Jefferson, NC: McFarland, 2014), 45.

72. "Notes and Comments," *Sporting Life,* July 13, 1887, 10.

73. The headline was reported by a St. Louis newspaper. See "Diamond Sparks," *St. Louis Post-Dispatch,* July 2, 1887, 9.

74. "The Baltimore Series. Barnie's Club and the 'Reception' Proposed for Them Thursday," *St. Louis Post-Dispatch,* July 5, 1887, 8.

75. "Base Ball Notes," *St. Louis Republican,* July 5, 1887, 6.

76. "All Enjoyed the Game Played in Baltimore as Well as in St. Louis—A Great Feat," *Baltimore American,* July 10, 1887, 4.

77. "Given Out in Great Style. 'The American' Shows the Multitude How the Game Was Played," *Baltimore American,* July 9, 1887, 4.

78. "Baltimores, 4; Browns, 3," *St. Louis Globe-Democrat,* July 9, 1887, 6.

79. One of the cornerstones of the American Association was playing games on Sunday. Since the inception of the Association in 1882, the Browns had played on Sundays in Sportsman's Park, usually to large crowds. In the spring of 1887, the Sabbatarians in the Missouri legislature passed an act to take effect in mid–June, forbidding a wide range of amusements. On July 15, Judge Noonan accepted the argument that baseball was recreation or entertainment and therefore did not qualify as one of the amusements prohibited in the recent legislation. Furthermore, and more to the point, baseball was not a "business that compelled ballplayers to work on Sundays," and thus the 1839 blue law preventing such labor on a Sunday did not apply. For a more detailed account of this case and Judge Noonan's decision, see Jon Cash, *Before They Were Cardinals: Major League Baseball in Nineteenth-Century St. Louis* (Columbia: University of Missouri Press, 2002), 155–160.

80. "Knocking King Kilroy. Baltimore's Left-Hand Wizard Almost Annihilated," *St. Louis Republican,* July 12, 1887, 6.

81. In the first phase of the season, O'Neill scored 41 runs and had 33 RBI. Fourteen of these runs made a difference in the game. Ten of the runs tied the game or put the Browns into the lead, and four represented the winning runs.

82. Two other Association batsmen hovered near the top of the leader board. Reddy Mack, the Louisville second baseman, had a batting average on July 11 of .412, hitting .420 in phase one (April 16 to May 24) and .406 in phase two (May 25 to July 11). Denny Lyons, the Philadelphia third baseman, had a batting average on July 11 of .449, hitting .434 in phase one and .458 in phase two. Chapters 10, 12, and 14 follow the batting performances of these two batsmen in relation to the achievements of O'Neill and Browning.

Chapter 9

1. "Sporting. The Browns Covering Themselves All Over with Glory," *St. Louis Republican,* May 8, 1887, 15.

2. "Baseball Surprises. The Champion Browns Scalped by the Indians," *New York Herald,* June 7, 1887, 8.

3. The seven games that featured O'Neill's batting and fielding included the following: May 14—Browns beat Baltimore, 8–3, and O'Neill had two hits in four times at bat (base on balls, home run) and three putouts; May 18—Browns beat Philadelphia, 12—and O'Neill

had three hits in five times at bat (base on balls, single, triple) and three putouts; June 22—Browns lost to Cincinnati, 8–4, and O'Neill had two hits in four times at bat (single, home run) and three putouts; July 8—Browns lost to Baltimore, 4–3, and O'Neill had four hits in four times at bat (two bases on balls, single, double) and four putouts; August 7—Browns beat Cleveland, 10–7, and O'Neill had three hits in five times at bat (base on balls, two doubles) and three putouts; August 16—Browns beat Cleveland, 11–4, and O'Neill had four hits in five times at bat (four singles) and one putout; and August 28—Browns beat New York, 9–2, and O'Neill had two hits in five times at bat (single, double) three putouts, and one error.

4. "Browns, 8; Baltimores, 3," *St. Louis Globe-Democrat,* May 15, 1887, 10.

5. Weidman, the New York pitcher, had a "splendid game," delivering numerous difficult pitches that only O'Neill, Latham, and Boyle were able to handle with some success, lining out "several nice hits." "Prettily Played. Good Pitching, Fine Batting and the Browns Win," *St. Louis Republican,* August 29, 1887, 5.

6. "Browns, 9; Metropolitans, 2," *St. Louis Globe-Democrat,* August 29, 1887, 3.

7. "Prettily Played," 5.

8. "The Browns Win Easily: As the Necessary Consequence of the Athletics' Poor Fielding," *Philadelphia North American,* September 10, 1887, 1.

9. "Eggs. Nine of the Overripe Variety. The World-Beaters Take Their Second Dose of Whitewash," *Cincinnati Enquirer,* September 23, 1887, 2.

10. "Notes," *Cincinnati Enquirer,* September 23, 1887. Dickson defines a circus catch as follows: "A spectacular catch suggesting the moves of a circus acrobat. Such a catch may involve a jump, dive, flip, roll, or combination thereof." Paul Dickson, *The Dickson Baseball Dictionary,* 3d ed. (New York: W.W. Norton, 2009), 190.

11. "000000000=0. The Above Represents the Work of Von der Ahe's Men Yesterday," *Cincinnati Commercial Gazette,* September 23, 1887, 3.

12. "Nine Goose-Eggs for the Browns," *St. Louis Republican,* September 23, 1887, 6.

13. "Cincinnatis, 6; St. Louis, 0," *St. Louis Globe-Democrat,* September 23, 1887, 8.

14. O'Neill was also credited with an assist in this game. However, there was no information in any of the game accounts about when or how O'Neill earned the assist.

15. In 1883 and 1884, O'Neill was a pitcher. In New York (1883), he played seven games in the outfield. In his first year with St. Louis (1884), he was the Browns' Opening Day pitcher and was considered part of the pitching rotation for all of 1884 and even into the early weeks of 1885. However, once he hurt his arm in June of 1884, when he returned to the lineup a few weeks later, Comiskey moved him to the outfield. Even though he was injured and appeared in only 52 games, the 1885 season was the first time that O'Neill regularly played as the Browns' left fielder. Thus, when I refer to O'Neill's career as an outfielder, I concentrate on those years when he was recognized as the regular, full-time left fielder (1885–1892).

16. J. C. Kofoed, "The Greatest Outfield," *Baseball Magazine,* XI, no. 3 (July 1913), 30.

17. Fred Pfeffer played against O'Neill in two World Championship Series (1885 and 1886) and in exhibition games, and thus witnessed his defensive play in left field on numerous occasions. He also interviewed numerous outfielders, including O'Neill, for the book. See N. Fred Pfeffer, *Scientific Ball* (Chicago: N. Fred Pfeffer, Publisher, 1889), 37–38.

18. Ibid.

19. Ibid., 70.

20. O'Neill was hit on the hand by a pitched ball twice, the first time in his second pre-season game (April 4) and the second time in a game on May 20. On July 4, he hurt his finger on a fly ball.

21. One of O'Neill's few efforts in 1887 to throw out a runner resulted in a double play. On August 13, in a game that the Browns lost to Louisville, 13–3, Guy Hecker, the Louisville first baseman, was on second with Pete Browning coming to the plate. Browning hit a fly ball that O'Neill caught. He quickly threw the ball to Robinson, who tagged out Hecker, slow getting back to second base. "Louisvilles, 13; Browns, 3," *St. Louis Globe Democrat,* August 14, 1887, 9.

22. David Nemec notes: "Among all gardeners in a minimum of 750 AA games, his 59 career assists are a whopping 92 short of the next-lowest man on the list, Jim McTamanay (151)." David Nemec, *Major League Baseball Profiles: 1871–1900, Volume 1, the Ballplayers Who Built the Game* (Lincoln: University of Nebraska Press, 2011), 589.

23. O'Neill had an error on a ground ball on July 1 as part of the 16–4 loss against Louisville. Browning, the Louisville center fielder, hit a line drive at Latham, who dodged the screaming shot, "barely escaping with his life." On this "Arlie Latham," a term later used to refer to any time a fielder avoided a hard-hit ball by stepping aside to let it pass into the outfield, O'Neill was faced with stopping this blast as it bounded towards his feet, a challenge that he was not up to. The ball skipped between his legs, and three runs scored on O'Neill's error. "Easy to Beat 'Em. The St. Louis Browns Defeated by the Louisvilles," *Louisville Commercial,* July 2, 1887, 3.

24. "High Flyers. The Correct and Incorrect Way of Taking in Sky-Scrapers," *St. Louis Post-Dispatch,* August 7, 1886, 9.

25. "Diamond Sparks," *St. Louis Post-Dispatch,* August 13, 1887, 9.

26. "Diamond Sparks," *St. Louis Post-Dispatch,* July 1, 1887, 3.

27. "Bunched Hits," *St. Louis Sunday Sayings,* May 22, 1887.

28. "Long Swim. Sunday Sports Varied by an Exciting River Contest," *St. Louis Chronicle,* August 27, 1887, 2.

29. After a 6–3 loss to Baltimore, the *St. Louis Post-Dispatch* stated that "O'Neill played a lazy game," while the *St. Louis Globe-Democrat* noted that Tip's "chief offense was sleepiness." "The Dress of Bad Ball, That was the Cause of the Browns' Defeat Yesterday," *St. Louis Post-Dispatch,* July 29, 1888, 6; "Baltimores, 6; St. Louis, 3," *St. Louis Globe-Democrat,* July 29, 1888.

30. "Ten Innings. The Visitors' Errors Give the Cincinnatis the Victory in the Tenth," *Cincinnati Commercial Gazette,* May 11, 1888.

31. "Hughes Did It. O'Neill in Left," *St. Louis Post Dispatch,* July 8, 1888, 15.

32. Of the 285 chances O'Neill had in the outfield, he made only 13 errors on fly balls. If he had no further errors, his fielding percentage in 1887 would have been .952. His fielding percentage fell below .900 largely due to his ten errors on ground balls, relatively higher than

other outfielders on his team. From my review of the game reports, it is evident that Welch, in center field, and Foutz and Caruthers, who shared the duties in right field, made comparatively fewer errors in fielding ground balls.

33. O'Neill's ability to cover a lot of territory was a source of some debate. In 1887, there were a few mutterings in this regard, but little or no concerted effort to criticize his fielding on this basis. By May 14, for example, the *St. Louis Globe-Democrat* noted that O'Neill was "covering more territory than he ever has" (Note 4). More than a century later, some scholars were critical of O'Neill's fielding record. For example, Nemec claimed that "O'Neill covered little ground in the field," an assessment that points to a career-long problem that I feel does not apply to O'Neill's fielding performance in 1886 or 1887, nor is it relevant for much of his time in St. Louis and Chicago. David Nemec, *Major League Baseball Profiles: 1871-1900, Volume 1, the Ballplayers Who Built the Game* (Lincoln: University of Nebraska Press, 2011), 589. Bill Sharsig, co-owner and general manager of the Philadelphia Athletics, suggested in the *Philadelphia Record* that Pop Corkhill, Harry Stovey, and O'Neill would be a great outfield next season. The *St. Louis Globe-Democrat* added: "That is a pretty fair outfield and one that would cover considerable ground. With Corkhill in Cincinnati, O'Neill in St. Louis and Stovey in Philadelphia no outfield in the world would cover as much ground." "Diamond Dust," *St. Louis Globe-Democrat,* August 24, 1887, 8.

34. In his final five years (1888–1892), O'Neill's fielding percentage was over .900 every year (high of .937 in 1889 with St. Louis; low of .922 in 1892 with Cincinnati in the National League). For four of the five years, O'Neill ranked in the top ten in putouts in the league (high of 264 in 1889 with St. Louis; low of 188 in 1892 with Cincinnati). O'Neill also significantly reduced his number of errors, with fewer than 20 in each of his final five seasons, well down the list among all outfielders (low of 14 in 1891 with St. Louis; high of 19 in 1889 with St. Louis and in 1890 with Chicago, in the Players' League). O'Neill's throwing statistics, specifically his numbers of assists and double plays, were consistently among the worst for outfielders in the majors and in each of the leagues in which he played (1888–1889, 1891 with St. Louis in the American Association; 1890 with Chicago in the Players' League; and 1892 with Cincinnati in the National League).

35. The phase-by-phase breakdown of games in which O'Neill was featured for batting and fielding was as follows: Phase One (April 16 to May 24): in 24 games, 13 times for batting and three times for fielding; Phase Two (May 25 to July 11): in 28 games, four times for batting and nine times for fielding; Phase Three (July 12 to August 10): in 25 games, nine times for batting and three times for fielding; Phase Four (August 12 to September 8): in 24 games, 13 times for batting and two times for fielding; and Phase Five (September 9 to October 9): in 23 games, eight times for batting and once for fielding.

Chapter 10

1. By almost any measure, it would be difficult to describe O'Neill's batting performance in any of the five phases of his season as "poor" or "in a slump." However, in the record-breaking 1887 season, the bar was set higher. O'Neill's batting average in phases two and three, especially during certain series within these two phases, was considerably below his own batting average in the other three phases. In these one-to-two-series dips, O'Neill's average was also lower than the batting averages of some of his teammates (notably Caruthers, Robinson, Foutz), his team as a whole, and the leading batsmen in the American Association. Thus, by comparison, in these times of struggle, O'Neill's hitting was "poor or below normal," and thus, by definition, a slump. Paul Dickson, *The Dickson Baseball Dictionary*, 3d ed. (New York: W.W. Norton, 2009), 794.

2. This adage has frequently been attributed to Confucius. However, the Quote Investigator argues that this adage first appeared in 1760–1761 in a series of letters by a fictitious Chinese traveler published in *The Public Ledger* magazine in London. The author of the letters was an Irishman, Oliver Goldsmith. See "Our greatest glory is not in never falling, but in rising every time we fall." Quote Investigator, accessed August 27, 2017, https://quoteinvestigator.com/2014/05/27/rising/. I am sure O'Neill, a player of Irish descent, would appreciate that the adage I use to describe his significant improvement in batting was first coined by a fellow Irishman.

3. Although the five phases are not divided into months, comparing O'Neill's batting record by months is also instructive. His batting averages by month were (Hits—At-Bats): April .480 (24–50); May .636 (42–66); June .432 (41–95); July .354 (35–99); August .557 (68–122); September .506 (44–87); and October .511 (23–45). July was clearly O'Neill's worst month, while May and August were his best months.

4. In the 15 July games in phase three, O'Neill hit two doubles, one triple, and one home run for 15 total bases. In the ten games in the August portion of phase three, he had six doubles, one triple, and two home runs for 23 total bases. O'Neill also scored 21 of his 31 runs and added 11 of his 19 runs batted in during the ten games in August.

5. "From St. Louis. News Notes and Comments," *Sporting Life,* July 27, 1887, 4.

6. "Bunched Hits," *St. Louis Sunday Sayings,* July 31, 1887.

7. For the season, the Browns averaged 8.2 runs per game, while in this phase they only scored 6.1 runs per game. The Browns' seasonal average for stealing bases was 4.2 per game. In this phase, they stole only 3.3 bases per game.

8. In 1887, the Browns averaged 3.49 errors per game. In this third phase, they made 2.92 errors per game. The Browns made 12 errors against Baltimore on July 29, their worst fielding game of the season, yet still won the game, 12–9. Excluding this error-filled game, in the other 24 games in this phase, the Browns averaged 2.54 errors per game.

9. Browns pitchers averaged 3.77 earned runs per game across the season. The pitchers also contributed to the tough defensive stand of the Browns in this phase by holding their opponents to 2.48 earned runs per game.

10. "Base Ball Notes," *St. Louis Republican,* July 17, 1887, 14.

11. "Won by the Browns," *St. Louis Republican,* July 25, 1887, 5.

12. "Baseball and Sporting News," *Brooklyn Citizen,* July 25, 1887, 2.

13. "Von der Ahe and Wikoff. Description of Byrne and Von der Ahe's Quarrel at Brooklyn," *The Sporting News,* August 6, 1887, 1.

14. "Base Ball Notes," *St. Louis Republican*, July 17, 1887, 14.
15. "Fielded Flagrantly. Ragged Support for Good Pitching Beats the Athletics," *St. Louis Republican*, July 17, 1887, 14.
16. "Still a Tie Game. A Great Contest of Pitchers," *Baltimore Sun*, July 20, 1887, 5.
17. "A Great Game It Was. A Tie in Fourteen Innings," *Baltimore American*, July 20, 1887, 2.
18. "Still a Tie Game," 5.
19. "St. Louis, 2; Baltimores, 2," *St. Louis Globe-Democrat*, July 20, 1887, 8.
20. "A Great Game It Was," 2.
21. Ibid.
22. "Still a Tie Game," 5.
23. Ibid.
24. In 1887, the umpire could call a strike on "any obvious attempt to make a foul hit." Sometimes a batter would deliberately and repeatedly bunt a ball foul to frustrate and tire an opposing pitcher or to increase the chance of getting a base on balls. In this case, the umpire determined that Caruthers purposely hit the ball foul and consequently called each ball that was bunted foul a strike. "The National Playing Rules 1887," *Reach's Official American Association Base Ball Guide 1887* (1887; Reprinted New York: Horton, 1989), 154.
25. "Still a Tie Game," 5.
26. Ibid.
27. Ibid.
28. "Tied in Eleven Innings," *New York Times*, July 23, 1887, 2.
29. "Three Interesting Games," *New York Herald*, July 23, 1887, 8. The *New York Clipper* also felt that "Umpire Curry had erroneously decided it not out." "Metropolitans vs. St. Louis," *New York Clipper*, July 30, 1887, 312–13.
30. The prize of a bottle of Pond's Extract for a home run hit by a visiting player to New York was first announced early in the season by the *New York World*. Other newspapers cited this announcement at different points in the season. "An Offer That Will Please Base-Ball Players," *St. Louis Post-Dispatch*, May 14, 1887, 12. I could not find any report to confirm that O'Neill actually received a bottle of *Pond's Extract*.
31. Seven of O'Neill's 16 hitless games in 1887 occurred in this phase, six in July. O'Neill had three hitless games in phase two of his season (May 25 to July 11) and two hitless games in each of the other three phases (April 16 to June 24, August 12 to September 8, September 9 to October 9). Across the 16 hitless games, O'Neill was on base ten times, five times on an error and five times on a fielder's choice. He also scored three runs and had three runs batted in.
32. "The Bachelor Browns," *St. Louis Republican*, August 14, 1887, 14.
33. "The Married Browns," *St. Louis Republican*, July 3, 1887, 14.
34. "Base Ball Notes," *St. Louis Post-Dispatch*, October 2, 1887, 10.
35. Local teams sometimes named themselves after one of the Browns. There also was a team named the Silver Tips. "The Little Diamond," *St. Louis Post-Dispatch*, July 18, 1887, 8; "The Little Diamond," *St. Louis Post-Dispatch*, July 23, 1887, 9; "The Little Diamond," *St. Louis Post-Dispatch* 25, 1887, 5.
36. "Mauled Mr. Mullane. The Browns Beat Cincinnati and Earn Every Run," *St. Louis Republican*, August 5, 1887, 6.
37. "Browns, 7; Cincinnatis, 2," *St. Louis Globe Democrat*, August 5, 1887, 6.
38. "Mauled Mr. Mullane," 6.
39. "Local Hits," *The Sporting News*, July 30, 1887, 5.
40. "Browns, 7; Cincinnatis, 2," *St. Louis Globe Democrat*, August 5, 1887, 5.
41. "The Bachelor Browns," 14.
42. Balls hit into the seats were considered still in play. On balls hit into the seats, fielders sometimes jumped the short fence in front of the benches to retrieve the ball and throw it back to one of the infielders with the hope of catching the runner before he scored a triple or home run. On hits into the seats by opposing batters, the St. Louis fans sometimes tried to help the Browns' outfielder in his pursuit of the ball by letting the ball hit them or even by kicking the ball back towards the fielder so that he did not have to scurry under benches. If one of the Browns hit the ball into the seats, the fans tried to get out of the way so that the ball would go further into or under the benches, making it all the more difficult for the opposing fielder to get the ball in time to throw out the St. Louis runner. "Notes on Yesterday's Game," *St. Louis Post-Dispatch*, August 5, 1887, 5.
43. In the four games in the April 27–May 1 series in St. Louis, the Browns scored 74 runs while Cleveland scored 38. In the August 7–10 series, the Browns scored 41 runs and Cleveland scored 23.
44. See Chapter 7, "Two Cycles," for a discussion of the concept of a near-cycle.
45. Many newspapers reported on O'Neill's nine hits in nine times at bat, failing to note that he also had a hit in his first at-bat on Wednesday August 10, thus making it ten hits in a row. "Local Hits," *The Sporting News*, August 13, 1887, 5.
46. "Long and Short Hits," *St. Louis Post-Dispatch*, August 11, 1887, 5.
47. "Clips and Chips," *St. Louis Post-Dispatch*, July 28, 1887, 5.
48. "Diamond Doings," *St. Louis Post-Dispatch*, August 2, 1887, 8.
49. "Pete and Tip," *St. Louis Post-Dispatch*, August 5, 1887, 5.
50. "Local Hits," *The Sporting News*, August 13, 1887, 5.
51. "Base Ball Notes," *St. Louis Republican*, August 9, 1887, 6.
52. The official averages of the leading Association batsmen were not available until weeks after the end of the season. Those who followed the batting race had to rely on the various unofficial compilations that were periodically published in the newspapers and weeklies. Locally, the *St. Louis Post-Dispatch* provided weekly summaries of the batting and fielding of each of the Browns. In this phase, the *Post-Dispatch's* statistics on July 16, 23, 27, 30, and August 9 showed that O'Neill did not have the highest batting average on the team. Each report had Caruthers, Foutz, or both ahead of O'Neill. For example, on August 9, the *St. Louis Post-Dispatch* reported that as of August 8, Caruthers led the Browns with an average of .461. Foutz was second at .455 and O'Neill third with .447. "The Champion's Averages," *St. Louis Post-Dispatch*, August 9, 1887, 5. However, the batting averages listed for Caruthers and Foutz included only at-bats in games when they pitched, omitting their batting record in games in which they played in the field. Other newspapers, likely influenced by the *St. Louis Post-Dispatch* weekly reports, also noted that O'Neill was no longer the Browns' batting leader. "Base Ball Notes," *St. Louis Republican*, July 17, 1887, 14. It must have come as a surprise when the summaries of the Association averages published by numerous newspapers in early August had O'Neill firmly in the lead in both the Association and on the Browns. Various newspapers, after Caruthers' and Foutz's hitting statistics in all games

were considered, reported that, as of August 1, Caruthers and Foutz trailed O'Neill in batting average. For example, *The Sporting News* indicated that O'Neill led the American Association with an average of .486. Caruthers was ranked sixth at .408, and Foutz was eighth at .398. "Tip O'Neill, The Leading Batsman According to the Official Averages," *The Sporting News*, August 6, 1887, 2.

Chapter 11

1. Henry Chadwick, *The Art of Baseball Batting* (Chicago: A. G. Spalding & Bros., 1885), 47–48.
2. *Ibid*.
3. "The Batting of 1887," *Spalding's Base Ball Guide and Official League Book for 1888* (1888; Reprinted New York: Horton, 1989), 19–20.
4. A record player was "more concerned about personal statistics than winning." Paul Dickson, *The Dickson Baseball Dictionary*, 3d ed. (New York: W.W. Norton, 2009), 693.
5. "The Batting of 1887," *Spalding's Base Ball Guide and Official League Book for 1888* (1888; Reprinted New York: Horton, 1989), 20.
6. Other writers echoed Chadwick's views on scientific batting. For example, Edward Prindle declared: "The progressive ball player is the one who uses his skill to the best advantage of the team to which he belongs and not solely for the purpose of running up a long list of 'home runs' ... Light, quick blows are the ones which yield the best results in the end. The slow, powerful blows which yield home runs when they *do* [italics in the original] hit, will miss the ball entirely in about four cases out of five where the sharp quick strokes would prove effective and called strikes are of course the result." Edward J. Prindle, "Light vs Heavy Blows," *The Art of Batting* (Philadelphia: A. J. Reach, 1888), 27. John Ward, a player on the New York club in the National League and President of the Brotherhood of Professional Base Ball Players, also warned against trying to hit the ball for home runs: "A great fault of many batters is that they try to hit the ball too hard. This is especially true of the younger players, the 'colts,' as they are called. A young player with a reputation as a hitter in some minor league, goes into the big club and at once thinks he must hit the ball over the fence. The result is that he doesn't hit it at all, and unless he corrects his fault, he goes on 'fanning the atmosphere' until he is handed his release." John Montgomery Ward, *Base-Ball: How to Become a Player* (1888; Reprint, Filiquarian Publishing, 2010), 52.
7. "How the Sluggers are Cheated Out of Their Dues," *St. Louis Post-Dispatch*, August 6, 1887, 9.
8. Interestingly, given Chadwick's abiding opposition to long hits, in the 1860s he was the first to suggest a measure based on the total number of bases divided by the number of games, what Thorn and Palmer called a "primitive version of the slugging percentage." A proposal in 1887 put forward by the *St. Louis Post-Dispatch* outlined a formula that years later was used to calculate slugging percentage, a tabulation that was accepted as an official statistic by the National League in 1923 and by the American League in 1946. John Thorn and Pete Palmer, *The Hidden Game of Baseball. A Revolutionary Approach to Baseball and Its Statistics* (Garden City, NY: Doubleday, 1984), 17.
9. In their first four years in the American Association (1882–1885), with the exception of 1882, the Browns were below the Association average in long hits, especially in triples and home runs. By 1886, the Browns had become more of a slugging team, leading the Association in doubles, extra-base hits, and total bases. In 1887, they led in doubles, home runs, extra-base hits, and total bases. For three years (1887–1889), they led the Association in home runs, a dramatic change from the relatively low power numbers in their early years.
10. "How the Sluggers are Cheated Out of Their Dues," 9.
11. "The Batting of 1887," *Spalding's Base Ball Guide and Official League Book for 1888* (1888; Reprinted New York: Horton, 1989), 20.
12. "From the Mound City," *Sporting Life*, April 21, 1886, 3.
13. See Chapter 6 for a further description of O'Neill's promise to hit the hat sign and how his two doubles fared in his attempt to achieve this pledge.
14. "From St. Louis. Squiblets," *Sporting Life*, August 17, 1887, 5.
15. *Ibid*. Note that this was the same home run that was reported in Chapter 10, where the ladies in the left field seats were commended for their baseball knowledge as they scrambled out of the way of a ball hit by O'Neill so that it would travel further under the seats and thus make it difficult for the Cincinnati left fielder to retrieve the ball in time to stop Tip from getting a home run. The young lady in the *Sporting Life* story apparently did not get out of the way of the ball in time, or so we are to believe. Pritchard may have embellished this tale, especially in his reference to "taking her meals standing," no doubt an exaggeration designed to amuse his readers. Even so, such accounts were part of the growing legend that surrounded O'Neill, that he was bigger than life and could not only hit the ball a long way but do so at will or on demand.
16. Although Comiskey and Chadwick both worried about any changes that might encourage players to try for long hits, Comiskey did not share Chadwick's belief that those who hit home runs were record players.
17. O'Neill had 15 doubles, six triples, and five home runs in 24 games in the first phase of the season (April 16 to May 24). In the 53 games of next two phases (May 25 to July 11 and July 12 to August 10), he had similar numbers, except for a drop in triples, with 15 doubles, two triples, and five home runs.
18. "The Long Hitters," *St. Louis Republican*, August 12, 1887, 6.
19. In addition to the 19 triples identified by the Information Concepts Incorporated (ICI) research conducted in the late 1960s, I discovered three other triples not on the ICI list, one against Cleveland on April 30 and two against New York, one on September 2 and another in the second game of a doubleheader on September 3. See the section on Triples in Appendix A.
20. The game reports of O'Neill's triples and home runs included details of the field in which these hits landed for 16 of the 22 triples and 13 of the 14 home runs. Although O'Neill hit many of his doubles to left field or left-center, he also hit comparatively more to center and right field than was the case with triples and home runs.
21. O'Neill's four-long-hit game was on April 30 (double, triple, two home runs). His three three-long-hit games were: May 7 (double, triple, home run), August 24 (three doubles), and August 30 (double, two triples). His 12 two-long-hit

games were: April 28 (double, triple), May 1 (two doubles), May 12 (two doubles), August 9 (double, triple), August 25 (double, triple), August 26 (two doubles), September 2 (double, triple), September 3 (double, triple), September 5 (two doubles), September 7 (two triples), October 4 (double, triple), and October 6, second game (triple, home run).

22. Some bulletin-board blasts by O'Neill went for a home run or a triple. On April 30, "He lined out a home run down back of the bulletin board." "Sporting. Great Batting Records Made by the Browns," *St. Louis Republican,* May 1, 1887, 15. On May 18, his bulletin-board shot went for a triple: "O'Neill besides making three beautiful catches slugged the ball in his inimitable manner, his three base hit being a line drive to the bulletin board." "Base-Ball and Athletics. Browns. 12; Athletics, 4," *St. Louis Globe-Democrat,* May 19, 1887, 8.

23. "Browns Victorious. The Quaker City Lads are Too Slow for Us," *St. Louis Chronicle,* May 19, 1887, 1.

24. As noted in earlier chapters, from time to time O'Neill took chances on the base paths and was thrown out trying to stretch a single into a double, a double into a triple, or a triple into a home run.

25. Ground rules are "special rules unique to the specific conditions and dimensions of a given park." Paul Dickson, *The Dickson Baseball Dictionary* 3d ed. (New York: W.W. Norton, 2009), 391.

26. "The National Playing Rules," *Reach's Official American Association Base Ball Guide, 1887,* (1887; Reprinted New York: Horton, 1989), 119.

27. In a game in Cincinnati, the reported crowd of 15,000 was described by the *Cincinnati Commercial Gazette* as "the largest ever seen at a ball game in the city." It also stated: "There would have been several home runs in the game had it not been for the ground rule." O'Neill's double in the fourth inning could have been one of those home runs. "Base Ball. Cincinnatis Badly Beaten by the Champions," *Cincinnati Commercial Gazette,* June 20, 1887, 3. See also the *Cincinnati Enquirer's* comment: "Latham, O'Neill, Foutz and Caruthers each made two-baggers, any one of which would have been longer hits on a clean field." "A Batted Ball Club. The Browns knock the Cincinnatis Very Dizzy," *Cincinnati Enquirer,* June 20, 1887, 2.

28. Larry Lupo, *When the Mets Played Baseball on Staten Island* (New York: Vantage, 2000), 14–16.

29. *Ibid.* Lupo notes that in 1886 "a ball hit into Babylon counted as a ground rule single." By 1887, this had changed to a ground-rule double. On August 12, Philadelphia lost a game to New York by forfeit over a dispute of the umpire's decision to award a ground-rule double on a ball hit into the Fall of Babylon structures. David Nemec and Eric Miklich, *Forfeits and Successfully Protested Games in Major League Baseball: A Complete Record, 1873–2013* (Jefferson, NC: McFarland, 2014), 46–47.

30. "Metropolitan vs St. Louis," *New York Clipper,* September 10, 1887, 409.

31. "Mets Beaten in Two Games," *New York Evening Sun,* September 3, 1887, 1.

32. "Clips and Chips," *St. Louis Post-Dispatch,* September 14, 1887, 8.

33. "Notes," *Cincinnati Enquirer,* October 16, 1887, 2. Joe Pritchard added: "His record on home runs would have been very large—at least thirty—had he been playing on grounds that would allow the ball full play." See "From St. Louis. Chips," *Sporting Life,* September 7, 1887, 4. While O'Neill led the Association on home runs, three sluggers in the National League hit more home runs in 1887: Billy O'Brien (Washington)—19; Roger Connor (New York)—17; and Fred Pfeffer (Chicago)—16.

34. As previously noted, balls hit into the benches in left field were in play. An outfielder could run into or under the seats to retrieve the ball and relay it to the infield with the hope of preventing the batsman from getting a triple or home run.

35. "Sporting. The Browns and Louisvilles Divide Yesterday's Honors," *St. Louis Republican,* October 7, 1887, 6.

36. *Ibid.*

37. There were no published records of long hits until the 1920s. Since the ICI research in the 1960s, most sources (e.g., Baseball Reference, Retrosheet) list O'Neill with 85 long hits, a mark that was tied by Hugh Duffy in 1894. Whether on his own with 88 long hits or tied with Duffy with 85 long hits, O'Neill had the record, or a share of it, until Babe Ruth broke it with 99 extra-base hits in 1920. Babe Ruth established the all-time record of 119 extra-base hits in one season in 1921. In the years after 1920, 88 extra-base hits would have led the major leagues in 53 of the next 97 years: 1926, 1939, 1941–1947, 1950–1952, 1956–1958, 1960–1961, 1963–1972; 1974–1994 (tied in 1993), 2008, 2011–2012, 2014, 2016–2017 (tied in 2017).

Chapter 12

1. "Batting lines" refers to the batter's box in which a batman must stay while he is at bat. Playing Rule 10 stated: "*The batsman's Lines* must be straight lines forming the boundaries of a space on the right, and a similar space on the left of the Home Base, six feet long by four feet wide, extending three feet in front of and three feet behind the center of the Home Base, and with its nearest line distant six inches from the Home Base." "The National Playing Rules," *Reach's Official American Association Base Ball Guide 1887* (1887; Reprinted New York: Horton, 1989), 150.

2. See Chapter Six for a discussion of his small bat, batting stance, and swing.

3. O'Neill had only two hitless games in phase four, both against Philadelphia. He had no hits in four times at bat in a 10-2 loss on August 20 and no hits in two times at bat in a 5-1 loss on August 21. On August 31, he had only one hit, a triple in four times at bat in a 6-4 win over Brooklyn.

4. In magnitude, the 142-point swing in batting average from phase three to phase four was close to the 136-point drop O'Neill experienced between phases one and two.

5. The last time that O'Neill topped .500 was after his third time at bat against New York on July 1. He started the season slowly but was hitting .500 or better by April 29, a threshold that he maintained for two months.

6. "Base Ball Notes," *Philadelphia Inquirer,* August 3, 1887, 3.

7. Caruthers was spotted in the stands at a Chicago White Stockings game. "Is Caruthers Sick?" *St. Louis Post-Dispatch,* August 10, 1887, 5.

8. "Diamond Notes," *Cleveland Leader,* August 10, 1887, 3.

9. Unsure of his readiness to assume his catching duties, Bushong opted to give his injured finger

a less pounding experience in his first games back by playing right field and at first base. He was not able to field the ball or hold the bat easily without pain, and therefore was deemed unfit to resume play. "Bushong and Foutz will Probably Not Play this Year," *St. Louis Post-Dispatch,* August 27, 1887, 8.

10. Boyle wore down after 44 consecutive games behind the plate. On August 20, in a game against Philadelphia, his hands were so sore that he came out in the fourth inning. Latham caught the final five innings. In the next game, Boyle was still plagued with sore hands and moved to right field. Robinson replaced him in the catcher's spot. Boyle returned to his catching position in the next series against Baltimore. "Sporting. The Athletics Turn the Tables on the Browns," *St. Louis Republican,* August 21, 1887, 14; "Athletics, 5; Browns, 1," *St. Louis Globe-Democrat,* August 22, 1887, 8.

11. "Comiskey a Cripple," *St. Louis Post-Dispatch,* August 31, 1887, 5.

12. "Yesterday's Game," *St. Louis Republican,* August 31, 1887, 6.

13. On July 22, the game between the Browns and New York ended in a 2–2 tie after 11 innings. Baseball games on Sunday were prohibited in New York, so the drawn game was replayed at a nearby park in Weehawken, New Jersey. "Games Played Sunday, Sept. 4," *Sporting Life,* September 14, 1887, 2.

14. Comiskey's injury occurred during the first series in phase five (September 9 to October 9). I include his injury in this chapter because it is linked to the Welch injury. Welch was called into service because Comiskey got hurt and, with no one else available, had to substitute into the game, otherwise the Browns would lose by forfeit because they no longer would have had nine players on the field. Rule 21 stated: "Every Club shall be required to adopt uniforms for its players, and in no case shall less than nine men be allowed to play on each side." "The National Playing Rules," *Reach's Official American Association Base Ball Guide 1887* (1887; Reprinted New York: Horton, 1989), 152.

15. "Athletics, 5; St. Louis, 4," *St. Louis Globe-Democrat,* September 11, 1887, 9.

16. "The Association. The Athletics Brace Up and Win a Creditable Victory from St. Louis," *Philadelphia Press,* September 11, 1887, 7.

17. "Nat Hudson's Mother Dead," *St. Louis Globe-Democrat,* September 1, 1887, 8.

18. This portrayal of the Browns made the rounds, appearing in newspapers in most of the National League and American Association cities, including the *Baltimore Sun*: "Gossip of the Diamond," *Baltimore Sun,* July 12, 1887, 6.

19. "Long and Short Hits," *St. Louis Post-Dispatch,* August 20, 1887, 9.

20. "Browns, 22; Athletics, 8," *St. Louis Globe-Democrat,* August 20, 1887.

21. In this phase, O'Neill (left field) and Gleason (shortstop) were the only players who did not play another position.

22. "Athletics, 10; Browns, 2," *St. Louis Globe-Democrat,* August 21, 1887, 9.

23. "Chips and Clips," *St. Louis Post-Dispatch,* September 1, 1887, 5.

24. "The National Playing Rules," *Reach's Official American Association Base Ball Guide 1887* (1887; Reprinted New York: Horton, 1989), 154.

25. In the game against Cleveland on August 15, Latham bunted several pitches foul before making "first on a pet of that kind." "The World of Sport. The Clevelands Make but Eight Hits While Crowell is Pounded for Twenty," *Cleveland Leader,* August 16, 1887, 3.

26. "Base Ball Notes," *Philadelphia Evening Bulletin,* August 23, 1887, 6.

27. "Made Ramsey Retire. Louisville's 'Phenomenal' Smith Knocked Out by the Browns," *St. Louis Republican,* August 13, 1887, 6.

28. "Base Ball Notes," *St. Louis Republican,* August 12, 1887, 6.

29. "From St. Louis. The Browns' Jonah," *The Sporting Life,* August 31, 1887, 4.

30. A "baser" is a single. The nine hits Tip had against Cleveland were all singles. "From Cleveland," *The Sporting Life,* August 24, 1887, 2.

31. The expression "berries" or "the berries" is slang that traces back to the nineteenth century in both the United States and the United Kingdom. While there is some disagreement on its exact meaning and origins, most define it as an "excellent person or thing," "the height of excellence," or "that which is attractive or pleasing." The statement, "All the local twirlers proved 'berries' to Tip O'Neill," then, suggested that the Cleveland pitchers did a good thing for O'Neill by delivering pitches he could readily hit. See "If something is considered the best why is it said to be 'the berries'?" at the English Language & Usage Stack Exchange. Accessed October 19, 2017, at http://english.stackexchange.com/questions/157816/If-something-is-the-best-why-is-it-the-berriesX

32. The seven games between April 27 and May 7 stand alone as O'Neill's historic week of 1887. I refer to the seven games between August 24 and August 30 and the seven games between September 2 and September 8 as his two near-historic or noteworthy weeks. As will become evident by the end of the chapter, most of the numbers achieved in the April 27–May 7 week were significantly higher than the numbers achieved in both of the noteworthy weeks in this phase. For example, O'Neill's statistics in his historic week exceeded the September 2–8 week (shown in parentheses), the next-best of the three weeks, in every category on a per-game basis as follows: Hits 3.9 (3.0); Long hits 2.0 (1.4); Total Bases 7.4 (5.1); and runs plus runs batted in 5.0 (3.6).

33. "Seventeen Singles. Baltimore's Left-Hand Wizard Hit Hard by the Browns," *St. Louis Republican,* August 24, 1887, 6.

34. "Notes of the Game," *St. Louis Post-Dispatch,* August 24, 1887, 8.

35. "In Fourth Place Again. Latham Furnishes the Entertainment on a Cold Day," *Baltimore American,* August 24, 1887, 3.

36. "Sport for Sportsmen," *St. Louis Chronicle,* August 25, 1887, 2.

37. "Long and Short Hits," *St. Louis Post-Dispatch,* August 26, 1887, 8.

38. The medal was designed and donated by the Mermod and Jaccard Jewelry Company. It was "one of the prettiest designs ever made. It is of solid gold, the pendant being a wheel, with bats for spokes." "Base Ball Notes," *St. Louis Republican,* August 26, 1887, 6.

39. "Lively Running," *St. Louis Republican,* August 28, 1887, 14.

40. "Caruthers Wins the Medal," *St. Louis Globe-Democrat,* August 28, 1887, 9.

41. On August 25, in the Browns' 14–8 win against Baltimore, O'Neill also had a near-cycle with three hits in five times at bat (single, double, triple). In the game on August 30

and the one on August 25, O'Neill was a home run shy of the cycle. See Chapter 7 for a review of O'Neill's near-cycles.

42. "Games Played on Sunday Sept. 4," *Sporting Life*, September 14, 1887, 2.

43. "A Lively Game of Ball. An Experiment That will not be Tried Again," *New York Times*, September 5, 1887, 8.

44. "The National Playing Rules," *Reach's Official American Association Base Ball Guide 1887* (1887; Reprinted New York: Horton, 1989), 152.

45. "Batters and Toughs. The St. Louis-Metropolitan Game Stopped by a Mob," *New York Star*, September 5, 1887, 5.

46. "Roughs at a Ball Game. An Unruly Mob Have Fun on the Weehawken Grounds," *New York World*, September 5, 1887, 6.

47. "A Riot in New York. The St. Louis Browns Tendered a Very Warm Reception at Weehawken," *The Sporting News*, September 10, 1887, 1.

48. "The Browns Mobbed. Weehawken Roughs Throw Rocks at the Champions," *St. Louis Chronicle*, September 5, 1887, 4.

49. "Won at Weehawken. The Browns Beat the Mets Among Untamed Jersey Natives," *St. Louis Republican*, September 5, 1887, 5.

50. "The Game at Weehawken," *New York Sun*, September 5, 1887, 3.

51. "Roughs at a Ball Game," 6.

52. "Batters and Toughs," 5.

53. "A Lively Game of Ball," 8.

54. "Sunday Ball Games. St. Louis and the 'Mets' Play Under Difficulties at Weehawken," *New York Herald*, September 5, 1887, 6.

55. "Batters and Toughs," 5.

56. Ibid.

57. "A Lively Game of Ball," 8.

58. Ibid.

59. A "sweat" board, also known as a "shuck," consisted of "a green cloth marked 1 to 6 and dice." S. L. Kotar and J. E. Gessler, *The Rise of the American Circus, 1716–1899* (Jefferson, NC: McFarland, 2011), 325. Games with three shells or three-card monte were similar in that the player or mark had to identify the shell under which lay a pea or the money card in monte. These were confidence games where another person, sometimes known as the "shill" or "bunco steerer," pretended to work with the mark to beat the dealer. As the mark's confidante, the "shill" first encouraged the mark to play against the dealer, then convinced him to lay down a wager, and finally helped him choose which was the winning shell or card. The swindle was on in that the "shill" was really working with the dealer to take the mark's money. See Tom Ogden, *The Complete Idiot's Guide to Magic Tricks* (Jefferson, NC: McFarland, 1998), 123. The words in quotation in the text, "pitch, steal, and hit," refer to the "pitch" of the "shill," the "theft" of the dealers or pickpockets, and the "hit" perpetrated by any confidence game, that is, being "hit on," or to the fights that broke out among fans engaged in these "games" while the Browns and Mets were playing baseball.

60. "Roughs at a Ball Game," 6. The *New York Times* also called the game a "farce." "A Lively Game of Ball," 8.

61. "Batters and Toughs," 5.

62. "A Checkered Game of Baseball. Almost a Riot at Monitor Park," *New York Tribune*, September 5, 1887, 8.

63. "Base Ball on Sunday. A Burlesque Affair at Weehawken," September 4, 1887. *1887. American Association. National League & American Association Box Scores*. Compiled by Information Concepts, Inc., National Baseball Hall of Fame Library. Microfilmed, 2002.

64. "Sunday Ball Games. St. Louis and the 'Mets' Play Under Difficulties at Weehawken," *New York Herald*, September 5, 1887, 6.

65. "Batters and Toughs," 5.

66. "Games Played Sunday, Sept. 4," *Sporting Life*, September 14, 1887, 2. See also "Baseball. Notes," *New York Clipper*, September 17, 1887, 428.

67. "Batters and Toughs," 5.

68. "Chips from the Diamond," *New York Sun*, September 5, 1887, 3.

69. O'Neill had previous bat-throwing incidents. A finger-wagging reporter from the Eastern Exchange chided O'Neill on his "childish habit of allowing his temper to get the best of him when he fails to connect with the ball in batting," a comment that seemed to refer to his tendency to throw his bat when he did not perform well at the plate. "Base Ball Notes," *St. Louis Republican*, June 22, 1887, 6. In 1886, O'Neill "gave his bat a violent throw after striking out, and it sailed by Comiskey, just missing his head." "Base Ball Briefs," *Pittsburgh Dispatch*, June 24, 1886, 6.

70. "From St. Louis," *Sporting Life*, September 14, 1887, 4.

71. "The Gladiator Drunk," *St. Louis Post-Dispatch*, August 26, 1887, 8.

72. "From the Falls City," *Sporting Life*, September 7, 1887, 4.

73. Ibid.

74. "Diamond Dust," *St. Louis Globe-Democrat*, August 31, 1887, 8.

75. It was possible that either Browning or Caruthers could get close to or even surpass O'Neill. If O'Neill did not hit as well in the final phase, Browning and Caruthers could overtake him if one or both had a hot bat for the last 23 games. For example, based on 100 times at bat, if O'Neill had 47 hits, Browning had 64 hits, and Caruthers had 61 hits, O'Neill would finish third with a batting average of .4902 (277 hits in 565 at-bats). Caruthers would win the batting crown with a .4908 average (215 hits in 438 at-bats) and Browning would come in second at .4907 (291 hits in 593 at-bats).

Chapter 13

1. O'Neill was injured on May 20, did not return to the lineup until June 6, and consequently was not part of the Browns' ten-game winning streak between May 24 and June 4.

2. It is more common to focus on the number of consecutive plate appearances with a hit. As discussed in Chapter 6, three players, Pinky Higgins, Walt Dropo, and Johnny Kling, share the record of 12 consecutive plate appearances with a hit. In this chapter, I focus on on-base streaks, which here include any time O'Neill reached base by a hit, base on balls, hit by pitch, error, fielder's choice, dropped third strike, catcher's interference, fielder's obstruction, etc. In my view, getting on base by any means can contribute to the offensive advancement of the team. To reach base in consecutive plate appearances over two or more games can have a significant cumulative impact on the outcome of these games, as O'Neill's four on-base streaks illustrate.

3. For comments on O'Neill's consecutive-at-bat hitting streak on April 30 to May 1, see "Base Ball Notes," *St. Louis Republican*, May 3, 1887, 6. On his consecutive-at-bat hitting streak from August 7–10, see "Base Ball Notes," *Cleveland Plain Dealer*, August 10, 1887, 4.

4. I previously described the first three on-base streaks in Chapters 6 (April 30–May 1), 7 (May 4–7), and 8 (August 8–10). In Chapter 12, I introduced the fourth on-base streak, and, in this chapter, I describe it in greater detail.

5. In 1887, there were no rules that defined what constituted a cumulative record. In the current "Official Rules of Baseball," in section 9.23, the "Guidelines for Cumulative Performance Records" states: "A consecutive hitting streak shall not be terminated if a batter's plate appearance results in a base on balls, hit batsman, defensive interference or obstruction or a sacrifice bunt. A sacrifice fly shall terminate the streak." See "Official Rules of Baseball. 2017 Edition," accessed October 10, 2017, http://mlb.com/documents/Official_Baseball_Rules_dbt69t59.pdf. Under today's rules, O'Neill would be credited with nine hits in a row in both streaks (April 30–May 1 and August 8–10). The base on balls would not count as a hit. Furthermore, a base on balls and a hit by pitch would not interrupt the streak. In the rules of 1887, O'Neill had two ten-hit streaks.

6. As in the last endnote, under 2017 rules, the base on balls would not be counted as a hit, and so O'Neill would be credited with only seven hits in a row.

7. In 1887, there were five streaks in the American Association with 20 or more games in a row with at least one hit: Tip O'Neill (St. Louis)—25 games (August 23 to September 21); Pete Browning (Louisville)—24 games (September 10 to October 9); Tip O'Neill (St. Louis)—22 games (October 4, 1887 to May 10, 1888); Denny Lyons (Philadelphia)—21 games (June 24 to July 20), and Denny Lyons (Philadelphia)—21 games (July 25 to August 17). Trent McCotter, "American Association Hitting Streaks," *Nineteenth Century Notes* (Summer 2010), 8.

8. *Ibid.* The top seven streaks all time in the American Association were: Jimmy Wolf (Louisville)—31 games (August 16, 1885 to April 21, 1886); Dave Orr (New York)—28 games (August 4 to September 7, 1886); Harry Taylor (Louisville)—27 games (June 29 to August 2, 1890); Pete Browning (Louisville)—26 games (May 9 to June 15, 1885); Tip O'Neill (St. Louis)—25 games (August 23 to September 21, 1887); Hick Carpenter (Cincinnati)—25 games (May 16 to June 28, 1882); and Perry Werden (Baltimore)—25 games (April 21 to May 22, 1891).

9. "Behind in the Race. Brooklyn's Professional Club Defeated by the St. Louis Browns," *Brooklyn Citizen*, August 30, 1887.

10. "Base Ball Notes," *St. Louis Republican*, August 31, 1887, 6.

11. "How Nine Men Play Ball. Just Enough Browns to Fill Positions and Win," *St. Louis Republican*, August 31, 1887, 2.

12. "Browns, 6; Brooklyn, 4," *St. Louis Globe-Democrat*, September 1, 1887, 8.

13. "Mets Beaten in Two Games," *New York Evening Sun*, September 3, 1887, 1. For a further description of O'Neill's Babylon double, see Chapter 11.

14. "From St. Louis. Chips," *The Sporting Life*, September 7, 1887, 4.

15. Paul Waner had an extra-base hit in 14 consecutive games between June 3 and June 19, 1927. Chipper Jones accomplished the same feat between June 26 and July 16, 2006.

16. O'Neill's 17-out-of-18 games with one or more extra-base hits compares favorably to the post-streak numbers of Paul Waner and Chipper Jones. Paul Waner had extra-base hits in 17 of 19 games in 1927 (June 3–28), while Jones had extra-base hits in 18 of 20 games in 2006 (June 26–July 28).

17. The record for consecutive games with a run batted in is 17, set by Ray Grimes of the Chicago Cubs in 1923.

18. Billy Hamilton, of the Philadelphia Phillies, holds the record for the most consecutive games scoring one or more runs, 24 in a row in 1894.

Chapter 14

1. The Cuban Giants were an African American professional team formed in late summer of 1885. Though none of the players were from Cuba, they pretended to be "Cuban," with the hope that white audiences would be more accepting if they thought they were watching a more exotic and foreign-born baseball team. In 1886 and 1887, they played exhibition games against semi-professional and professional teams, some of whom were in the National League and American Association. For example, after their cancelled game with the St. Louis Browns (September 11, 1887), the Cuban Giants defeated Baltimore (American Association) twice, 8–3 and 12–2; lost 13–6 to Philadelphia (American Association); tied with New York (National League), 2–2; and split two games with Cincinnati (American Association), winning the first game, 6–5, and losing the second, 18–6. Earlier in the season, they lost, 8–4, to Detroit (National League). "A Great Game. The Cuban Giants Make Detroit Work," *Daily True American*, May 26, 1887, 5.

2. The *St. Louis Post-Democrat* described Gleason as "the man who had drawn up the protest." "That Revolt. A dramatic Account of the Mutiny Among the World's Champions," *St. Louis Post-Democrat*, September 13, 1887, 8. The letter referred to the poor condition of the Browns, a concern likely shared by all of the players. While some of the players may have been bothered by the prospect of playing a black team, Latham was the only one who, in an interview, commented on refusing to play a "nigger club." "The Browns' Color Line," *St. Louis Globe-Democrat*, September 13, 1887, 8. Years later, Latham added that they tried to appeal to Von der Ahe's Democratic leanings. When Von der Ahe asked: "Do you mean to say you won't play the Cuban Giants?" Latham, as the one "salted for spokesman," responded: "We're all good Democrats and can't think of meeting the black birds." "Another on Von der Ahe. Latham Springs a new One about the Only Chris," *Sporting Life*, June 2, 1894, 3. Based on these two reports, I infer that Latham was likely the one who proposed the argument of not playing the Cuban Giants because of their color.

3. "A Color Line in Baseball. The St. Louis Browns Refuse to Play with the Cuban Giants," *New York Times*, September 12, 1887, 1. Only eight of the players signed the letter. Comiskey was not aware of the protest. Knouff had just joined the team and decided not to sign the letter. Bushong and Foutz were still injured and were not with the team on this road trip.

4. *Ibid.*

5. *Ibid.*

6. "The Browns' Color Line," 8.

7. "A Color Line in Baseball," 1.

8. "Rebellion in the Ranks. Von der Ahe's Men Draw the Color Line. They Flatly Refuse to Play the Famous Negro Team," *St. Louis Republican*, September 12, 1887, 5.

9. "The Browns Refuse to Play," *St. Louis Globe-Democrat*, September 12, 1887, 8.
10. "Base Ball Color Line. The Browns Draw It Very Plainly," *St. Louis Chronicle*, September 12, 1887, 1.
11. "The Revolt of the Players. Why the Browns Failed to Play the Cuban Giants," *New York Evening Telegram*, September 12, 1887, 4.
12. "That Revolt. A Dramatic Account of the Mutiny Among the World's Champions," *St. Louis Post-Dispatch*, September 13, 1887, 8.
13. "The Browns' Color Line," 8.
14. "The Color Line in Base Ball" *New York Evening Sun*, September 13, 1887, 3.
15. "The Browns Go on Strike. They Refuse to Come to New York to Play the Cuban Giants," *New York Sun*, September 13, 1887, 3.
16. "The Browns' Color Line," 8.
17. "The Color Line in Baseball," 3. Comiskey was the first to point out the inconsistency in the players' alleged concern about playing a colored team. "A Color Line in Baseball. The St. Louis Browns refuse to Play the Cuban Giants," *New York Times*, September 12, 1887. 1. In a game in late May 1886, the Browns beat the Cuban Giants, 9–3. O'Neill had five hits in the game. Five of the players who signed the letter to Von der Ahe played in the 1886 game against the Cuban Giants (O'Neill, Latham, Gleason, Robinson, and Welch). "Their First Defeat. The St. Louis Champions Down the Trentons," *Trenton Times*, May 29, 1886, 1. Welch played with Fleet Walker, an African American catcher, on the Toledo Club in the American Association in 1884. O'Neill pitched against a black team when he played for the Hartford Club in 1883. "Swinging the Ash. The Hartfords Beat the West Ends," *Hartford Times*, September 15, 1883.
18. The *Boston Globe* reported that the "color line had nothing to do with the refusal of the Browns to play the Cuban Giants. It was merely an excuse to get a day off." "Diamond Points," *Boston Globe*, September 16, 1887, 5. Years later, Latham claimed that some of the players had plans to spend the day in Atlantic City. "Another on Von der Ahe," 3.
19. "The Browns' Color Line," 8.
20. *Ibid.*
21. "The Browns Go on Strike," 3.
22. The game in Weehawken, New Jersey, was supposed to be a championship game. However, given the difficult conditions under which the game was played, both teams agreed that it would be considered an exhibition game. See Chapter 12 for a description of the Weehawken game.
23. "Clips and Chips," *St. Louis Post-Dispatch*, September 8, 1887, 8; "The Browns' Color Line," 8; "The Browns Go on Strike," 3.
24. The players' letter clearly stated that they refused to play the Cuban Giants because of the color of their skin. It was a segregationist stance that today many would call "racist" in word and deed. Once it was determined that there were other reasons behind the refusal of the eight players to play the Cuban Giants, the press, with the possible exception of the *New York Times* and *New York Evening Sun*, no longer accused the players of drawing the color line. They believed that the players' failure to go to West Farms was based on reasons other than color. In Von der Ahe's statement to the players, "As it seems to be a matter of principle with you, you need not play tomorrow," there was no comment or criticism in the press of his implied claim that "drawing the color line" constituted some kind of principle. In short, although the actions of the players raised two major issues, one related to segregation and the other to revolt, it was their mutiny that lingered in the minds of the observers of the day. Contemporary scholars tend to focus more on the racism inherent in the players' refusal to play the Cuban Giants. For example, Cash argues that "by the late nineteenth century, racism had become so ingrained in American society that weary and gimpy ballplayers turned to it as a convenient excuse for getting the day off." Jon Cash, *Before They Were Cardinals: Major League Baseball in Nineteenth-Century St. Louis* (Columbia: University of Missouri Press, 2002), 204. Gregory Bond highlights the acceptability of segregation in organized baseball in 1887: "Players who, for any reason, like the St. Louis Browns' conspirators, acted improperly, were still criticized by the sporting community. Players who honestly and diligently advocated segregation, though, were no longer anathema to organized baseball. Instead, drawing the color line had become, in the words of Chris Von der Ahe, 'a matter of principle.'" Gregory Bond, "Whipped Curs and Real Men: Race, Manliness, and the Segregation of Organized Baseball in the Late Nineteenth Century," Unpublished Master Thesis, University of Wisconsin–Madison, 1999, 85.
25. "Notes and Comments," *Sporting Life*, September 28, 1887, 6.
26. "The Browns' Color Line," 8.
27. "The Champion's Captain Returns," *St. Louis Globe-Democrat*, September 14, 1887, 8.
28. Tip's 14 long hits in phase five matched his modest output in phase three (July 12 to August 10).
29. "Base Ball Notes," *Cleveland Plain Dealer*, September 20, 1887, 4.
30. "Clips and Chips," *St. Louis Post-Dispatch*, September 14, 1887, 8. The idiom "handsome is as handsome does" means "that you should judge someone by their actions and not by their appearance." The note still acknowledged O'Neill's good looks ("Tip is really a handsome fellow") but then reminded readers that O'Neill's image would be in the *Reach's Guide* for his outstanding achievements in 1887 as a batsman.
31. The Browns had only nine men and so when Comiskey went down, rather than lose the game by forfeit, Welch was sent in to play center field, with Caruthers moving from right field to first base and King shifting from center field to right field.
32. "Base Ball Notes," *St. Louis Republican*, September 23, 1887, 6.
33. "Cleveland's Good Game," *St. Louis Republican*, September 18, 1887, 14.
34. Bushong started the first of seven games against Cincinnati. After Cincinnati jumped out to a 10–0 lead in the first two innings, Comiskey replaced Bushong with Boyle for the rest of the game and for the six games against Cincinnati that followed. Bushong next played behind the plate in three of the five games against Louisville (October 4–6) and in one game against Cleveland (October 8).
35. In September, Cincinnati had a 16–5 record. In the season's series against St. Louis, going into the seven-game set in late September, Cincinnati had six wins and five losses. After beating the Browns in six of seven games, Cincinnati finished the season's series against St. Louis with a 12–6 record.
36. The 12-run deficit in the Browns' 15–3 loss to Cincinnati matched their 16–4 loss to Louis-

ville on July 1. "Smashed the Ball. The Way the Louisvilles Won Yesterday's Game from the Champions," *Louisville Courier-Journal,* July 2, 1887, 2.

37. "Chicagoed" was a term used when a team won by a shutout. Cincinnati Chicagoed the Browns twice, the first time on August 5, 5–0. "Ring the Bells! The Reds Shut Out the St. Louis Champions," *Cincinnati Commercial Gazette,* August 6, 1887, 7.

38. "000000000=0. The Above Represents the Work of Von der Ahe's Men Yesterday," *Cincinnati Commercial Gazette,* September 23, 1887, 3.

39. "From Cincinnati. Notes and Comments," *Sporting Life,* October 5, 1887, 3.

40. "Association Batting," *St. Louis Globe-Democrat,* September 25, 1887, 11.

41. "Clips and Chips," *St. Louis Post-Dispatch,* September 24, 1887, 12.

42. "Pete Browning, writing to a friend, says he intends to beat O'Neill for the batting honors next season and will not drink a drop." "From the Falls City. Notes," *Sporting Life,* September 21, 1887, 2. Hugh Nicol, O'Neill's former teammate and now the right fielder for Cincinnati, after a recent batting streak, promised that in 1888, he would "give 'Tip' O'Neill a tight brush for first place." "Diamond Dust," *St. Louis Globe-Democrat,* October 2, 1887, 11.

43. On October 6, in the ninth inning of the second game of the doubleheader, O'Neill hit a second home run that did not count in his record. The umpire called the game on account of darkness with the inning still in progress. The final score and official record of the game reverted to the end of the eighth inning, disallowing any individual achievements in the ninth inning. For a discussion of the ninth inning and O'Neill's second home run, see Chapter 11, "Long Hits." Also see Chapter 7, "Two Cycles," for a review of O'Neill's near-cycle games.

44. Although the series was originally scheduled to be played in Cleveland, Von der Ahe promised Cleveland "a handsome surety," $2,000 to be precise, if the club moved the venue to Sportsman's Park. It was Fair Week in St. Louis, and Von der Ahe felt that the games would attract a large crowd. He also wanted his boys at home and well rested for the World Championship Series, which started in St. Louis the day after the last game against Cleveland. "From Cleveland. Cleveland Club News," *Sporting Life,* October 5, 1887, 4; "Closing of the Championship Season," *St. Louis Post-Dispatch,* October 4, 1887, 8.

45. Detroit finished the season with a 79–45 record, 3½ games ahead of Philadelphia. On September 15, Philadelphia, sitting in fourth place, 9½ games behind Detroit, began a 16-game win streak, surging ahead of Chicago and New York who both faltered down the stretch.

46. "Thinks They'll Win. President Von der Ahe Talks about the Great Series with Detroit," *St. Louis Post-Dispatch,* September 27, 1887, 8.

47. "The World Beaters. They Will Be Seen in Detroit Next Wednesday," *Detroit Free Press,* October 9, 1887, 6.

48. "Bunched Hits," *St. Louis Sunday Sayings,* September 25, 1887.

49. "Diamond Dust," *St. Louis Globe-Democrat,* October 8, 1887, 7.

50. "Liners," *Detroit Free Press,* September 16, 1887, 2; "Liners," *Detroit Free Press,* September 28, 1887, 2.

51. "Diamond Dust," *St. Louis Globe-Democrat,* October 1, 1887, 6.

52. The O'Neill-Brouthers matchup never happened. Brouthers was injured and missed most of the series, playing in only one game. He had two hits in three times at bat in Game Twelve (October 22).

53. Von der Ahe offered no reason why he wanted to replace Gleason at the end of the season, though the implication seemed to be that he had concerns about his deteriorating play at shortstop. It was also possible that Von der Ahe turned against Gleason for his role in formulating the letter announcing the players' refusal to play the Cuban Giants. "Diamond Dust," *St. Louis Globe-Democrat,* September 22, 1887, 8. In a later article on the moves of Gleason and Welch to Philadelphia and Foutz, Caruthers, and Bushong to Brooklyn, Pritchard, the St. Louis correspondent to *Sporting Life,* indicated that Gleason had been critical of Von der Ahe for some time, so much so that he would "quit the diamond rather than play another season with the Browns." For Von der Ahe's part, he felt a similar animosity towards his shortstop, especially upset by Gleason's poor play in the World Championship Series against Detroit. "St. Louis Siftings," *Sporting Life,* February 1, 1888, 2.

54. Von der Ahe had an argument with Bushong over his refusal to catch one of the games in the Cincinnati series. "Inside Information," *St. Louis Post-Dispatch,* October 2, 1887, 10. After Bushong was sold to Brooklyn, Von der Ahe said that he believed that Bushong never fully recovered from his injury in 1887 and that he believed that his "best days behind the bat had passed and gone." "St. Louis Siftings," *Sporting Life,* February 1, 1888, 2.

55. Von der Ahe was still bothered by how long it took for Caruthers to return to the team after he fell ill in early August and went home to Chicago to recuperate. In addition, Caruthers repeatedly asserted that he wanted to leave the Browns. "Inside Information," *St. Louis Post-Dispatch,* October 2, 1887, 10. After Caruthers was sold to Brooklyn, Von der Ahe reiterated that Caruthers was adamant about not playing with the Browns and said he had little choice except to sell Caruthers.

56. Foutz was sold to Brooklyn in late November. After the sale, Von der Ahe commented that "old reliable was growing weaker as a pitcher as the years rolled by." He also explained that he did not need Foutz at first base or in right field. He conceded "that Dave was an excellent sticker and a valuable man to have on the club, but he figured he could get along as well without him as with him and be in pocket a good roll of money." "St. Louis Siftings," *Sporting Life,* February 1, 1888, 2.

57. "Clips and Chips," *St. Louis Post-Dispatch,* October 3, 1887, 10.

58. "Diamond Points," *Boston Globe,* September 27, 1887, 5.

59. In the weeks leading up to the world championship, there was the occasional suggestion of a lack of harmony, even dissension among some of the players. "Clip and Chips," *St. Louis Post-Dispatch,* October 4, 1887, 10; "Notes," *Cincinnati Enquirer,* October 9, 1887, 10.

60. Although not published until the Browns had played three games against Detroit, the interview took place when the Browns visited Louisville on October 3–4. "From the Falls City. A Chat with Comiskey," *Sporting Life,* October 12, 1887, 4.

61. Many of the offensive categories listed for the Browns and for O'Neill were not part of the official statistics reported by the Association. In most game reports, the box scores included who hit doubles, triples, or home runs, who got their base on a walk or hit by pitch, who stole a base, etc. Newspapers usually described how runs were scored, including information on who drove in each run, thus enabling the tabulation of most of the runs batted in for a team or an individual. A few newspapers kept track of and periodically reported on some of these categories (e.g., long hits, stolen bases) during the year. The ICI-based research in the late 1960s provided some RBI data, with research in subsequent years completing this process.

Chapter 15

1. "Had to Bring Out Our Rooster Again," *St. Louis Republican,* October 24, 1886, 14.
2. "Our Flag in Not There," *St. Louis Republican,* October 22, 1887, 6.
3. In his book on the World Series played in the nineteenth century, Jerry Lansche entitled his chapter on the 1887 world championship, "The Series That Went On Forever." Jerry Lansche, *Glory Fades Away. The Nineteenth-Century World Series Rediscovered* (Dallas: Taylor, 1991), 95–125.
4. Frederick Stearns, the president of the Detroit Wolverines, and Chris Von der Ahe had previously agreed to play all 15 games, even if one team won the championship in an earlier match. Detroit won the world championship in the 11th game. For all intents and purposes, the last four games were exhibition contests.
5. In St. Louis, the players, the newspapers, and likely the fans were surprised and upset by the limited number of games scheduled for Sportsman's Park. "A Great Record. What the Champion Browns Have Done During the Season of '87," *St. Louis Post-Dispatch,* September 17, 1887, 12.
6. "The Triumphal Tour," *St. Louis Republican,* October 12, 1887, 6; "The Great Tour. The Most Extensive and Costly Base Ball Aggregation on its Travels," *St. Louis Post-Dispatch,* October 12, 1887, 5; "The Champions Arrive," *Philadelphia Inquirer,* October 17, 1887, 3.

7. "The Lightning Special Train. Scenes and Incidents Connected with the World Championship Trip," *The Sporting News,* December 24, 1887, 2.
8. "Red-Eyed Champions. How the Faithful Browns Work Both Night and Day," *St. Louis Post-Dispatch,* October 16, 1887, 5.
9. "Der Prowns Drink, Play Poker, and Fight," *St. Louis Post-Dispatch,* October 18, 1887, 8.
10. "Saved a Shut-Out. The League Champions Received a Sharp Lesson from the Browns," *St. Louis Post-Dispatch,* October 11, 1887, 5.
11. "One for the Browns. They Outplayed Detroit on All Points," *Detroit Free Press,* October 11, 1887, 2.
12. Following the Browns' 8–0 loss on October 13 in Pittsburgh (Recreation Park), they beat Detroit, 5–2, in Brooklyn (Washington Park) on October 14 and then lost four games in a row: 9–0 on October 15 in New York (Polo Grounds); 3–1 on October 17 in Philadelphia (Philadelphia Base Ball Grounds), 3–1 on October 17 in Boston (Union Park), and 4–2 in Philadelphia (Jefferson Street Grounds).
13. "A Week in the Pool-Rooms. Local Disappointment," *St. Louis Globe-Democrat,* October 16, 1887, 9.
14. While the odds varied among the betting establishments in St. Louis, most favored Detroit to win the Series. On each game, the odds fluctuated from one inning to the next as bettors wagered on such things as the winner of the game, the number of runs scored by one or both teams by game's end, or the records of particular players. "Down-town Betting," *St. Louis Globe-Democrat,* October 11, 1887; "Today's Betting," *St. Louis Post-Dispatch,* October 13, 1887, 5; "Betting in St. Louis," *St. Louis Globe-Democrat,* October 14, 1887, 8. Betting also occurred in the community. "The story is told, on very good authority, that a certain baseball 'crank' living in the western suburbs, who swears by the Browns, wagered his house and lot against $1500, the latter furnished by a sporting man who took the Detroit end of the bet." "A Week in the Pool-Rooms," 9.
15. A few days later, the *St. Louis Chronicle* published an account of a five-inning game where the Browns overwhelmed Detroit, 23–0. It turned out to be a game played out in one of Von der Ahe's dreams where in the end he won a million dollars for the win. Unlike the poem, the dream win did not come down to a heroic hit made by O'Neill. However, O'Neill did contribute a double, triple, and home run to this fantasy win. On the day that the dream was published, Detroit had won seven games and lost two, and thus needed to win only one more game to claim the world championship. In an inspirational flourish, the *Chronicle* boldly declared: "They'll win every game from now on," which of course the Browns needed to do if they wanted to retain their world title. "We've Won at Last! Chris Von der Ahe Pockets a Cool Million. 'Der Poss Club' Plays as Never a Club has Played Before," *St. Louis Chronicle,* October 20, 1887, 22.
16. "The Last Game. A Metrical Forecast of the Detroit-Browns Series," *St. Louis Post-Dispatch,* October 16, 1887, 22.
17. Ibid.
18. Ibid. The expression "Chestnuts" is British slang meaning a "trite old story, joke, song" or in this case, poem. Accessed December 22, 2017. http://Dictionary.com.
19. "Saved a Shut-Out," 5.
20. Many of the Browns did not hit well in the Series. Among the St. Louis batsman who had 45 or more times at bat, Robinson led the team with 25 hits in 56 times at bat for a .446 average. Latham had 26 hits in 67 times at bat for a .388 average, and Comiskey had 20 hits in 63 times at bat for a .317 average. Among those who struggled at the bat, Caruthers had a .255 average on 12 hits in 47 times at bat. Gleason had 11 hits in 52 times at bat for a .212 average, and Welch had 12 hits in 58 times at bat for a .207 average. Then came O'Neill at .200 with Foutz last at .197 on 12 hits in 61 times at bat. John Thorn, Phil Birnbaum, and Bill Deane, *Total Baseball. The Ultimate Encyclopedia, 8th Edition.* Toronto: SPORT Media Publishing, 2004), 324.
21. "Gossip of the Game. The Playing of the Browns and Detroits Reviewed," *St. Louis Globe-Democrat,* October 23, 1887, 11.
22. "Diamond Dust," *St. Louis Globe-Democrat,* October 11, 1887, 8.
23. "A Good Club. The Betting," *St. Louis Post-Dispatch,* October 11, 1887, 5.
24. "Today's Betting," 5.
25. "Red-Eyed Champions. How

the Men Talk," *St. Louis Post-Dispatch,* October 16, 1887, 5.

26. "Whitewashed Again. The Browns are Traveling in Too Fast Company," *Detroit Free Press,* October 16, 1887, 6.

27. *Ibid.*

28. "Hard Work on the Diamond. St. Louis Defeats Detroit at Washington Park, Brooklyn," *New York Herald,* October 15, 1887, 9.

29. During the 1887 season, O'Neill created 278 runs (167 runs scored plus 125 runs batted in minus 14 home runs, for a contribution rate of 25 percent of the 1,131 runs scored by the Browns. In the world championships, he scored seven runs and batted in another nine, one by a home run. His run contribution rate was 15 of 54 runs scored by the Browns, or 28 percent.

30. "O'Neill's Great Catch," *St. Louis Post-Dispatch,* October 18, 1887, 8.

31. *Ibid.*

32. On October 26, the Browns returned to St. Louis for the 15th game. The fans were disgruntled by the humiliating loss of the series to Detroit and thus were not in the mood to show their usual support to the home team. In the first inning, "O'Neill stalked up to the plate and the usual cry of 'Kill it, Jim' was not heard." O'Neill nonetheless hit a triple to deep left field, knocking in two runs to give the Browns an early lead. "In Form Again. The Last Game of the World's Series Won by the Browns," *St. Louis Globe-Democrat,* October 27, 1887, 8.

33. It was the only game of the Series in which the Browns scored ten or more runs, a feat that they had achieved 46 times in the regular season. They had 20 hits, including a triple by Foutz and home runs by Latham and Welch. Eight of the Browns had two or more hits, with O'Neill hitting two singles. Caruthers scattered nine hits for the win.

34. Larry G. Bowman, *Before the World Series: Pride, Profits, and Baseball's First Championships* (DeKalb: Northern Illinois University Press, 2003), 107.

35. "Bushong Mad," *St. Louis Post-Dispatch,* October 23, 1887, 6.

36. "Why the Browns Lose," *St. Louis Republican,* October 21, 1887, 6.

37. *Ibid.* For a further comment on Bushong and Caruthers, see "Caruthers and Bushong. Their Probable Transfer and Sale to Brooklyn," *St. Louis Post-Dispatch,* October 27, 1887, 8.

38. "Will Gleason Lay Off?" *St. Louis Post-Democrat,* October 16, 1887, 5; "Caruthers and Bushong. Their Possible Transfer and Sale to the Brooklyn Team," 8; and "St. Louis Siftings. Why a Number of the Browns Were Sold," *Sporting Life,* February 1, 1888, 2.

39. "After the 1886 world championship, Von der Ahe paid each player $625. In the 1887 Series, Stearns and Von der Ahe created a $1,200 purse to be shared with the players on the winning team. Stearn also promised to give each of the Wolverines $400. Von der Ahe put aside $100 per player if the Browns won the world championship. Many of the players did not seem to be aware of this hundred-dollars-per-player pot. There was no monetary provision stipulated if the Browns lost the Series. In the end, the Browns played 16 games, the 15-game Series against Detroit and an exhibition game against Brooklyn (October 16), without any compensation. Larry G. Bowman, *Before the World Series,*" 103–04, and J. Thomas Hetrick, *Chris Von der Ahe and the St. Louis Browns* (Lanham, MD: Scarecrow, 1999), 75.

40. Bill Barnie, the manager of the Baltimore club, was surprised at the poor play of the Browns. He added: "I don't know whether the players are trying to get even with Chris for not offering to share profits, or whether it is case of rattle. It certainly ought not to be the former. Chris has been very liberal with his men—always has—too liberal in fact. Last year he paid them between $600 and $700 apiece, and now if they are trying to do him up they ought to suffer for it. But I hardly think they are." "Chips and Clips," *St. Louis Post-Dispatch,* October 27, 1887, 8.

41. "Gossip of the Games. The Playing of the Browns and Detroits Reviewed," *St. Louis Globe-Democrat,* October 23, 1887, 11.

42. The *Detroit Free Press* took exception to the claim by the Browns that they played well but had just not been lucky. "The Team Work," *Detroit Free Press,* October 22, 1887, 2.

43. "Detroit and St. Louis," *The Sporting News,* October 22, 1887, 4.

44. Attendance at the final four games was: 1,138 in Brooklyn (October 22), 3,389 in Detroit (October 24), 378 in Chicago (October 25), and 659 in St. Louis (October 26). At a previous game in Brooklyn on October 14, 6,796 fans attended. In the first two games in St. Louis (October 10–11) 4,208 cranks were at Game One and 6,468 at Game Two. "From St. Louis," *Sporting Life,* November 2, 1887, 5.

45. "A Grand Finale. Brilliant Ending of the Base Ball Season in Detroit," *Detroit Free Press,* October 25, 1887, 2.

46. *Ibid.* In the first inning, with Sy Sutcliffe, the Detroit first baseman, at bat, the umpire called time. Dan Brouthers was called to the plate to receive a zylonite bat from Albert Spalding, the owner of the Chicago club, as the best batter on the Detroit club. In the second inning, there was another pause in the game, this time to present Charley Sutcliffe, the Detroit catcher that day, with a gold watch and chain.

47. *Ibid.*

48. *Ibid.*

49. *Ibid.*

50. "Batting and Fielding Averages," *The Sporting News,* October 22, 1887, 3.

51. "Association Averages for 1887," *St. Louis Republican,* October 23, 1887, 14.

52. "O'Neill's batting has been a great disappointment; no more to his friends than to himself." "The Work of the Two Clubs," *St. Louis Republican,* October 23, 1887, 14.

53. "Presentation of Medals," *St. Louis Sunday Sayings,* October 23, 1887.

54. O'Neill might have also wanted the ceremony cancelled or postponed. As the designated winner of the batting medal, he might have been too embarrassed by his inability to hit for average or power in the world championship to walk across a stage to accept a medal for batting, even if it was based on his success in the regular season.

55. On November 5 and in the 1888 *Reach's Guide,* O'Neill was listed with 123 games played. In the research reported by Information Concepts Incorporated, in *The Baseball Encyclopedia: The Complete and Official Record of Major League Baseball* (1969), and in all subsequent encyclopedias (e.g., *Total Baseball. The Ultimate Baseball Encyclopedia, 8th Edition*) and online databases (e.g., Baseball Reference), O'Neill is credited with 124 games played. These post-1960 sources follow the contemporary practice

of counting any game in which a player appears, even if he was in the game for only a brief period and did not have a time at bat. O'Neill's 124th game occurred on May 30 in the first game of a doubleheader in Brooklyn. He played in left field for a half-inning, making one putout. He had injured his hand in a game on May 20. The hand had not healed sufficiently, so he left the game in the bottom of the first without taking his turn at bat.

56. On October 22, in the first official list of Association batting averages, O'Neill's announced batting average was .495, based on 270 hits in 545 times at bat in 117 games. The list also reported that he scored 169 runs. "Batting Averages," *The Sporting News*, October 22, 1887, 3. In the November 5 publication of the official averages, Wikoff stated: "It was only today that I was able to complete the official averages of the American Association so that all records previously published were unofficial." In the revised list, O'Neill had a batting average of .492 on 277 hits in 123 games. There was no information on times at bat or runs scored. It did include a column that indicated that O'Neill had 30 stolen bases. "American Association. Official Averages of the Players of this Organization," *The Sporting News*, November 5, 1887, 6.

57. "Association Official Averages," *St. Louis Globe-Democrat*, November 6, 1887, 11; "Clips and Chips," *St. Louis Post-Dispatch*, November 7, 1887, 8.

58. Comiskey and most of the Browns left on Sunday, October 30, for an extended series of exhibition games. The trip started in the South and then veered west, eventually landing in San Francisco. In the first leg, they played in such cities as Memphis and Nashville, Tennessee, and Charleston, South Carolina. On November 5, the day when the official batting averages were published, the Browns beat Chicago, 6–5, in Charleston. O'Neill had a single and a double in four times at bat. As was the case with the papers in the National League and American Association cities, the newspapers in the cities where the Browns played on this tour did not feature O'Neill's batting title, nor did they publish comments from Von der Ahe, Comiskey, or O'Neill on the official announcement of his average. "St. Louis and Chicago," *The Sporting News*, November 12, 1887, 3.

59. In the front pages of 1888 *Reach's Guide*, there was a one-page story about O'Neill, the champion batsman of the American Association, with a full-page portrait of him on the opposite page. "James E. O'Neill," *Reach's Official American Association Base Ball Guide 1888* (1888; Reprinted New York: Horton, 1989), page numbers not included in the reprint.

60. On February 20, 1888, the *St. Louis Republican* announced that medals would be awarded to O'Neill for best batting and Latham for base running during the first game of the forthcoming season. "Base Ball Briefs," *St. Louis Republican*, February 20, 1888, 20. The presentations were made by Judge Scott in late April 1888. "Grand Stand Chat," *St. Louis Post-Dispatch*, April 25, 1888, 3. See the Preface for the testimonial to O'Neill made by Judge Scott. "Latham and O'Neill," *The Sporting News*, May 5, 1888, 5.

61. David Nemec, ed. *Major League Baseball Profiles: 1871–1900, Volume 1.* (Lincoln: University of Nebraska Press, 2011), 589.

Chapter 16

1. Appendix B is entitled, "Tip O'Neill–Single-Season Batting Records and Feats in 1887." It summarizes the records that O'Neill set in 1887 (e.g., leading in the most batting categories, runs, consecutive games with an extra-base hit) as well as his more noteworthy batting feats (e.g., Triple Crown, games with five or more hits). As noted in the Preface, I honor the conventionalist position in the conduct of my research and in the writing of this book. In Appendix B, however, I also note the revisionist perspective when I reference O'Neill's batting average, his number of hits, and some of his records or feats in recognition of the fact that most record books include numbers or percentages that apply the revisionist position. Thus, for those statistics that are affected by the 1887 rules, I include two numbers or percentages for a record or feat, one based on a tally or calculation that counts a base on balls as a hit and a time at bat (conventionalist position) and, in parentheses, one based on a tally or calculation that scores a base on balls as in any other season where it is not counted as a hit or a time at bat (revisionist position). See the Preface for a further discussion of the debate between conventionalist and revisionist positions on record-keeping in baseball. In this chapter, the statistics follow the 1887 rules for scoring bases on balls.

2. O'Neill led the Browns in most offensive categories except for singles and stolen bases. His 135 singles were fourth-highest on the team, behind Gleason, who led with 152, Latham with 151, and Comiskey with 149. O'Neill's 33 stolen bases were well behind his more fleet-footed teammates. Latham led the team with 129 stolen bases, Comiskey came next with 117, followed by Welch with 89. O'Neill had the sixth-highest total on the Browns.

3. Caruthers and Robinson were also relatively close to O'Neill's .492 on-base percentage (OBP). Caruthers had an OBP of .463, and Robinson .445. Caruthers had a slugging percentage (SLG) of .547 and an on-base plus slugging percentage (OPS) of 1.010, in both cases second to O'Neill, who had a SLG of .732 and an OPS of 1.224.

4. O'Neill scored and batted in 278 or 25 percent of the Browns' 1,131 runs. Robinson and Caruthers were over 100 runs behind O'Neill in run contribution. Robinson created 175 runs (102 runs scored plus 74 runs batted in minus one home run) and Caruthers 167 runs (102 runs scored plus 73 runs batted in minus eight home runs), in both cases scoring and batting in 15 percent of the Browns' 1,131 runs.

5. O'Neill's 167 runs scored were the highest in the American Association. In my view, a batting category includes a statistic that represents the frequency (expressed as a number or percentage) with which a batsman hits a pitched ball for a particular result (e.g., for a single, double, run batted in, etc.). While "runs scored" is an important offensive category, scoring a run occurs after a player gets on base and does not directly reflect the immediate outcome of a ball hit by the player, and thus I omit this category from the batting table.

6. For a more detailed account of O'Neill's 88 long hits, see Chapter 13.

7. The formula for calculating total bases involves the addition of the following: singles plus two times doubles plus three times triples plus four times home runs. In 1887, the figure for singles includes both one-base hits plus bases

on balls. Thus, O'Neill had 413 total bases, based on the following calculation: 187 bases on one-base hits (135 singles + 52 bases on balls) + 104 bases on doubles (2 × 52 doubles) + 66 bases on triples (3 × 22 triples) + 56 bases on home runs (4 × 14 home runs).

8. "Scoring," *Reach's Official American Association Base Ball Guide 1887* (1887; Reprinted New York: Horton, 1989), 164.

9. The addition of runs batted in (RBI), on-base percentage (OBP), slugging percentage (SLG), and on-base percentage plus slugging percentage (OPS) complements and supplements the numbers and percentages used in the 1876–1892 era. These also provide a more comprehensive set of batting categories for comparing O'Neill's 1887 season to those of leading batsmen in other eras (addressed in a later section of this chapter). Runs Batted In became an official statistic in baseball in 1920, SLG in 1923, OBP in 1984, and OPS in the latter part of twentieth century. In the nineteenth-century, versions of these concepts appeared from time to time in some newspapers or guides, usually suggested by some of the baseball commentators of the day. In earlier chapters, I have referred to RBI in relation to O'Neill's run production. Most newspapers in the 1880s included a description of how each run was scored, often with accounts that report RBI events in statements like "player A batted in player B" or "player B scored on player A's double." In 1887, by counting bases on balls as hits, the rule makers were, in effect, converting the traditional formula for determining a batting average (hits divided by times at bat) to something akin to the approach used today to calculate OBP (hits plus bases on balls plus hit by pitch divided by times at bat plus bases on balls plus hit by pitch plus sacrifice flies). As noted in Chapter 11 on "Long Hits," the *St. Louis Post-Dispatch* recommended a different approach to calculating a batting average, one that was based on total bases, which is the basis of today's formula for computing a player's slugging percentage (total bases divided by times at bat). And in an OPS-style debate on whether a batsman should hit to get on base or try for a long hit, numerous pundits tried to reconcile hitting for average and power. The current OPS measure (OBP plus SLG) evaluates a hitter's ability to do both. For a further discussion on the development of these three statistics (and others), see John Thorn and Pete Palmer, *The Hidden Game of Baseball: A Revolutionary Approach to Baseball and Its Statistics* (Garden City, NY: Doubleday, 1984), 1–62; John Thorn, Peter Palmer, and Joseph M. Wayman, "The History of Major League Baseball Statistics," in John Thorn, Phil Birnbaum, and Bill Deane, *Total Baseball: The Ultimate Baseball Encyclopedia,* 8th ed. (Toronto: SPORT Media Publishing, 2004), 951–962.

10. Pete Browning also had 275 hits in 1887. Browning and O'Neill held the all-time hit record in the Association (1882–1891) and in the major leagues in 1892. O'Neill's 14 home runs in 1887 tied the single-season record in the Association, set in 1883 by Harry Stovey, the first baseman for Philadelphia. Stovey and Bug Holliday, an outfielder with Cincinnati, broke the Association record in 1889, each hitting 19 home runs. O'Neill did not break the all-time record for triples. In 1886, Dave Orr, the first baseman on the New York club in the American Association, set the record of 31 triples in one season. In 1884, Ned Williamson, the third baseman for Chicago in the National League, set the National League and major league record of 27 home runs in a season. Tip O'Neill's runs batted in 1887 set the single-season record in the American Association. However, it was considerably behind the mark set by Sam Thompson, who in 1887 led the National League and the major leagues with 166 RBI.

11. Gary Gillette and Pete Palmer, *The ESPN Baseball Encyclopedia* 5th ed. (New York: Sterling, 2008), 1856. In their lists of single-season leaders, Gillette and Palmer present two lists, one for the all-time leaders and a second for the top ten players in each era, for the following categories: runs, doubles, triples, home runs, home run percentage, runs batted in, strikeout percentage, and batting average. For another example of a source that includes records listed both for all-time and by era, see Lyle Spatz, ed., *The SABR Baseball List & Record Book* (New York: Scribner, 2007).

12. As noted in the Preface, O'Neill's leadership in three categories in the same season was first listed in *The Little Red Book of Major League Baseball* under the following heading: "leading in all three departments—Doubles, triples, homers-season—James E. O'Neill." F. C. Lane, ed., *The Little Red Book of Major League Baseball* (New York: Al Munro Elias Baseball Bureau, 1948), 15. This record also appeared in the final issue of *The Little Red Book*. "Leading League, Doubles-Triples-Home Runs, Season," Seymour Siwoff, *The Little Red Book of Major League Baseball 1971* (New York: Elias Sports Bureau, 1971), 19.

13. "1887 Baseball Season in Review." Accessed December 6, 2016, from https://tops.files.wordpress.com/2011/05/oneill.jpg.

14. Seymour Siwoff, *The Little Red Book of Major League Baseball 1971* (New York: Elias Sports Bureau, 1971), 19.

15. The category of "extra bases" refers to the number of bases beyond a single that a batter earned on each long hit. A batter achieved one extra base on a double, two extra bases on a triple, and three extra bases on a home run. In *The Little Red Book of Major League Baseball* published in 1971, Babe Ruth is listed with the "Most extra bases on long hits, season," at 253, a record set in 1921 on 44 doubles, 16 triples, and 59 home runs. The category of extra bases was discontinued, possibly because it did not offer a statistic that was sufficiently distinct from other long-hit statistics (e.g., number of long hits, total bases).

16. I did not use some of the categories listed in the table for Cobb, Medwick, and Musial. In addition to dropping the category of "Extra Bases," I also excluded "Games" and "At-Bats." I appreciate that if a batsman plays in more games and has more times at bat, he has a greater opportunity to increase his number of hits or improve his average in various categories. Although game and at-bat statistics provide numbers that, when combined with hitting numbers, generate hitting statistics (e.g., hits divided by times at bat=batting average), the game and at-bat numbers by themselves offer no information about what happens when a player hits the ball. Similarly, while "runs scored" and "stolen bases" are important offensive categories, these statistics occur after a player gets on base and do not directly reflect the immediate outcome of a ball hit by the player who is now on base, and thus are also omitted from the batting table.

17. Seventeen players have hit

.400 or higher in 28 seasons. Five of these seasons are represented on this table: Tip O'Neill (1887), Ross Barnes (1876), Nap Lajoie (1901), Ty Cobb (1911), and Rogers Hornsby (1922). Only Cobb (1911, 1912, 1922) and Hornsby (1922, 1924, 1925) have hit over .400 three times apiece. Trent McCotter, "The .400 Club," *Baseball Research Journal* 33, no. 7 (2004): 64–70.

18. Fifteen players have earned a Triple Crown in 17 seasons. Five of the Triple Crowns are included in this table: Tip O'Neill (1887), Nap Lajoie (1901), Rogers Hornsby (1922), Chuck Klein (1933), and Joe Medwick (1937).

19. When I transferred Medwick's statistics to my batting table, he fell from leading in 12 categories in the Cobb-Medwick-Musial table to leading in nine categories in my revised 12–category batting table. The exclusion of the categories for games, at-bats, and extra bases were responsible for the drop. In addition, I added Musial's 1948 season and dropped his 1946 season (in the Cobb-Medwick-Musial table). Without games, at-bats, runs, and extra bases, Musial led in eight categories (nine including OPS). Given their status in the 1971 record noted in *The Little Red Book* (tied for leading in 12 categories), I was committed to retaining Cobb, Medwick, and Musial in my 12-category table. Lajoie (1904), Cy Seymour (1905), Cobb (1909), Heinie Zimmerman (1912), Hornsby (1920), Musial (1943, 1946), and Carl Yastrzemski (1967) also led their respective leagues in nine batting categories.

20. The statistics of total bases, slugging percentage, and on-base percentage plus slugging percentage (OPS) are dominated by long-hit sluggers.

21. Numerous sluggers led their respective leagues in five of seven long-hit categories, including: Deacon White (1877), Harry Stovey (1883, 1891), Hugh Duffy (1894), Ed Delahanty (1899), Honus Wagner (1904, 1908), Babe Ruth (1919, 1921, 1923, 1924, 1926, 1928), Lou Gehrig (1934), Johnny Mize (1939), Ted Williams (1947, 1949), Al Rosen (1953), Mickey Mantle (1956), Hank Aaron (1963), Frank Robinson (1966), Carl Yastrzemski (1967), Willie Stargell (1973), Mike Schmidt (1981), Robin Yount (1982), Don Mattingly (1986), Barry Bonds (1993), Albert Belle (1995), Larry Walker (1997), Todd Helton (2000), Albert Pujols (2009), and Miguel Cabrera (2012).

22. In 1911, Cobb broke the American League records for hits, singles, runs batted in, long hits, and total bases. In 1921, Hornsby established a new National League record for hits. In 1922, Hornsby again broke the National League record for hits and established new records in the National League for home runs, long hits, total bases, and slugging percentage.

23. Since the National League was the only recognized major league in 1876, Barnes' ten firsts were also major league records. In my view, any distinction or comparison between League or Association records and Major League records is only meaningful when there are two or more major leagues in operation at the same time. Consequently, I consider Barnes' marks in each of the categories in which he led as National League records only.

24. Of those batsmen who led in ten or more batting categories in one season, only Ross Barnes and James O'Neill are not in the National Baseball Hall of Fame. Those who have been inducted in the Hall of Fame include (year elected in parentheses): Nap Lajoie (1937), Honus Wagner (1936), Ty Cobb (1936), Rogers Hornsby (1942), Chuck Klein (1980), Joe Medwick (1968), and Stan Musial (1969).

25. The expression "first among equals" comes from the Latin expression "primus inter pares." It refers to "a member of a group who is officially on the same level as the other members but who in fact has slightly more responsibility or power." Although originally used in the context of political or religious organizations, I adopt this expression in the end of the chapter to suggest that O'Neill was "on the same level" for one season as the other eight distinguished batsmen in my 12-category table. O'Neill had a similar record to these eight batsmen in terms of the number of batting categories in which they led in the seasons represented in the table. I also note the comment "slightly more power" to emphasize the fact that O'Neill was the only batsman in the group to lead in all seven long-hit (power) categories. He also was the batsman who registered the greatest number of record-breaking firsts. "First Among Equals." Accessed December 15, 2017. http://dictionary.cambridge.org/dictionary/english/first-among-equals.

Epilogue

1. After the end of the American Association in 1891, eight teams from the National League and four teams from the Association consolidated into the National League and American Association of Base Ball Clubs. In 1892, the new league competed in a split season, with the winner of each half-season playing in a post-season series for the pennant. Boston won with first half, with Cincinnati finishing fourth, while Cleveland won the second half, with Cincinnati dropping to eighth. David Nemec, *The Great Encyclopedia of the Nineteenth Century Major League Baseball*, 2d ed. (Tuscaloosa: University of Alabama Press, 2006), 607–610.

2. *Ibid.*, 445.

3. As of 2017, Tip is one of only 31 batters to win the batting title in consecutive years.

4. Tommy Tucker, the Baltimore first baseman, won the batting championship in 1889 with an average of .372.

5. "Base Ball Notes," *Cleveland Plain Dealer*, September 20, 1887, 4; "Diamond Points," *Boston Globe*, October 15, 1887, 3; and "St. Louis Siftings: O'Neill Again Leads the Procession," *Sporting Life*, December 5, 1888, 5.

6. I compared O'Neill to the leading batsmen on the Browns, in the American Association, and in the major leagues for two-year (1885–1886, 1886–1887, 1887–1888, 1888–1889), three-year (1885–1887, 1886–1888, 1887–1889), four-year (1885–1888, 1886–1889), and five-year (1885–1889) periods.

7. In this chapter, I report on one of the three–year periods (1887–1889) and on the only five-year period (1885–1889). To develop a list of batsmen for these comparisons, I reviewed the leading batsmen on the Browns and in each league in the major batting categories (hits, singles, doubles, triples, home runs, runs batted in, extra-base hits, total bases, on-base percentage, slugging percentage, OPS, and batting average). I focused on those batsmen who led in two or more categories in more than one year and those who played in all three years for the 1887–1889 comparison and in all five years for the 1885–1889 comparison. While I had more than 40 batsmen on the initial list for both comparisons, in addition to O'Neill, I was able to pare down this list to the following leading batsmen in

each group: Browns—Charles Comiskey, Arlie Latham, and Yank Robinson; American Association—Pete Browning, Henry Larkin, Dave Orr, John Reilly, and Harry Stovey; National League—Cap Anson, Dan Brouthers, Roger Connor, Buck Ewing, King Kelly, Jimmy Ryan, and Sam Thompson.

In these three years (1887–1889), O'Neill led the Association and the major leagues with the following numbers and percentages: hits (631), doubles (109), long hits (177), total bases (904), runs batted in (333), batting average (.388), on-base percentage (.431), slugging percentage (.556), and OPS (.987).

8. Based on his Win Shares system, Bill James claimed that "Thirty Win Shares is a Great Season." O'Neill reached this mark only once with 36 win shares in 1887, so James concluded that Tip had "one Great Season." He had 28 win shares in 1888. Bill James, "Great Seasons by Left Fielders," *The New Bill James Historical Baseball Abstract* (New York: Free Press, 2003), 680–682, 716–719.

9. In the five-year period (1885–1889), O'Neill played in 578 games. He led the Association in hits (893), total bases (1,255), runs batted in (478), batting average (.370), on-base percentage (.449), slugging percentage (.520), OPS (.969). Stovey played in 626 games. He led the Association with 149 doubles, compared to O'Neill's 144. Stovey knocked out 52 home runs, while O'Neill hit 34 four-baggers. In long hits, Stovey had 266 and O'Neill had 236. Roger Connor, the first baseman of the New York Giants in the National League, was the five-year (1885–1889) leader in the Major Leagues in triples (91) and home runs (tied with Stovey with 52).

10. Cap Anson, the first baseman for Chicago, played in 627 games between 1885 and 1889, and led the Major Leagues in hits (909) and runs batted in (558). Dan Brouthers, the first baseman for Buffalo (1885), Detroit (1886–1888), and Boston (1889) in this five-year period, played in 597 games. He had the second-highest number of hits (908) among the leading batsmen. O'Neill ranked third in the major leagues in hits (893) and second in runs batted in (478). Sam Thompson, the right fielder for Detroit (1885–1888) and Philadelphia (1889), played in 496 games. Among the leading batsmen in the majors, he had the third-most runs batted in (450). On a per-game basis, O'Neill had the most hits per game (1.54), followed by Brouthers (1.52) and Anson (1.45). In runs batted in, Thompson led the way with .907 RBIs per game, Anson was second at .890, and O'Neill was third at .827.

11. In comparison to the other leading batsmen, Dan Brouthers was the cumulative leader over five years (1885–1889) in the major leagues in doubles (167), extra-base hits (279), total bases (1,345), on-base percentage (.468), slugging percentage (.544), and OPS (1.012). O'Neill was second in on-base percentage (.449) and third in slugging percentage (.520) and OPS (.969). Anson was second in on-base percentage (.448), and Connor was second in OPS (.984). Although O'Neill was fourth in total bases, he was second in total bases per game at 2.17, just behind Brouthers at 2.25 and ahead of Connor in third place with 2.11.

12. O'Neill was one of 14 Association batsmen who hit .300 or better in 1891. The Association average was .255. O'Neill finished in the top ten in most batting categories, ranking third in doubles (28), fourth in home runs (10), and sixth in hits (166), on-base percentage (.404), and total bases (232).

13. "Editorial Views, News and Comment," *Sporting Life*, April 15, 1893, 2.

14. In both 1888 and 1892, and periodically in the seasons in between, O'Neill complained of malarial attacks and dysentery. "O'Neill Goes to Kansas City," *St. Louis Globe-Democrat*, July 11, 1888, 8; Daniel M. Pearson, *Baseball in 1889. Players vs. Owners* (Bowling Green: Bowling Green State University Popular Press, 1993), 205.

15. "St. Louis Siftings, The Disadvantages Under Which the Browns Won the Pennant," *Sporting Life*, November 17, 1888, 3.

16. O'Neill missed a game on May 13, 1892. "Tip's stomach was indulging in a bit of rebellion." "Called Bawls," *Cincinnati Times-Star*, May 14, 1892, 62; "The big fielder is laid up with a severe strain in the groin, and it may be several days before he is able to resume his position." "Base Ball Gossip," *Cincinnati Commercial Gazette*, May 14, 1892; and "Tip will not Rejoin the Cincinnatis This Season—Diamond Gossip," *Cincinnati Commercial Gazette*, September 19, 1892.

17. "A Beauty. Not a Break in the Game," *Cincinnati Enquirer*, August 21, 1892, 2. "Tip O'Neill is still complaining, and in the seventh inning Comiskey took him out of the game and played Genins in his place. Ever since the Red's fielder slid into Reilly in one of the Philadelphia games, he has been complaining of a severe pain in his side. A physician told O'Neill that two of his ribs were fractured. In case he is unable to play, Pete Browning will be secured to fill his position." "Base Ball Gossip," *Cincinnati Commercial Gazette*, August 31, 1892.

18. Von der Ahe accused Byrne, the president of the Brooklyn club, of tampering. He alleged that Byrne encouraged Bushong to send O'Neill a letter indicating that Brooklyn would make every effort to sign him if he played for his release. The owner lifted the suspension after O'Neill missed two games. "A Bad Break. The Case of O'Neill," *Sporting Life*, July 17, 1888, 1.

19. O'Neill agreed to a medical examination shortly thereafter. The doctor indicated that O'Neill did not have malarial fever, but rather "a bad case of stomach trouble that would require some time and care to radically overcome." He also advised that the illness did not require O'Neill to stop playing baseball. "O'Neill's Side. The Browns' Left Fielder Pronounced Sick by a Physician," *St. Louis Post-Dispatch*, July 10, 1888, 8.

20. Later that same season, O'Neill was sick and felt he could not "play good ball." Once again, Von der Ahe directed O'Neill to go to a doctor of the owner's choosing, and once again O'Neill refused, responding with "somewhat warm language," which got him a second suspension, this time for impertinence. Comiskey had previously agreed to the day off requested by O'Neill. When he heard of O'Neill's suspension, after he missed the one game that he had originally requested off, Comiskey declared that O'Neill had served his suspension and could resume play. Von der Ahe reluctantly supported the reinstatement. "O'Neill Suspended," *St. Louis Post-Dispatch*, September 23, 1888, 16.

21. After this series in May, the Browns beat Kansas in 13 of the remaining 16 games, for a final 14-6 record in six series that season. When the Browns finished the season in second place, just two games back of Brooklyn, some observers pointed to the three losses in May

as one of the reasons why the Browns failed to win their fifth American Association championship in a row. "Ball Players Strike. The Fining of Robinson Causes Trouble in the Browns," *St. Louis Post-Dispatch*, May 3, 1889, 3; Jean-Pierre Caillault, *A Tale of Four Cities: Nineteenth Century Baseball's Most Exciting Season, 1889, In Contemporary Accounts* (Jefferson, NC: McFarland, 2003), 280–281; Al Kermisch, "From a Researcher's Notebook … Yank Robinson's One-Man Strike in 1889," SABR Research Archives, accessed July 15, 2016, https://www.research.sabr.org.

22. "The 'Quitters' Return. President Von der Ahe and his Conquered Heroes Home Again," *St. Louis Post-Dispatch*, May 7, 1889, 8.

23. Most players were required to return to their former clubs. Of the seven players who left to join the Players' League in 1890, only Comiskey, Boyle, and O'Neill returned to the Browns. Robinson went to Cincinnati, King to Pittsburgh, and Milligan to Philadelphia. Latham moved to Cincinnati in the middle of the 1890 season.

24. As previously noted, of the nine core Browns in 1887–1889 (see Chapter 3), Von der Ahe sold or traded five of these players in late 1887: Gleason and Welch to Philadelphia and Bushong, Foutz, and Caruthers to Brooklyn. In 1890, Robinson went to the Pittsburgh Burghers in the Players' League. Latham was suspended by the Browns in the latter part of the 1889 season and then reunited with Comiskey and O'Neill when he signed with the Chicago Pirates in the Players' League in 1890. By midseason in 1890, Comiskey released Latham, who then signed with Cincinnati in the National League. Latham played with Cincinnati from 1890 to 1896 and thus played again with two of the core Browns when Comiskey and O'Neill joined the Reds in 1892.

25. "Base Ball Briefs," *St. Louis Republican*, May 15, 1888, 6; "A Challenge Refused," *St. Louis Chronicle*, May 16, 1888. Comiskey eventually remitted the fine. "Base Ball Briefs," *St. Louis Republican*, June 17, 1888, 3.

26. "O'Neill and Comiskey have had a difference this season, but 'Commie' knows a hitter when he sees one." "St. Louis Siftings. Diamond Dust," *Sporting Life*, October 10, 1888, 9.

27. "Commie and Tip: The Two Had a Spat, and the Big Fielder was Ordered Home," *Cincinnati Commercial Gazette*, August 11, 1892.

28. "On Top Again: The Cleveland Club Fights its Way to the Front Rank Once More," *Cleveland Leader*, August 10, 1892.

29. O'Neill had made other miscues in recent games. For example, on the previous day (August 8), in a 12–8 loss to Chicago, Vaughn was on second base and O'Neill was on third when Comiskey hit a ground ball. Vaughn took off from second on the hit, but O'Neill chose not to run home. Vaughn reached third, forcing O'Neill off the base. O'Neill was tagged out. Comiskey was upset because he felt O'Neill should have run to the plate. "Little Tim. On Uncle's Staff," *Cincinnati Times-Star*, August 9, 1892, 6.

30. "A Lost Cause Well Saved. The Latest Gossip from the Club's Quarters," *Cincinnati Times-Star*, August 11, 1892, 2.

31. Comiskey wanted more hustle out of O'Neill in tracking down fly balls and in stealing bases: "Goodness knows I need Tip O'Neill's hitting but I can't stand his slow action." "'Tip' O'Neill to Resume Play," *Cincinnati Times-Star*, August 13, 1892.

32. "Welch Goes on a Tear: O'Neill Still Sulks," *Cincinnati Times-Star*, August 17, 1892.

33. Ibid.

34. In a list of the "string of ill fortune which beset his [Comiskey's] team on every side," one of the problems mentioned was "O'Neill's sulky fits." "Notes," *Cincinnati Commercial Gazette*, September 4, 1892.

35. "Base-Ball Gossip," *Cincinnati Enquirer*, August 14, 1892, 2.

36. The *Cincinnati Commercial Gazette* believed that O'Neill was "making a serious mistake" by not returning to play after five games. "Base-Ball Gossip," *Cincinnati Commercial Gazette*, August 16, 1892.

37. "A Beauty. Not a Break in the Game. The Reds Play in Clockwork Style," *Cincinnati Enquirer*, August 21, 1892, 2; "Base Ball Gossip," *Cincinnati Commercial Gazette*, August 31, 1892.

38. In Tip's last game, he went hitless in four times at bat, with two putouts in the field. Cincinnati beat Boston, 6–1. "Close Call for Boston. Two Hits in the Ninth Saved the Hub Team from a Shut Out," *Cincinnati Commercial Gazette*, August 31, 1892. Comiskey re-signed Pete Browning to take "Counterfeit Tip O'Neill's Place in the Field."

"Sporting," *Cleveland Leader*, September 1, 1892.

39. "Cincinnati Chips. Comiskey Agrees Upon Terms with his Club," *Sporting Life*, January 7, 1893, 3.

40. Since O'Neill still appeared on Cincinnati's reserve list, throughout the off-season newspapers repeatedly asked Stearns, the president of the Cincinnati Club, and Comiskey about O'Neill's status for the 1893 season. Those newspapers that were the most critical of O'Neill's play in 1892 argued against re-signing him. By November of 1892, the *Cincinnati Commercial Gazette* predicted that O'Neill "has played his last championship game as a member of Comiskey's team." "Base-Ball Gossip," *Cincinnati Commercial Gazette*, November 27, 1892.

41. As a reserved player without a contract, O'Neill was ineligible to play with another team in the National League and American Association of Baseball Clubs or any minor league team who were members of the Professional Base Ball Association, as stipulated by the terms and conditions of the National Agreement. O'Neill had to be released or traded by the Cincinnati club before he could sign with another team. See section 9 of the National Agreement. "The National Agreement," *Reach's Official American Association Base Ball Guide 1892* (1892; Reprinted New York: Horton, 1989), 102–103.

42. "Personals," *The Sporting News*, December 24, 1892, 2.

43. "Editorial Views, News, Comment," *Sporting Life*, July 1, 1893, 2.

44. "All of the sports smoke the 'Pug,' the best 10–cent cigar on earth, made by MacKay and O'Neill." "Hesitant Amsterdam," *Sporting Life*, April 21, 1894, 6. The cigar business also did well in Montreal, Quebec, Canada: "Tip O'Neill is prospering in the cigar business in Montreal," in association with his brothers George and D'Arcy." "Canada Cranks. Good Players," *Sporting Life*, July 11, 1896, 21. After a few years in Montreal, he also got into the restaurant business with George, co-managing the Hoffman Café. "News and Comment," *Sporting Life*, April 24, 1897, 5. After the death of George in 1909, O'Neill was the sole proprietor of the Hoffman Café. He sold the Café in 1912. "The Late Geo. O'Neill," *Woodstock Sentinel-Review*, December 22, 1909, 1.

45. "Hesitant Amsterdam," 6.

46. "Personal Paragraphs. The Movements of Woodstock Citizens and their Friends," *Woodstock Sentinel-Review*, September 17, 1894, 4. O'Neill's brother George had moved to Montreal in 1893.

47. Although numerous secondary sources suggest that after 1892, O'Neill played baseball on various minor league or independent teams, I was unable to find any primary sources to verify these claims. For two examples of sources that indicate that O'Neill played on other teams after 1892, see Neil Munro and STATS, Inc. "James 'Tip' O'Neill. 1883–92," *Canadian Players Encyclopedia* (STATS Publishing, 1996), 49, and Michel Vigneault, "O'Neill, James Edward (Tip)," *Dictionary of Canadian Biography Online*. Accessed December 8, 2011, at http://biographi.ca/009004-119.01-e.php?id_nbr=7629. Since he was still on Cincinnati's reserve list for at least 1893, it is doubtful that he played for any team in 1893. He was reported to be in bad health from 1894 to 1896 and might not have been able to play in these years as well. "Caught on the Fly," *The Sporting News*, February 22, 1896, 5.

48. "Saturday's Ball Game," *Montreal Gazette*, September 28, 1894, 8.

49. "The Match on Saturday," *Montreal Gazette*, October 29, 1894, 8.

50. The Hiawathas Grays was a barnstorming team in Detroit funded by the Hiawatha Tobacco Works as a vehicle to promote the company's various tobacco products. O'Neill and Page played together for a few weeks in the spring of 1881. For a short history of the Scottens, the family that owned the tobacco business, see "Mansion to Mission," Fort Street Presbyterian Church. Accessed November 22, 2012, at http://fortstreet.org/Facility/History/mansiontomission.html. X

51. In the 1889 entry of a recent history of baseball in Montreal published in *Montreal La Presse*, André Rivest described Joe Page as follows: "Canadian Pacific Employee Joe Page is considered the father of baseball in Quebec. A former player, he trains and trains a large number of teams using the train as a means of dissemination. He creates new leagues wherever he goes." *La Presse+*, March 29, 2014, at http://plus.lapresse.ca/4187-64ec-5335da14-b13d-138acc/XAMK27-RIxCq.hmtl. A recent nomination for the Baseball Foundation's Quebec Hall of Fame portrayed Page as follows: "Player, manager, promoter, journalist, scout, he was known as the father of baseball in Canada. Founder of the first professional baseball club in Montreal, he also played a crucial role in the arrival of the Royals in the city in 1897. He founded many leagues and led several clubs in addition to developing the Provincial League during a 60-year-old baseball career." Wednesday, April 5, 2017. RDS. Accessed December 10, 2017, at http://www.rds.ca/pied-de-page/contacts?property=RDSca.X

52. "Off for Boston," *Montreal Gazette*, May 8, 1897, 8.

53. O'Neill played various roles with the Montreal Reserves of the Canadian Baseball League in 1907, for example, representing the team at the league meeting and managing the team for some of its games, as well as being the umpire for some league games. "Baseball Meeting," *Montreal Star*, January 28, 1907; "Rock City Defeated," *Montreal Star*, May 27, 1907; "Canadian League Ball Tomorrow," *Montreal Star*, May 31, 1907.

54. William Brown, *Baseball's Fabulous Montreal Royals. The Minor League Team That Made Major League History* (Montreal: Robert Davies, 1996), 10.

55. "Montreal Mention. The New Club in Control of the Old Company's Stock and Assets," *Sporting Life*, December 17, 1898, 1.

56. "Merry Montreal. Delights to do Honor to the Veteran Henry Chadwick," *Sporting Life*, September 10, 1898, 13.

57. The notice of O'Neill's death in the first issue of *Sporting Life* in 1916 stated that after his career ended, "he became an umpire and a scout for various clubs." Presumably, he identified prospects from his work with various teams in the Montreal area, from his days as an umpire in the Eastern League, and from his visits to major league cities. "'Tip' O'Neill Dead. A Famous Hard-Hitting Outfielder of the Olden Times Passes Away," *Sporting Life*, January 8, 1916, 6.

58. "Boston Briefs. Old-Timers' Days," *Sporting Life*, August 3, 1907, 3.

59. "Montreal Merry," *Sporting Life*, February 5, 1898, 5.

60. *Sporting Life* published a note that conveyed O'Neill's concern about this false report and provided the address of the Hoffman Café, should anyone wish to write him directly to ask about his state of health. "News and Comment," *Sporting Life*, April 24, 1897, 5.

61. "The Only Tip O'Neill Objects to Lightweights Appropriating His Famous Title," *Sporting Life*, January 29, 1898, 3.

62. Ernest J. Lanigan, in his *Baseball Cyclopedia*, identified James O'Neill as "Tip the First," claiming that this was the name that most writers used for the "original" Tip. He called Norris L. O'Neill, the former president of the Western League, Tip II, and William John O'Neill, a fielder for a number of teams in the early years of the American League, Tip III. Ernest J. Lanigan, *Baseball Cyclopedia* (1922; Reprinted Jefferson, NC: McFarland, 2005), 71–72.

63. "'Tip' O'Neill Called by Death in Street. Had Great Reputation as Baseball Player Twenty Years Ago," *Montreal Gazette*, January 1, 1916, 7.

64. "Edward ('Tip') O'Neill, Famous Ball Player. Remains of Former Woodstock Man Brought to City for Burial—Brother and Sister Accompanied Body," *Woodstock Sentinel-Review*, January 3, 1916.

65. At the time of O'Neill's death, his brother, D'Arcy, and his sisters, Agnes O'Neill and Clara MacKay, were the only surviving family members. Theresa died in 1871 at two years of age. His father James died in 1883. Of his other three deceased brothers, John died in 1889, Joseph in 1898, and George in 1909. His mother died in 1915, just three months prior to Tip's death.

66. "Original 'Tip' Dies of Heart Attack," *St. Louis Globe-Democrat*, January 1, 1916. Also see "The man who made the name famous and the original J. E. 'Tip' O'Neill died yesterday. He was the only 'Tip' and there was only one 'I' in his name." "'Tip' O'Neill, Famous Old Brownie, is Dead," *Cincinnati Times-Star*, January 1, 1892. The *Chicago Herald* began its announcement with the following: "Death yesterday removed one of the two greatest natural baseball batters in the history of the American game when James (the original Tip) O'Neill succumbed to heart disease on a street car in Montreal, his home town." "O'Neill is Dead. Member of Comiskey's old St. Louis Browns Passes Away at Montreal," *Chicago Herald*, January 1, 1916. The tribute that Joe Page wrote following

O'Neill's death for the *St. John Times* in New Brunswick was reproduced in 1935 by *The Sporting News*. It made reference to the many stories told about "the original Tip O'Neill." "Tribute to O'Neill, Written in '16 by Joe Page, Former Teammate," *The Sporting News*, November 7, 1935, 5.

67. "Tip O'Neill Dies; St. Louis Player King of Hitters," *St. Louis Republic*, January 1, 1916.

68. "Tip O'Neill Dies in Montreal, Member of Old-Time Browns and Holder of Hitting Record," *The Sporting News*, January 6, 1916, 2.

69. "O'Neill is Dead. Member of Comiskey's old St. Louis Browns Passes Away at Montreal," *Chicago Herald*, January 1, 1916.

70. "Tribute to O'Neill," 5.

71. In the Preface, I reviewed or cited a number of articles that challenged O'Neill's batting average, two of which were published in *Baseball Magazine*: "1887, the Black Sheep of Baseball Records" by John Ward (1915) and "One Batting Championship That Never Was Deserved" by F. C. Lane (1923).

72. In most record books or compendia published before 1980, O'Neill was on two lists, one for being the batting champion of the American Association in 1887 and the other for hitting .400 or higher in a season. His .492 average was invariably followed by a note or parenthetical comment which indicated that in 1887, bases on balls were counted as hits.

73. The claim that O'Neill had the all-time highest batting average was based on the position that the history of the major leagues began with the National League in 1876. However, Levi Meyerle hit .492 in 1871 with the Philadelphia Athletics in the National Association. In 1968, the Special Baseball Records Committee did not recognize the National Association as a major league. *The Baseball Encyclopedia: The Complete and Official Record of Major League Baseball* (Toronto: Macmillan, 1969), 2328.

74. *Ibid.*

75. Information Concepts Incorporated (ICI) reported the following batting statistics for O'Neill in 1887: At-Bats—517; Runs—167; Hits—225; Doubles—52; Triples—19; Home Runs—14; Bases on Balls—50; Stolen Bases—30; Batting Average—435; Slugging Percentage—.691. There also was a column for Runs Batted In, with a number that was incomplete (103) and thus was not included in *The Baseball Encyclopedia*. The ICI statistics are available through the National Baseball Hall of Fame Library. *American Association, I.C.I. Statistics, 1887. Batting and Fielding Record, O'Neill* (Cooperstown, NY: National Baseball Hall of Fame Library, Microfilmed, 2002).

76. *The Baseball Encyclopedia* was published in 1969 by the Macmillan Company. In subsequent years, many people referred to the volume by the nickname "Big Mac." *The Baseball Encyclopedia: The Complete and Official Record of Major League Baseball* (Toronto: Macmillan, 1969).

77. Jerome Holtzman, "An Important Change to the Official Record of Major League Baseball." Accessed on May 13, 2017, from https://ourgame.mlbblogs.com/why-is-the-national-association-not-a-major-league-and-other-record-issues.

78. *The Baseball Encyclopedia* was based on the statistics generated by Information Concepts Incorporated: 517 times at bat, 225, hits, and 50 bases on balls. In 1969, O'Neill's batting average was recalculated: 225 hits divided by 517 times at bat or .435. Following the Holtzman declaration, 50 at-bats and 50 hits were added to the 1969 numbers. O'Neill's batting average changed to .485, based on 275 hits divided by 567 times at bat.

79. I noted in the Preface that *The Elias Book of Baseball Records* still lists O'Neill with a .442 batting average. Seymour Siwoff, ed., *The Elias Book of Baseball Records, 2016 Edition* (New York: Elias Sports Bureau, 2016), 7.

80. Cap Anson, the first baseman and captain of the Chicago club, was recognized as the champion batsman of the National League in 1887. "Adrian C. Anson," *Spalding's Official American Association Base Ball Guide 1888* (1888; Reprinted New York: Horton, 1989), 8–9. Dan Brouthers was second with a .420 average, and Sam Thompson, the right fielder on the Detroit club, was third with a .407 average. When bases on balls are not counted as hits and times at bat (revisionist calculation), as is the case with most sources of baseball records (e.g., Baseball Reference), Sam Thompson, had the highest average at .372, followed by Anson at .347 and Brouthers at .338.

81. In his review of key moments in the history of baseball statistics, Alan Schwarz referred to the 1887 approach to the calculation of batting averages (counting walks as hits) as a "spooky harkening of today's on-base baseball revolution." Alan Schwarz, "A Numbers Revolution," July 8, 2004. Accessed May 20, 2017, http://espn.com.

82. John Farrell, *Tip O'Neill and the Democrat Century* (Boston: Little, Brown, 2001), 41. Also see Tip O'Neill, with William Novak, *Man of the House: The Life and Political Memoirs of Speaker Tip O'Neill* (New York: Random House, 1987).

83. In its first decade, the Canadian Baseball Hall of Fame and Museum was located in Toronto. It moved to St. Marys, Ontario, in June of 1998.

84. In 1983, there were six inductees into the Canadian Baseball Hall of Fame and Museum: James "Tip" O'Neill, John Ducey, Phil Marchildon, George Selkirk, Lester B. Pearson, and Frank Shaughnessy.

85. "Tip's Name Tops Field at Park," *Woodstock Sentinel-Review*, June 8, 1984, 3.

86. The individual photo that hangs on the Woodstock Sports Wall of Fame is a picture of O'Neill in a Woodstock Actives uniform. The inscription reads: "Major League Baseball St. Louis Browns. Batting Champion All-Time. Highest Batting Average in 1887 of .492." He was also inducted to the Sports Wall of Fame in the team category. His photo appears with the Woodstock Actives, winners of the Canadian baseball championship in 1878. "Inductees Honoured on the Wall of Fame," Woodstock Sentinel-Review. Accessed April 5, 2018, at http://www.woodstocksentinelreview.com/2008/10/27inductees-honoured-on-the-wall-of-fame.

87. Canada's Sports Hall of Fame is located in Calgary, Alberta. "Honoured Member. James O'Neill. Inducted 1994." Accessed January 7, 2018, at http://sportshall.ca.

88. "James 'Tip' O'Neill," Honoured Members, The Ontario Sports Hall of Fame, Accessed April 5, 2018, at http://ophof.ca.

89. As noted in the Preface, the National Baseball Hall of Fame in Cooperstown, New York, recognizes O'Neill's record of 1887 (listed as .485 but then adjusted to .435) along with Hugh Duffy's record of 1894 (listed as .440) in a display entitled, "Highest Batting Average in a Season Since 1876."

90. "James 'Tip' O'Neill Award," Canadian Baseball Hall of Fame and Museum. Accessed January 7,

2018, at http://baseballhalloffame.ca.

91. *Ibid.*

Appendix A

1. The *New York Evening Sun* was the only newspaper I reviewed that provided a same-day, inning-by-inning report of most of the home games of New York and Brooklyn teams. It also included a line score but did not have a table with individual statistics or a summary of team statistics. In most cities, there were one or two newspapers who occasionally published more detailed inning-by-inning game reports, but not on a regular basis.

2. In most cases, I resolved discrepancies by considering one or more of the following: (1) game reports from local newspapers; (2) game reports that had both box scores and some details about O'Neill's times at bat (especially those in which he had a hit or base on balls); and (3) statistics supported by the majority of game reports.

3. In the description of LoC C, I indicate that that the "numbers outlined in box scores include consistent information in the ABs, Hs, and BBs in most of the reports." Six of the games with an LoC C rating did have consistent information in the box scores on AB, H, and BB. In the other six games with an LoC C rating, there were 1–3 reports with information on one of AB, H, and BB that differed from the majority of the other 6–10 game reports. In all cases, I was confident in the numbers listed in the majority reports because they included local accounts, some of which had details to support the numbers listed in the box scores. Although most of the other reports in the majority group were relatively brief, they corroborated the information from the local reports. In contrast, the few discrepant reports were brief, had few details, had gaps in information, and, in some cases, were internally inconsistent. In short, with the six games with a LoC rating based on inconsistent information, I had more confidence in the information reported in the majority than I did with the few reports that offered discrepant if not confusing information.

4. When O'Neill's 50 bases on balls are not considered as either hits or times at bat, his batting average was .435, based on 225 hits divided by 517 times at bat. This revised average was first reported in *The Baseball Encyclopedia: The Complete and Official Record of Major League Baseball* (Toronto: Macmillan, 1969), 58, 123, 1310.

5. When O'Neill's 50 bases on balls are considered as hits and times at bat, his batting average was .485, based on 275 hits divided by 567 times at bat. The first source to report O'Neill's .485 average was *Total Baseball*. John Thorn, Pete Palmer, and Michael Gershman, *Total Baseball: The Official Encyclopedia of Major League Baseball, Seventh Edition* (Kingston, NY: Total Sports Publishing, 2001), 551–552, 1066, 2065, 2326.

6. *American Association, I.C.I. Statistics, 1887. Batting and Fielding Record, O'Neill* (Cooperstown, NY: National Baseball Hall of Fame Library, Microfilmed, 2002).

7. Unless I quote from the newspaper, I do not always provide the full reference in an endnote for the relevant game report of the newspaper I cite as evidence in the determination of the batting statistic in question. In most cases, the game report was published in the next edition of the newspaper. The *New York Evening Sun* and the *St. Louis Chronicle* published their game reports on the same day in the evening edition of the newspaper. For all other daily newspapers cited in evidence, the game report appeared in the edition published the next day. The three weeklies, *Sporting Life, The Sporting News,* and the *New York Clipper,* published their game reports in the next edition, which came out a few days after the game was played. As an example, for the game played in New York on September 3, the report appeared in the *New York Evening Sun* in the evening edition published on the same day as the game. The game reports in the *New York Times, New York Star, New York World, New York Herald, New York Sun, St. Louis Globe-Democrat,* and *St. Louis Republican* were published in the September 4 edition of these newspapers. For the weeklies, the *New York Clipper* and *The Sporting News* published their game reports in the September 10 edition, while *Sporting Life* published its report on September 14.

8. "Sporting. The Browns Win a Six-Inning Game," *St. Louis Republican*, May 5, 1887, 6; "Sporting. Browns, 4; Louisvilles, 1," *St. Louis Globe-Democrat*, May 5, 1887, 4.

9. "Sporting. Great Slugging Match Between Browns and Brooklyns," *St. Louis Republican*, May 21, 1887, 6; "Browns, 15; Brooklyns, 9," *St. Louis Globe-Democrat*, May 21, 1887, 6.

10. "Great Slugging Match," 6.

11. "Browns, 15; Brooklyns, 9," 6.

12. "Mets Beaten in Two Games," *New York Evening Sun*, September 3, 1887. The *St. Louis Globe-Democrat* also published a detailed account of the game, one that replicated most of the report from the *New York Evening Sun*.

13. "Mets Beat St. Louis," *New York Evening Sun*, September 5, 1887, 1. The *St. Louis Globe-Democrat* and the *St. Louis Republican* also provided detailed reports on the game, in both cases relying on the accounts and often the wording from the *New York Evening Sun* to summarize some of the innings where runs were scored. These two St. Louis newspapers ended their reports with a more general statement on the ninth inning. The *St. Louis Republican* added a comment on the performances of King and Latham and the absence of Welch due to his injury in the previous day's game.

14. "The Association. Listless Work by the Athletics Gives a Game to the St. Louis Browns," *Philadelphia Press*, September 10, 1887, 6; "St. Louis Wins, Although the Athletic Club Earns the Most Runs," *Philadelphia Record*, September 10, 1887, 6; "American Association. The Athletics Laid Out by the St. Louis Browns," *Philadelphia Inquirer*, September 10, 1887, 3; "Beaten by the Champions," *Philadelphia Times*, September 10, 1887, 2. Note that the *St. Louis Globe-Democrat* relied on the game report of the *Philadelphia Times* for its game account, while the *St. Louis Republican* drew on the account by the *Philadelphia Press* for its report.

15. In addition to the *American Association, ICI. Statistics, 1887,* ICI made box scores available to the National Baseball Hall of Fame Library. For each game, the box scores included one game report, which consisted of a description of the game and a box score (tabular summary of individual statistics on batting and fielding, a list of other team statistics related batting, fielding, base running, and pitching, and a line score that displayed the number of runs scored in each in-

ning). While in most cases, the box score in this collection offered further information on the games, for the game played on September 9, it showed that O'Neill had one hit in four times at bat and thus was at odds with the numbers reported for this game in *ICI Statistics* (one hit in five times at bat). *National League & American Association Box Scores,* Cooperstown, NY: National Baseball Hall of Fame Library, Microfilmed 2002.

16. "Good for Brooklyn. The St. Louis Men Defeated, Score 4 to 2," *New York Evening Sun,* July 25, 1887, 1; "Smith's Great Work. Brooklyn Captures a Game from the Champions," *Brooklyn Citizen,* July 26, 1887, 2.

17. In the case of the *St. Louis Republican,* it published the report from the *New York Evening Sun,* which clearly described O'Neill with a base on balls in the sixth inning and a single in the eighth inning. Yet it included a box score that had O'Neill with one hit in four times at bat with no base on balls. "More Ninth-Inning Luck. Brooklyn Bats Out a Victory from St. Louis," *St. Louis Republican,* July 26, 1887, 6.

18. "Count Us One. Louisville Wins the First Championship Contest from St. Louis—A Hot One," *Louisville Commercial,* April 17, 1887, 2.

19. "Sporting. Opening of the Association Ball Season. The Browns score Another Defeat," *St. Louis Republican,* April 17, 1887, 12.

20. In 1887, reporters rarely travelled to cover away games. In this case, Sheridan likely wanted to get a first-hand account of the first game of the new season of the Browns, the reigning world champions and champions of the American Association. "Base Ball Notes," *Louisville Courier-Journal,* May 4, 1887, 14.

21. "Honors for Brooklyn. Byrne's Men Beat the Champions" *New York Evening Sun,* September 6, 1887, 1.

22. The *St. Louis Globe-Democrat* and the *St. Louis Republican* also provided detailed reports on the game, in both cases drawing on the *New York Evening Sun* accounts to introduce the game, with a particular focus on what transpired in the seventh and eighth innings. The *St. Louis Globe-Democrat* also used excerpts from the *New York Evening Sun* to describe what some of the Browns did in the fourth and fifth innings, using the accounts and often the wording from the *Sun* to summarize some of the innings. The *St. Louis Republican* reproduced the *Sun*'s report of the first inning. In addition, the *St. Louis Republican* ended its report with praise for the work of Comiskey and the fielding of three of the Brooklyn players. "Brooklyns, 8; St. Louis, 6," *St. Louis Globe-Democrat,* September 7, 1887, 8; "Beaten by Brooklyn. The Browns Lose a Game in the Seventh Inning," *St. Louis Republican,* September 7, 1887, 6; "Brooklyn Downs St. Louis," *New York Star,* September 7, 1887, 3.

23. "Honors for Brooklyn. Byrne's Men Beat the Champions," *New York Evening Sun,* September 6, 1887, 1.

24. "Brooklyns, 8; St. Louis, 6," *St. Louis Globe-Democrat,* September 7, 1887, 8.

25. "Brooklyn Downs St. Louis," *New York Star,* September 7, 1887, 3.

26. I also found the *Brooklyn Citizen* reports quite dependable. Unfortunately for this game, I was unable to get a copy of the *Brooklyn Citizen*'s game report.

27. "Sporting. Great Batting Records Made by the Browns," *St. Louis Republican,* May 1, 1887, 15.

28. "St. Louis vs. Cleveland at St. Louis, April 30," *Sporting Life,* May 11, 1887, 3.

29. "St. Louis vs. Cleveland," *New York Clipper,* May 7, 1887, 122.

30. "St. Louis Wins Easily," *New York Evening Sun,* September 2, 1887, 1. The *St. Louis Globe-Democrat* and the *St. Louis Republican* also published a detailed account of the game, one that replicated most of the report from the *New York Evening Sun.* The *St. Louis Republican* concluded its report with comments on Latham (e.g., "carried the honors in the game") and Caruthers.

31. "St. Louis Wins Easily. The Mets Make 4 Runs, the Visitors 12," *New York Evening Sun,* September 2, 1887, 1.

32. "Indians in Very Poor Form. Erastus Wiman's Pets are Slaughtered on Staten Island," *New York Star,* September 3, 1887, 5.

33. "O'Neill made five successive base hits, including a three-baser and a two bagger." "Metropolitan vs. St. Louis," *New York Clipper,* September 10, 1887, 409.

34. The *New York Evening Sun* did not report a full box score, only a line score. The *St. Louis Globe-Democrat* and the *St. Louis Republican* either had their own box score or relied on a box score from another New York newspaper.

35. "The Second Game," *New York Evening Sun,* September 3, 1887, 1.

36. "Mets Beaten in Two Games," *New York Evening Sun,* September 3, 1887, 1.

Appendix B

1. Unless otherwise noted, I rely on the "Leaders Index" of Baseball-Reference.com for baseball records and statistics reported in this appendix.

2. Steve Gietschier, "Extra-Base Hits: Career and Season," *The 2005 Complete Baseball Record Book* (St. Louis: The Sporting News, 2005), 36; Seymour Siwoff, *The Little Red Book of Major League Baseball 1971* (New York: Elias Sports Bureau, 1971), 19.

3. As explained in Chapter 16, scoring runs is not considered a batting category. O'Neill scored runs after he got on base by any means, which could range from a hit or base on balls to an error or a fielder's choice. Once on base, whether or not O'Neill scored was related to a number of factors such as the success of subsequent batters in advancing O'Neill one or more bases and eventually scoring. It also depended on O'Neill's base running ability and the extent to which the opposing team was able to prevent O'Neill from advancing bases and scoring runs. In short, O'Neill's runs scored were not a direct result of his own hit ball, except of course when he hit a home run.

4. Lyle Spatz, *The SABR Baseball List & Record Book* (New York: Society for American Baseball Research, 2007), 149.

5. Trent McCotter, "Johnny Kling's 12 Consecutive Hits," SABR Baseball Records Committee, April 2009. Accessed December 10, 2015, SABR-Baseball_Records_Cmte-2009-04.pdf.

6. Trent McCotter, "The .400 Club," *Baseball Research Journal* 33, no. 7 (2004), 64–70.

7. David Shoebotham, in a 1976 article in the *Baseball Research Journal,* adapted the formula for relative batting average. He subtracted the player's hits and at-bats from the league totals and recalculated the average of the rest of the league. He then divided the player's average by the revised league average. Shoebotham rea-

soned that it was "unfair to compare a player to himself." When I applied this formula, it increased O'Neill's relative batting average but did not alter his ranking. David Shoebotham, "Relative Batting Average," *Baseball Research Journal*, 1976. Research Journal Archives, Society for American Baseball Research. Last accessed March 19, 2018. http://research.sabr.org.

8. John Thorn, Pete Palmer, and Michael Gershwin, *Total Baseball: The Official Encyclopedia of Major League Baseball, Seventh Edition* (Kingston, NY: Total Sports Publishing, 2001), 2327.

9. Gary Gillette and Pete Palmer, *The ESPN Baseball Encyclopedia*, 5th ed. (New York: Sterling, 2008), 1781.

10. Ibid.

11. Jim Weigand, "The Road to 200 Hits," April 4, 2009. Accessed on March 16, 2018, at http://retrosheet.org/Research/WeigandJ/200%20Hits.pdf

12. Steve Gietschier, "Most Games with Five or More Hits, Season," *The Sporting News: The Complete 2008 Baseball Record Book* (Chesterfield, MO: The Sporting News, 2008), 20.

13. Trent McCotter suggested that Johnston's records for times on base in four, five, six, and seven consecutive games "have only been beaten by Billy Hamilton in 1894." He also noted that Cal McVey (1876) had 19 hits in five consecutive games and 24 hits in six consecutive games. "Memorable Week for Brooklyn's Jimmy Johnston," Society for American Baseball Research, Baseball Records Committee Newsletter, August 2007. Accessed September 19, 2016, at http://SABR-Baseball_Records_Cmte-2007-8.

14. Trent McCotter, "American Association Hitting Streaks," *Nineteenth Century Notes* (Summer 2010), 8.

15. I am not aware of a source that lists a record for the most number of games in a season with two or more extra-base hits.

16. "Most Extra-Base Hits, Two Consecutive Games," *The Elias Book of Baseball Records, 2013 Edition* (New York: Elias Sports Bureau, 2013), 15.

17. The other seven batters with five extra-base hits in a game are: Lou Boudreau (1946), Joe Adcock (1954), Willie Stargell (1970), Steve Garvey (1977), Shawn Green (2002), Kelly Shoppach (2008), and Josh Hamilton (2012). Seymour Siwoff, "Extra-base Hits," *The Elias Book of Baseball Records*, (New York: Elias Sports Bureau, 2013), 15.

Appendix C

1. The batting tables do not include a column for singles (1B). O'Neill led the Association in singles in 1886 and 1888.

2. As noted in Appendix A, I reviewed nine to 16 sources for each game in 1887. I consulted a similar number of sources for 1886. I found a few discrepancies between my game-based statistics for these two seasons and those in the game-by-game reports generated by Information Concepts Incorporated (ICI). The discrepancies were mainly related to times at bat, hits, bases on balls, and, in some cases, the types of hits identified. The statistics published at baseball-reference.com are based on the numbers identified by ICI. Given the evidence from my sources for 1886 and 1887, I altered the statistics for some games, which in turn resulted in changes in these two seasons in the number or percentages in some of the batting and fielding categories.

Bibliography

Books and Articles

"1887 Baseball Season in Review." Accessed December 6, 2016, from http://tops.files.wordpress.com/2011/05/oneill.jpg.

Achorn, Edward. *The Summer of Beer and Whiskey: How Brewers, Barkeeps, Rowdies, Immigrants, and a Wild Pennant Fight Made Baseball America's Game.* New York: Public Affairs, 2013.

Axelson, G.W. *"Commy": The Life Story of Charles A. Comiskey.* Jefferson, NC: McFarland, 2003.

The Baseball Encyclopedia: The Complete and Official Record of Major League Baseball. Toronto: Macmillan, 1969.

Baseball Foundation's Quebec Hall of Fame, Wednesday, April 5, 2017. RDS. Accessed December 10, 2017, at http://www.rds.ca/pied-de-page/contacts?property=RDSca.

Bloodgood, Clifford. "Ted Williams Vs. Tip O'Neill." *Baseball Magazine* 80, no.6 (1948): 403, 427.

Bouchier, Nancy. *For the Love of the Game: Amateur Sport in Small-Town Ontario 1838–1895.* Montreal: McGill-Queen's University Press, 2003.

Bowman, Larry G. *Before the World Series: Pride, Profits, and Baseball's First Championships.* DeKalb: Northern Illinois University Press, 2003.

Brown, William. *Baseball's Fabulous Montreal Royals: The Minor League Team That Made Major League History.* Montreal: Robert Davies, 1996.

Burk, Robert. *Never Just a Game: Players, Owners, and American Baseball to 1920.* Chapel Hill: University of North Carolina Press, 1994.

Caillault, Jean-Pierre. *A Tale of Four Cities: Nineteenth Century Baseball's Most Exciting Season, 1889, In Contemporary Accounts.* Jefferson, NC: McFarland, 2003.

Cash, Jon David. *Before They Were Cardinals: Major League Baseball in Nineteenth-Century St. Louis.* Columbia: University of Missouri Press, 2002.

Chadwick, Henry. *The Art of Batting.* Chicago: A. G. Spalding & Bros., 1885.

_____. *The Art of Pitching and Fielding.* Chicago: A.G. Spalding & Bros., 1885.

_____. *Haney's Base Ball Player's Book of Reference for 1867.* New York: J.C. Haney, 1867.

_____. "The New Playing Rules of Base-Ball." *Outing* 10, no. 1 (April 1887): 77–78.

_____. "The New Rules of Base-Ball." *Lippincott Magazine,* May 1887, 836–40.

"Chestnuts." Accessed December 22, 2017, http://Dictionary.com.

Comiskey, Charles A. "How to Play the Infield." In *The National Game. Second Edition,* edited by Alfred H. Spink. Carbondale: Southern Illinois University Press, 2000, 395.

_____. "Thirty-Seven Years of Baseball." *Pearson's Magazine* 31, no. 3 (March 1914): 311–17.

Dickson, Paul. *The Dickson Baseball Dictionary. Third Edition.* New York: W.W. Norton, 2009.

Donner, Joseph G. "Hitting for the Cycle." *Baseball Research Journal* 10, 1981. Accessed on November 3, 2017, through SABR Research Journal Archives at http://research.sabr.org/hitting-for-the-cycle.

Egenriether, Richard. "Chris Von Der Ahe: Baseball's Pioneering Huckster." Accessed on April 18, 2017, from SABR Research Journal Archives at http://research.sabr.org/journals/chris-von-der-ahe-baseballs-pioneering-huckster.

Elliott, Bob. *The Northern Game: Baseball the Canadian Way.* Toronto: Sport Classic, 2005.

Farrell, John. *Tip O'Neill and the Democrat Century.* Boston: Little, Brown, 2001.

Felber, Bill. *Inventing Baseball: The 100 Greatest Games of the Nineteenth Century.* Phoenix: Society for American Baseball Research, 2013.

"First Among Equals." Accessed December 15, 2017, http://dictionary.cambridge.org/dictionary/english/first-among-equals.

Foster, John B. "The First Five Batters." *Baseball Magazine* 61, no. 2 (July 1938): 371–72, 374.

Fullerton, Hugh. "Winning Baseball Pennants. Brains Beat Hands and Feet in the Game." *Collier's* (September 11, 1909), 13–14, 28.

General Register of Ingersoll's Mission Including Ingersoll, Woodstock, Norwich, and East Oxford 1850–1879: Baptisms, Deceases, and Marriages Performed or Witnessed from the Year 1850 to 1879. Accessed May 20, 2016, from the Diocese of London Archives, London Ontario.

Gettelson, Leonard. *The Sporting News 1975 Official Baseball Record Book.* St. Louis: Sporting News, 1975.

Gietschier, Steve, ed. *Sporting News: The Complete 2008 Baseball Record Book.* Chesterfield, MO: Sporting News, 2008.

Gillette, Gary, and Pete Palmer, eds. *The ESPN Baseball Encyclopedia.* 4th Edition. New York: Sterling, 2007.

Golenbock, Peter. *The Spirit of St. Louis: A History of the St. Louis Cardinals and Browns.* New York: Harper Entertainment, 2000.

Hetrick, J. Thomas. *Chris Von Der Ahe and the St. Louis Browns.* Lanham: Scarecrow, 1999.

Holtzman, Jerome. "An Important Change to the Official Record of Major League Baseball." Our Game (blog of MLB official historian, John Thorn), 2001. Accessed on May 13, 2017, from http://ourgame.mlbblogs.com/why-is-the-national-association-not-a-major-league-and-other-record-issues.

"Honoured Member. James O'Neill. Inducted in 1994." Canada's Sports Hall of Fame. Accessed January 7, 2017, at http://www.sportshall.ca.

Hornbaker, Tim. *Turning the Black Sox White: The Misunderstood Legacy of Charles A. Comiskey.* New York: Sports Publishing, 2014.

Humber, William. *Diamonds of the North: A Concise History of Baseball in Canada.* Toronto: Oxford University Press, 1995.

"If Something Is Considered the Best Why Is It Said to Be 'The Berries'?" English Language & Usage Stack Exchange (online). Accessed October 19, 2017, at http://english.stackexchange.com/questions/157816/If-something-is-the-best-why-is-it-the-berries.

Information Concepts Incorporated. *American Association I. C. I. Statistics 1887.* Cooperstown: National Baseball Hall of Fame Library. Microfilmed, 2002.

_____. *1887 National League & American Association. National League & American Association Box Scores.* Cooperstown: National Baseball Hall of Fame Library. Microfilmed, 2002.

Ivor-Campbell, Frederick, Robert L. Tiemann, Mark Rucker, eds. *Baseball's First Stars.* Cleveland: Society for American Baseball Research, 1996.

James, Bill. *The New Bill James Historical Abstract.* New York: Free Press, 2003.

"James 'Tip' O'Neill Award." Canadian Baseball Hall of Fame and Museum. Accessed January 7, 2018, at http://baseballhalloffame.ca.

Kermisch, Al. "Yank Robinson's One-Man Strike in 1889." From "A Researcher's Notebook," *Baseball Research Journal* 10 (1981): 66–67. Accessed July 15, 2016, from SABR Research Journal Archives, at http://research.sabr.org/journals/from-a-researchs-notebook.

Kotar, S.L., and J.E. Gessler. *The Rise of the American Circus, 1716–1899.* Jefferson, NC: McFarland, 2011.

Koyfoed, J. C. "The Greatest Outfield." *Baseball Magazine* 11, no. 3 (July 1913): 29–31.

Krabbenhoft, Herm. "Quasi-Cycles—Better than Cycles?" *Baseball Research Journal* 46, no. 2 (Fall 2017): 107–11.

Lane, F. C., ed. *The Little Red Book of Major League Baseball.* New York: Al Munro Elias Baseball Bureau, 1948.

_____. "One Batting Championship That Never Was Deserved." *Baseball Magazine* 30, no. 6 (1923): 547–48, 575.

_____. "Who Is the Greatest Player in the History of Baseball?" *Baseball Magazine* 8, no. 3 (1911): 27–34.

Lanigan, Ernest J. *Baseball Cyclopedia.* New York: Baseball Magazine, 1922; Jefferson, NC: McFarland, 2005.

Lansche, Jerry. *Glory Fades Away: The Nineteenth-Century World Series Rediscovered.* Dallas: Taylor, 1991.

Light, Jonathan Fraser. *The Cultural Encyclopedia of Baseball.* Jefferson, NC: McFarland, 1997.

Logan, Mrs. John A. *The Home Manual: Everybody's Guide in Social, Domestic and Business Life.* Philadelphia: H.J. Smith, 1889.

Lowry, Philip. *Green Cathedrals: The Ultimate Celebration of Major League and Negro League Ballparks.* New York: Walker, 2006.

Lupo, Larry. *When the Mets Played Baseball on Staten Island.* New York: Vantage, 2000.

MacLean, Malcolm. "Anson to Comiskey to Chase." *Collier's* (September 20, 1913), 28–29.

"Mansion to Mission." Fort Street Presbyterian Church. Accessed November 22, 2012, at http://fortstreet.org/Facility/History/mansiontomission.html.

McCotter, Trent. "American Association Hitting Streaks." *Nineteenth Century Notes* (newsletter of SABR's Nineteenth Century Committee), summer 2010, 8. Accessed June 20, 2016, SABR-Nineteenth–Century_Cmte-2010-08.pdf.

_____. "The .400 Club." *Baseball Research Journal* 33 (2004): 64–70.

_____. "Johnny Kling's 12 Consecutive Hits." Newsletter of SABR's Baseball Records Committee, April 2009, 2. Accessed December 10, 2015, https://sabr.org/cms-files/files/records_apr2009.pdf.

_____. "Memorable Week for Brooklyn's Jimmy Johnston." Newsletter of SABR's Baseball Records Committee Newsletter, August 2007. Accessed September 19, 2016, at http://SABR-Baseball_Records_Cmte-2007-8.

McKenna, Brian. "Doc Bushong." *SABR Baseball Biography Project.* Accessed April 17, 2017, https://sabr.org/bioproj/person/5d4b5fe8.

Miklich, Eric. *The Rules of the Game: A Compilation of the Rules of Baseball, 1845–1900.* Published 2005, through 19C Base Ball (website), http://www.19cbaseball.com/baseball-rules-1845–1900.html

Miller, Stuart. *Good Wood: The Story of the Baseball Bat.* Chicago: ACTA, 2011.

Morgan, Brother George. *La Sallian Education: 150 Years in Toronto.* Toronto: Brothers of the Christian Schools, 2001.

Morrill, John F., and T. O'Keefe. *Batting and Pitching, Illustrated.* Boston: Wright & Ditson, 1884.

Morris, Peter. *Catcher: How the Man Behind the Plate Became an American Folk Hero* Chicago: Ivan R. Dee, 2009.

_____. *A Game of Inches: The Story Behind the Innovations That Shaped Baseball.* Chicago: Ivan R. Dee, 2010.

Morton, John Maddison. *Slasher and Crasher! An Original Farce.* New York: Samuel French & Son, 1895.

_____. *Who Stole the Pocket-Book; or, a Dinner for Six.* Boston: W.V. Spencer, 1857.

Munro, Neil, ed. *STATS Canadian Players Encyclopedia: The Complete Statistical Record of Canadians Who Played in the Major Leagues.* Morton Grove, IL: STATS, 1996.

Nemec, David. *The Beer and Whiskey League: The Illustrated History of the American Association—Baseball's Renegade Major League.* Guilford, CT: Lyons Press, 2004.

_____. *The Great Encyclopedia of the Nineteenth Century Major League Baseball.* Second Edition. Tuscaloosa: University of Alabama Press, 2006.

_____, ed. *Major League Baseball Profiles. 1871–1900.* Volume 1. Lincoln: University of Nebraska Press, 2011.

_____, ed. *Major League Baseball Profiles. 1871–1900.* Volume 2. Lincoln: University of Nebraska Press, 2011.

_____. *The Official Rules of Baseball Illustrated.* Guilford, CT: Lyons Press, 2006.

Nemec, David, and Eric Miklich. *Forfeits and Successfully Protested Games in Major League Baseball: A Complete Record, 1871–2013.* Jefferson, NC: McFarland, 2014.

"Official Rules of Baseball. 2017 Edition." Accessed October 10, 2017, http://mlb.com/documents/Official_Baseball_Rules_dbt69t59.pdf.

Ogden, Tom. *The Complete Idiot's Guide to Magic Tricks.* New York: Alpha, 1998.

O'Neill, Tip, with William Novak. *Man of the House: The Life and Political Memoirs of Speaker Tip O'Neill.* New York: Random House, 1987.

"Our greatest glory is not in never falling, but in rising every time we fall." Quote Investigator. Accessed August 27, 2017, at http://quoteinvestigator.com/2014/05/27/rising/.

Pearson, Daniel M. *Baseball in 1889: Players Vs. Owners.* Bowling Green, OH: Bowling Green State University Popular Press, 1993.

Pfeffer, N. Fred. *Scientific Ball.* Chicago: N. Fred Pfeffer, 1889.

Prindle, Edward J. *The Art of Batting.* Philadelphia: A. J. Reach, 1888.

Reach's Official American Association Base Ball Guide 1886. New York: Horton, 1989.

Reach's Official American Association Base Ball Guide, 1887. New York: Horton, 1989.

Reach's Official American Association Base Ball Guide 1888. New York: Horton, 1989.

Reach's Official American Association Base Ball Guide 1892. New York: Horton, 1989.

Reichler, Joseph L. *The Great All-Time Baseball Record Book.* New York: Macmillan, 1993.

Richter, Francis C. *Richter's History and Records of Base Ball: The American Nation's Chief Sport.* Philadelphia: F. C. Richter, 1914; reprinted Jefferson, NC: McFarland, 2005.

Rivest, André. *La Presse+*, March 29, 2014. Accessed November 12, 2017, at http://plus.lapresse.ca/4187-64ec-5335da14-b13d-138acc/XAMK27-RIxCq.hmtl.

Rogers, Mike. "The Greatest Season You Don't Know About." Beyond the Box Score (website), January 5, 2011. Accessed May 10, 2016, http://www.beyondtheboxscore.com.

Ross, Robert B. *The Great Baseball Revolt: The Rise and Fall of the 1890 Players League.* Lincoln: University of Nebraska Press, 2016.

"Runs Produced." Accessed July 30, 2015, http://baseball-reference.com.

Schwarz, Alan. *The Numbers Game: Baseball's Lifetime Fascination with Statistics.* New York: Thomas Dunne, 2004.

_____. "A Numbers Revolution." ESPN.com, July 8, 2004. Accessed May 20, 2017, http://www.espn.com/mlb/columns/story?columnist=schwarz_alan&id=1835745.

Seymour, Harold, and Dorothy Seymour Mills. *Baseball: The Early Years.* New York: Oxford University Press, 1960.

Shearon, Jim. *Canada's Baseball Legends: True Stories of Canadians in the Big Leagues Since 1879.* Kanata, ON: Malin Head, 1994.

_____. *Over the Fence and Out! The Larry Walker Story and More of Canada's Baseball Legends.* Kanata, ON: Malin Head, 2009.

Shoebotham, David. "Relative Batting Average." *Baseball Research Journal* 5 (1976): 37–42. Accessed March 19, 2018, from SABR Research Archives http://research.sabr.org/journals/relative-batting-average.

Simmons, Harry. "The National League of 1887." *Baseball Magazine* 69, no. 6 (November 1942): 549.

Siwoff, Seymour, ed. *The Elias Book of Baseball Records, 2016 Edition.* New York: Elias Sports Bureau, 2016.

_____. *The Little Red Book of Major League Baseball 1971.* New York: Elias Sports Bureau, 1971.

Smith, Robert. *Baseball: A Historical Narrative of the Game, the Men Who Played It, and Its Place in American Life.* New York: Simon & Schuster, 1947.

Snyder, John. *Cardinals Journal: Year by Year and Day by Day with the St. Louis Cardinals Since 1882.* Cincinnati: Clerisy Press, 2010.

Spalding's Official Base Ball Guide, 1894. Chicago: A. G. Spalding and Bros., 1894.

Spalding's Official Base Ball Guide. Official League Book for 1886. New York: Horton, 1989.

Spalding's Official Base Ball Guide. Official League Book for 1888. New York: Horton, 1989.

Spatz, Lyle, ed. *The SABR Baseball List & Record Book.* New York: Scribner's, 2007.

Spink, Alfred H. *The National Game.* 2d Edition, 1911. Carbondale: Southern Illinois University Press, 2000.

Sporting Life's Official Base Ball Guide 1891. Philadelphia: Sporting Life, 1891.

Sutter, L.M. *Arlie Latham: A Baseball Biography of the Freshest Man on Earth.* Jefferson, NC: McFarland, 2012.

Symons, Doug M. *Giants of Oxford: Women and Men Who Changed Our World.* Woodstock, ON: Woodstock Historical Society, 2001.

Thorn, John, and Pete Palmer. *The Hidden Game of Baseball: A Revolutionary Approach to Baseball and Its Statistics.* Garden City, NY: Doubleday, 1984.

Thorn, John, Pete Palmer, and Michael Gershman, eds. *Total Baseball: The Ultimate Baseball Encyclopedia.* 7th Edition. Toronto: SPORT Media, 2004.

Thorn, John, Pete Palmer, Michael Gershwin, and David Pietrusza, eds. *Total Baseball: The Official Encyclopedia of Major League Baseball.* 5th Edition. New York: Viking, 1997.

Thorn, John, Phil Birnbaum, and Bill Deane, eds. *Total Baseball: The Ultimate Baseball Encyclopedia.* 8th Edition. Toronto: SPORT Media, 2004.

Tiemann, Robert, and Mark Rucker, eds. *Nineteenth Century Stars.* Kansas City: Society for American Baseball Research, 1989.

_____. *Nineteenth Century Stars.* 2012 Edition. Phoenix: Society for American Baseball Research, 2012.

Turkin, Hy, and S.C. Thompson. *The Official Encyclopedia of Baseball.* Jubilee Edition. New York: A. S. Barnes, 1951.

_____. Revisions by Pete Palmer. *The Official Encyclopedia of Baseball.* Tenth Revised Edition. Garden City, NY: Dolphin, 1979.

Vigneault, Michel. "O'Neill, James Edward (Tip)." Dictionary of Canadian Biography Online. Accessed December 8, 2011, at http://biographi.ca/009004-119.01-e.php?id_nbr=7629.

Voigt, David. *American Baseball. Volume 1. From Gentleman's Sport to the Commissioner System.* University Park: Pennsylvania University Press, 1983.

_____. "Denny Lyons' 52–Game Hitting Streak." *National Pastime: A Review of Baseball History* 13 (1993): 45–49.

_____. "Fie on Figure Filberts: Some Crimes Against Clio." *Baseball Research Journal* 12 (1983): 35–36. Accessed May 13, 2017, from SABR Research Archives http://sabr.org/researchjournalarchives/BRJ-1983.

Ward, John J. "1887, the Black Sheep of Baseball Records." *Baseball Magazine* 15, no. 2 (1915): 69–74.

Ward, John Montgomery. *Base-Ball: How to Become a Player.* 1888. Filiquarian, 2010.

_____. "Is the Base Ball Player a Chattel?" *Lippincott's Magazine* 40 (August 1887): 310–19.

Weigand, Jim. "The Road to 200 Hits." Retrosheet (website), April 4, 2009. Accessed on March 16, 2018, at http://retrosheet.org/Research/WeigandJ/200%20Hits.pdf

Weir, Hugh. "The Real Comiskey." *Baseball Magazine* 12, no. 4 (February 1914): 21–28.

White, Charles. *The Little Red Book: Spalding's Official Base Ball Record*. New York: American Sports, 1932.

Newspapers

Baltimore American
Baltimore Sun
Batavia (NY) *Times*
Boston Globe
Boston Herald
British Whig (Kingston, Ontario)
Brooklyn Citizen
Brooklyn Daily Times
Brooklyn Eagle
Brooklyn Standard Union
Chicago Chronicle
Chicago Daily News
Chicago Herald
Chicago Inter Ocean
Chicago Times
Chicago Tribune
Cincinnati Commercial Gazette
Cincinnati Enquirer
Cincinnati Post
Cincinnati Times-Star
Cleveland Leader
Cleveland Plain Dealer
Daily True American (Trenton, NJ)
Detroit Free Press
Detroit News
Guelph Mercury (Ontario)
Hartford Times
Ingersoll Chronicle (Ontario)
London Free Press (Ontario)
Louisville Commercial
Louisville Courier-Journal
Louisville Evening Post
Louisville Times
Montreal Gazette (Quebec)
Montreal La Presse (Quebec)
Montreal Star (Quebec)
National Daily Baseball Gazette
National Police Gazette
New York Clipper
New York Evening Sun
New York Herald
New York Star
New York Sun
New York Telegram
New York Times
New York Tribune
New York World
Ottawa Citizen (Ontario)
Philadelphia Evening Bulletin
Philadelphia Inquirer
Philadelphia North American
Philadelphia Press
Philadelphia Record
Philadelphia Times
Pittsburgh Dispatch
Providence Evening Bulletin
St. Louis Chronicle
St. Louis Globe-Democrat
St. Louis Post-Dispatch
St. Louis Republican
St. Louis Sunday Sayings
San Francisco Chronicle
Sporting Life
Sporting News
Springfield Daily Republican
Syracuse Daily Journal
Syracuse Evening Herald
Syracuse Standard
Toronto Daily Star (Ontario)
Toronto Globe (Ontario)
Toronto Mail (Ontario)
Toronto Times (Ontario)
Toronto World (Ontario)
Trenton Times
Woodstock Sentinel-Review (Ontario)
Woodstock Weekly Review (Ontario)

Websites

www.19cbaseball.com
www.baseball-almanac.com
www.baseball-reference.com
www.fangraphs.com
www.la84.org
www.mlb.com
www.paperofrecord.hypernet.ca
www.retrosheet.org

Collections

Canada's Sport Hall of Fame
Canadian Baseball Hall of Fame
Library of Congress
National Baseball Hall of Fame
Society for American Baseball Research (SABR)

Index

Numbers in *bold italics* indicate pages with illustrations

Adcock, Joe 188
Allentown 27
American Association 5, 6, 11, 13, 23, 27, 30–31, 33, 44, 46, 48, 50, 54, 56–58, 60, 64, 66, 70, 73, 75, 79, 85, 95–96, 98, 102, 108–9, 112–13, 115, 126, 128, 130, 134, 136, 140–41, 143, 145–46, 152, 154–55, 157–58, 159–61, 168–70, 181, 183–84, 187, 188
American League 157–58
Amsterdam, New York 165
Anson, Adrian "Cap" 18–21, 51, 144, 160, 167–68
Atkinson, Al 72
Aulick, William W. (sportswriter) 9

Baldwin, Mark 21, 152
Baltimore American 86–87, 93, 103, 104
Baltimore Orioles 29, 54, 72–73, 78, 79, 81–83, 84–91, 92–93, 95, 101–5, 117, 121–22, 130–31, 139
Baltimore Sun 86, 88, 89, 93, 104, 121
Barnes, Ross 157–58, 186–88
Barnie, Billy 86, 89, 92
base running skills and headwork 35–36, 39, 44–46, 83–84
base-stealing contest 122
Baseball Cyclopedia 8
The Baseball Encyclopedia: The Complete and Official Record of Major League Baseball 10, 12
Baseball Magazine 7, 9, 96
Baseball Reference 189
Battin, Joe (umpire) 124
batting average based on on-base percentage 168

batting average based on total bases 110
batting skills and headwork 35, 37–39, 46
Bauer, Al (umpire) 64, 68–69
Bay, Jason 170
Beer and Whiskey League 66
The Beer and Whiskey League: The Illustrated History of the American Association—Baseball's Renegade Major League 13
Beltre, Adrian 75, 186
Bennett, Charlie 149–51
betting 19, 66, 122, 141, 145–49, 165, 220ch15n14
Bloodgood, Clifford 9, 12
Bonds, Barry 185
Boston Globe 84
Boston Red Sox 169
Boston Reds 142, 159
Bottomley, Jim 156
Bouchier, Nancy (historian) 24
Boyle, John "Jack" 59–60, 84, 91, 95, 104–5, 117–19, 135, 140
Breckenbaugh, W.W. (auctioneer) 87
Bright, John 135, 138
broadcasts and reports of games 66, 86–87, 89, 93, 104, 208ch8n52
Brodie, Steve 96
Brooklyn Citizen 102, 176, 177
Brooklyn Daily Times (BDT) 177, 178, 179
Brooklyn Eagle (BE) 176, 177, 178, 179
Brooklyn Grays 72–73, 78–79, 82–83, 99, 101–2, 105, 114, 118, 121–23, 125–27, 130–33, 137, 142, 159, 162, 175, 177–79, 181
Brooklyn Standard Union (BSU) 177, 179

Brotherhood of Professional Baseball Players 59–60
Brouthers, Dan 141, 156–57, 160
Brown, Tom 186
Browning, Pete 30, 94, 108–9, 112, 120, 126–28, 140, 143, 152, 155, 158, 160, 183, 185
Brunell, Frank H. (sportswriter) 120
Buffalo Bill's Wild West Show 114
Burns, Thomas "Oyster" 87–89, 104, 112–13, 181
Burns, Tom 18, 22
Bushong, Albert "Doc" 18–19, 22, 24, 33, 39–42, 47–48, 53, 56, 60, 76, 88–89, 91, 105, 117, 138–40, 142, 151, 159, 162
Byrne, Charles 103, 162

Campbell, first name unknown (sportswriter) 25
Canada's Sports Hall of Fame 26, 169
Canadian Baseball Hall of Fame and Museum 169–70
Carroll, Fred 75
Caruthers, Bob 17–18, 20–22, 24, 29–30, 33, 39–42, 45, 48, 51, 54, 60–61, 73, 80–83, 84, 103–5, 109, 112, 117–19, 121–22, 126–27, 132, 135, 140–43, 149, 151, 154, 159, 177
Caylor, Oliver Perry "O.P." 50
Chadwick, Henry 37, 110
Chamberlain, Elton "Icebox" 115
Champion's March 63
Chicago Daily News 21
Chicago Pirates 159–60, *162*, 163–64
Chicago Record 167
Chicago Times 21

237

Chicago Tribune 21
Chicago White Stockings 17, 19–22, 33, 51, 57, 59–61, 64, 114, 136, 144, 157
Cincinnati Commercial Gazette (CCG) 19, 96, 140, 178, 180
Cincinnati Enquirer (CE) 44, 51, 68, 96, 165, 178, 180
Cincinnati Reds 54, 63, 68–69, 81–83, 91, 96, 106, 108, 111, 114, 138–40, 142, 159–61, 163–65, 167, 169
Clark, Bob 83, 122
Clarkson, John 22–23
Cleveland Blues 70–71, 73, 75–76, 78, 82, 91, 101, 106–9, 115, 117–18, 120, 129–30, 139–41, 164–65, 180–81
Cleveland Leader (CL) 164, 180
Cleveland Plain Dealer (CPD) 70, 139, 180
coaching 20, 33, 36–38, 44, 49–50, 54, 59, 64, 72, 82–84, 87, 91, 93, 102–3, 119, 121, 148, 194*ch1n*26
Cobb, Ty 7, 156–58, 186–87
Collins, Hubert "Hub" 120
color line 136–38, 217*ch14n*2, 218*ch14n*24
Colorado Rockies 169–70
Comiskey, Charles 9, 17, 20–22, 24, 28, 31, 33–34, **35**, 35–37, 43–54, 56, 60, 64, 69, 70–73, 76, 81–83, 85, 88–92, 103, 105, 107, 111–12, 115, 118–19, 121–22, 125, 131–33, 135, 137–42, 152, 161, 163–65, 167–68, 175
Connelly, John "Red" (umpire) 115
Connor, Roger 156, 160
conventionalist vs. revisionist positions 6, 8, 11–13, 184, 191*Pref.n*7
Corkhill, John "Pop" 80
Crawford, Sam 156
Cuban Giants 135–38, 217*ch14n*1

Dalrymple, Abner 17, 19, 22
Danbury Club 136
Davis, Jumbo 88, 112, 181
defensive skills and headwork 33–35, 37–38, 41–42, 46–48, 84, 96, 102
Delahanty, Ed 156, 184–86, 188
De La Salle Institute 24
Detroit Free Press 141, 142, 146
Detroit Hiawatha Grays 166
Detroit Tigers 156
Detroit Wolverines 118, 136, 140–43, 144–51
dirty ball 43–44, 48–49, 54, 68
Doescher, Herman (umpire) 166
Dropo, Walt 185

Duffy, Hugh 8, 11–12, 160, 185–86, 188
Dunlap, Fred 150, 188

Easterbrook, Tom 95
Eastern League 166
Elias, Al Munro (statistician) 8
The Elias Book of Baseball Records 12
Elias Sports Bureau 12
Elk Club 56
Emslie, Bob 29
The ESPN Baseball Encyclopedia 155, 187
Everything Is Fair in Baseball 44

The Fall of Babylon 114
fans (cranks) at games 20, 23, 65–67, 86–89, 93, 103–4, 106, 111–12, 121, 123–25, 147, 151
Fennelly, Frank 83
Ferguson, Bob (umpire) 114, 124
For the Love of the Game. Amateur Sports in Small-Town Ontario 1838–1895 24
forfeited games 51, 92, 115, 207*ch8n*5
Foster, John (writer) 9
Foulon, I. D. (editor) 63
Foutz, Dave 19–21, 23–24, 29, 33, **40**, 40–42, 48–50, 53, 60–61, 64, 68, 73, 76, 84, 88, 94, 104–7, 109, 112, 117–18, 120, 138–39, 141–42, 150, 159, 175

Gaffney, "Honest John" (umpire) 163
game-based statistics 171
Gardner, Gid 29
Gehrig, Lou 156, 186
Getzein, Charlie "Pretzels" 148
Gillette, Gary 155
Gleason, Bill 18–22, 24, 33, **37**, 37–38, 45–46, 49–54, 60–61, 71, 73, 76, 81–84, 88–89, 104–5, 131–33, 135, 141–42, 147, 151, 159, 175–76, 181
Gore, George 18, 188
Greenberg, Hank 157
Greenwood, Bill 89–92, 103, 139
Griffin, Mike 104
ground rules 66, 86, 113–15, 124–25, 132, 195*ch1n*31, 213*ch11n*27
Gwynn, Tony 187

Hamilton, Billy 185–87
Hartford Club 27
Hecker, Guy 29, 64
Henderson, Hardie 29
Herman, Babe 75, 186
Higgins, Michael "Pinky" 185
Hill, Aaron 75, 186
Hines, Paul 186

Holliday, James "Bug" 184
Holmes, Tommy 157
Holtzman, Jerome 11–12, 168, 174, 184, 193*Pref.n*41
Holyoke 27
Hornsby, Rogers 156–58, 185–86
Hotaling, Pete 107
Hudson, Nat 21, 68, 88, 105, 117–18, 142

Information Concepts Incorporated (ICI) 10, 12–13, 168, 171–72, 174–82

James "Tip" O'Neill Award 169
Johnston, Jimmy 187–88
Jones, Charley 114
Jones, Chipper 133, 185

Kansas City Cowboys 163
Kansas City Journal 118
Keeler, Willie 8, 96, 188
Kelley, Joe 96, 185
Kelly, "Honest John" 17–18, 109, 127–28
Kelly, Michael "King" 17, 21, 23
Kerins, John 71, 112, 181
kicking 17, 20, 38, 44, 49–52, 54–55, 59, 64, 69, 83, 87–89, 91, 93, 102–3
Kilroy, Matt 88
King, Charles "Silver" 68, 84, 88, 105, 117–19, 126, 135, 142
Klein, Chuck 157–58
Kling, Johnny 185
Knouff, Ed 117, 125
Koyfoed, J.C. 96
Krebbenhoft, Herm 116

ladies at games 67, 106, 111–12
Lajoie, Nap 157–58, 183, 186
Lane, Ferdinand Cole (editor) 7–8, 12–13
Lanigan, Ernest 8, 12
The Last Game. A Metrical Forecast of the Detroit-Browns Series 147–48
Latham, Arlie 17–22, 24, 33, **36**, 36–38, 44–46, 49, 51–54, 56, 60–61, 64, 73, 76, 81–83, 87–88, 91–92, 95, 102, 104–5, 110, 112, 118–22, 131–32, 135–36, 138, 141, 147–49, 154, 175
League Alliance 27
level of confidence in game-based statistics 172–74
Lewis, Fred 28–29
Lifetime Topps Project 156
Linden House 29
The Little Red Book of Major League Baseball 13, 156
The Lost Game 19–20
Louisville Colonels 63–64, 68, 70–71, 73, 75–78, 79, 81–83,

91–92, 95, 99, 102, 108–9, 115, 118, 120, 126–28, 129, 136, 139–40, 175, 178
Louisville Commercial (LC) 175, 177, 178
Louisville Courier-Journal (LCJ) 83, 92, 127, 175, 177, 178, 180
Louisville Evening Post (LEP) 175, 178
Louisville Hotel 64
Lyons, Denny 30, 102, 109, 112–13, 127, 143

Mack, Reddy 109, 127, 143
MacKay, Max 165
MacLean, Malcolm (sportswriter) 33–34
MacMillan Company 10
major leagues 29–30, 96, 98, 100, 120, 136, 154–55, 158, 159, 165, 170, 183–88
Maude Abbey House 29
McCormick, Jim 17–19, 21
McCotter, Trent 130, 187
McKean, Ed 118
McLellan, Bill 132
McNish, Johnson and Slavin Minstrels 57
McPhee, Bid 75, 83, 112, 181
McQuaid, Jack (umpire) 17, 83, 89, 122
Medwick, Joe 156–57
Mermod & Jaccard Jewelry Company (also E. Jaccard Company) 7, 30, 56, 152
Merrell's Penetrating Oil 79
Meusel, Bob 75, 186
Milligan, Jack 72, 120
Minnesota Twins 169
Mitchell, first name unknown (umpire) 102
The Monarchs of the Sphere 22
Monitor Park 123–24
Montreal 15, 165–67
Montreal Expos 169
Montreal Gazette 165, 167
Montreal Royals 166
Morcau, Justin 169
Murphy, Joe (sportswriter) c119
Musial, Stan 156–58, 187
Musical Review 63
Mutrie, Jim 29

National Daily Base Ball Gazette (NDBBG) 178
National Baseball Hall of Fame 11–12, 169, 174
National League 5, 18, 23, 54, 58–59, 64, 66, 70, 75, 111, 136, 140–42, 145–46, 155, 157–58, 159–61, 164, 168, 184
near-cycle 77–78, 107, 122–23, 140, 216*ch*12*n*43

Nelson, John "Candy" 84
Nemec, David 13, 84
The New York Clipper (NYC) 27–28, 175, 176, 177, 179, 180, 181
New York Evening Sun (NYES) 136, 176, 177, 178, 179, 181
New York Giants 59, 159
New York Gothams 27
New York Herald (NYH) 95, 176, 177, 178, 181
New York Metropolitans 27–28, 78, 79, 82, 84, 92, 95, 102, 104–5, 113–14, 117, 121–27, 130–33, 137, 176, 181
New York Star (NYST) 123, 125, 176, 177, 178, 179, 181
New York Sun (NYS) 136, 137, 176, 177, 178, 181
New York Telegram 137
New York Times (NYT) 9, 124, 136, 138, 176, 177, 179, 180, 181
New York Tribune (NYTR) 181
New York World (NYW) 105, 123, 176, 177, 181
Nicol, Hugh 45, 59, 81, 84, 140
Noonan, Edward A. (judge) 93

O'Brien, Darby 105, 112
O'Brien, Jack 30
The Official Encyclopedia of Baseball 12, 168
Olympic Theater 152
O'Neill, Agnes "Aggie" 165, 167
O'Neill, D'Arcy 165, 167
O'Neill, George 165–66
O'Neill, James (father) 24
O'Neill, James "Tip" **7**, 24, **25, 26,** 33, **34,** 56–58, 60–62, **70, 97, 99,** 101, 106, 135, 142, **143, 149, 160, 162,** 165–68, **169,** 170, 195*ch*2*n*2; base running 21–22, 31, 54, 71, 80–82, 164; bat 69, 116, 149, 205*ch*6*n*36, 205*ch*6*n*37; bat throwing 118, 125, 149, 152, 216*ch*12*n*70; batting statistics (1884–1886) 23, 28–30, 189–90, 198*ch*2*n*41, 198*ch*2*n*45; batting statistics (1887) 6, 8–12, 60–61, 69, 70, 73–74, 75, 78, 80, 85, 91, 93–94, 101, 106–9, 112–13, 116–17, 121–22, 126–28, 129–30, 132–34, 138–41, 143, 148–50, 152, 154–55, 157, 170, 224–25, 174, 179, 181–82, 189–90, 212–13*ch*10*n*52, 213–14*ch*11*n*21, 224–25*Epil.n*7; batting statistics (1888–1892) 159–61, 189–90; batting style and strategy 46, 54, 58–59, 69, 149; batting title based on on-base percentage 168; character 28–29, 31, 57, 168; and Comiskey 9, 28,

31, 53–54, 71, 81–82, 97, 105, 161, 164–65, 167–68, 208*ch*8*n*22; commendations 7, 10, 12, 19, 27, 29–30, 32, 56–57, 69–70, 72, 93, 95–98, 104, 107, 114, 120–22, 131, 133, 139–42, 152–53, 161, 166, 167–69, 209–10*ch*9*n*3; defensive plays 30–31, 54, 63, 67–68, 71–72, 93, 95–96, **97, 99,** 98–100, 102, 120, 140, 150, 163–64, 211*ch*9*n*33; defensive statistics 96–98, 100, 190, 211*ch*9*n*34; final days as a major league player 164–65; honors 169–70; injuries or health problems 27–28, 53–55, 60–62, 63, 72, 79, 92–93, 98, 161, 164–65, 225*Epil.n*19; kicks, tricks, and rough plays 18, 51, 53–55; leading batsman 1885–89 160; Little O'Neills 106; nickname "Tip" 14, 25–26, 166–67, 170, 196*ch*2*n*15, 196*ch*2*n*16, 196*ch*2*n*17; and the new rules of 1887 58–59; as a pitcher 14, 25–28, 190, 197*ch*2*n*26, 197*ch*2*n*29; popularity 31, 57, 60, 106, 111–12, 149; records for leading in most batting categories, one season 15, 158, 170, 183–84, 222*ch*16*n*5, 223–24*ch*16*n*16; records in American Association (1882–1891) 155, 157, 170, 183–85; records in major leagues as of 1892 155, 157–58, 184–86, 214*ch*11*n*37; run impact 73, 77, 94, 107, 117, 126, 129–30, 133, 139, 154; run production 73, 75–77, 107, 117, 126, 129–30, 133, 150, 154; tributes following his death 167–68; as an umpire 166; and Von der Ahe 23, 53, 60, 161–63, 225*Epil.n*20
O'Neill, Joseph 165
O'Neill, Mary (mother) 24, 165
O'Neill, Thomas "Tip," Jr. (politician) 169
O'Neill House 24
Ontario Sports Hall of Fame 169
Orr, Dave 30, 53, 75, 108, 160, 184
Otterson, Billy 178

Page, Joe 166, 168
Palmer, Pete 155
Pfeffer, Fred 18, 97–98
Philadelphia Athletics 72, 79–80, 82, 85, 95, 102–3, 105, 109, 113, 117–20, 127, 135–37, 139, 157, 159, 161, 165, 176–77

Philadelphia Inquirer (PI) 177
Philadelphia North American (PNA) 85, 96, 177
Philadelphia Press (PP) 177
Philadelphia Record (PR) 177
Philadelphia Times (PT) 177
Phillips, Bill 102, 112
Pinkney, George 83, 102, 131
Pitching Skills and Headwork 39–42, 48
Pittsburgh Alleghenys 46, 53
Pittsburgh Pirates 157, 169
Players' League 155, 159–60, 163–64
Pond's Extract 105
Poorman, Tom 112, 181
Pope's Theatre 122
Porter, Henry 128
Princeton 27–28
Pritchard, Joe 43, 63, 73, 93, 112, 161
Pug Cigars 165
Pullman cars 145
Purcell, William "Blondie" 104, 121

quasi-cycle 76–78
Quest, Joe (umpire) 17

Ramsey, Thomas "Toad" 64
Reach's Official American Association Base Ball Guide 1888 6, 7, 11, 45, 139, 152–53
Reccius, Phil 64
Reilly, John 75, 81, 112, 186
Reiser, Pete 157
Rice, Jim 157
Richardson, Hardy 149
Robinson, William "Yank" 18–19, 22–23, 24, 33, **35**, 35–36, 38, 44–45, 49, 51–54, 60, 64, 72, 76, 82–84, 94, 102–5, 109, 118–22, 127, 135, 139, 141–43, 150, 154, 163
rough plays 19, 35, 38, **44**, 49, 51–55, 64, 68, 83–85, 88–93, 102–3
Rowe, Jack 149
rule changes 1887 6–7, 9–10, 12, 50, 58–59, 61, 73, 119, 159, 168
Russell House 151
Ruth, Babe 185, 1888
Ryan, Jim 21

St. George Cricket Grounds, Staten Island 113–14
St. Louis Browns 5, 17, **22**, 19–23, 24, 33, **34**, 43–44, 46, 48–49, 51–52, 56, 60–61, 63–65, 70, 77–78, 79, 82, 85, 101–2, 105, 116–18, 121–22, 128, 129, 138, 140–43, **145**, 144–46, 148, 150–51, 154, 159, **160**, 162–64, 167

St. Louis Cardinals 156–57
St. Louis Chronicle (SLC) 99, 122, 124, 136, 152, 176
St. Louis Globe-Democrat (G-G) 23, 40, 61, 63, 92, 93, 95, 96, 99, 119, 136, 140, 141, 142, 146, 148, 152, 175, 177, 178, 179, 180, 181
St. Louis Maroons 33, 56, 111
St. Louis Merchants' Exchange 56
St. Louis Post-Dispatch 25, 29, 37, 44, 49, 53, 81, 99, 107, 108, 110, 111, 112, 114, 119, 122, 127, 136, 140, 145, 147–50, 152
St. Louis Republican (REP) 19, 31, 71, 77, 92, 95, 96, 102, 103, 105, 106, 109, 112, 115, 118, 124, 131, 136, 144, 150, 152, 167, 175, 177, 178, 179, 180, 181
St. Louis Sunday Sayings 29, 89, 99, 101, 141, 152
St. Marys Cemetery 167
Schoendienst, Albert "Red" 188
Scientific Ball 97
Scott, first name unknown (Judge) 7
Sexton, Clay 91
Seymour, Cy 157
Sheeley, Earl 188
Sheepshead Bay 165
Sheridan, Ed (editor) 178
Shreve, Lev 142
Simmons, Al 187
Sisler, George 186
Siwoff, Seymour 156
Smith, John "Phenomenal" 103–4
Sommer, Joe 88, 104
Spalding, Albert Goodwin 21, 51, 59, 144
Spalding's Official Base Ball Guide 1888 110
Special Baseball Records Committee 1968 10–12, 167, 174
Spink, Alfred 38, 41
The Sporting Life (SL) 25–26, 29, 32, 43, 57, 63, 73, 93, 112, 120, 133, 161, 166–67, 175, 176, 177, 178, 180, 181
The Sporting Life's Official Base Ball Guide 1891 7
The Sporting News (SN) 32, 57, 107, 108, 109, 123, 145, 151, 152, 167, 175, 176, 177, 178, 180, 181
Sportsman's Park 6, 21, 23, **65**, 65–69, 72, 79, 91–93, 101, 105–6, 111–14, 122, 146, 160, 186, 204*ch*6*n*11, 208*ch*8*n*29, 219*ch*14*n*44
Springfield, Ontario 24
Stearns, Frederick 141, 144, 147

Stenzel, Jake 185
Stovey, Harry 113, 156, 159, 183–85
Strief, George 188
Sunday games 66, 93, 123, 209*ch*8*n*79
Suzuki, Ishiro 185, 187–88
Sweatman, Rice and Fagan's Minstrels 152
Sylvester, Lou 117, 120

Thompson, Sam 141, 149, 156, 187–88
Tiemann, Bob 38
Tip and Slasher 26
Tip O'Neill Sportsfield 169
Total Baseball 11, 13, 184, 187
tricks 35, 44, 49, 52–53, 64, 72, 83–84, 88, 92–93, 102–3, 120, 146
Trott, Sam 84, 88, 104
Tucker, Tommy 88–89, 104, 112
Turner, George "Tuck" 187
Twitchell, Larry 188

Union Association 155

Valentine, John (umpire) 77
Vandalia Railroad 145
Van Haltren 185
Voigt, David (historian) 11
Von der Ahe, Chris 19–21, 26, 28–29, 52–53, 56, 59–60, 63–65, **67**, 67–69, 72, 81, 85, 89, 91–93, 102–3, 105, 117–19, 122, 124, 135–38, 140–42, 144, 147–48, 150–52, 161–64
Von der Horst 89
Votto, Joey 169

Wagner, Honus 157–58
Walker, Larry 169, 188
Waner, Paul 133, 185
Ward, John (prosecutor) 90
Ward, John Montgomery 7, 12, 59
Waverly Station-House 89
Webb, Earl 184–85
Weehawken 118, 123–25, 137, 139
Weigand, Jim 187
Welch, Curt 19, 22–23, 24, 29–30, 33, **39**, 38–39, 44–45, 47, 49, 51–54, 60–61, 76, 82–85, **90**, 89–92, 96, 100, 103–5, 118–19, 121–22, 125, 132, 135, 139, 141–42, 149, 159
Welch Arrested to Prevent a Riot 90
Weyhing, Gus 85
White, Bill 81
White, Jim 141
Williams, Jimmy 48

Williams, Ted 9, 157, 186
Williamson, Ned 18, 21, 51
Wiman Trophy 64, 85
Woodstock, Ontario 24–25, 27, 56–57, 151–52, 165, 167, 169
Woodstock Actives 25, 27–29, 169
Woodstock Sentinel-Review 25, 56
Woodstock Sports Wall of Fame 169
Woodstock Young Canadians 24–25
Wikoff, Wheeler 6, 85

Yeamans, Jennie (singer) 122
Young, Benjamin "Ben" (umpire) 83, 92
Young, Nick 122

Zimmer, Charles "Chief" 164
Zimmerman, Heine 157

www.ingramcontent.com/pod-product-compliance
Lightning Source LLC
Chambersburg PA
CBHW081551300426
44116CB00015B/2834